Collected Hutc… 2

WHO WRITES THIS CRAP?! DID YOU WRITE THIS?!?

by Tom Hart

Top Shelf Productions, Marietta, GA

For Mom.

INTRODUCTION

TOM HART'S WORKING HARD: SELLING FUTURES IN HOPE

*"People who talk about revolution and class struggle without referring explicitly to everyday life, without understanding what is subversive about love and what is positive in the refusal of constraints, such people have a corpse in their mouth." -Raoul Vaneigem, **The Revolution Of Everyday Life.***

The problem with Americans, Jean Giraud (Moebius) once complained, is that they have no politics.

Any foreigner who's had a lot to do with America (and that's most of us, as we emerge from the so-called "American Century") knows what he means. It's not that Americans have no interest in who's president or what party dominates Congress (although that seems to be true of most, given voter turnout). What Giraud was talking about, I think, is the lack of political analysis, or even instincts, in American social, economic and even everyday life.

I remember seeing "Hype," Doug Pray's excellent documentary about the Seattle music scene a few years back. Giraud's comment kept coming back to me and I kept thinking: "God, if only more of those people had had some politics about the whole thing." The process they'd been put through by the corporate music/entertainment/hype machine seemed to have taken them largely by surprise - so it had chewed them up and spat them out before they'd even had the chance to try and work out what was going on. Afterwards, there was plenty of bitterness and bewildered hostility towards "the Man." But it was as if they were having to invent a vocabulary with which to understand what had happened; and the easiest vocabulary for them, as young Americans, to fall back on was that of the Individual being gobbled up by Big Business - or of an alternative counter-culture being co-opted by the corporate mainstream.

All of which is, on one level, quite accurate. But a while later, I saw an equally amazing film - Julien Temple's "The Filth and the Fury", an account of the Sex Pistols. Now, it's pretty commonplace to point to the Seattle scene as having been America's equivalent to England's Punk explosion in the late 1970s. But what's really interesting is the differences, which these two films illustrate beautifully. From the get-go, British Punk was political, in every meaningful sense of the world. The Sex Pistols were managed by Malcolm McLaren, an enthusiastic follower of the French Situationists, who - along with their graphic artist, Jamie Reid - covered their clothes, their posters and their lyrics with Situationist slogans from the 1968 Paris uprising: "Demand the impossible," "Club Med: a cheap holiday in other people's misery."

For Johnny Rotten, the music business was as corrupt and - well - fucked up as the rest of cosy, oppressive, brain-dead 1970s Britain and the job of the Sex Pistols was to tear the whole fucking edifice down. No mercy, no compromise - and No Future. McLaren added his own particular brand of sabotage, by infiltrating the music industry with record deal after record deal - all of which imploded in controversy as the band pushed the establishment past its limits. By exposing the hypocrisy of the "rock and roll" establishment, they revealed the huge construction of lies that makes up modern capitalist society: what Guy Debord called "the Society of the Spectacle."

Of course, even the Sex Pistols were defeated in the end (read pg. 34 of the first story in this book: "Punk Car - Get Angry For It"). The death of Sid Vicious was to Punk what Kurt Cobain's was to the Seattle scene: a sign that the hoped-for revolution hadn't come and now it was eating its own children.

But anyway, all this is a digression. What, you're wondering, has all this to do with Tom Hart?

Okay, let's start again. When I first met Tom, it was 1994 and he'd just brought out the first Xeric-funded edition of Hutch Owen's Working Hard. I met him at the aptly-named San Diego Comic Con - a temple to the almighty Spectacle if ever there was one. Tucked away in a dark corner, away from the gigantic Marvel booth (full of loud tv screens), the Barbie Twins signing queues and the souped-up, mag-wheeled Spawnmobile, a small group of sweet, gentle geniuses sat at the small press tables. I'd come all the way from New Zealand to promote my comic book Pickle and was feeling a little overwhelmed by all the noise and, well, horror of it all. But these lovely people soon took me under their wing and showed me a good time. It soon became clear that most of them came from Seattle: Megan Kelso, Jon Lewis, Ed Brubaker, Jon Snyder, James Sturm, David Lasky and, of course, Tom Hart. I now realise that many of these guys weren't Seattle born & bred, but had drifted there over the previous few years - drawn by the twin beacons of the Fantagraphics-centred comics scene and the more famous "seattle scene."

They were all (and are still) mighty fine cartoonists and I've followed their work enthusiastically since. But Tom is the one I'm writing about here, so back to Hutch Owen.

Before Hutch, most of Tom's comics (so far as I could tell) had been lovely, lyrical little minicomics - full of poetry and whimsy, inspired by British cartoonist Glen Dakin and his idol, Finnish writer and cartoonist Tove Jansson (creator of the Moomins). But with Hutch Owen, Tom had taken a huge step in terms of ambition and scope. It was long, hilarious, beautifully drawn and - surprise - political! In light of the atmosphere in Seattle post-Nirvana, it's not surprising that that politics was primarily an attack on the Man. But what saved it from being just another shallow sophomoric rebellion was, of course, the analysis.

"Working Hard" is an attack on the Spectacle. From the hilarious opening scene, in which Worner outlines a plan to market "Malcolm X" merchandise (as Carver says "so long as no one gets hurt") to the epilogue (which I won't give away here, but when you've read it you'll know what I mean), this is a story about the way corporate power co-opts rebellious counter-cultures and movements, rendering them harmless - all in the pursuit of profit.

-->>>

by Dylan Horrocks

But however the plot turns out, this is also an optimistic, joyful story - the satire is urgent and pleasurable. Hutch Owen really does represent an alternative to the bleak hegemony headed by Worner. He lives by an economy in which poetry is the most precious currency and love the commodity it buys. Hutch himself has opted out of the whole sick trip, living in a cabin in the woods and getting by on the pennies he earns from his self-published pamphlets (or zines). However Worner might try to crush Owen and his message, we can't help feeling his victory will be hollow.

Back in 1994 this was such a breath of fresh air - and still is. Even alternative comics - though full of depth and poetry - are rarely openly political, in contrast to the Underground comix (dripping with anarchism, Maoism, feminism and, perhaps most convincingly, Crumb's scathing but ideologically impure socialism). A few welcome exceptions like Rob Walton and Peter Kuper aside, the cartoonists of the 80s and 90s have tended to focus on the internal, personal and individual, rather than the social, political or - heavens help us - economic. In Tom Hart, we're lucky to have a cartoonist who's passionately interested in all of these things. Since the first Hutch Owen, Tom's gone on to draw a number of books of extraordinary intelligence and subtlety: The Sands, Banks/Eubanks, New Hat - all of which break new ground formally and explore relationships and our internal lives. They've earned him a place alongside Chris Ware and Chester Brown as one of the most interesting cartoonists of our generation.

Thankfully, though, he has also continued to revisit Hutch Owen at fairly regular intervals - hence this very welcome collection. Reading them all together like this, it's interesting to see how Tom's analysis has extended in reach (looking at global capitalism in "Emerging Markets") and depth (the complexity and ambivalence of the last two stories). It's also interesting - if a little depressing - to see the change in tone. As we move through the late nineties in "Stocks are Surging!"and "The Road to Self," we find a much less hopeful Hutch. It's as if things have passed him by and no-one's listening anymore. His friends are too busy surfing the net or spending money and even Hutch seems full of doubt now: "I'm broken down. I've been living under a bridge for two weeks - I'm soaked, I smell, I'm completely exhausted... All my books and things are smelly and mouldy - shaking people up just isn't profitable anymore since the economy started "booming". On top of that, now I'm saying things like 'profitable.' "

asked Tom if this shift in tone was a response to the change in the political atmosphere in America during the economic "bubble"of the late nineties. It reminded me of the comics I was doing here in New Zealand during the mid-80s when we experienced a similar share market boom as the result of financial deregulation. Back then the whole country seemed to have gone insane: obsessed with BMWs, yachts, champagne and futures markets. Any kind of alternative dissenting viewpoint was derided and mocked; literary journals began to publish essays arguing that the only meaningful test of an artistic work's value was the one that could be measured in dollars. It was a stark illustration of Marx's observation on the effect of Capitalism on cultural and ethical values: "all that is solid melts into air." Of course the party came to an abrupt end (as they always do) with the 1987 stock market crash, which hit New Zealand harder than most. Through the 1990s, while America was building its current head of steam, we were in the depths of recession, turning the political atmosphere nasty. By the end of that decade the battle lines had finally been redrawn and in 1999 we elected our first centre-left government since the seventies.

Tom agreed that the nineties had taken its toll on Hutch: "except that I really can't be sure of how much of the doubt and pessimism of the later two stories are attributable to the pornography of our recent boom years and how much of it is really attributable to my growing older and more complex myself- more able to see more of the whole picture. I doubt I can ever isolate those two explanations, actually, but I would say certainly that the drive to do more stories is fuelled by the former, for sure. The latter two were very urgent for me- being 4 or 5 years after the first one (and the 2nd story being a sort of build up to that urgency again)."

In a sense this collection provides a chronological chart of the political atmosphere as it evolved during the 1990s - as viewed by our conscience, Hutch Owen. Note, however, that this is only "Volume One"of the Collected Hutch Owen - a fact that fills my heart with joy. It will be interesting to see, as the years progress and future stories are collected, where things will go from here. There are reasons to think the world has begun to turn once again: the Seattle WTO riots and subsequent high profile anti-capitalist demo's in Washington, Europe, Australia etc are just the most obvious signs of a growing breach in that stifling orthodoxy. I keep remembering an essay I once read from the very beginning of the sixties in which a left-wing American academic bemoaned the fact that the younger generation had no interest in politics or social justice and seemed obsessed only with getting good grades, a lucrative job and the latest hot consumer items. Little did he suspect what that same generation was about to do to the world.

As Tom explains, "I sometimes view it as a pleasant personal challenge to do more Hutch Owen stories throughout my life and to hopefully find myself, in the end, with the same exuberence and optimism that the first story had."

For Tom's sake - and ours - let us hope he succeeds.

dylan horrocks

Maraetai Beach
New Zealand, 2000

I. Hutch Owen's Working Hard

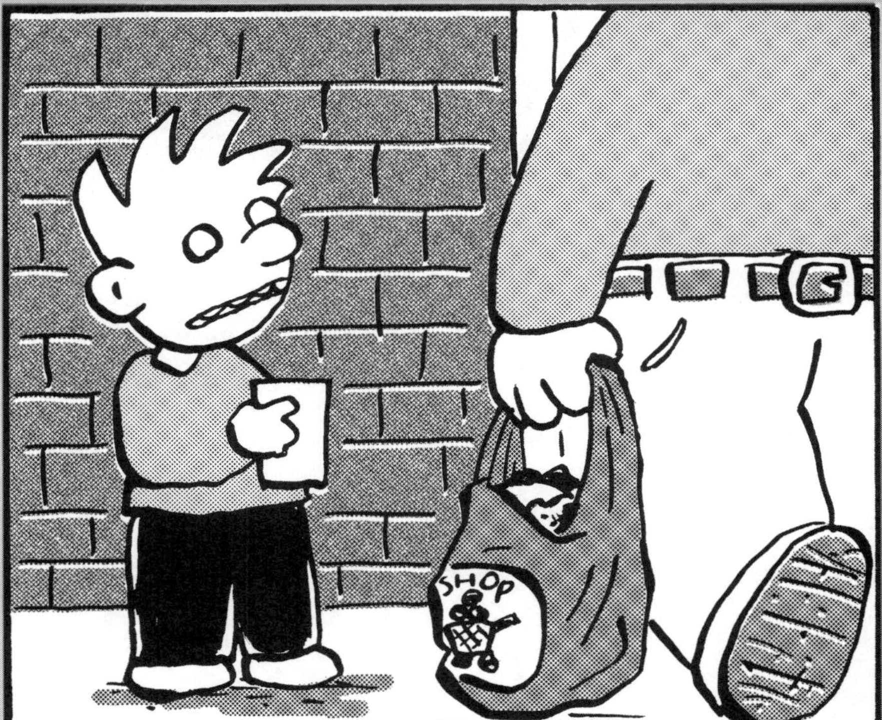
SHOP

for Dad

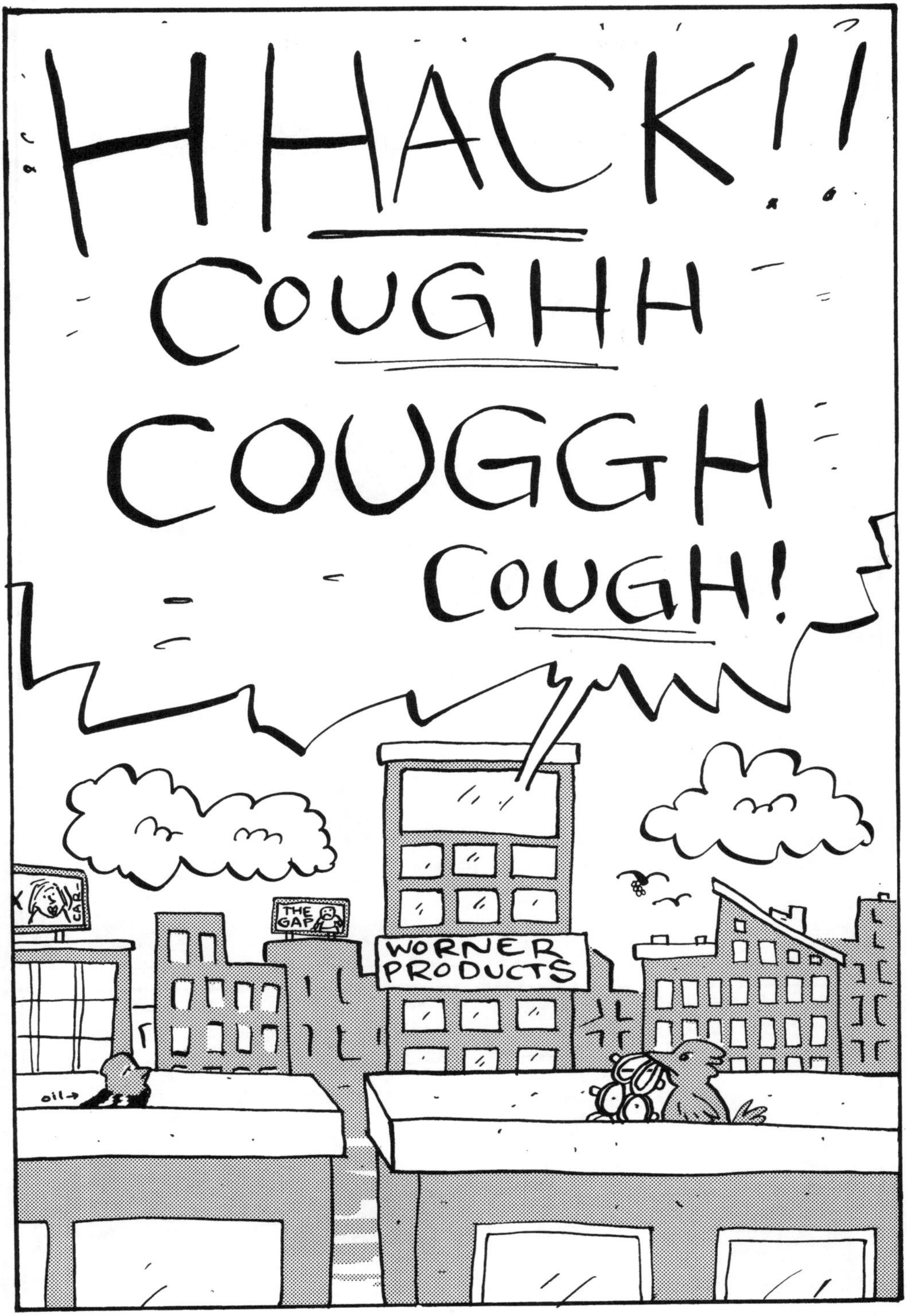
HHACK!!
COUGHH
COUGGH
COUGH!
CAR-
THE GAP
WORNER PRODUCTS
oil→

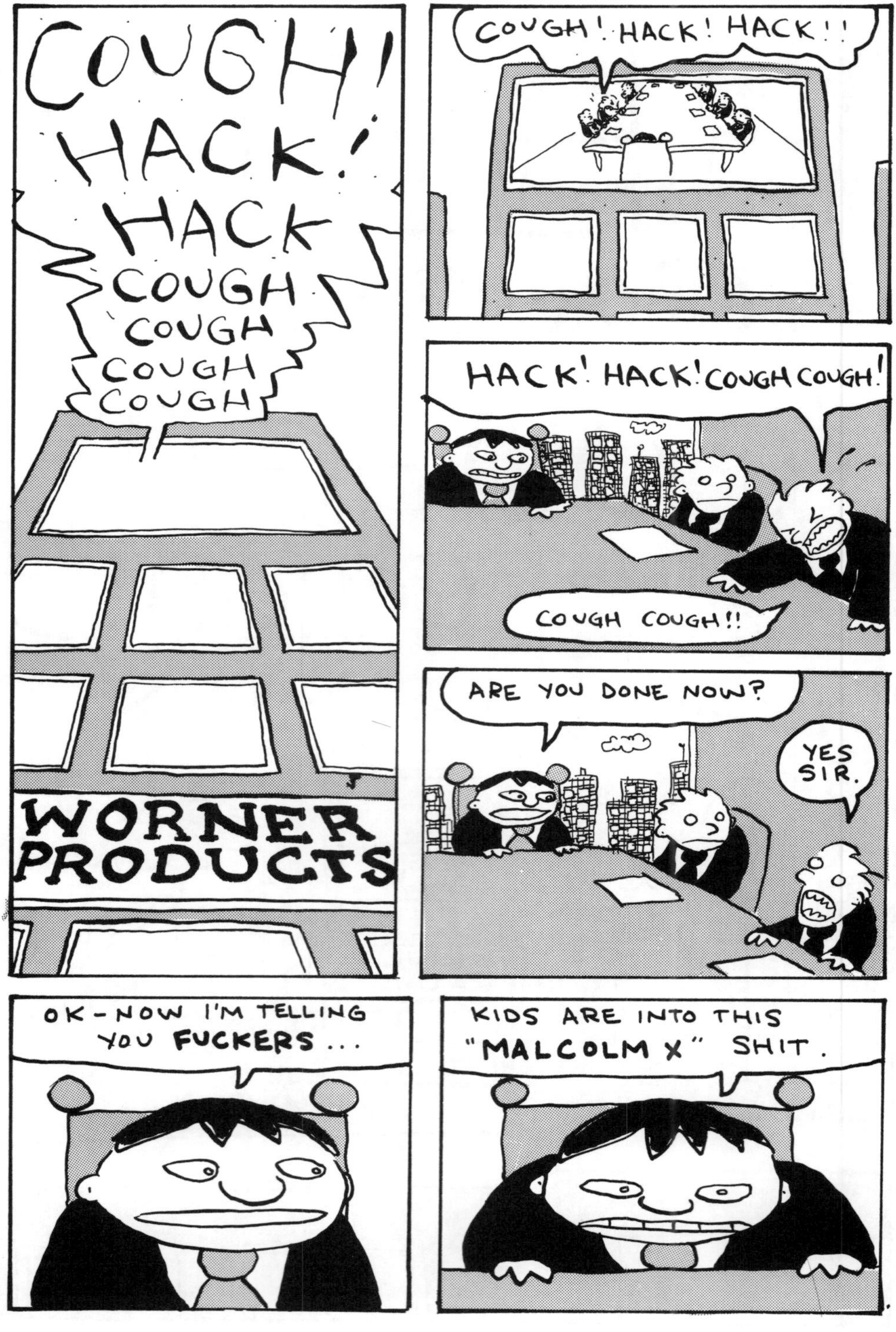

COUGH! HACK! HACK COUGH COUGH COUGH COUGH
WORNER PRODUCTS
COUGH! HACK! HACK!!
HACK! HACK! COUGH COUGH!
COUGH COUGH!!
ARE YOU DONE NOW?
YES SIR.
OK - NOW I'M TELLING YOU **FUCKERS** ...
KIDS ARE INTO THIS "**MALCOLM X**" SHIT.

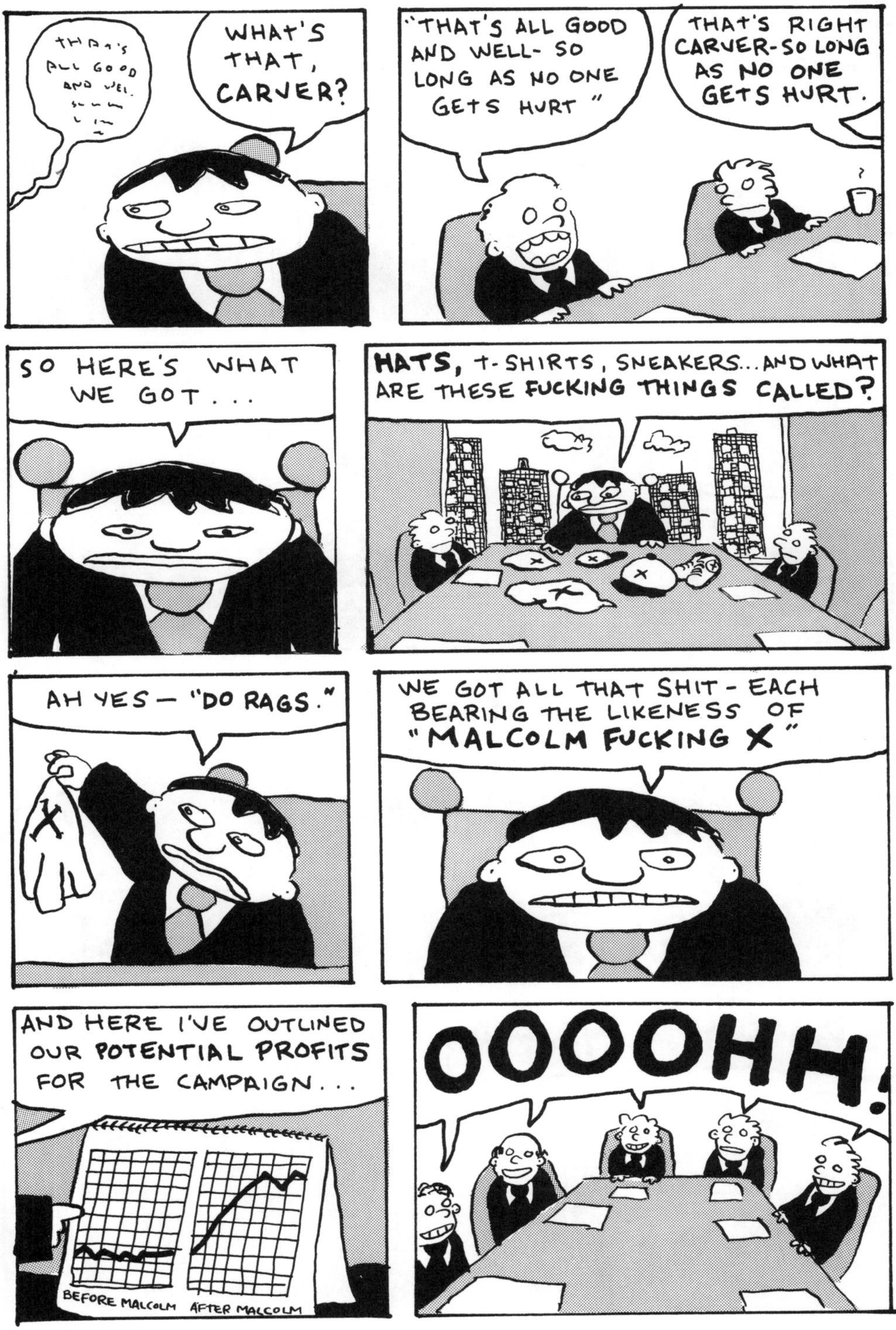
WHAT'S THAT, CARVER?
"THAT'S ALL GOOD AND WELL- SO LONG AS NO ONE GETS HURT"
THAT'S RIGHT CARVER- SO LONG AS NO ONE GETS HURT.
SO HERE'S WHAT WE GOT . . .
HATS, T-SHIRTS, SNEAKERS... AND WHAT ARE THESE FUCKING THINGS CALLED?
AH YES — "DO RAGS."
WE GOT ALL THAT SHIT - EACH BEARING THE LIKENESS OF "MALCOLM FUCKING X"
AND HERE I'VE OUTLINED OUR POTENTIAL PROFITS FOR THE CAMPAIGN . . .
BEFORE MALCOLM
AFTER MALCOLM
OOOOHH!

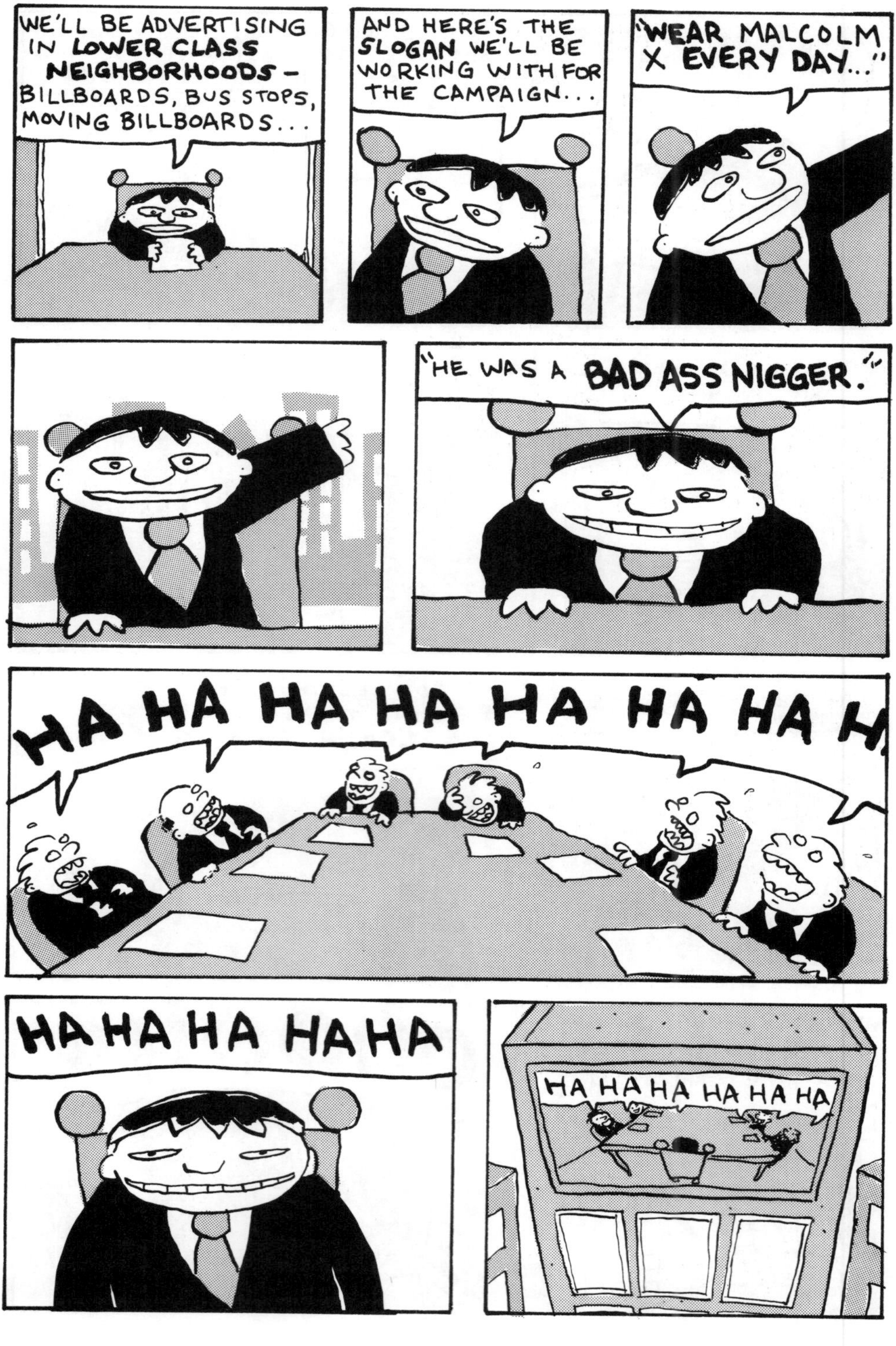
WE'LL BE ADVERTISING IN LOWER CLASS NEIGHBORHOODS – BILLBOARDS, BUS STOPS, MOVING BILLBOARDS...
AND HERE'S THE SLOGAN WE'LL BE WORKING WITH FOR THE CAMPAIGN...
"WEAR MALCOLM X EVERY DAY..."
"HE WAS A BAD ASS NIGGER."
HA HA HA HA HA HA HA H
HAHAHA HA HAHA
HA HAHA HA HA HA HA

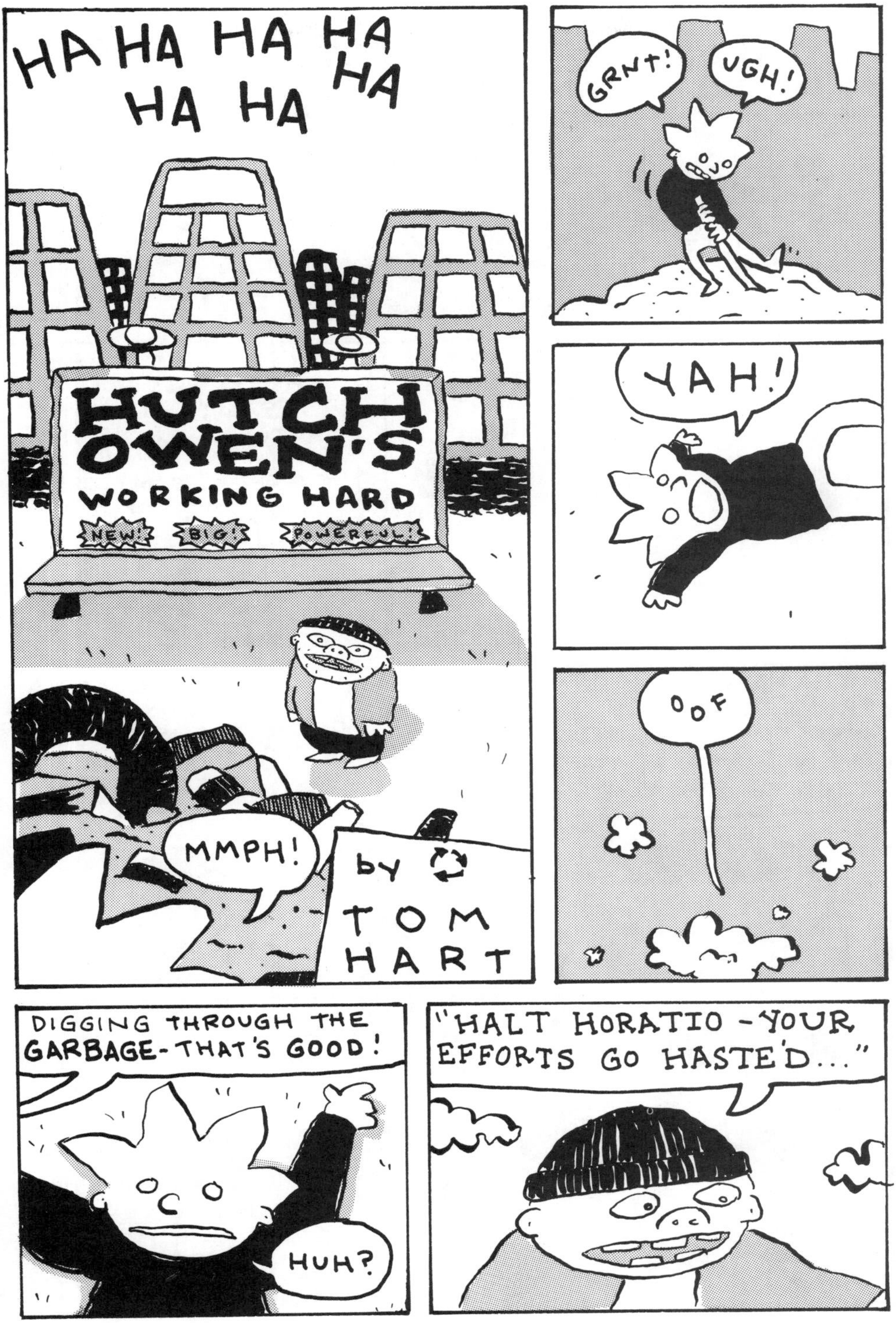
HA HA HA HA HA HA HA
HUTCH OWEN'S
WORKING HARD
NEW! BIG! POWERFUL!
MMPH!
by TOM HART
GRNT!
UGH!
YAH!
OOF
DIGGING THROUGH THE GARBAGE- THAT'S GOOD!
HUH?
"HALT HORATIO - YOUR EFFORTS GO HASTE'D..."

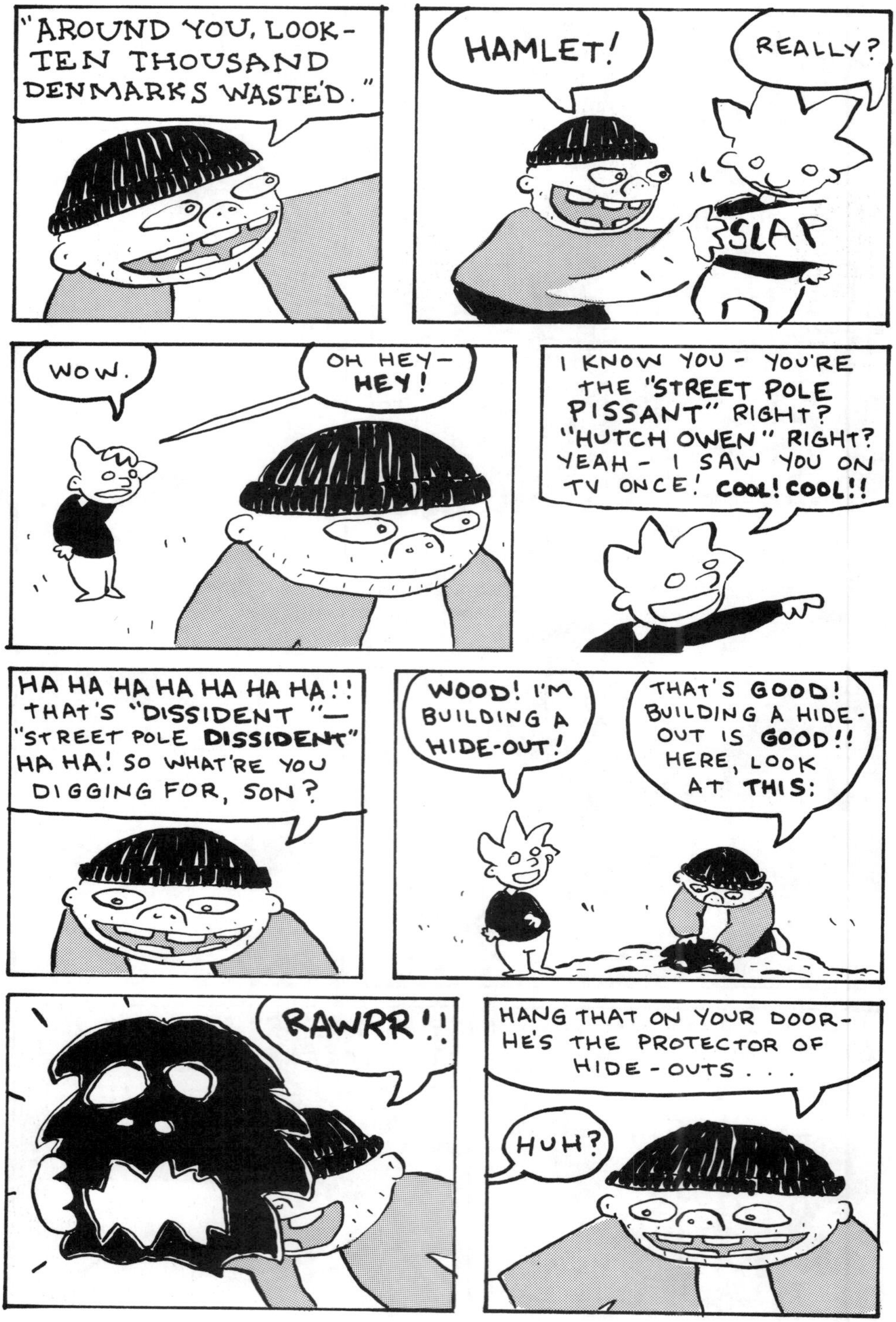
"AROUND YOU, LOOK- TEN THOUSAND DENMARKS WASTE'D."
HAMLET!
REALLY?
SLAP
WOW.
OH HEY- HEY!
I KNOW YOU - YOU'RE THE "STREET POLE PISSANT" RIGHT? "HUTCH OWEN" RIGHT? YEAH - I SAW YOU ON TV ONCE! COOL! COOL!!
HA HA HA HA HA HA HA HA!! THAT'S "DISSIDENT"— "STREET POLE DISSIDENT" HA HA! SO WHAT'RE YOU DIGGING FOR, SON?
WOOD! I'M BUILDING A HIDE-OUT!
THAT'S GOOD! BUILDING A HIDE-OUT IS GOOD!! HERE, LOOK AT THIS:
RAWRR!!
HANG THAT ON YOUR DOOR- HE'S THE PROTECTOR OF HIDE-OUTS...
HUH?

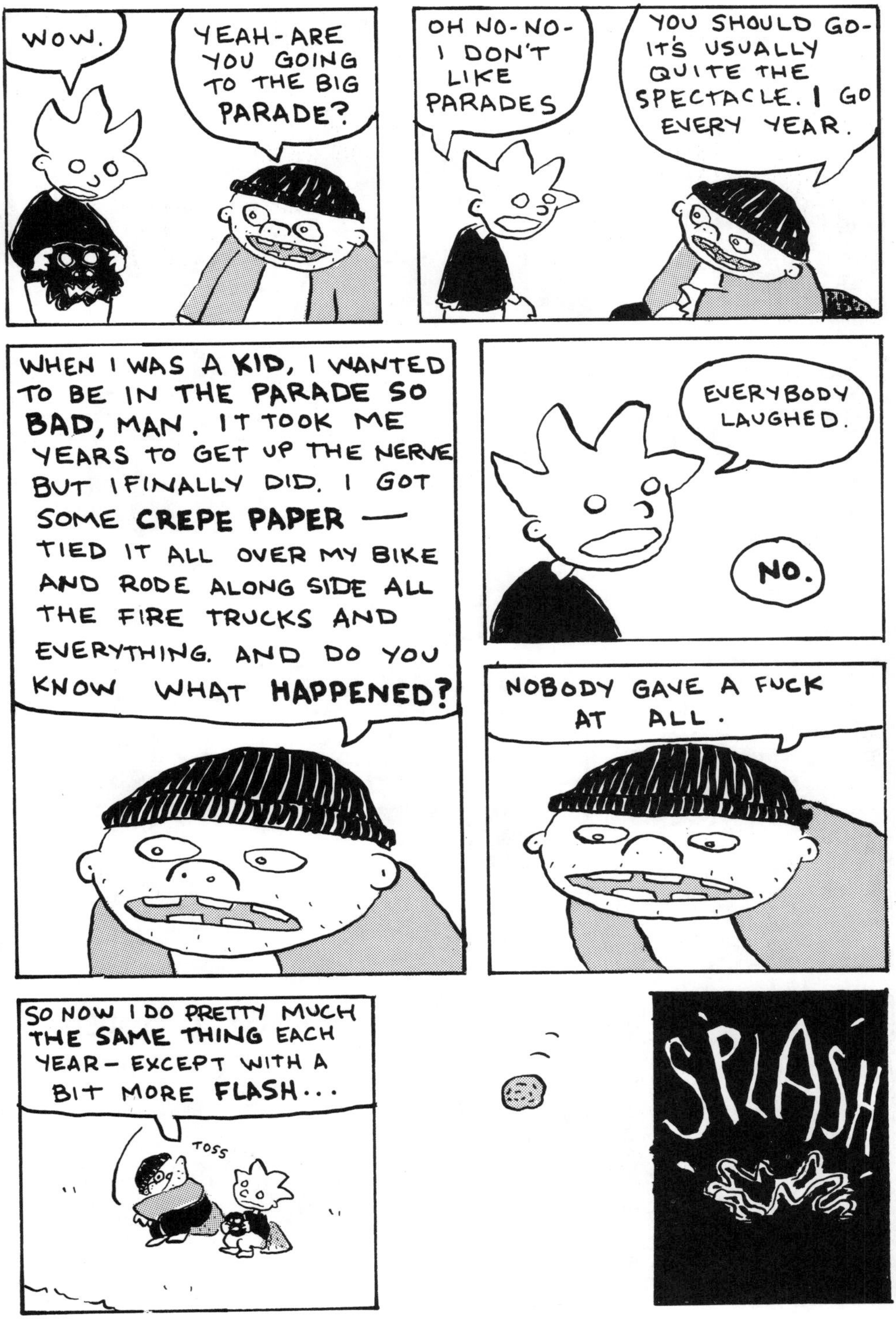

WOW.
YEAH-ARE YOU GOING TO THE BIG PARADE?
OH NO-NO- I DON'T LIKE PARADES
YOU SHOULD GO- IT'S USUALLY QUITE THE SPECTACLE. I GO EVERY YEAR.
WHEN I WAS A KID, I WANTED TO BE IN THE PARADE SO BAD, MAN. IT TOOK ME YEARS TO GET UP THE NERVE BUT I FINALLY DID. I GOT SOME CREPE PAPER — TIED IT ALL OVER MY BIKE AND RODE ALONG SIDE ALL THE FIRE TRUCKS AND EVERYTHING. AND DO YOU KNOW WHAT HAPPENED?
EVERYBODY LAUGHED.
NO.
NOBODY GAVE A FUCK AT ALL.
SO NOW I DO PRETTY MUCH THE SAME THING EACH YEAR- EXCEPT WITH A BIT MORE FLASH...
TOSS
SPLASH

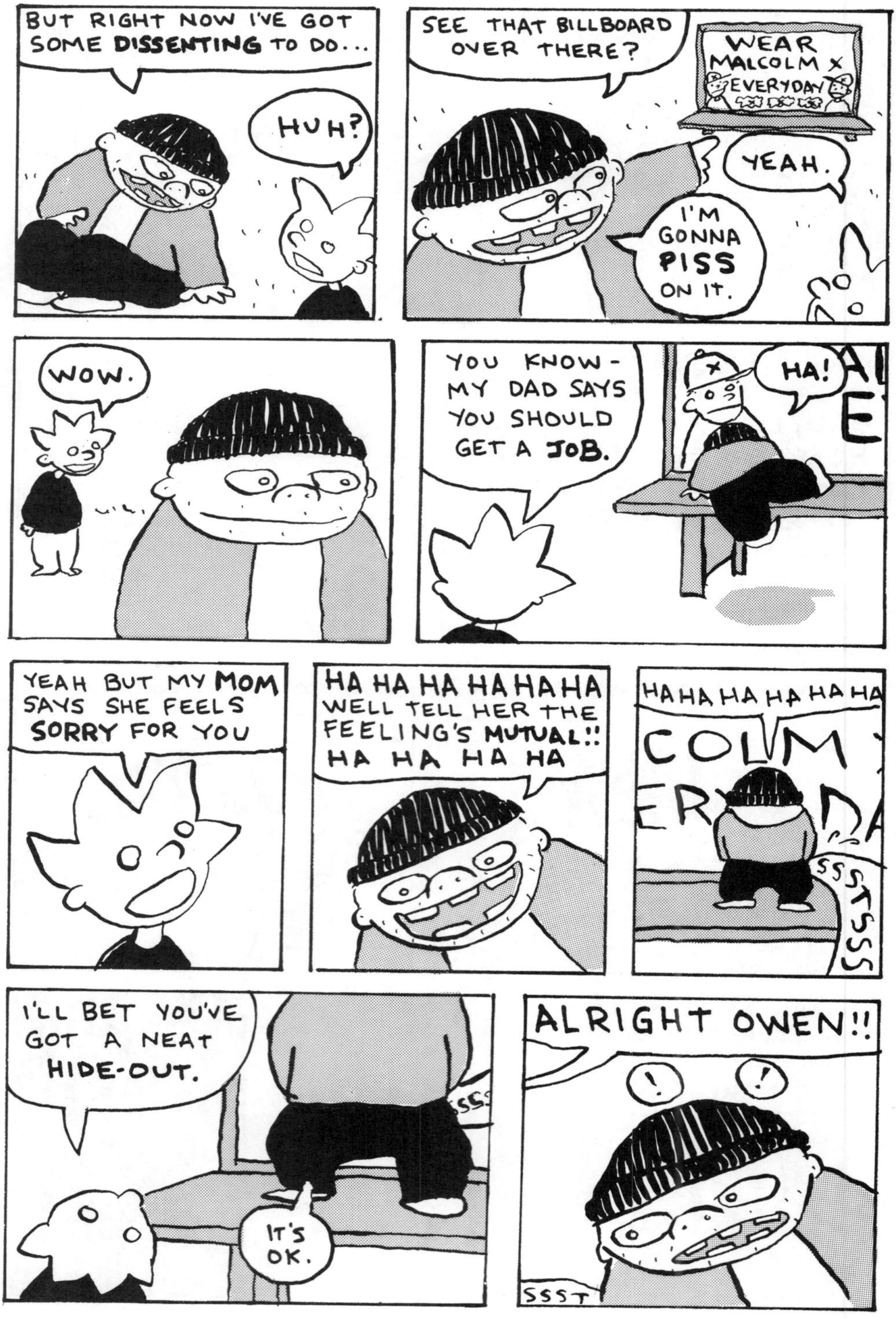
BUT RIGHT NOW I'VE GOT SOME DISSENTING TO DO...
HUH?
SEE THAT BILLBOARD OVER THERE?
WEAR MALCOLM X EVERYDAY
YEAH.
I'M GONNA PISS ON IT.
WOW.
YOU KNOW- MY DAD SAYS YOU SHOULD GET A JOB.
HA!
YEAH BUT MY MOM SAYS SHE FEELS SORRY FOR YOU
HA HA HA HA HA HA HA WELL TELL HER THE FEELING'S MUTUAL!! HA HA HA HA
HA HA HA HA HA HA HA
COLM
SSSTSSSSS
I'LL BET YOU'VE GOT A NEAT HIDE-OUT.
IT'S OK.
ALRIGHT OWEN!!
! !
SSST

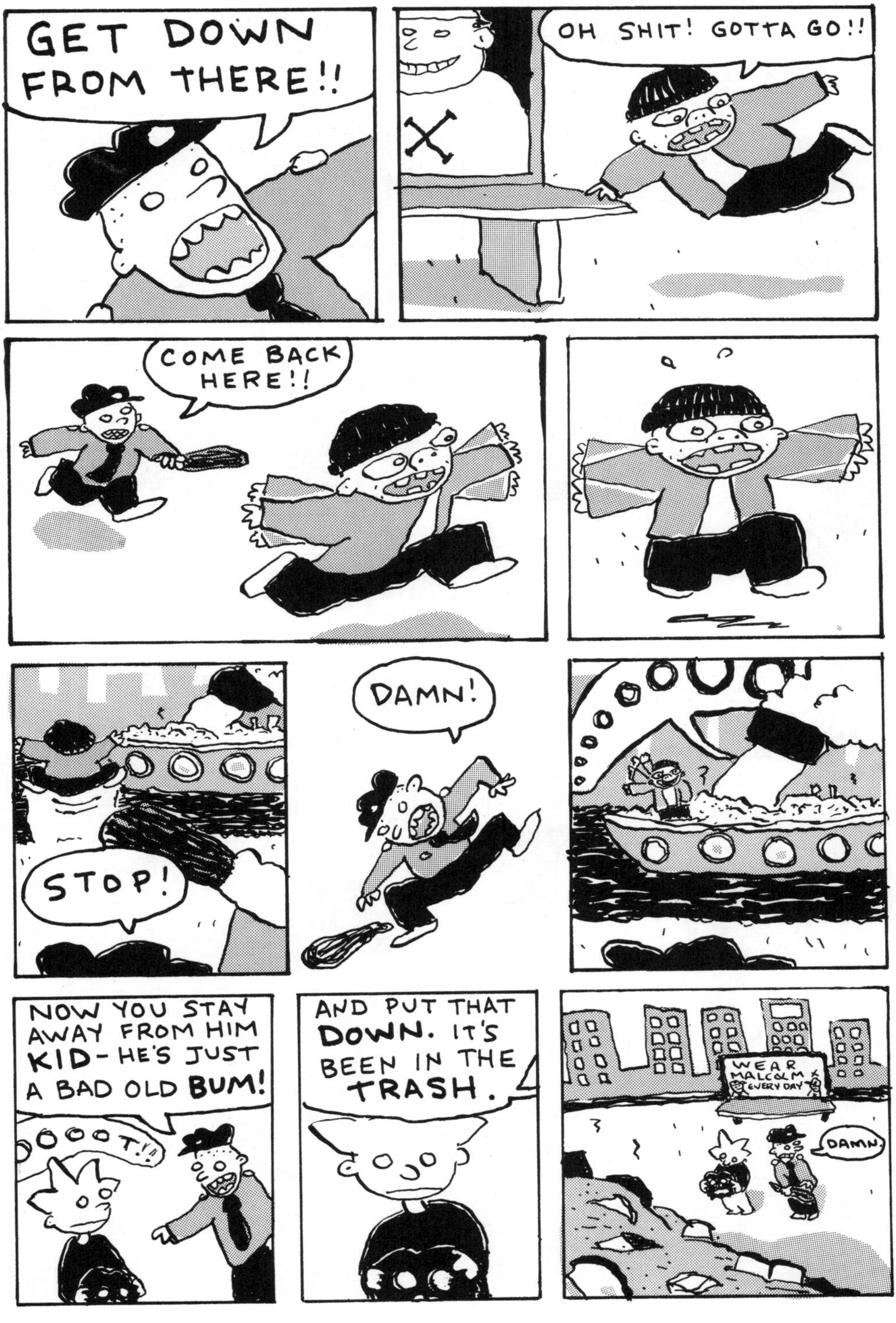
GET DOWN FROM THERE!!
OH SHIT! GOTTA GO!!
COME BACK HERE!!
STOP!
DAMN!
NOW YOU STAY AWAY FROM HIM KID - HE'S JUST A BAD OLD BUM!
OOOOT!!
AND PUT THAT DOWN. IT'S BEEN IN THE TRASH.
WEAR MALCOLM X EVERY DAY
DAMN.

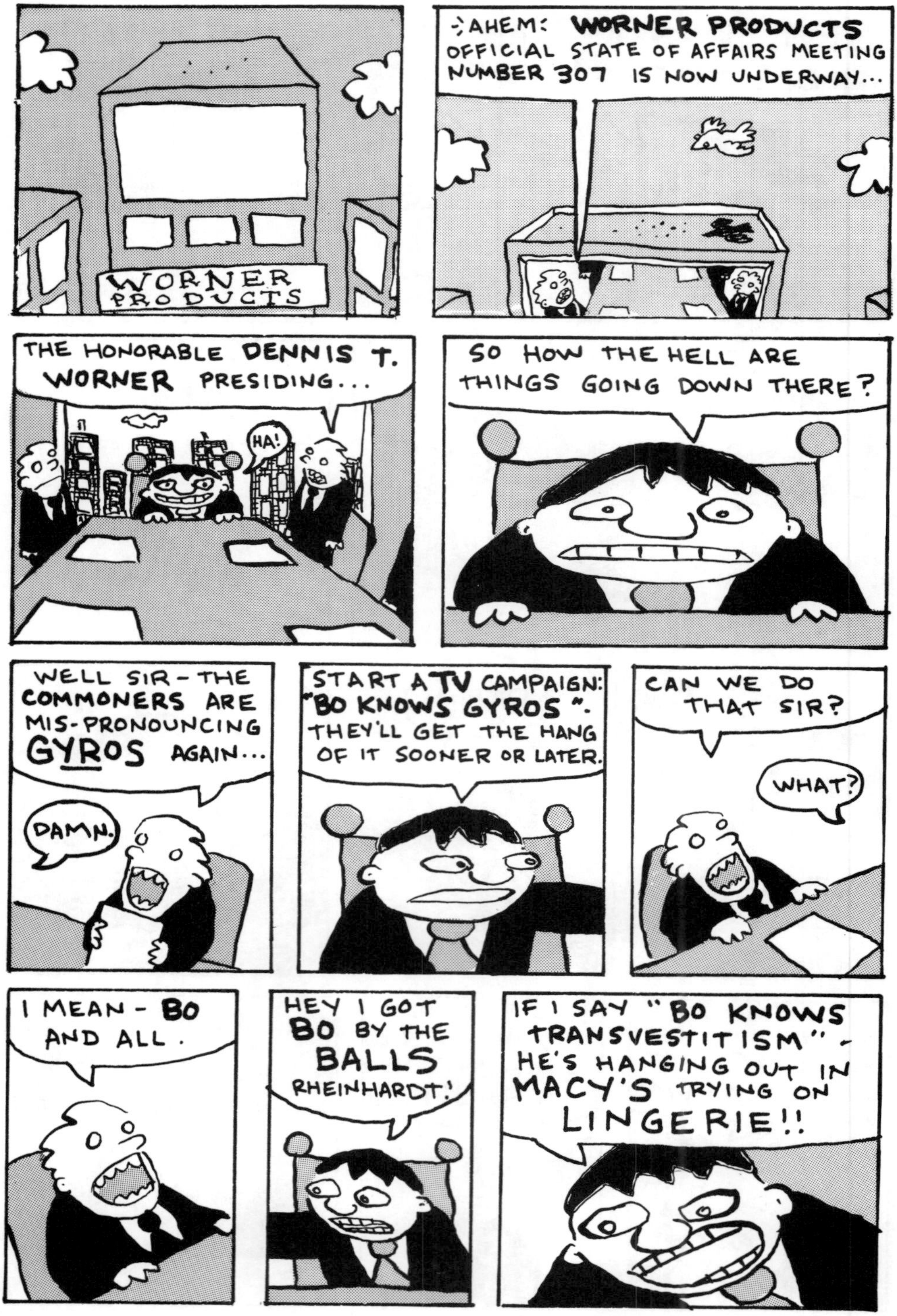
WORNER PRODUCTS
:AHEM: WORNER PRODUCTS OFFICIAL STATE OF AFFAIRS MEETING NUMBER 307 IS NOW UNDERWAY...
THE HONORABLE DENNIS T. WORNER PRESIDING...
HA!
SO HOW THE HELL ARE THINGS GOING DOWN THERE?
WELL SIR - THE COMMONERS ARE MIS-PRONOUNCING GYROS AGAIN...
DAMN.
START A TV CAMPAIGN: "BO KNOWS GYROS". THEY'LL GET THE HANG OF IT SOONER OR LATER.
CAN WE DO THAT SIR?
WHAT?
I MEAN - BO AND ALL.
HEY I GOT BO BY THE BALLS RHEINHARDT!
IF I SAY "BO KNOWS TRANSVESTITISM" - HE'S HANGING OUT IN MACY'S TRYING ON LINGERIE!!

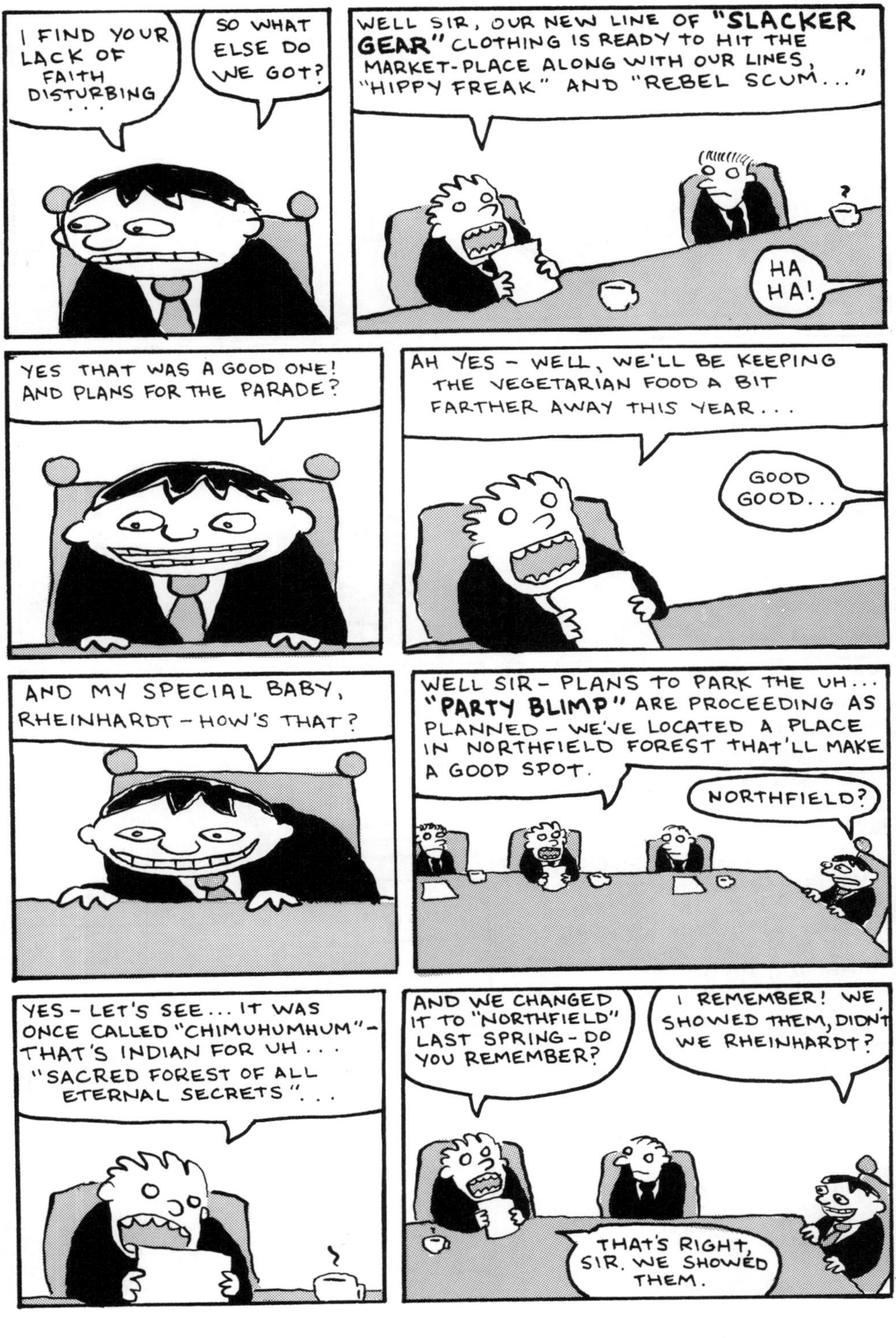
I FIND YOUR LACK OF FAITH DISTURBING . . .
SO WHAT ELSE DO WE GOT?
WELL SIR, OUR NEW LINE OF "SLACKER GEAR" CLOTHING IS READY TO HIT THE MARKET-PLACE ALONG WITH OUR LINES, "HIPPY FREAK" AND "REBEL SCUM..."
HA HA!
YES THAT WAS A GOOD ONE! AND PLANS FOR THE PARADE?
AH YES - WELL, WE'LL BE KEEPING THE VEGETARIAN FOOD A BIT FARTHER AWAY THIS YEAR...
GOOD GOOD...
AND MY SPECIAL BABY, RHEINHARDT - HOW'S THAT?
WELL SIR - PLANS TO PARK THE UH... "PARTY BLIMP" ARE PROCEEDING AS PLANNED - WE'VE LOCATED A PLACE IN NORTHFIELD FOREST THAT'LL MAKE A GOOD SPOT.
NORTHFIELD?
YES - LET'S SEE... IT WAS ONCE CALLED "CHIMUHUMHUM" - THAT'S INDIAN FOR UH . . . "SACRED FOREST OF ALL ETERNAL SECRETS". . .
AND WE CHANGED IT TO "NORTHFIELD" LAST SPRING - DO YOU REMEMBER?
I REMEMBER! WE SHOWED THEM, DIDN'T WE RHEINHARDT?
THAT'S RIGHT, SIR. WE SHOWED THEM.

AND FRISTON HAS THE MAIL, SIR.

FRISTON?

AH YES— THIS CAME IN FROM "MATTY PLEVA" OF THE LOWER DISTRICT: "DEAR SIRS, RECENTLY I SAW YOUR "GRATUITATOR 2" MOVIE. THIS MOVIE WAS ADVERTISED AS HAVING "TWICE THE CARNAGE" WHEN IN FACT IT HAD NOWHERE NEAR TWICE THE CARNAGE..."

"IT FEATURED, IN FACT, 22 CAR CHASES COMPARED TO NUMBER ONE'S 16. 430 ROUNDS OF GUN-FIRE COMPARED TO 320, AND 32 DEATHS TO 18. ITS ONLY "SUCCESS" OCCURRED IN ITS **NEAR-DEATH INJURIES** WITH 58 COMPARED TO NUMBER ONE'S 25..."

"THE QUESTION ARISES, HOWEVER, OF WHETHER IT IS EVEN **ETHICAL** TO CONSIDER **NEAR-DEATH INJURIES** TO BE "CARNAGE" AT ALL. PLEASE REFRAIN FROM MISLEADING YOUR AUDIENCE IN THE FUTURE. SINCERELY, MATTY PLEVA, LOWER DISTRICT."

YOU LISTEN TO ME, FRISTON...

YOU TELL THAT LITTLE HEART PATIENT TO GET HIS LITTLE SCORECARD READY CAUSE WE GOT **GRATUITATOR 3** COMING OUT WITH **THREE** TIMES THE CARNAGE OF **NUMBER 2**! THAT'S **SIX** TIMES THE CARNAGE OF FUCKING **NUMBER ONE**!! WE GOT BODIES FLYING ALL OVER, FUCKING **HEADS** BEING **BASHED APART**, GUTS AND SHIT HE CAN'T EVEN IMAGINE AND WE'RE GOING TO USE **HIM** AS A **PROP**.!! **WRITE IT DOWN!!**

YES, SIR.

SO WHAT ELSE WE GOT?

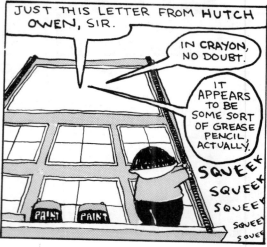

JUST THIS LETTER FROM **HUTCH OWEN**, SIR.

IN CRAYON, NO DOUBT.

IT APPEARS TO BE SOME SORT OF GREASE PENCIL, ACTUALLY.

SQUEEK SQUEEK SQUEEK SQUEEK SQUEEK

PAINT PAINT

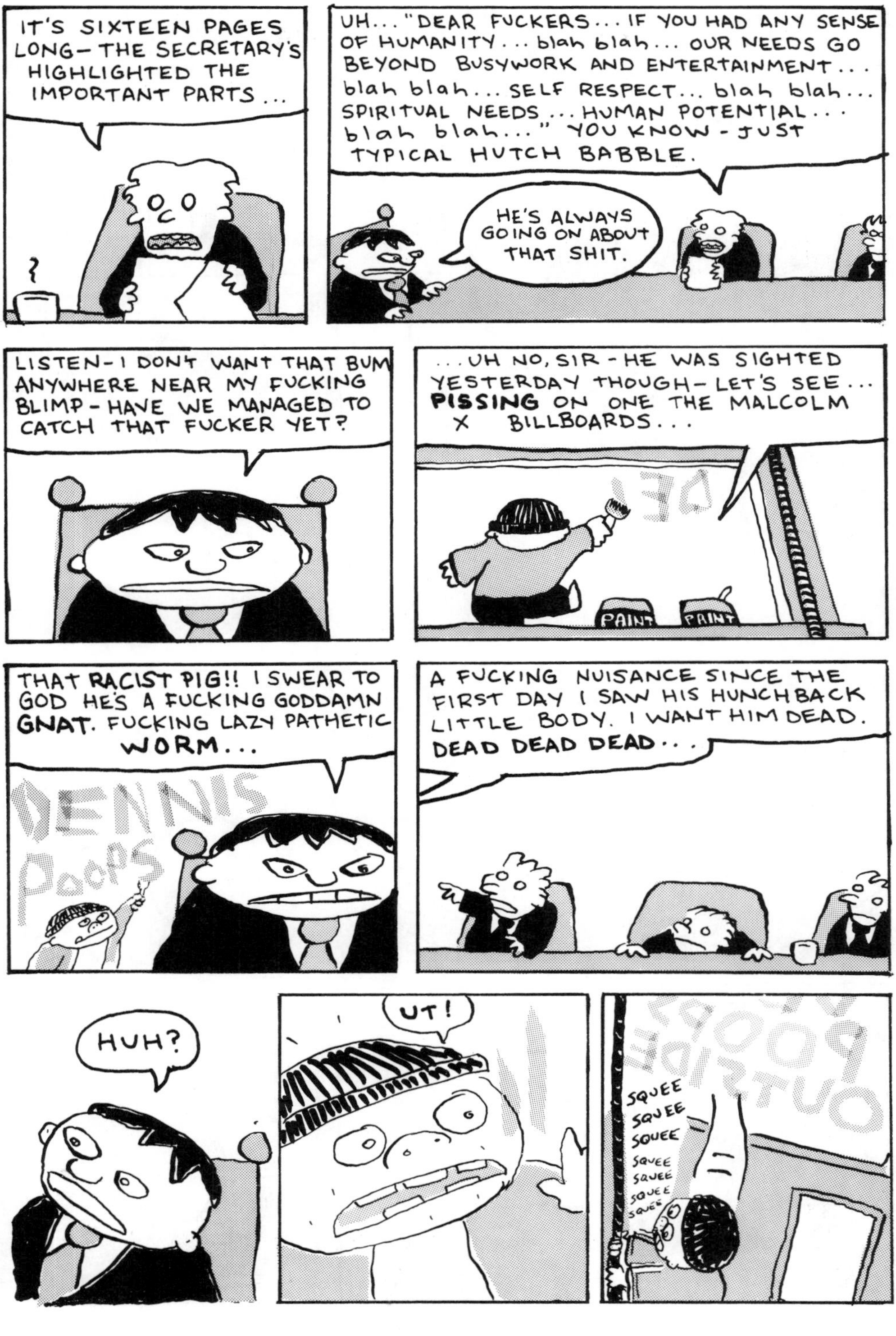
IT'S SIXTEEN PAGES LONG— THE SECRETARY'S HIGHLIGHTED THE IMPORTANT PARTS...
UH..."DEAR FUCKERS... IF YOU HAD ANY SENSE OF HUMANITY... blah blah... OUR NEEDS GO BEYOND BUSYWORK AND ENTERTAINMENT... blah blah... SELF RESPECT... blah blah... SPIRITUAL NEEDS... HUMAN POTENTIAL... blah blah..." YOU KNOW - JUST TYPICAL HUTCH BABBLE.
HE'S ALWAYS GOING ON ABOUT THAT SHIT.
LISTEN- I DON'T WANT THAT BUM ANYWHERE NEAR MY FUCKING BLIMP- HAVE WE MANAGED TO CATCH THAT FUCKER YET?
...UH NO, SIR - HE WAS SIGHTED YESTERDAY THOUGH- LET'S SEE... PISSING ON ONE THE MALCOLM X BILLBOARDS...
PAINT
PAINT
THAT RACIST PIG!! I SWEAR TO GOD HE'S A FUCKING GODDAMN GNAT. FUCKING LAZY PATHETIC WORM...
DENNIS Poops
A FUCKING NUISANCE SINCE THE FIRST DAY I SAW HIS HUNCHBACK LITTLE BODY. I WANT HIM DEAD. DEAD DEAD DEAD...
HUH?
UT!
SQUEE
SQUEE
SQUEE
SQUEE
SQUEE
SQUEE
SQUEE

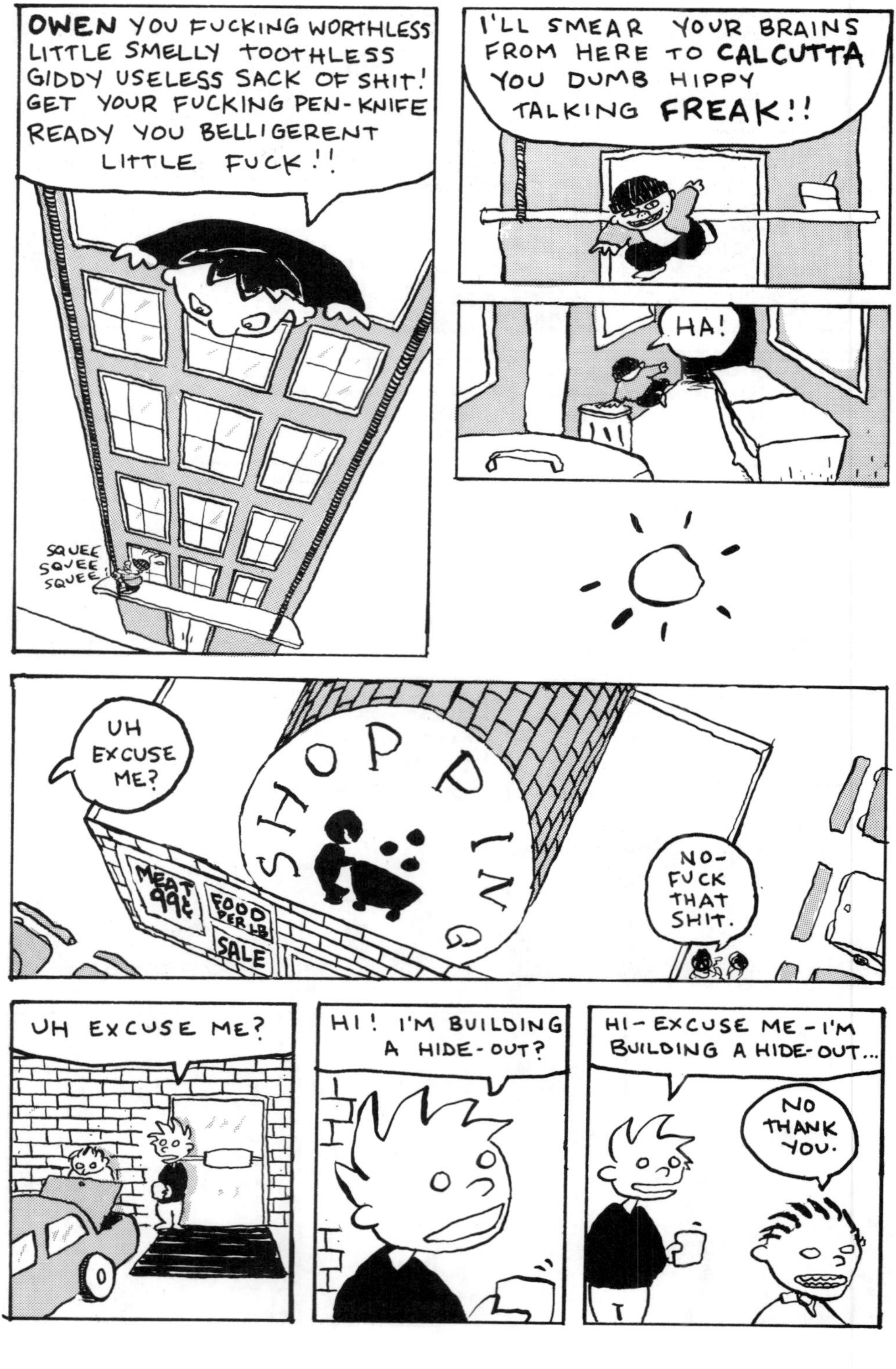
OWEN YOU FUCKING WORTHLESS LITTLE SMELLY TOOTHLESS GIDDY USELESS SACK OF SHIT! GET YOUR FUCKING PEN-KNIFE READY YOU BELLIGERENT LITTLE FUCK!!
SQUEE SQUEE SQUEE
I'LL SMEAR YOUR BRAINS FROM HERE TO CALCUTTA YOU DUMB HIPPY TALKING FREAK!!
HA!
UH EXCUSE ME?
SHOPPING
MEAT 99¢
FOOD PER LB
SALE
NO- FUCK THAT SHIT.
UH EXCUSE ME?
HI! I'M BUILDING A HIDE-OUT?
HI- EXCUSE ME- I'M BUILDING A HIDE-OUT...
NO THANK YOU.

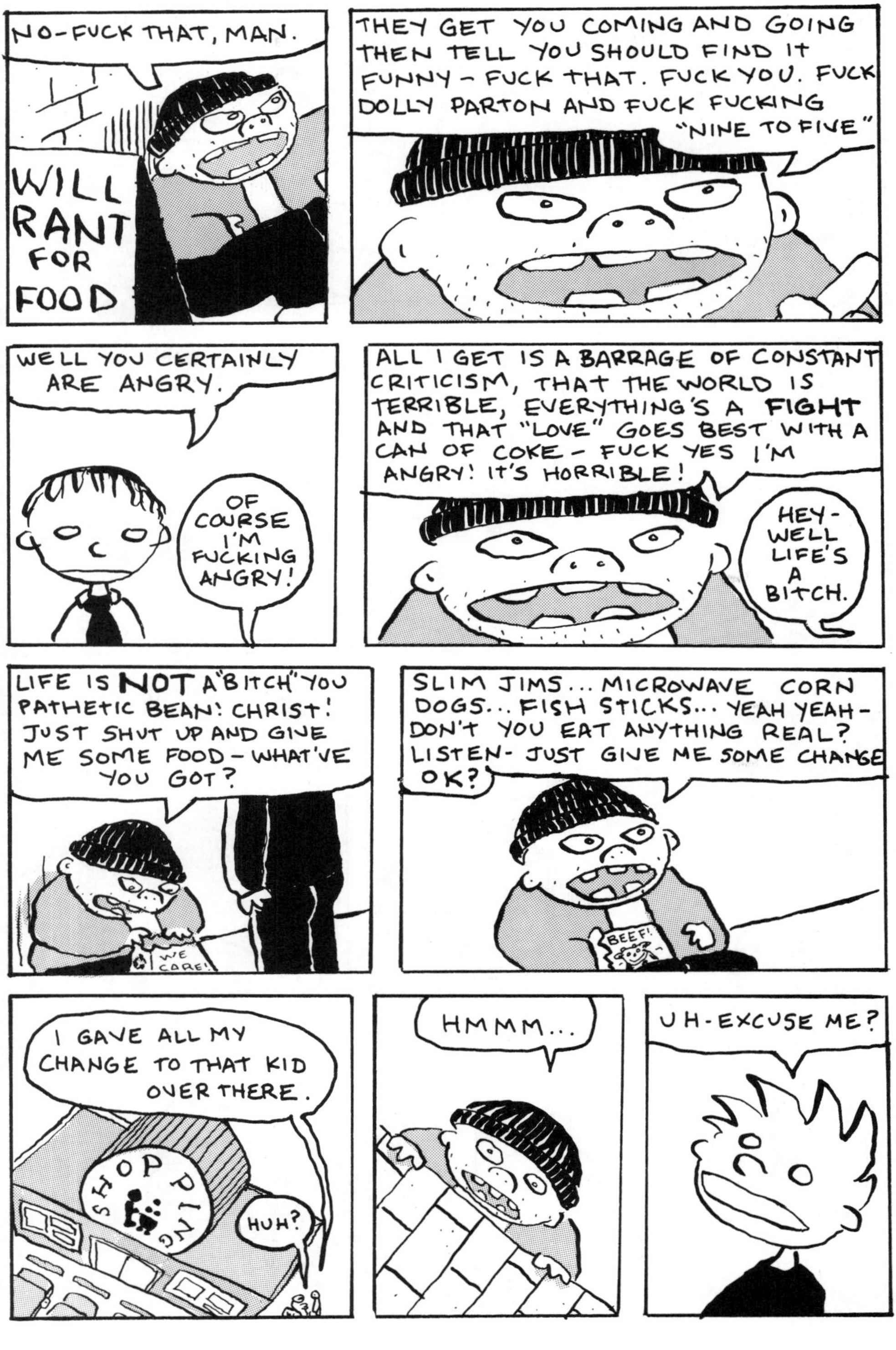
NO-FUCK THAT, MAN.
WILL RANT FOR FOOD
THEY GET YOU COMING AND GOING THEN TELL YOU SHOULD FIND IT FUNNY - FUCK THAT. FUCK YOU. FUCK DOLLY PARTON AND FUCK FUCKING "NINE TO FIVE"
WELL YOU CERTAINLY ARE ANGRY.
OF COURSE I'M FUCKING ANGRY!
ALL I GET IS A BARRAGE OF CONSTANT CRITICISM, THAT THE WORLD IS TERRIBLE, EVERYTHING'S A FIGHT AND THAT "LOVE" GOES BEST WITH A CAN OF COKE - FUCK YES I'M ANGRY! IT'S HORRIBLE!
HEY- WELL LIFE'S A BITCH.
LIFE IS NOT A "BITCH" YOU PATHETIC BEAN! CHRIST! JUST SHUT UP AND GIVE ME SOME FOOD - WHAT'VE YOU GOT?
WE CARE!
SLIM JIMS... MICROWAVE CORN DOGS... FISH STICKS... YEAH YEAH - DON'T YOU EAT ANYTHING REAL? LISTEN- JUST GIVE ME SOME CHANGE OK?
BEEF!
I GAVE ALL MY CHANGE TO THAT KID OVER THERE.
SHOPPING
HUH?
HMMM...
UH-EXCUSE ME?

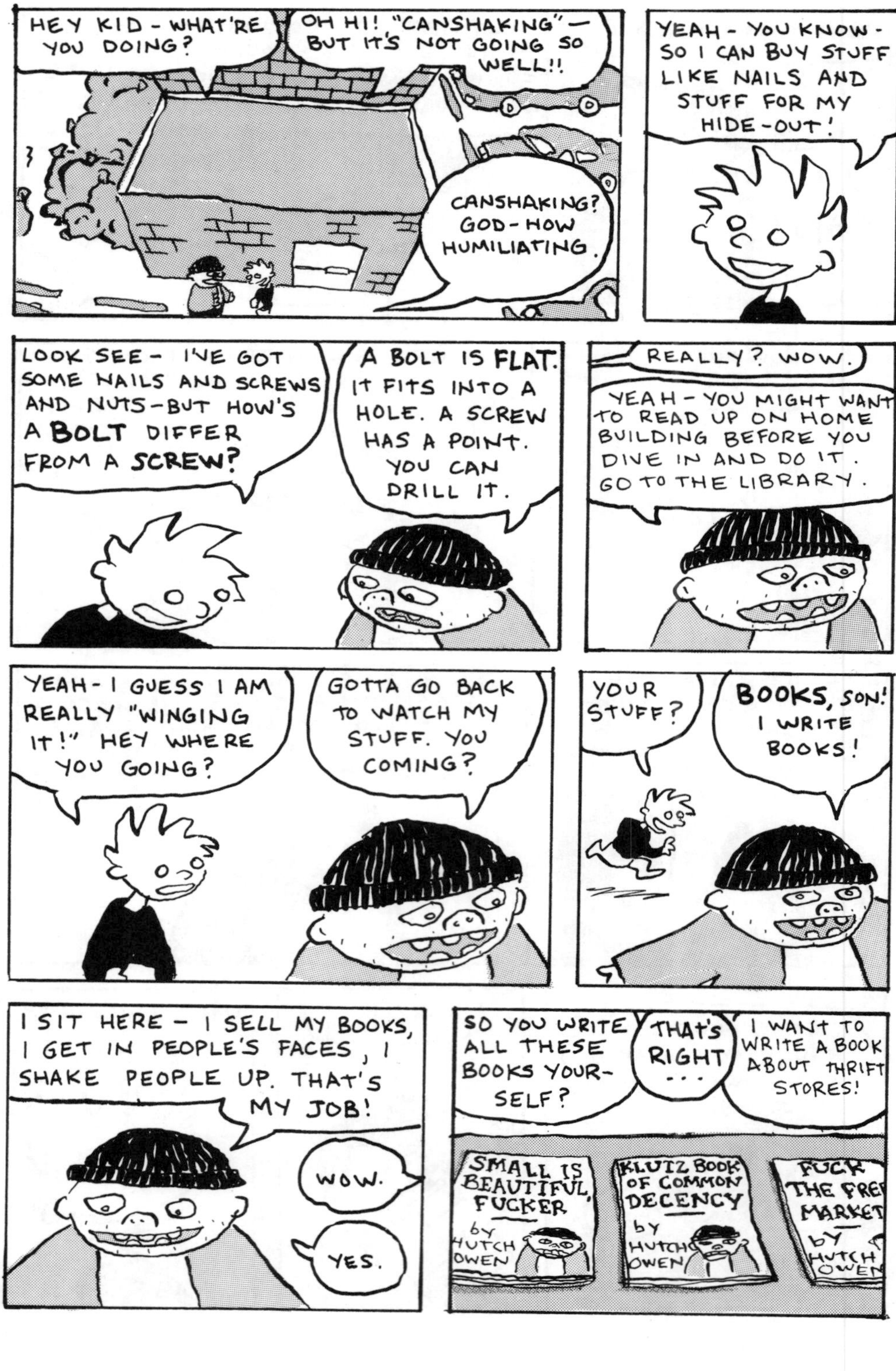

HEY KID - WHAT'RE YOU DOING?
OH HI! "CANSHAKING" — BUT IT'S NOT GOING SO WELL!!
CANSHAKING? GOD - HOW HUMILIATING.
YEAH - YOU KNOW - SO I CAN BUY STUFF LIKE NAILS AND STUFF FOR MY HIDE-OUT!
LOOK SEE - I'VE GOT SOME NAILS AND SCREWS AND NUTS - BUT HOW'S A BOLT DIFFER FROM A SCREW?
A BOLT IS FLAT. IT FITS INTO A HOLE. A SCREW HAS A POINT. YOU CAN DRILL IT.
REALLY? WOW.
YEAH - YOU MIGHT WANT TO READ UP ON HOME BUILDING BEFORE YOU DIVE IN AND DO IT. GO TO THE LIBRARY.
YEAH - I GUESS I AM REALLY "WINGING IT!" HEY WHERE YOU GOING?
GOTTA GO BACK TO WATCH MY STUFF. YOU COMING?
YOUR STUFF?
BOOKS, SON! I WRITE BOOKS!
I SIT HERE - I SELL MY BOOKS, I GET IN PEOPLE'S FACES, I SHAKE PEOPLE UP. THAT'S MY JOB!
WOW.
YES.
SO YOU WRITE ALL THESE BOOKS YOURSELF?
THAT'S RIGHT ...
I WANT TO WRITE A BOOK ABOUT THRIFT STORES!
SMALL IS BEAUTIFUL, FUCKER by HUTCH OWEN
KLUTZ BOOK OF COMMON DECENCY by HUTCH OWEN
FUCK THE FREE MARKET by HUTCH OWEN

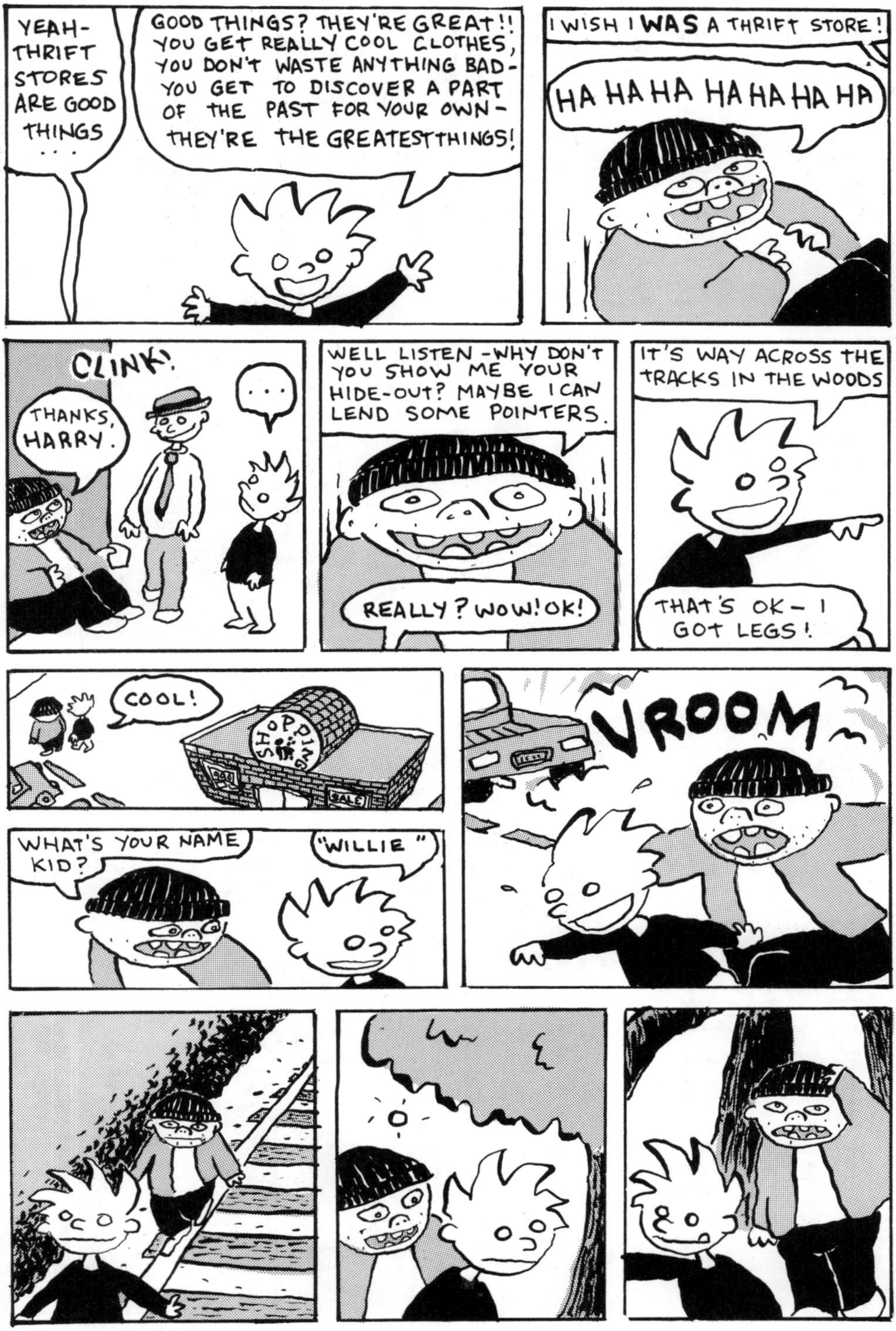

YEAH- THRIFT STORES ARE GOOD THINGS . . .
GOOD THINGS? THEY'RE GREAT!! YOU GET REALLY COOL CLOTHES, YOU DON'T WASTE ANYTHING BAD- YOU GET TO DISCOVER A PART OF THE PAST FOR YOUR OWN- THEY'RE THE GREATEST THINGS!
I WISH I WAS A THRIFT STORE!
HA HA HA HA HA HA HA
CLINK!
THANKS, HARRY.
. . .
WELL LISTEN - WHY DON'T YOU SHOW ME YOUR HIDE-OUT? MAYBE I CAN LEND SOME POINTERS.
REALLY? WOW! OK!
IT'S WAY ACROSS THE TRACKS IN THE WOODS
THAT'S OK - I GOT LEGS!
COOL!
SHOPPING
SALE
VROOM
WHAT'S YOUR NAME KID?
"WILLIE"

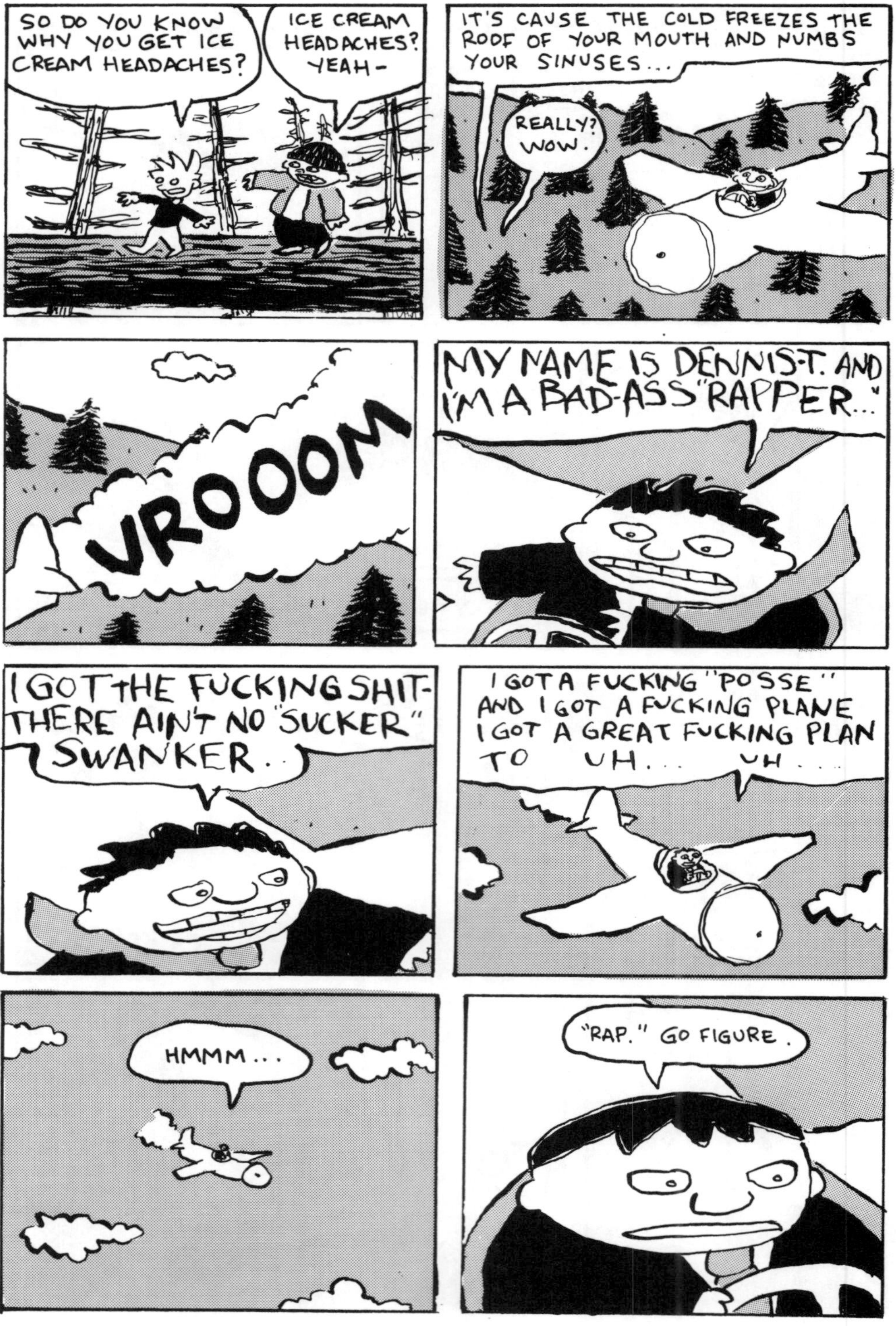

SO DO YOU KNOW WHY YOU GET ICE CREAM HEADACHES?
ICE CREAM HEADACHES? YEAH -
IT'S CAUSE THE COLD FREEZES THE ROOF OF YOUR MOUTH AND NUMBS YOUR SINUSES...
REALLY? WOW.
VROOOM
MY NAME IS DENNIS-T. AND I'M A BAD-ASS "RAPPER..."
I GOT THE FUCKING SHIT- THERE AIN'T NO "SUCKER" SWANKER..
I GOT A FUCKING "POSSE" AND I GOT A FUCKING PLANE I GOT A GREAT FUCKING PLAN TO UH... UH...
HMMM...
"RAP." GO FIGURE.

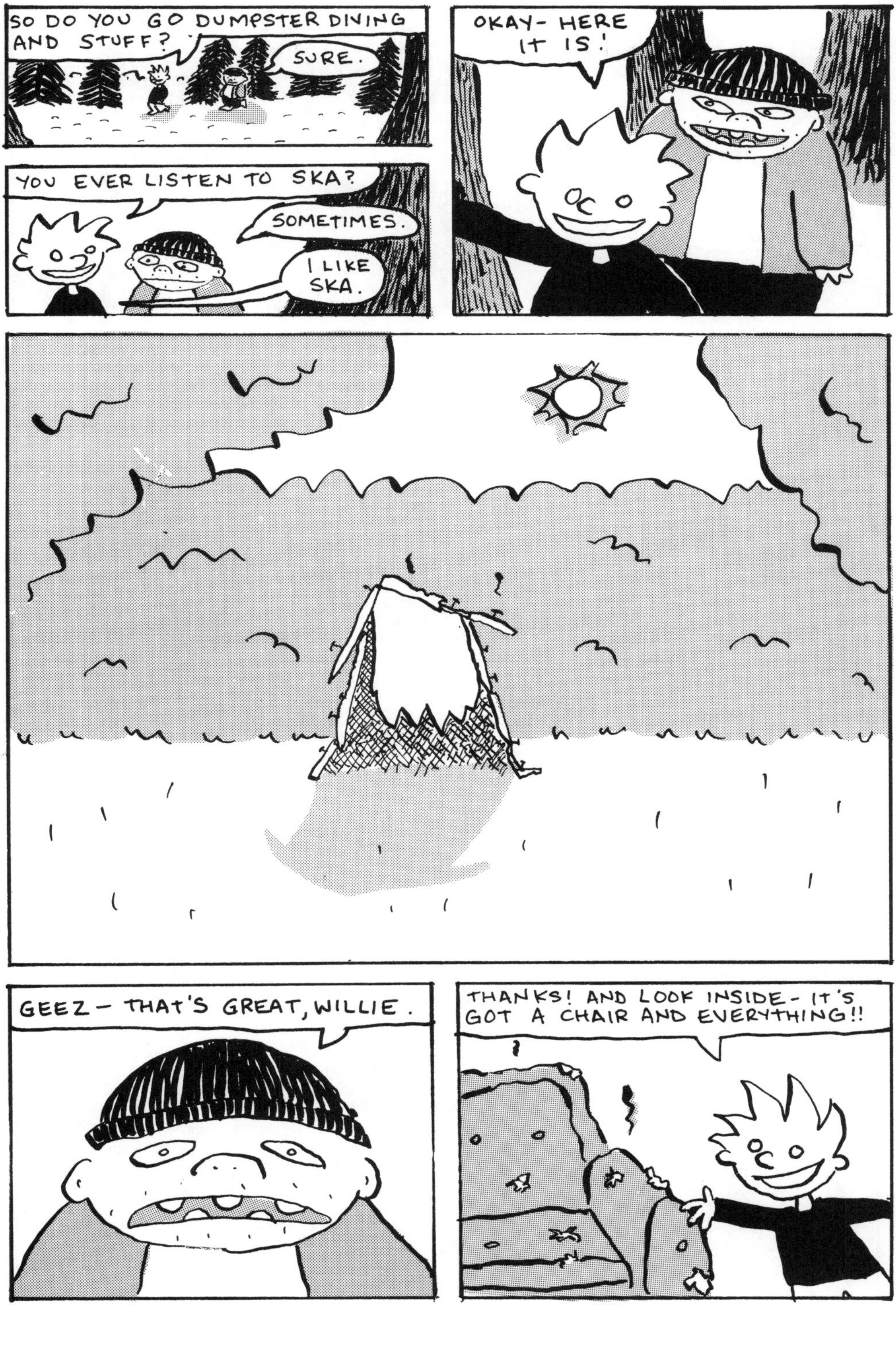
SO DO YOU GO DUMPSTER DIVING AND STUFF?
SURE.
OKAY- HERE IT IS!
YOU EVER LISTEN TO SKA?
SOMETIMES.
I LIKE SKA.
GEEZ- THAT'S GREAT, WILLIE.
THANKS! AND LOOK INSIDE- IT'S GOT A CHAIR AND EVERYTHING!!

WHERE'D YOU FIND THIS?

JUST OVER THERE - A COUPLE YARDS AWAY. IT MUST HAVE BEEN THERE A **LONG** TIME!

MMM.

WELL YOU REALLY GOT A GOOD START HERE, WILLIE.

YEAH! I'M GONNA GET IT ALL SET UP NICE AND THEN ANNIE BAXTER WILL COME AND REALLY LIKE IT AND WE'LL TALK AND

"ANNIE BAXTER" HUH?

OOOPS.

HA HA HA OK - SO WHO'S ANNIE??

OH YOU KNOW - SHE'S JUST THIS GIRL, YOU KNOW JUST THIS GIRL I KINDA LIKE . . .

UH-HUH. DOES SHE KNOW YOU EXIST?

UH...

WELL - SHE SMILED AT ME ONCE.

THAT'S GREAT **MAN**!!

YEAH - BUT I DON'T KNOW HOW TO IMPRESS HER - I DON'T KNOW WHAT SHE LIKES, YOU KNOW . . .

LISTEN - FUCK THAT TALK. JUST BE YOURSELF.

I'LL GIVE YOU TWO PIECES OF ADVICE - THE MOST IMPORTANT TWO THINGS YOU'LL EVER HEAR: ONE IS **BE YOURSELF.** YOU KNOW THAT LINE ABOUT THE ONLY TWO INEVITABILITIES BEING DEATH AND TAXES?

YEAH.

WELL IT'S WHITE SLAVE OWNER BULLSHIT. THE ONLY TAXES YOU SHOULD EVER PAY ARE EXISTENTIAL ONES. THE TWO INEVITABILITIES ARE YOU'LL DIE AND IN THE MEANTIME YOU'RE **YOU** AND NO ONE ELSE SO JUST RELAX AND BE YOURSELF ...

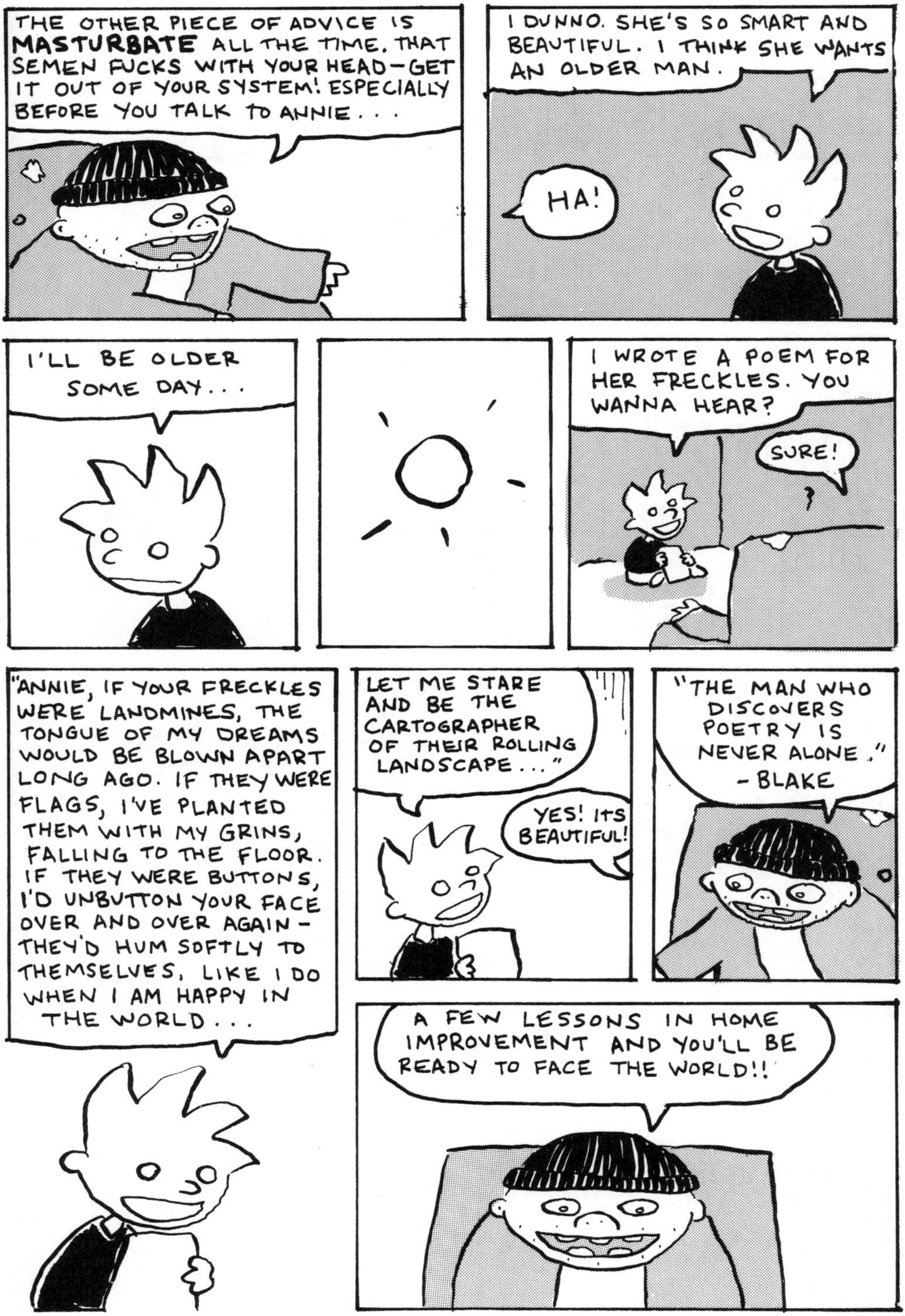
THE OTHER PIECE OF ADVICE IS MASTURBATE ALL THE TIME. THAT SEMEN FUCKS WITH YOUR HEAD—GET IT OUT OF YOUR SYSTEM! ESPECIALLY BEFORE YOU TALK TO ANNIE...
I DUNNO. SHE'S SO SMART AND BEAUTIFUL. I THINK SHE WANTS AN OLDER MAN.
HA!
I'LL BE OLDER SOME DAY...
I WROTE A POEM FOR HER FRECKLES. YOU WANNA HEAR?
SURE!
"ANNIE, IF YOUR FRECKLES WERE LANDMINES, THE TONGUE OF MY DREAMS WOULD BE BLOWN APART LONG AGO. IF THEY WERE FLAGS, I'VE PLANTED THEM WITH MY GRINS, FALLING TO THE FLOOR. IF THEY WERE BUTTONS, I'D UNBUTTON YOUR FACE OVER AND OVER AGAIN—THEY'D HUM SOFTLY TO THEMSELVES, LIKE I DO WHEN I AM HAPPY IN THE WORLD...
LET ME STARE AND BE THE CARTOGRAPHER OF THEIR ROLLING LANDSCAPE..."
YES! ITS BEAUTIFUL!
"THE MAN WHO DISCOVERS POETRY IS NEVER ALONE." -BLAKE
A FEW LESSONS IN HOME IMPROVEMENT AND YOU'LL BE READY TO FACE THE WORLD!!

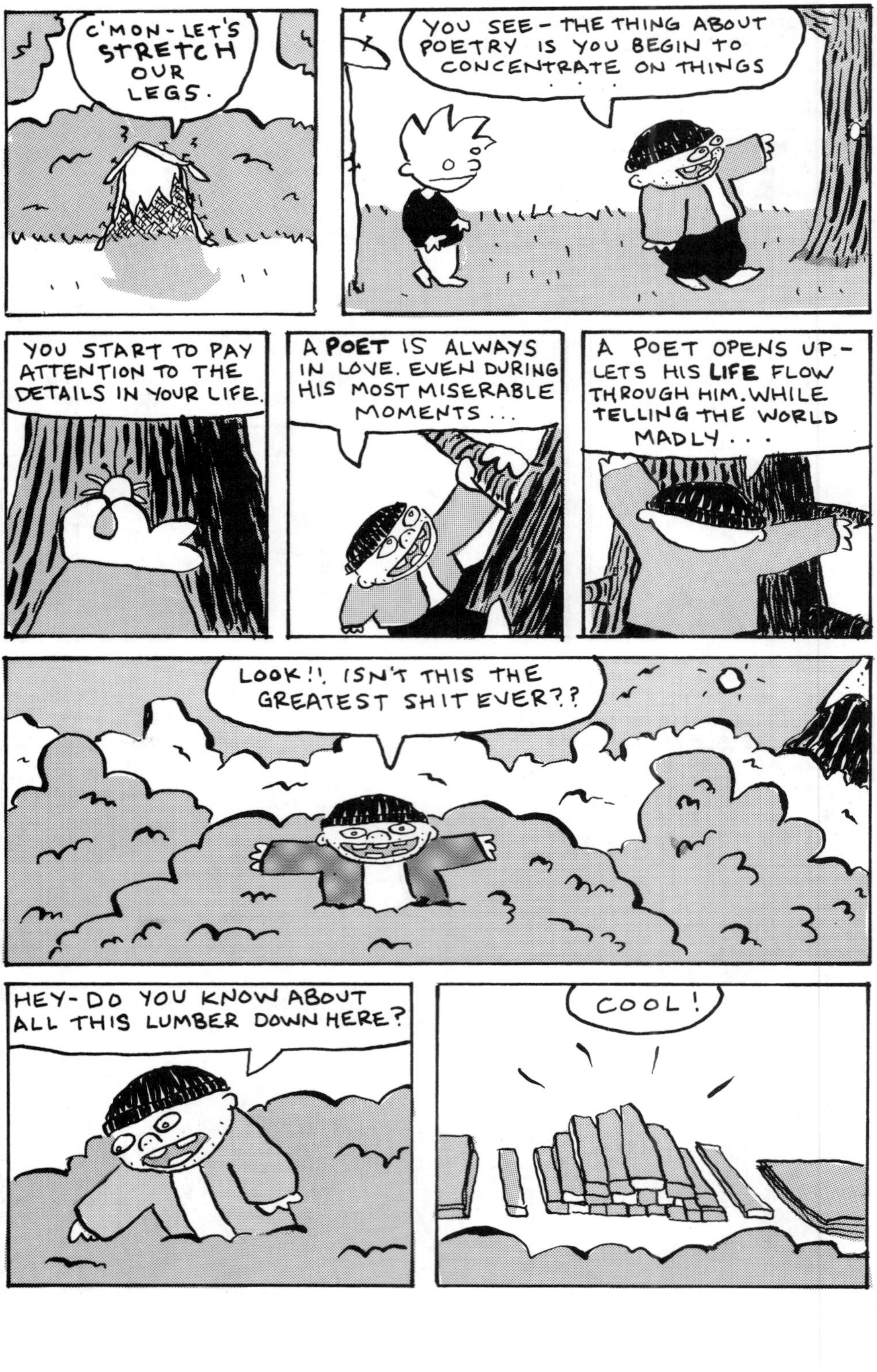
C'MON - LET'S STRETCH OUR LEGS.
YOU SEE - THE THING ABOUT POETRY IS YOU BEGIN TO CONCENTRATE ON THINGS . . .
YOU START TO PAY ATTENTION TO THE DETAILS IN YOUR LIFE.
A POET IS ALWAYS IN LOVE. EVEN DURING HIS MOST MISERABLE MOMENTS . . .
A POET OPENS UP - LETS HIS LIFE FLOW THROUGH HIM. WHILE TELLING THE WORLD MADLY . . .
LOOK!! ISN'T THIS THE GREATEST SHIT EVER??
HEY - DO YOU KNOW ABOUT ALL THIS LUMBER DOWN HERE?
COOL!

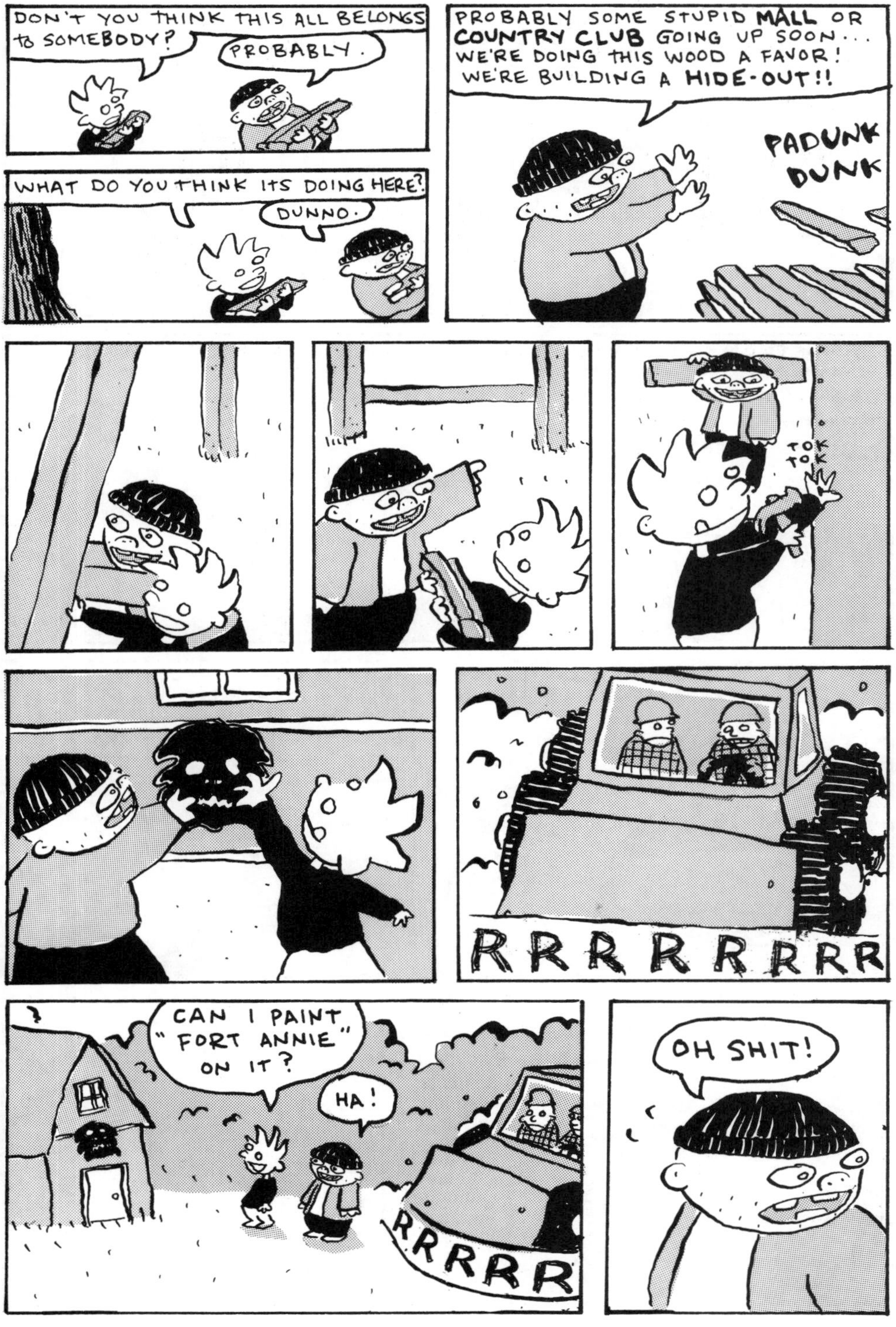
DON'T YOU THINK THIS ALL BELONGS TO SOMEBODY?
PROBABLY.
WHAT DO YOU THINK ITS DOING HERE?
DUNNO.
PROBABLY SOME STUPID MALL OR COUNTRY CLUB GOING UP SOON... WE'RE DOING THIS WOOD A FAVOR! WE'RE BUILDING A HIDE-OUT!!
PADUNK DUNK
TOK TOK
RRRRRRRR
CAN I PAINT "FORT ANNIE" ON IT?
HA!
RRRRR
OH SHIT!

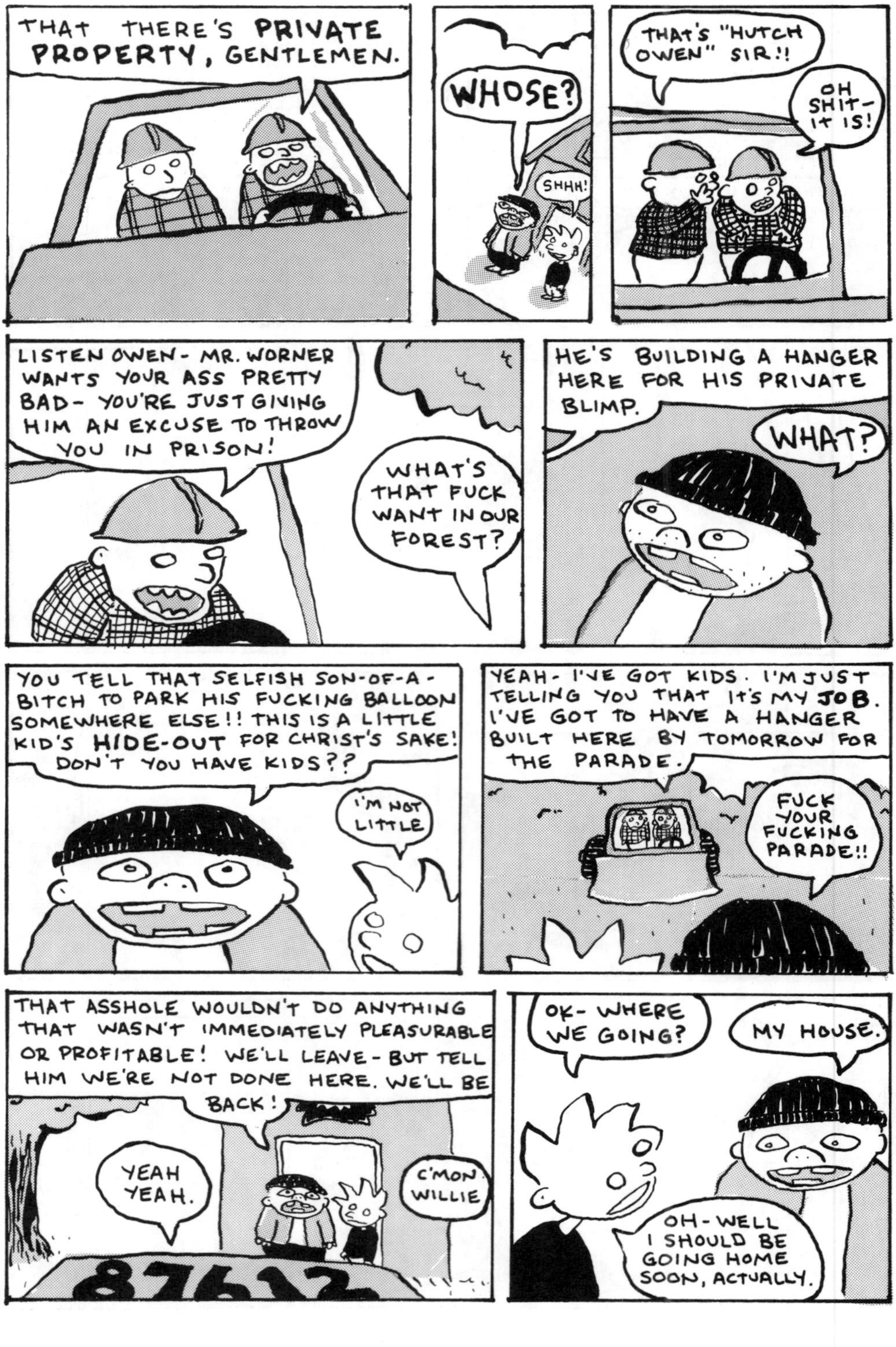
THAT THERE'S PRIVATE PROPERTY, GENTLEMEN.
WHOSE?
SHHH!
THAT'S "HUTCH OWEN" SIR!!
OH SHIT- IT IS!
LISTEN OWEN- MR. WORNER WANTS YOUR ASS PRETTY BAD- YOU'RE JUST GIVING HIM AN EXCUSE TO THROW YOU IN PRISON!
WHAT'S THAT FUCK WANT IN OUR FOREST?
HE'S BUILDING A HANGER HERE FOR HIS PRIVATE BLIMP.
WHAT?
YOU TELL THAT SELFISH SON-OF-A-BITCH TO PARK HIS FUCKING BALLOON SOMEWHERE ELSE!! THIS IS A LITTLE KID'S HIDE-OUT FOR CHRIST'S SAKE! DON'T YOU HAVE KIDS??
I'M NOT LITTLE
YEAH- I'VE GOT KIDS. I'M JUST TELLING YOU THAT IT'S MY JOB. I'VE GOT TO HAVE A HANGER BUILT HERE BY TOMORROW FOR THE PARADE.
FUCK YOUR FUCKING PARADE!!
THAT ASSHOLE WOULDN'T DO ANYTHING THAT WASN'T IMMEDIATELY PLEASURABLE OR PROFITABLE! WE'LL LEAVE- BUT TELL HIM WE'RE NOT DONE HERE. WE'LL BE BACK!
YEAH YEAH.
C'MON WILLIE
87612
OK- WHERE WE GOING?
MY HOUSE.
OH- WELL I SHOULD BE GOING HOME SOON, ACTUALLY.

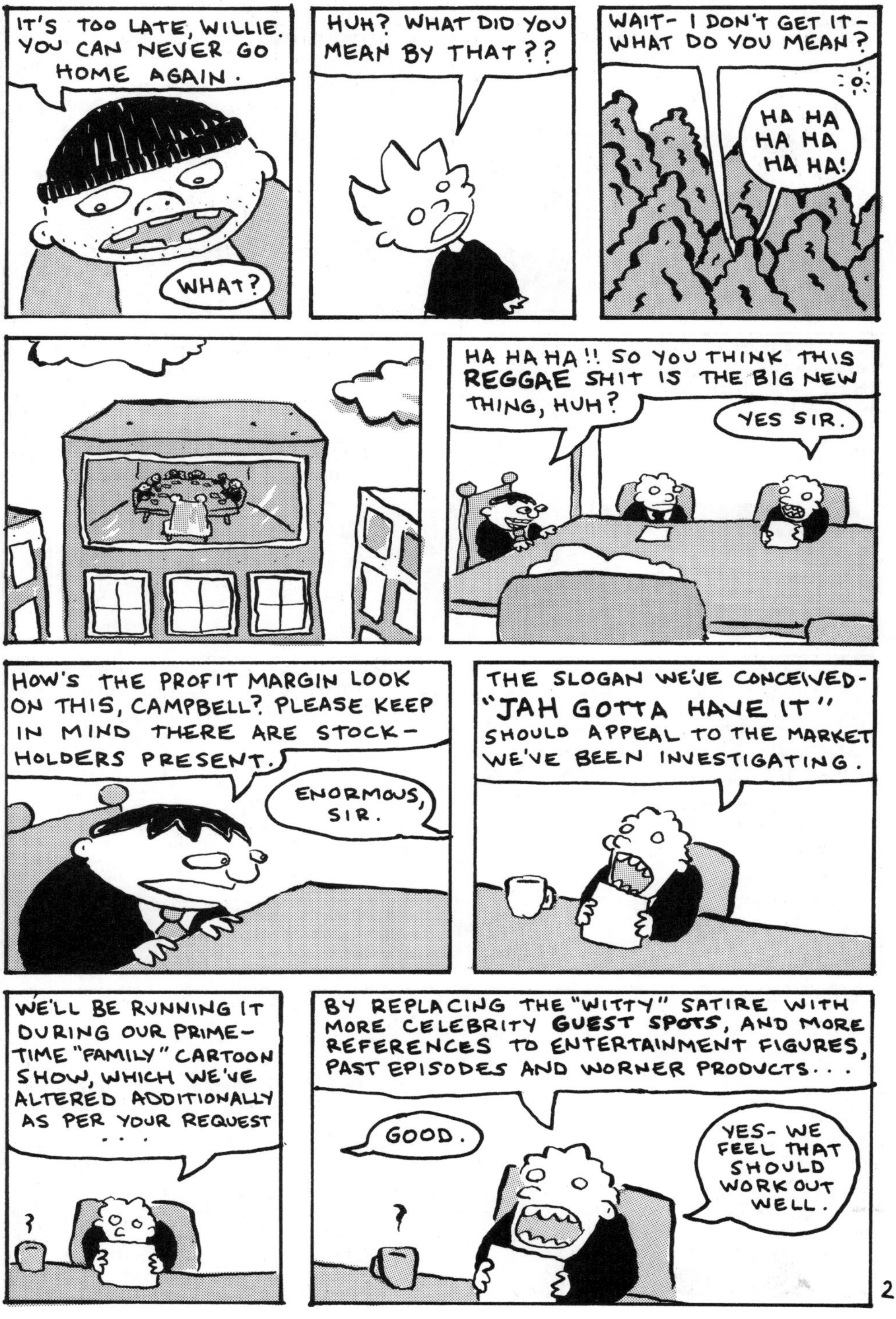
IT'S TOO LATE, WILLIE. YOU CAN NEVER GO HOME AGAIN.
WHAT?
HUH? WHAT DID YOU MEAN BY THAT??
WAIT- I DON'T GET IT- WHAT DO YOU MEAN?
HA HA HA HA HA HA!
HA HA HA!! SO YOU THINK THIS REGGAE SHIT IS THE BIG NEW THING, HUH?
YES SIR.
HOW'S THE PROFIT MARGIN LOOK ON THIS, CAMPBELL? PLEASE KEEP IN MIND THERE ARE STOCK-HOLDERS PRESENT.
ENORMOUS, SIR.
THE SLOGAN WE'VE CONCEIVED- "JAH GOTTA HAVE IT" SHOULD APPEAL TO THE MARKET WE'VE BEEN INVESTIGATING.
WE'LL BE RUNNING IT DURING OUR PRIME-TIME "FAMILY" CARTOON SHOW, WHICH WE'VE ALTERED ADDITIONALLY AS PER YOUR REQUEST . . .
BY REPLACING THE "WITTY" SATIRE WITH MORE CELEBRITY GUEST SPOTS, AND MORE REFERENCES TO ENTERTAINMENT FIGURES, PAST EPISODES AND WORNER PRODUCTS . . .
GOOD.
YES- WE FEEL THAT SHOULD WORK OUT WELL.

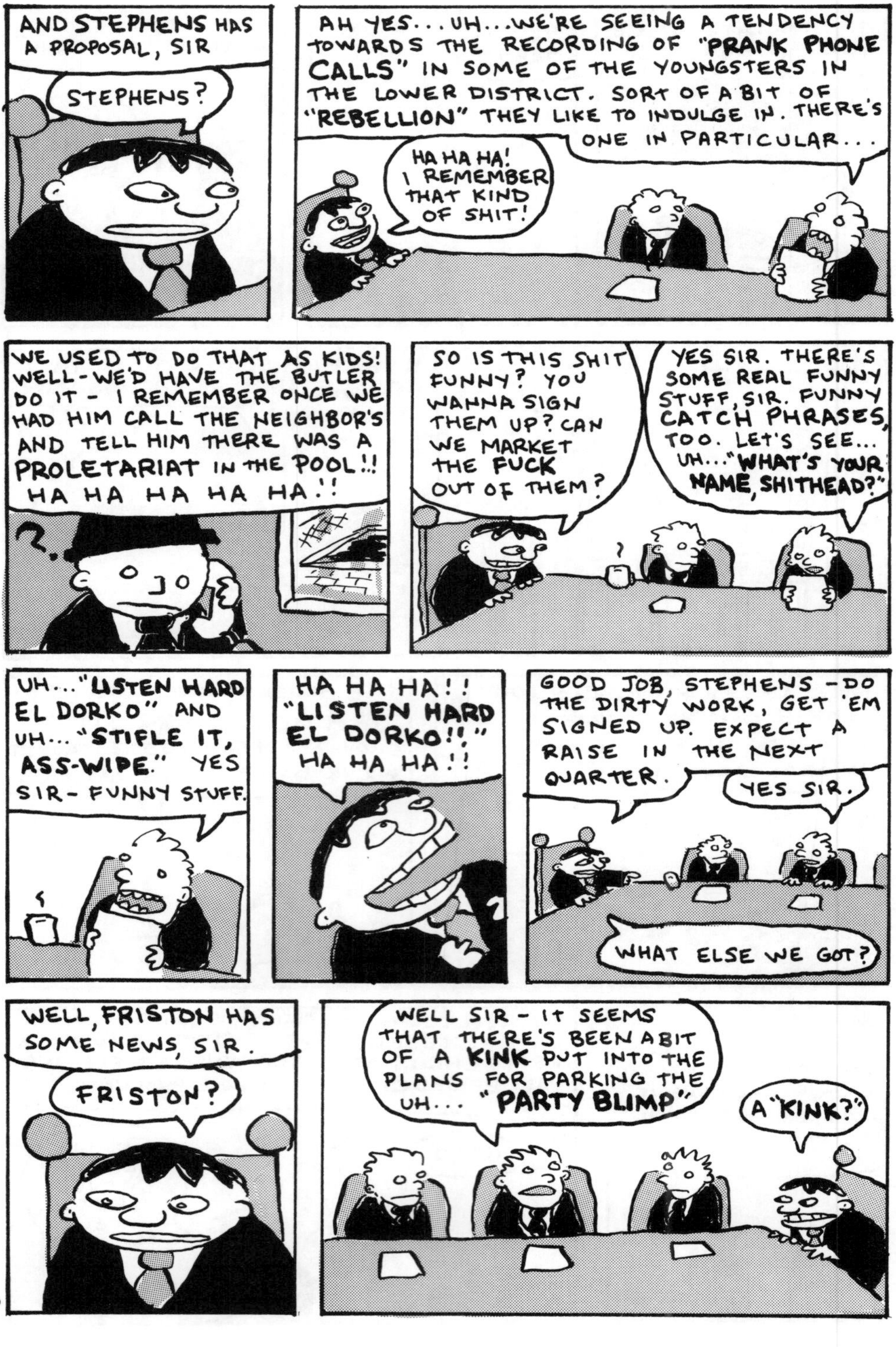
AND STEPHENS HAS A PROPOSAL, SIR
STEPHENS?
AH YES... UH... WE'RE SEEING A TENDENCY TOWARDS THE RECORDING OF "PRANK PHONE CALLS" IN SOME OF THE YOUNGSTERS IN THE LOWER DISTRICT. SORT OF A BIT OF "REBELLION" THEY LIKE TO INDULGE IN. THERE'S ONE IN PARTICULAR...
HA HA HA! I REMEMBER THAT KIND OF SHIT!
WE USED TO DO THAT AS KIDS! WELL - WE'D HAVE THE BUTLER DO IT - I REMEMBER ONCE WE HAD HIM CALL THE NEIGHBOR'S AND TELL HIM THERE WAS A PROLETARIAT IN THE POOL!! HA HA HA HA HA!!
SO IS THIS SHIT FUNNY? YOU WANNA SIGN THEM UP? CAN WE MARKET THE FUCK OUT OF THEM?
YES SIR. THERE'S SOME REAL FUNNY STUFF, SIR. FUNNY CATCH PHRASES, TOO. LET'S SEE... UH..."WHAT'S YOUR NAME, SHITHEAD?"
UH..."LISTEN HARD EL DORKO" AND UH..."STIFLE IT, ASS-WIPE." YES SIR - FUNNY STUFF.
HA HA HA!! "LISTEN HARD EL DORKO!!" HA HA HA!!
GOOD JOB, STEPHENS - DO THE DIRTY WORK, GET 'EM SIGNED UP. EXPECT A RAISE IN THE NEXT QUARTER.
YES SIR.
WHAT ELSE WE GOT?
WELL, FRISTON HAS SOME NEWS, SIR.
FRISTON?
WELL SIR - IT SEEMS THAT THERE'S BEEN A BIT OF A KINK PUT INTO THE PLANS FOR PARKING THE UH... "PARTY BLIMP"
A "KINK?"

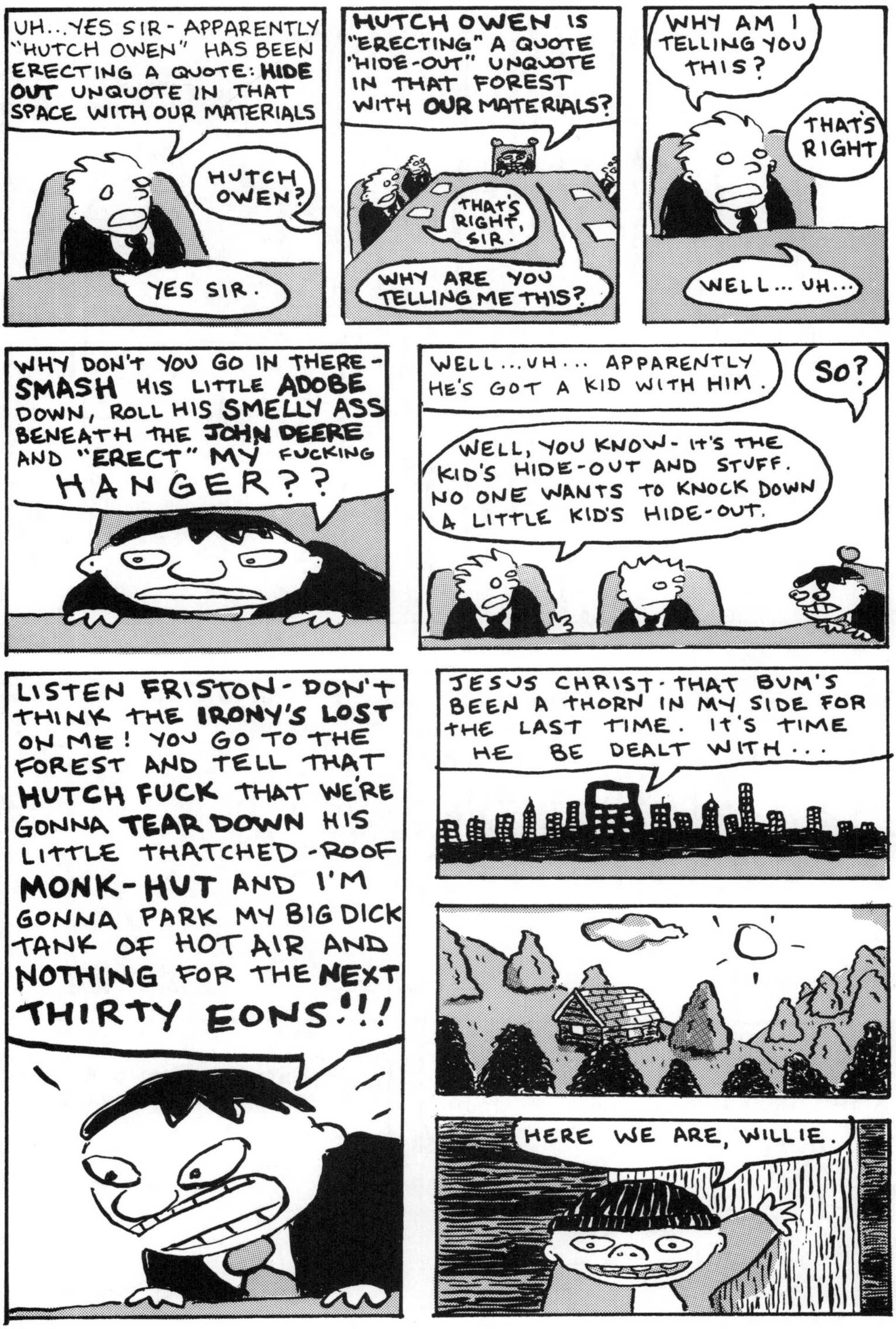
UH...YES SIR- APPARENTLY "HUTCH OWEN" HAS BEEN ERECTING A QUOTE: HIDE OUT UNQUOTE IN THAT SPACE WITH OUR MATERIALS
HUTCH OWEN?
YES SIR.
HUTCH OWEN IS "ERECTING" A QUOTE "HIDE-OUT" UNQUOTE IN THAT FOREST WITH OUR MATERIALS?
THAT'S RIGHT, SIR.
WHY ARE YOU TELLING ME THIS?
WHY AM I TELLING YOU THIS?
THAT'S RIGHT
WELL... UH...
WHY DON'T YOU GO IN THERE- SMASH HIS LITTLE ADOBE DOWN, ROLL HIS SMELLY ASS BENEATH THE JOHN DEERE AND "ERECT" MY FUCKING HANGER??
WELL...UH... APPARENTLY HE'S GOT A KID WITH HIM.
SO?
WELL, YOU KNOW- IT'S THE KID'S HIDE-OUT AND STUFF. NO ONE WANTS TO KNOCK DOWN A LITTLE KID'S HIDE-OUT.
LISTEN FRISTON- DON'T THINK THE IRONY'S LOST ON ME! YOU GO TO THE FOREST AND TELL THAT HUTCH FUCK THAT WE'RE GONNA TEAR DOWN HIS LITTLE THATCHED-ROOF MONK-HUT AND I'M GONNA PARK MY BIG DICK TANK OF HOT AIR AND NOTHING FOR THE NEXT THIRTY EONS!!!
JESUS CHRIST- THAT BUM'S BEEN A THORN IN MY SIDE FOR THE LAST TIME. IT'S TIME HE BE DEALT WITH...
HERE WE ARE, WILLIE.

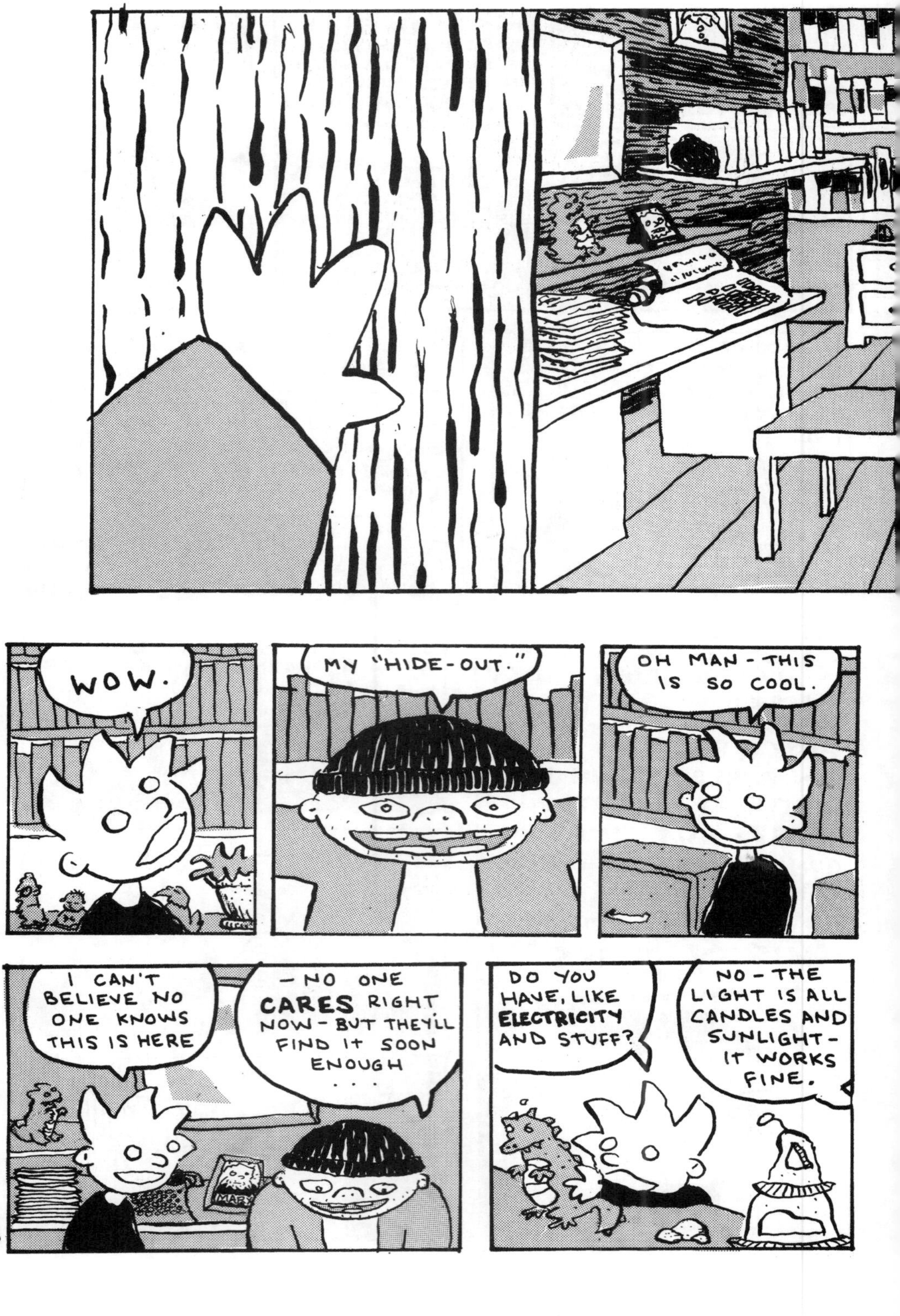
WOW.
MY "HIDE-OUT."
OH MAN - THIS IS SO COOL.
I CAN'T BELIEVE NO ONE KNOWS THIS IS HERE
-NO ONE **CARES** RIGHT NOW - BUT THEY'LL FIND IT SOON ENOUGH . . .
MARY
DO YOU HAVE, LIKE **ELECTRICITY** AND STUFF?
NO - THE LIGHT IS ALL CANDLES AND SUNLIGHT - IT WORKS FINE.

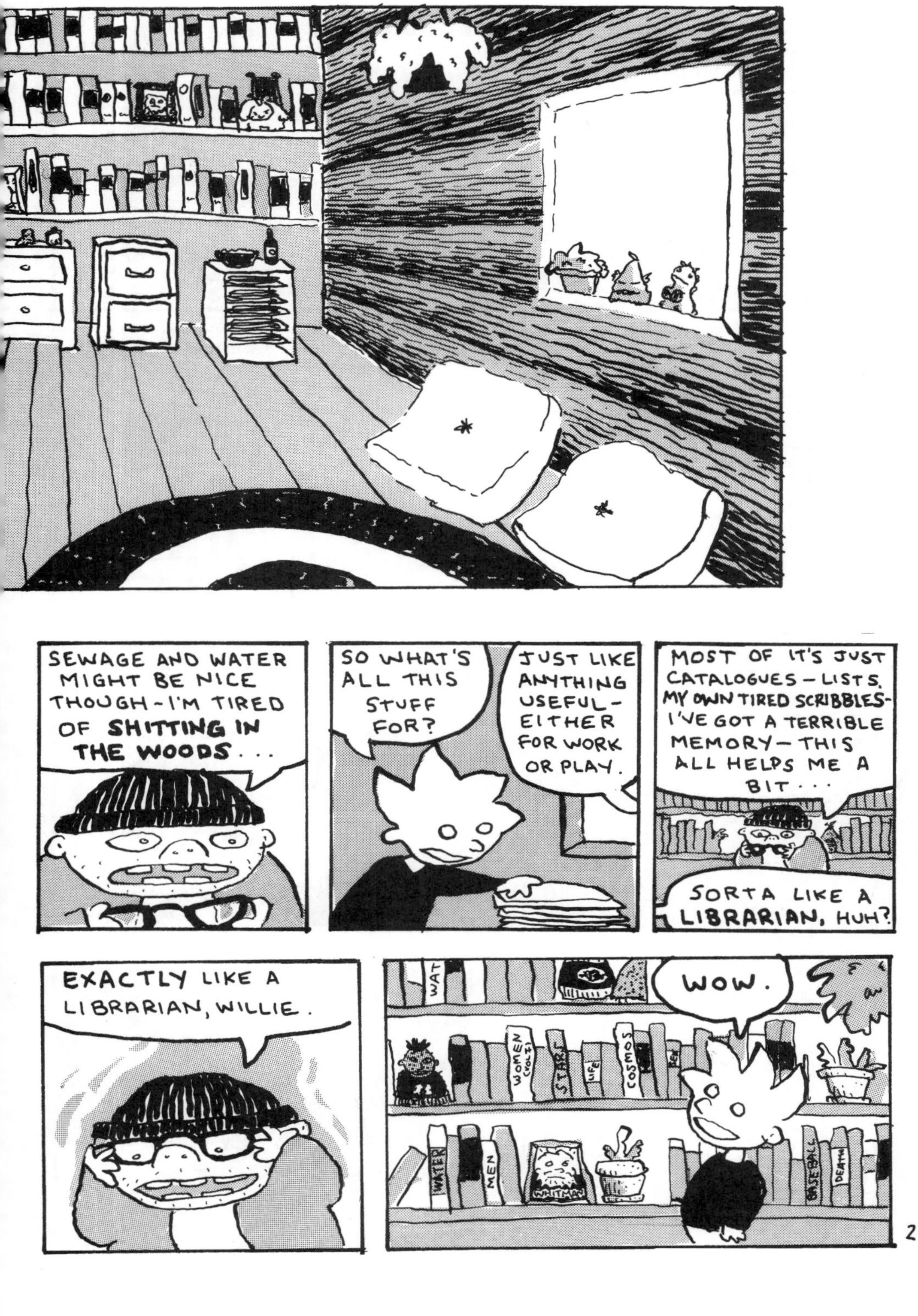
SEWAGE AND WATER MIGHT BE NICE THOUGH - I'M TIRED OF **SHITTING IN THE WOODS**...
SO WHAT'S ALL THIS STUFF FOR?
JUST LIKE ANYTHING USEFUL - EITHER FOR WORK OR PLAY.
MOST OF IT'S JUST CATALOGUES - LISTS. MY OWN TIRED SCRIBBLES - I'VE GOT A TERRIBLE MEMORY - THIS ALL HELPS ME A BIT...
SORTA LIKE A **LIBRARIAN**, HUH?
EXACTLY LIKE A LIBRARIAN, WILLIE.
WOW.
COSMOS
LIFE
WATER
MEN
WHITMAN
BASEBALL
DEATH

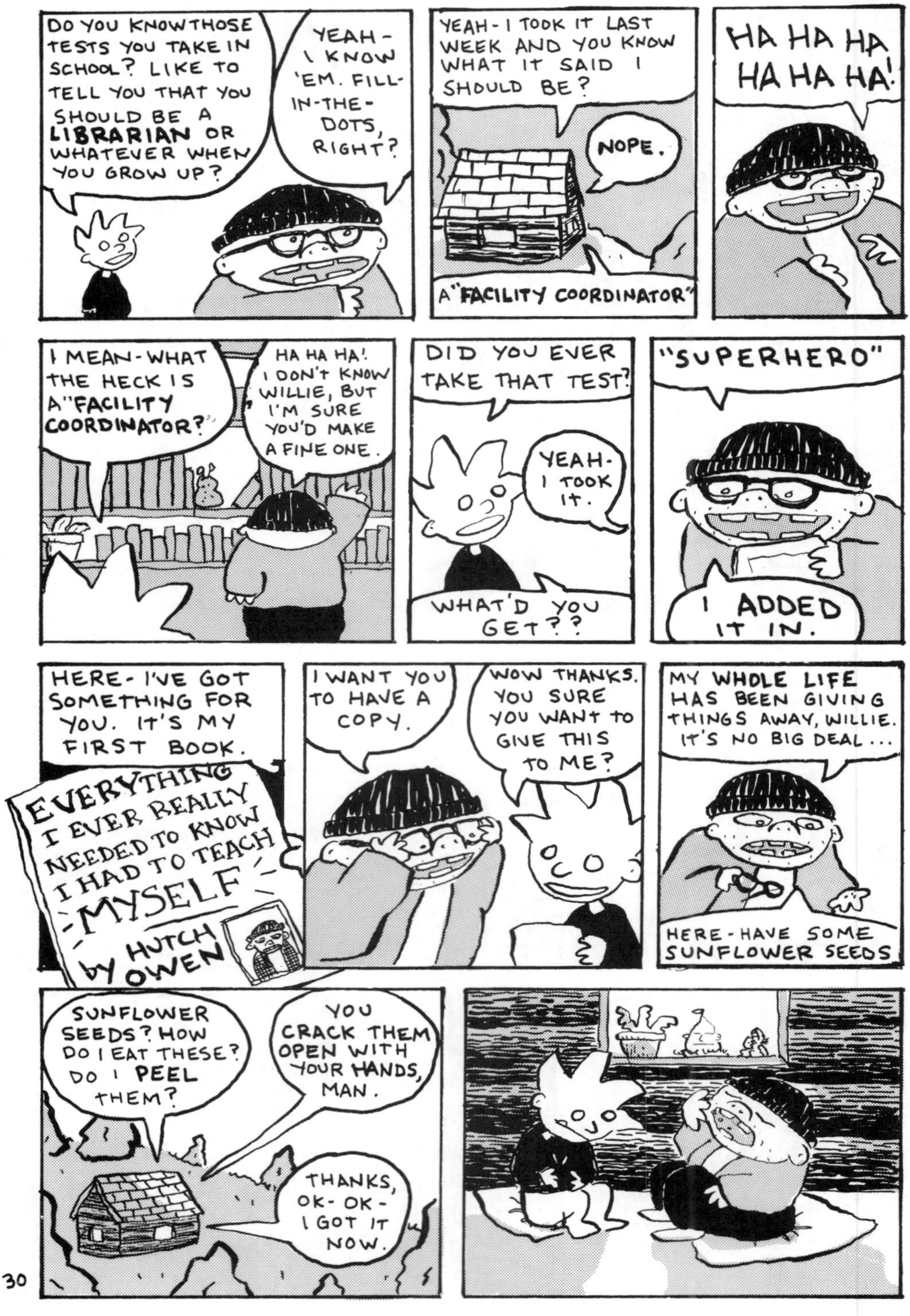
DO YOU KNOW THOSE TESTS YOU TAKE IN SCHOOL? LIKE TO TELL YOU THAT YOU SHOULD BE A LIBRARIAN OR WHATEVER WHEN YOU GROW UP?
YEAH - I KNOW 'EM. FILL-IN-THE-DOTS, RIGHT?
YEAH - I TOOK IT LAST WEEK AND YOU KNOW WHAT IT SAID I SHOULD BE?
NOPE.
A "FACILITY COORDINATOR"
HA HA HA HA HA HA!
I MEAN - WHAT THE HECK IS A "FACILITY COORDINATOR?"
HA HA HA! I DON'T KNOW WILLIE, BUT I'M SURE YOU'D MAKE A FINE ONE.
DID YOU EVER TAKE THAT TEST?
YEAH - I TOOK IT.
WHAT'D YOU GET??
"SUPERHERO"
I ADDED IT IN.
HERE - I'VE GOT SOMETHING FOR YOU. IT'S MY FIRST BOOK.
EVERYTHING I EVER REALLY NEEDED TO KNOW I HAD TO TEACH MYSELF by HUTCH OWEN
I WANT YOU TO HAVE A COPY.
WOW THANKS. YOU SURE YOU WANT TO GIVE THIS TO ME?
MY WHOLE LIFE HAS BEEN GIVING THINGS AWAY, WILLIE. IT'S NO BIG DEAL...
HERE - HAVE SOME SUNFLOWER SEEDS
SUNFLOWER SEEDS? HOW DO I EAT THESE? DO I PEEL THEM?
YOU CRACK THEM OPEN WITH YOUR HANDS, MAN.
THANKS, OK - OK - I GOT IT NOW.

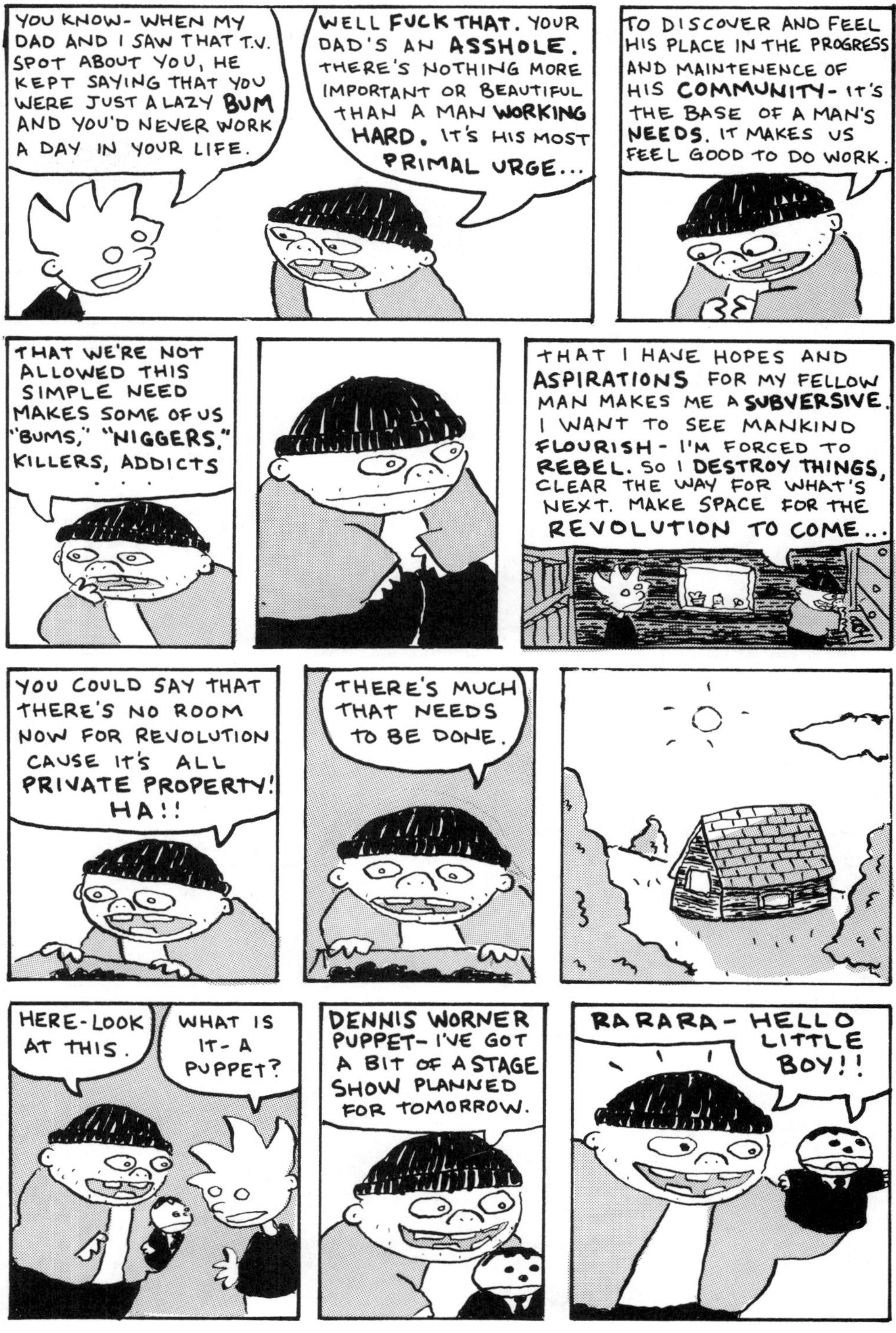
YOU KNOW- WHEN MY DAD AND I SAW THAT T.V. SPOT ABOUT YOU, HE KEPT SAYING THAT YOU WERE JUST A LAZY BUM AND YOU'D NEVER WORK A DAY IN YOUR LIFE.
WELL FUCK THAT. YOUR DAD'S AN ASSHOLE. THERE'S NOTHING MORE IMPORTANT OR BEAUTIFUL THAN A MAN WORKING HARD. IT'S HIS MOST PRIMAL URGE...
TO DISCOVER AND FEEL HIS PLACE IN THE PROGRESS AND MAINTENENCE OF HIS COMMUNITY- IT'S THE BASE OF A MAN'S NEEDS. IT MAKES US FEEL GOOD TO DO WORK.
THAT WE'RE NOT ALLOWED THIS SIMPLE NEED MAKES SOME OF US "BUMS," "NIGGERS," KILLERS, ADDICTS . . .
THAT I HAVE HOPES AND ASPIRATIONS FOR MY FELLOW MAN MAKES ME A SUBVERSIVE. I WANT TO SEE MANKIND FLOURISH- I'M FORCED TO REBEL. SO I DESTROY THINGS, CLEAR THE WAY FOR WHAT'S NEXT. MAKE SPACE FOR THE REVOLUTION TO COME...
YOU COULD SAY THAT THERE'S NO ROOM NOW FOR REVOLUTION CAUSE IT'S ALL PRIVATE PROPERTY! HA!!
THERE'S MUCH THAT NEEDS TO BE DONE.
HERE- LOOK AT THIS.
WHAT IS IT- A PUPPET?
DENNIS WORNER PUPPET- I'VE GOT A BIT OF A STAGE SHOW PLANNED FOR TOMORROW.
RARARA- HELLO LITTLE BOY!!

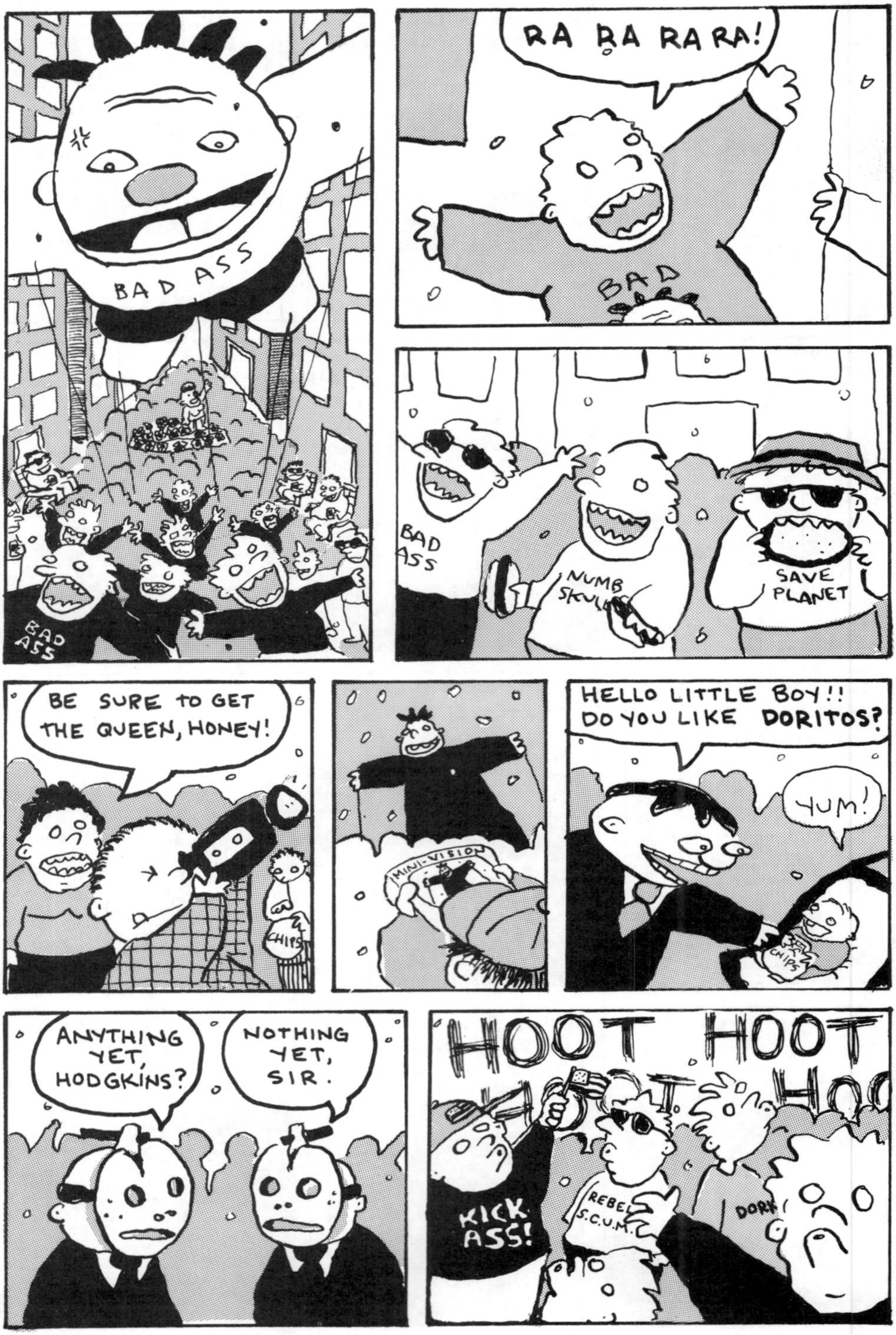
BAD ASS
BAD ASS
RA RA RA RA!
BAD
BAD ASS
NUMB SKULL
SAVE PLANET
BE SURE TO GET THE QUEEN, HONEY!
CHIPS
MINI-VISION
HELLO LITTLE BOY!! DO YOU LIKE DORITOS?
YUM!
CHIPS
ANYTHING YET, HODGKINS?
NOTHING YET, SIR.
HOOT HOOT
KICK ASS!
REBEL S.C.U.M.
DORK

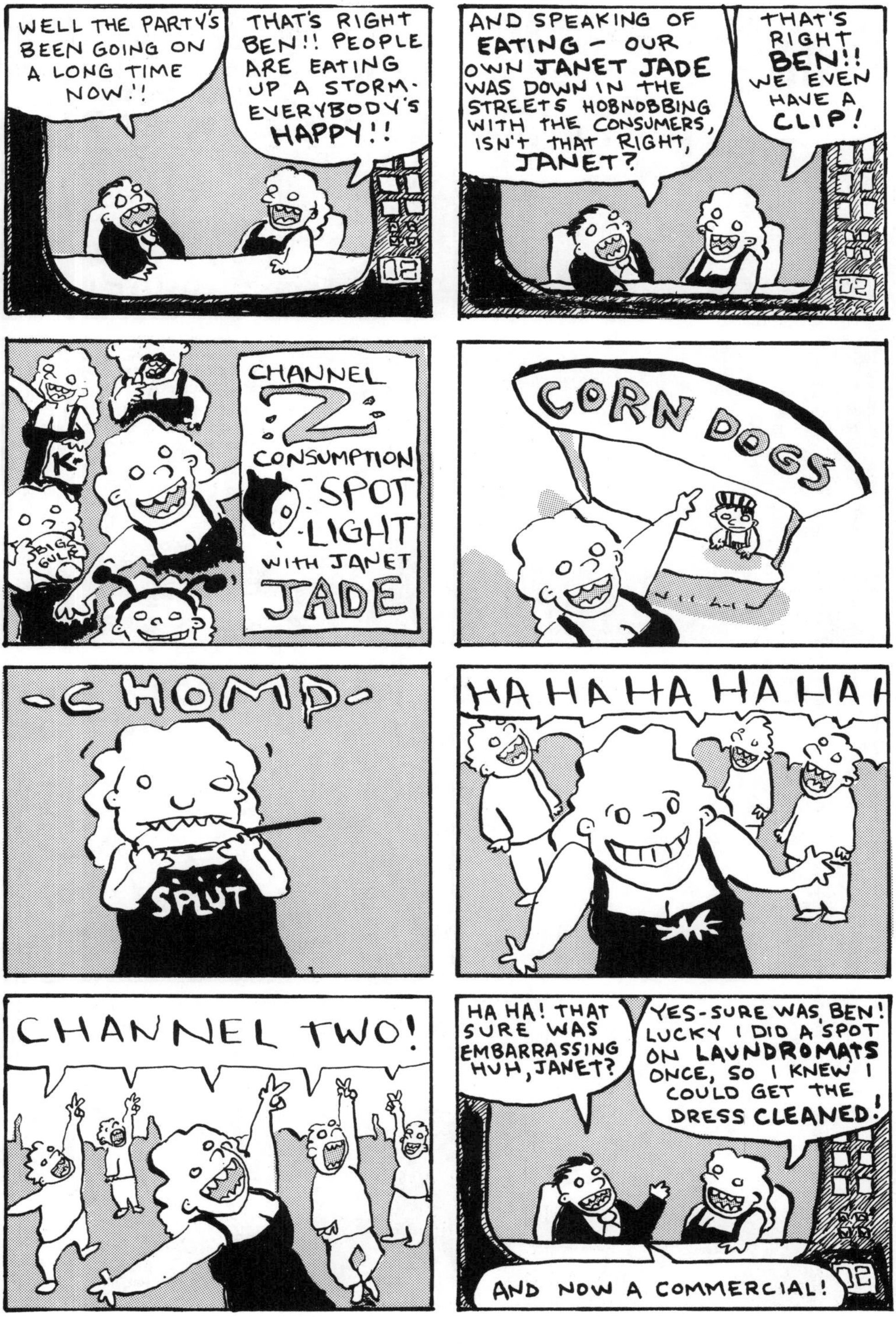

WELL THE PARTY'S BEEN GOING ON A LONG TIME NOW!!
THAT'S RIGHT BEN!! PEOPLE ARE EATING UP A STORM. EVERYBODY'S HAPPY!!
02
AND SPEAKING OF EATING - OUR OWN JANET JADE WAS DOWN IN THE STREETS HOBNOBBING WITH THE CONSUMERS, ISN'T THAT RIGHT, JANET?
THAT'S RIGHT BEN!! WE EVEN HAVE A CLIP!
02
K
BIG GULP
CHANNEL 2 CONSUMPTION SPOT LIGHT WITH JANET JADE
CORN DOGS
-CHOMP-
SPLUT
HA HA HA HA HA
CHANNEL TWO!
HA HA! THAT SURE WAS EMBARRASSING HUH, JANET?
YES-SURE WAS, BEN! LUCKY I DID A SPOT ON LAUNDROMATS ONCE, SO I KNEW I COULD GET THE DRESS CLEANED!
AND NOW A COMMERCIAL!
02

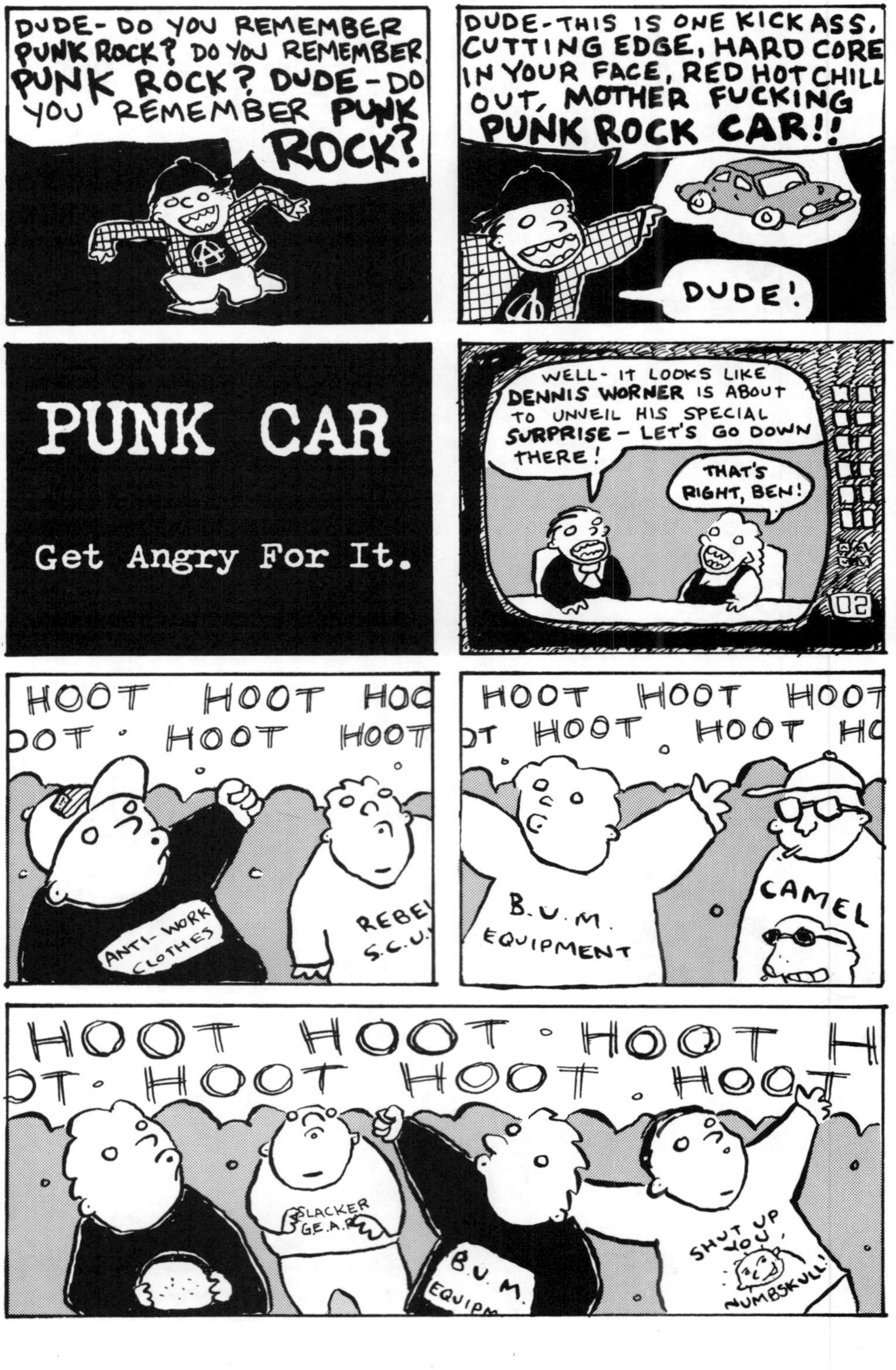
DUDE- DO YOU REMEMBER PUNK ROCK? DO YOU REMEMBER PUNK ROCK? DUDE - DO YOU REMEMBER PUNK ROCK?
DUDE-THIS IS ONE KICK ASS, CUTTING EDGE, HARD CORE IN YOUR FACE, RED HOT CHILL OUT, MOTHER FUCKING PUNK ROCK CAR!!
DUDE!
PUNK CAR
Get Angry For It.
WELL- IT LOOKS LIKE DENNIS WORNER IS ABOUT TO UNVEIL HIS SPECIAL SURPRISE - LET'S GO DOWN THERE!
THAT'S RIGHT, BEN!
02
HOOT HOOT HOO
OOT HOOT HOOT
ANTI-WORK CLOTHES
HOOT HOOT HOOT
OT HOOT HOOT HO
B.U.M. EQUIPMENT
CAMEL
HOOT HOOT HOOT H
OT HOOT HOOT HOOT
SLACKER GE.A.R
B.U.M. EQUIPM
SHUT UP YOU, NUMBSKULL!

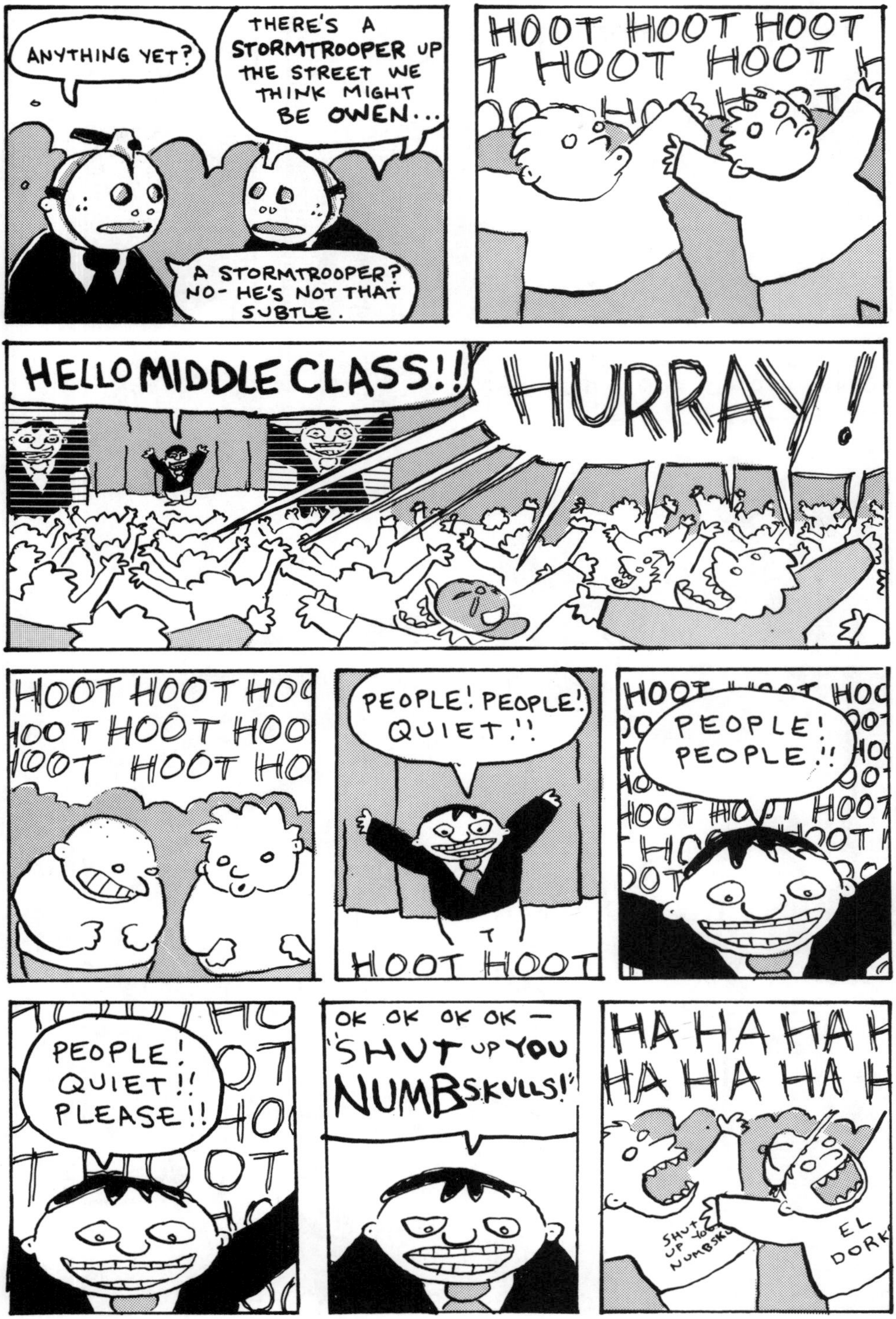
ANYTHING YET?
THERE'S A STORMTROOPER UP THE STREET WE THINK MIGHT BE OWEN...
A STORMTROOPER? NO- HE'S NOT THAT SUBTLE.
HOOT HOOT HOOT HOOT HOOT
HELLO MIDDLE CLASS!!
HURRAY!
HOOT HOOT HOOT HOOT HOOT HOOT HOOT HOOT
PEOPLE! PEOPLE! QUIET!!
HOOT HOOT
PEOPLE! PEOPLE!!
PEOPLE! QUIET!! PLEASE!!
OK OK OK OK — "SHUT UP YOU NUMBSKULLS!"
HA HA HA HA HA HA
EL DORK

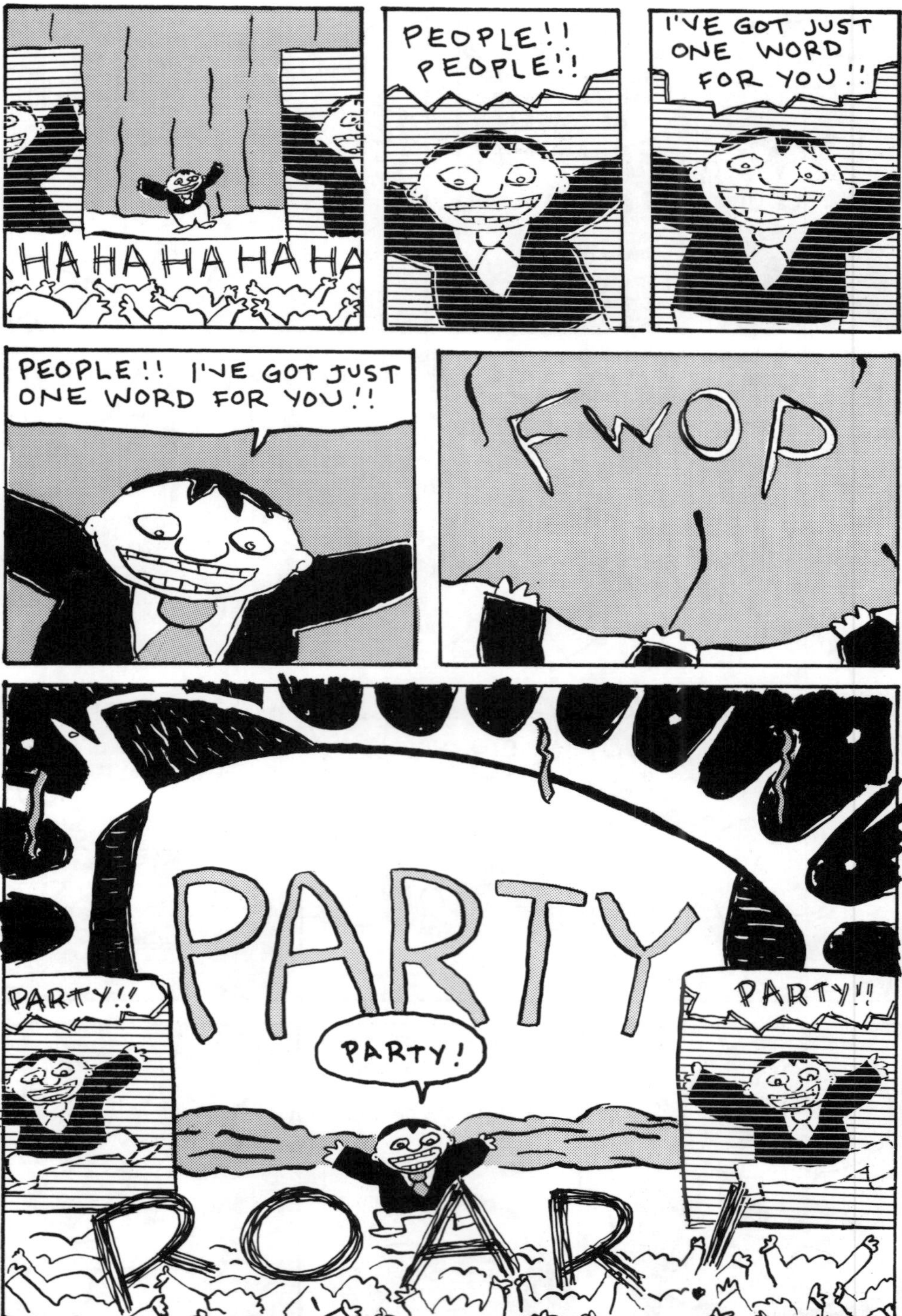
HAHAHAHAHAHA
PEOPLE!! PEOPLE!!
I'VE GOT JUST ONE WORD FOR YOU!!
PEOPLE!! I'VE GOT JUST ONE WORD FOR YOU!!
FWOP
PARTY
PARTY!!
PARTY!!
PARTY!
ROAR

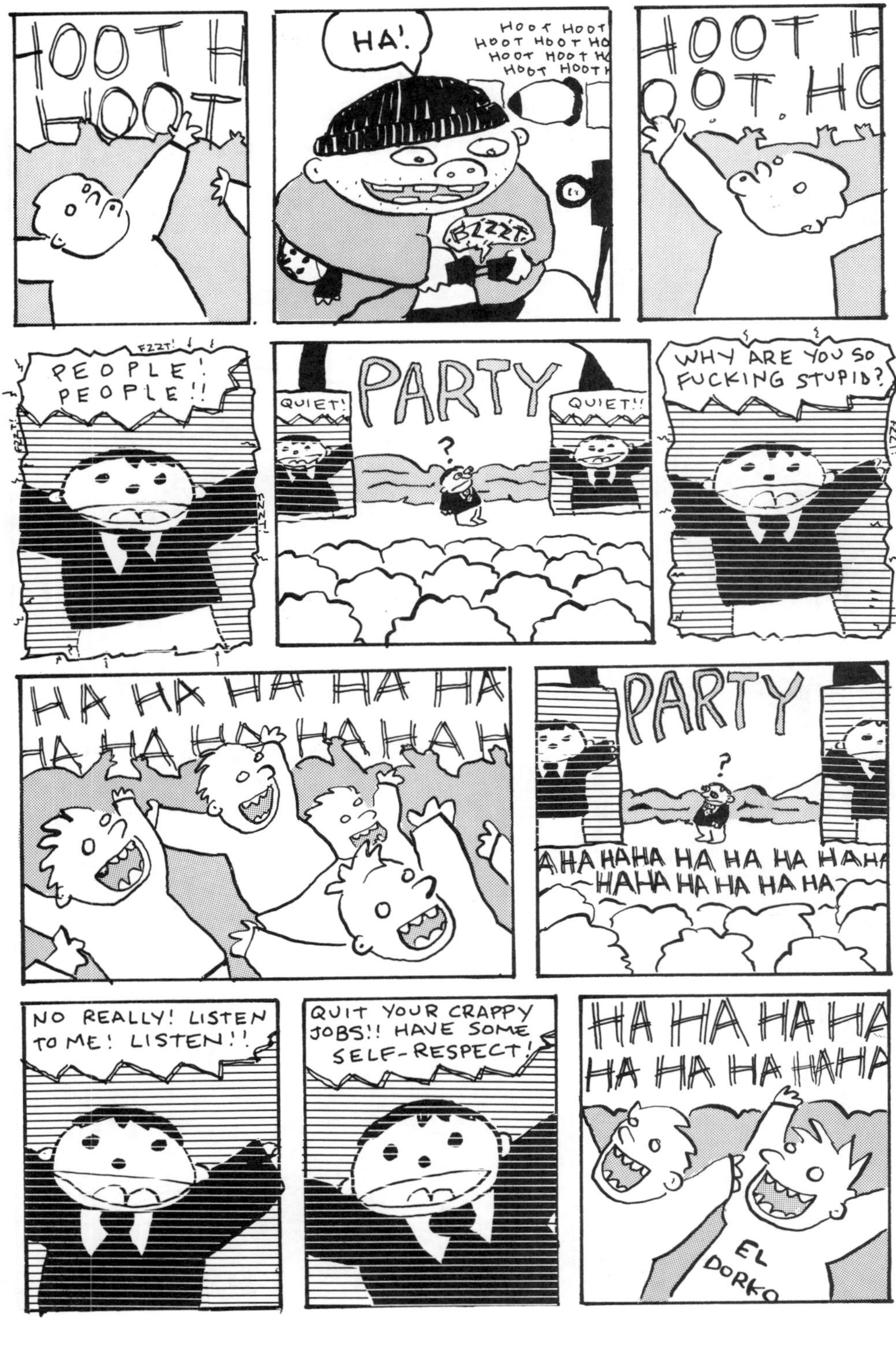
HOOT HOOT
HA!
HOOT HOOT HOOT HOOT HOOT HOOT HOOT HOOT
BZZZT
HOOT HOOT
FZZT!
PEOPLE! PEOPLE!!
FZZT!
QUIET!
PARTY
?
QUIET!!
WHY ARE YOU SO FUCKING STUPID?
FZZT!
HA HA HA HA HA HA HA HA HA HA
PARTY
?
HA HA HA HA HA HA HA HA HA HA HA HA HA HA HA
NO REALLY! LISTEN TO ME! LISTEN!!
QUIT YOUR CRAPPY JOBS!! HAVE SOME SELF-RESPECT!
HA HA HA HA HA HA HA HAHA
EL DORKO

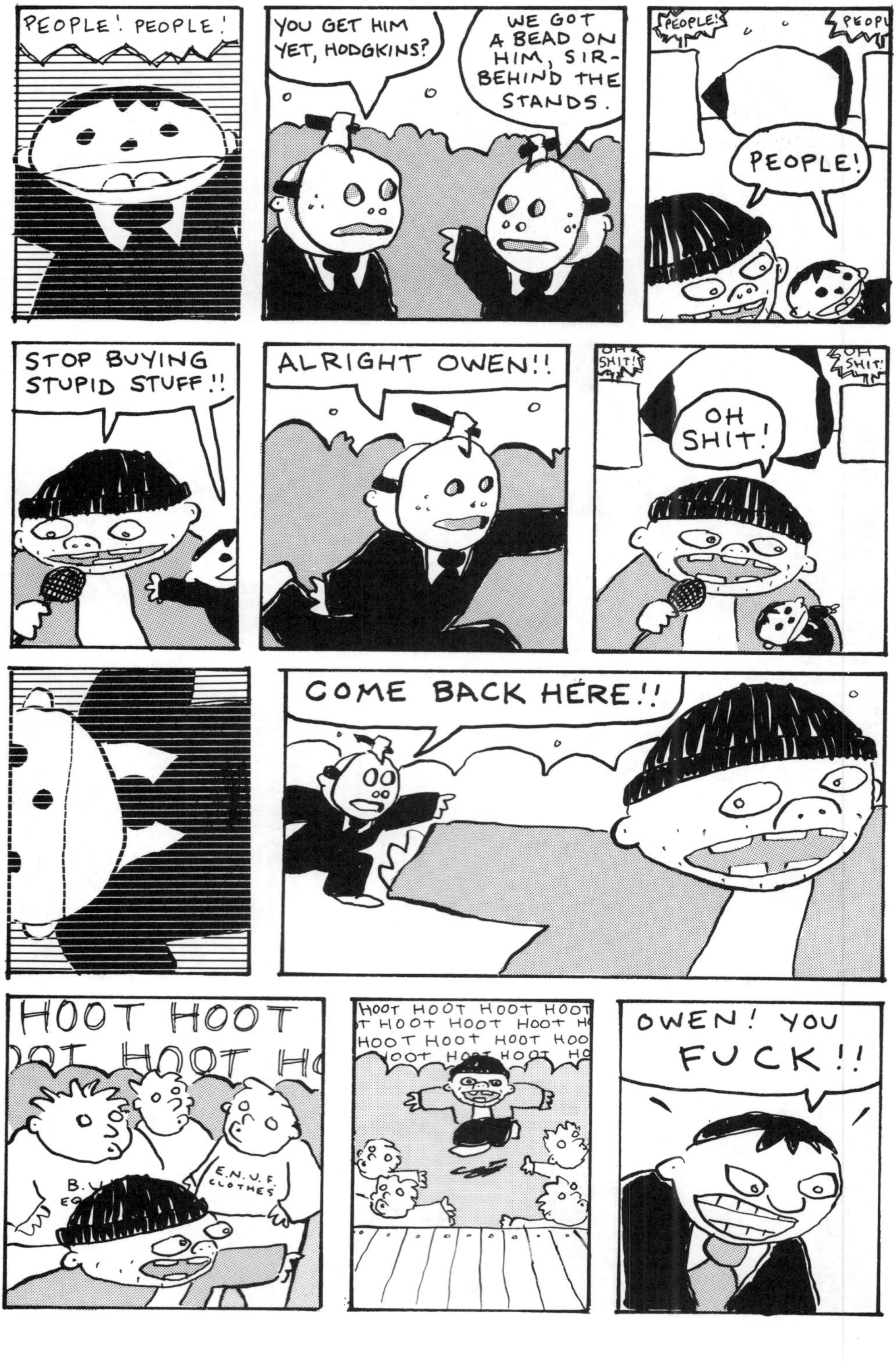
PEOPLE! PEOPLE!
YOU GET HIM YET, HODGKINS?
WE GOT A BEAD ON HIM, SIR- BEHIND THE STANDS.
PEOPLE!
PEOPLE!
PEOPLE!
STOP BUYING STUPID STUFF!!
ALRIGHT OWEN!!
OH SHIT!
OH SHIT!
OH SHIT!
COME BACK HERE!!
HOOT HOOT
HOOT HOOT HOOT HOOT
E.N.U.F. CLOTHES
OWEN! YOU FUCK!!

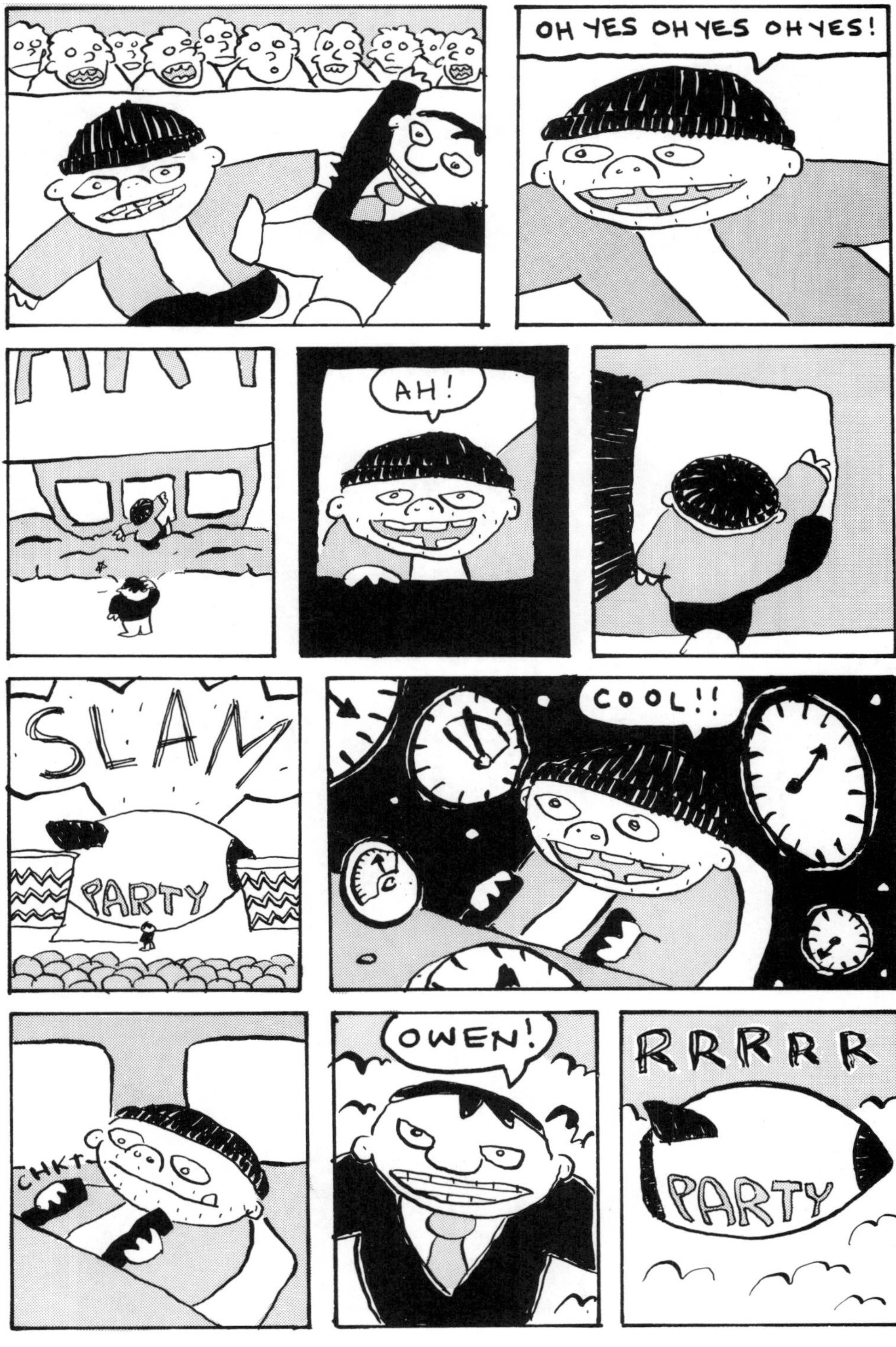

OH YES OH YES OH YES!
AH!
SLAM
PARTY
COOL!!
CHKT-
OWEN!
RRRRR
PARTY

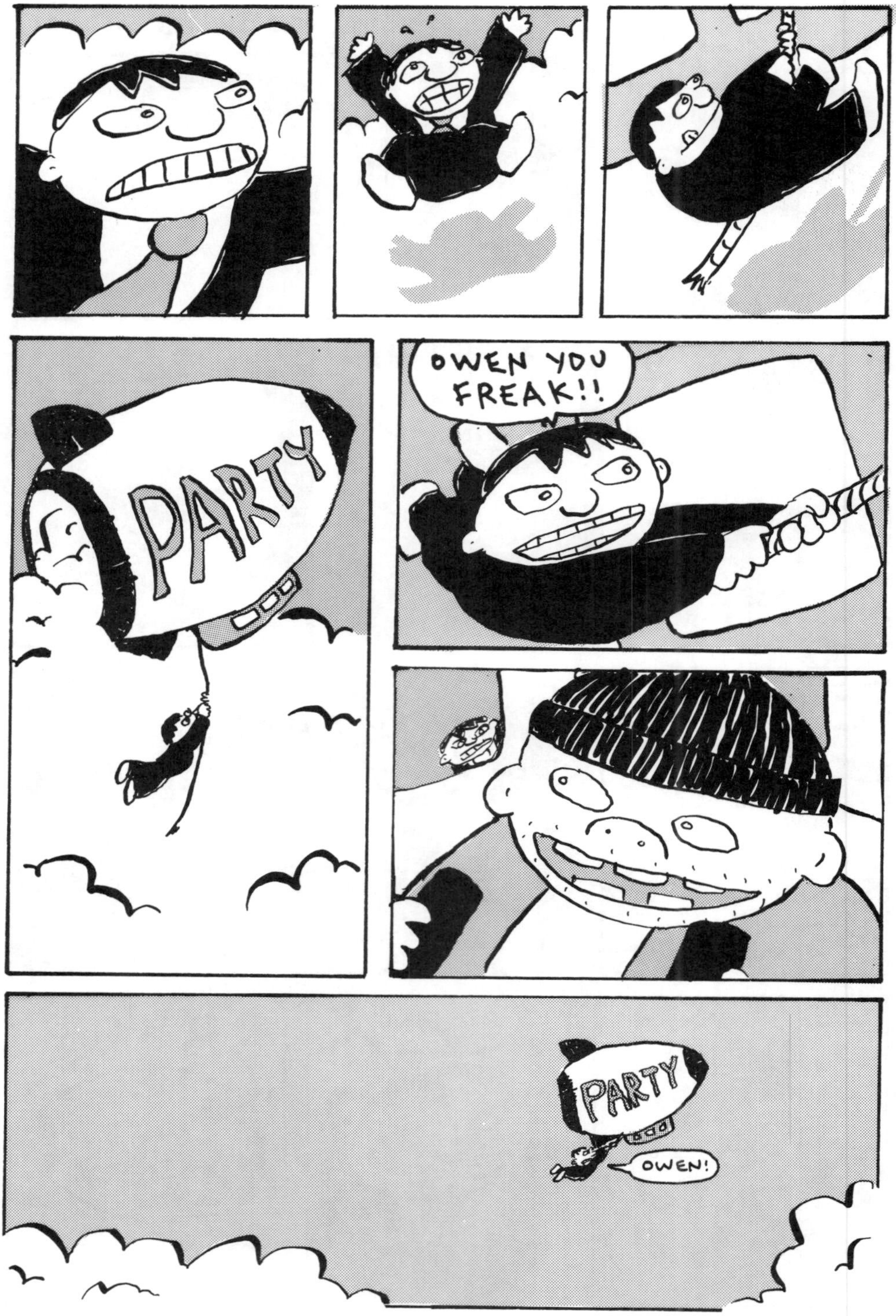
PARTY
OWEN YOU FREAK!!
PARTY
OWEN!

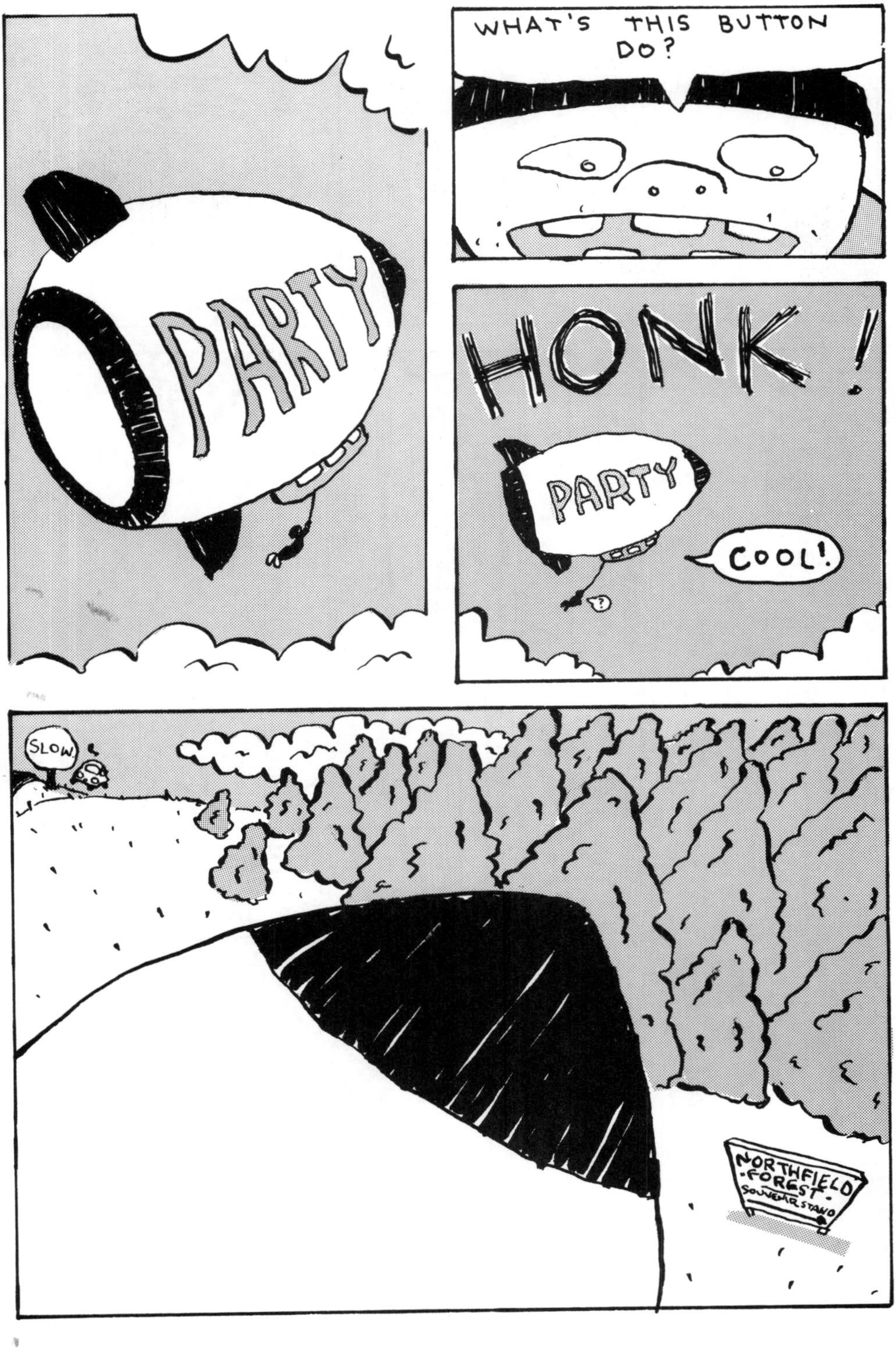
WHAT'S THIS BUTTON DO?
PARTY
HONK!
PARTY
COOL!
SLOW
NORTHFIELD FOREST
SOUVENIR STAND

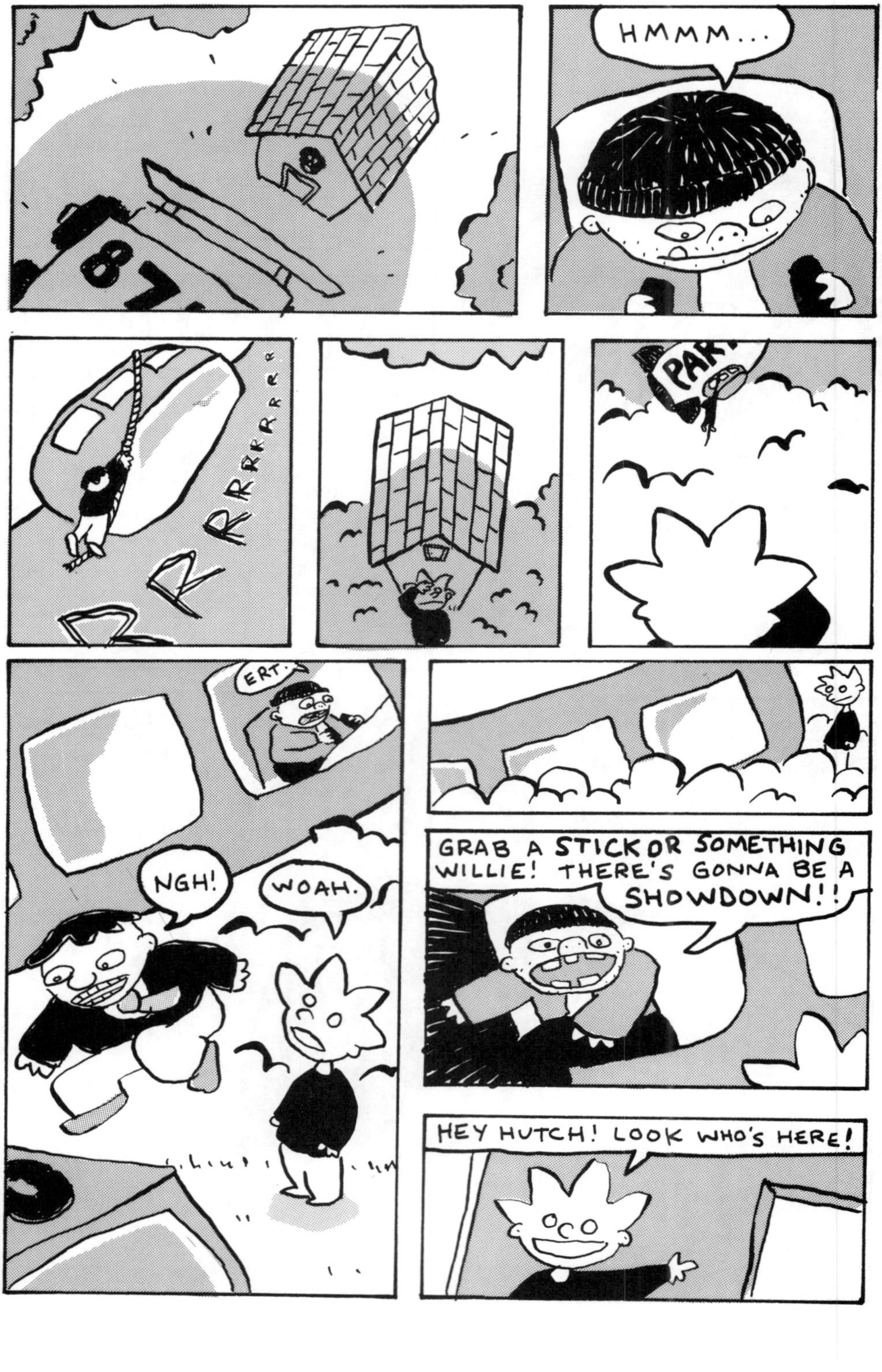
HMMM...
RRRRRRRRRR
PAR
ERT.
NGH!
WOAH.
GRAB A STICK OR SOMETHING WILLIE! THERE'S GONNA BE A SHOWDOWN!!
HEY HUTCH! LOOK WHO'S HERE!

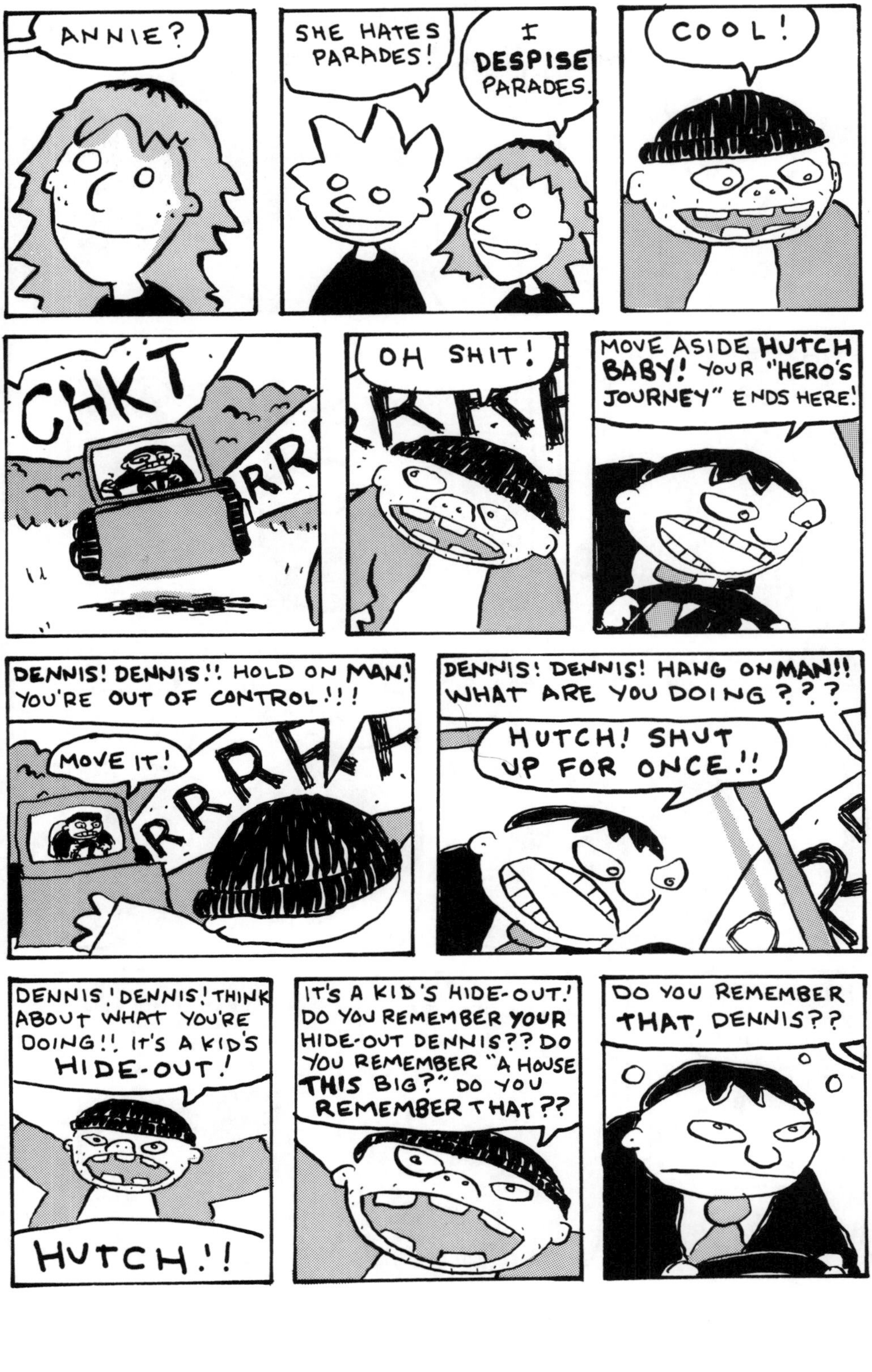

ANNIE?
SHE HATES PARADES!
I **DESPISE** PARADES.
COOL!
CHKT
RRR
OH SHIT!
RRRRH
MOVE ASIDE **HUTCH BABY!** YOUR "**HERO'S JOURNEY**" ENDS HERE!
DENNIS! DENNIS!! HOLD ON MAN! YOU'RE OUT OF CONTROL!!!
MOVE IT!
RRRRHH
DENNIS! DENNIS! HANG ON MAN!! WHAT ARE YOU DOING???
HUTCH! SHUT UP FOR ONCE!!
DENNIS! DENNIS! THINK ABOUT WHAT YOU'RE DOING!! IT'S A KID'S HIDE-OUT!
HUTCH!!
IT'S A KID'S HIDE-OUT! DO YOU REMEMBER **YOUR** HIDE-OUT DENNIS?? DO YOU REMEMBER "A HOUSE **THIS** BIG?" DO YOU **REMEMBER** THAT??
DO YOU REMEMBER **THAT**, DENNIS??

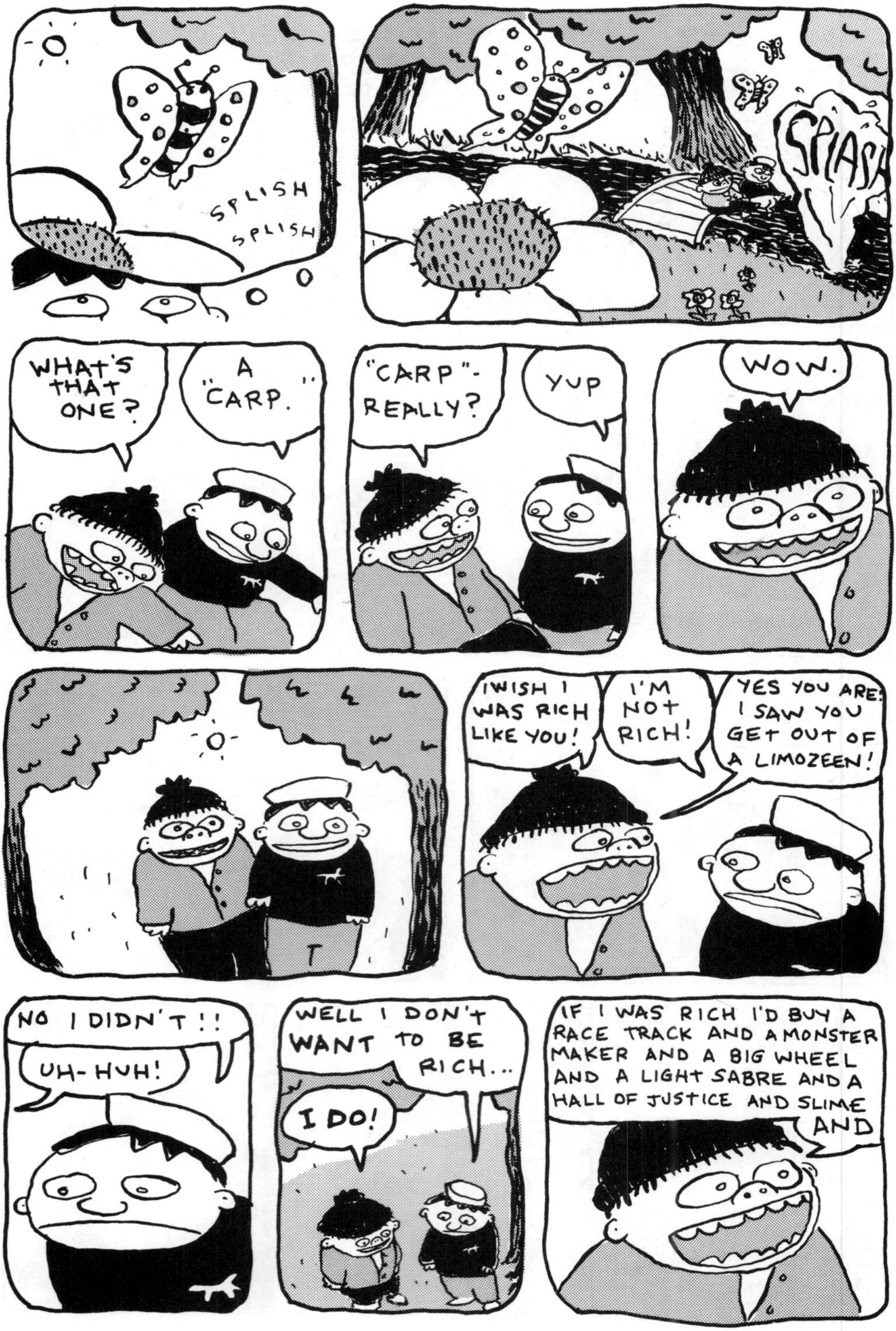
SPLISH
SPLISH
SPLASH
WHAT'S THAT ONE?
"A CARP."
"CARP"- REALLY?
YUP
WOW.
I WISH I WAS RICH LIKE YOU!
I'M NOT RICH!
YES YOU ARE! I SAW YOU GET OUT OF A LIMOZEEN!
NO I DIDN'T!!
UH-HUH!
WELL I DON'T WANT TO BE RICH...
I DO!
IF I WAS RICH I'D BUY A RACE TRACK AND A MONSTER MAKER AND A BIG WHEEL AND A LIGHT SABRE AND A HALL OF JUSTICE AND SLIME
AND

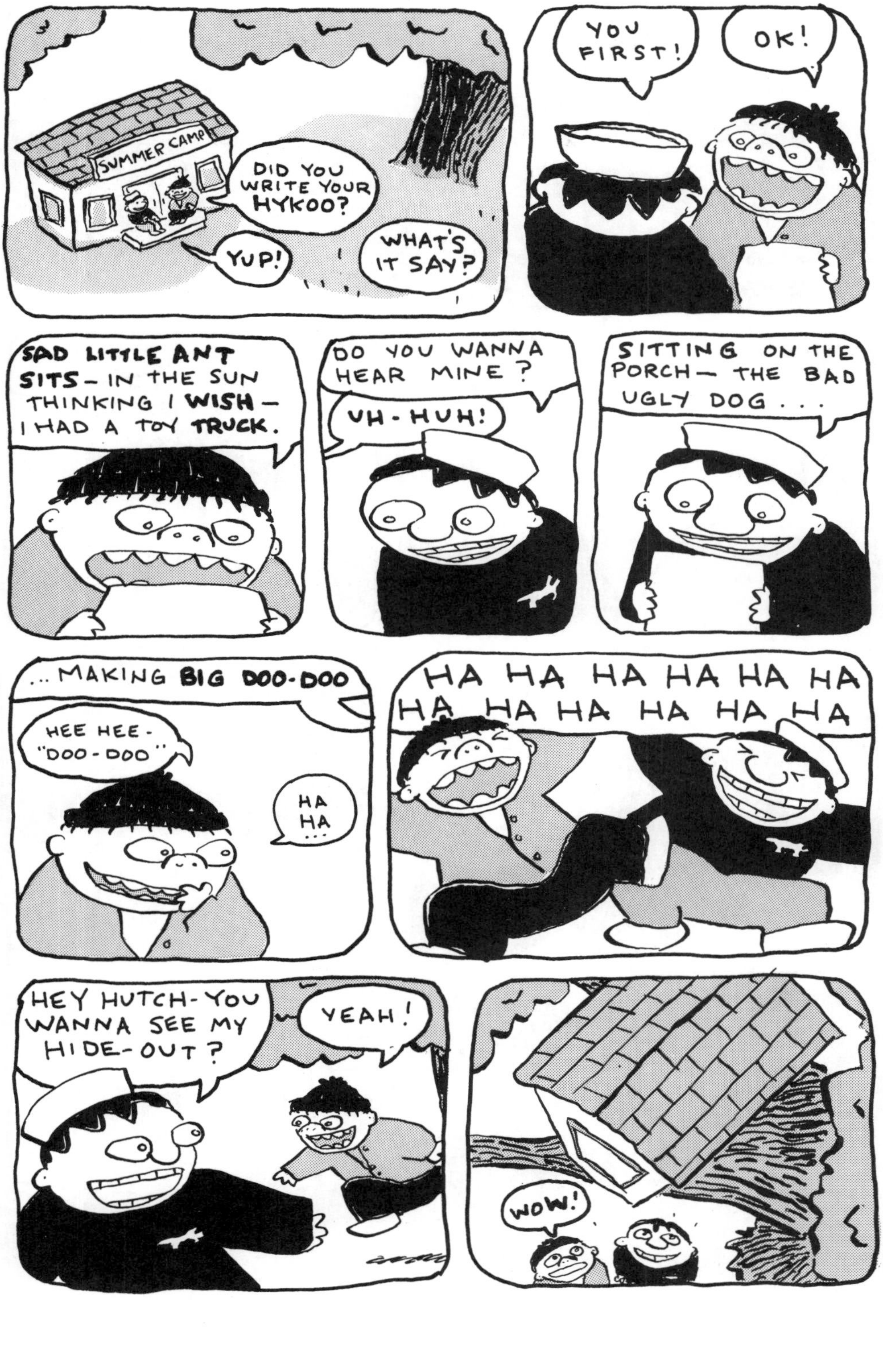
SUMMER CAMP
DID YOU WRITE YOUR HYKOO?
YUP!
WHAT'S IT SAY?
YOU FIRST!
OK!
SAD LITTLE ANT SITS— IN THE SUN THINKING I WISH— I HAD A TOY TRUCK.
DO YOU WANNA HEAR MINE?
UH-HUH!
SITTING ON THE PORCH— THE BAD UGLY DOG...
...MAKING BIG DOO-DOO
HEE HEE- "DOO-DOO"
HA HA
HA HA HA HA HA HA HA HA HA HA HA HA
HEY HUTCH- YOU WANNA SEE MY HIDE-OUT?
YEAH!
WOW!

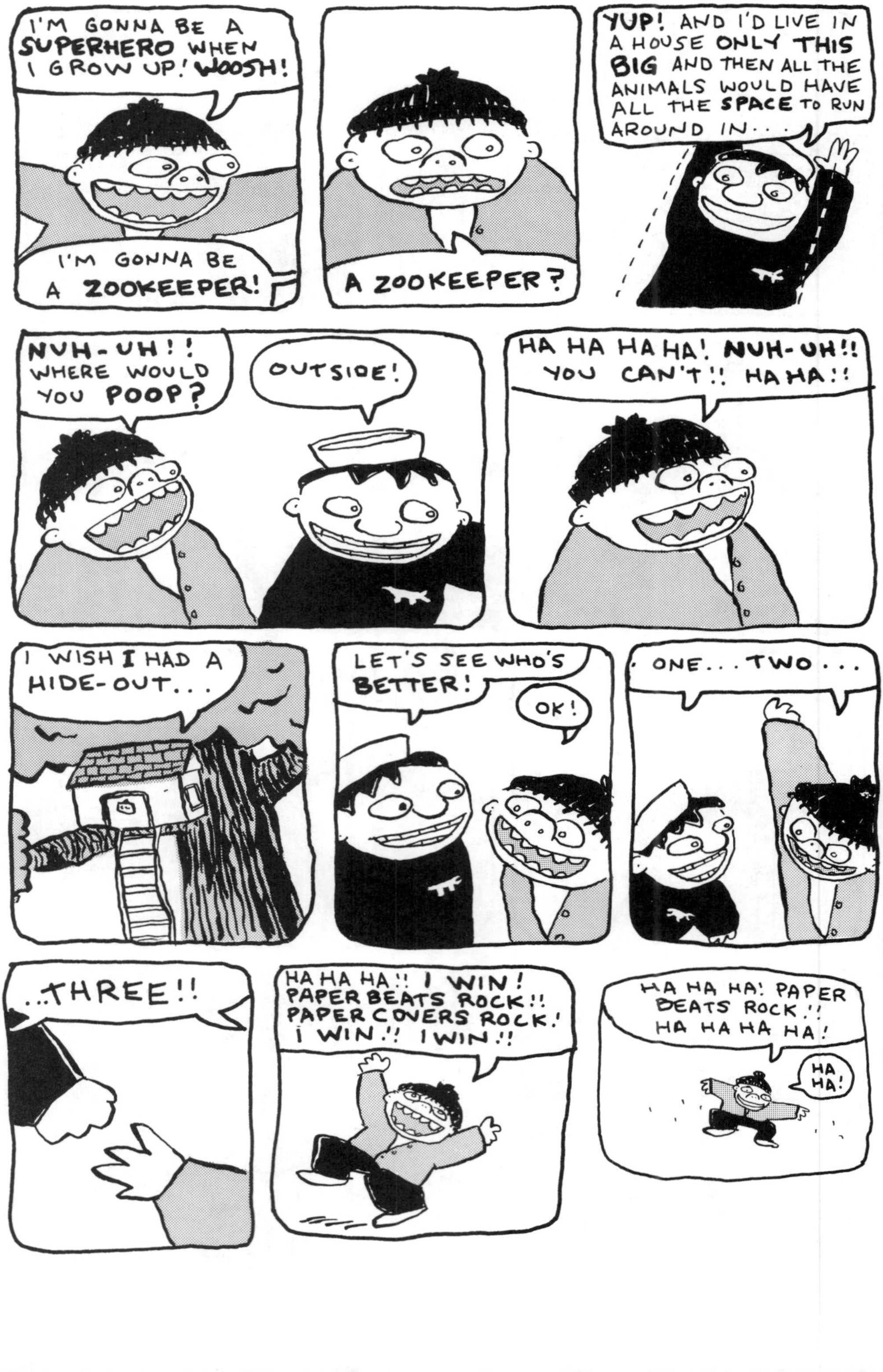
I'M GONNA BE A SUPERHERO WHEN I GROW UP! WOOSH!
I'M GONNA BE A ZOOKEEPER!
A ZOOKEEPER?
YUP! AND I'D LIVE IN A HOUSE ONLY THIS BIG AND THEN ALL THE ANIMALS WOULD HAVE ALL THE SPACE TO RUN AROUND IN...
NUH-UH!! WHERE WOULD YOU POOP?
OUTSIDE!
HA HA HA HA! NUH-UH!! YOU CAN'T!! HA HA!!
I WISH I HAD A HIDE-OUT...
LET'S SEE WHO'S BETTER!
OK!
ONE... TWO...
...THREE!!
HA HA HA!! I WIN! PAPER BEATS ROCK!! PAPER COVERS ROCK! I WIN!! I WIN!!
HA HA HA! PAPER BEATS ROCK!! HA HA HA HA!
HA HA!

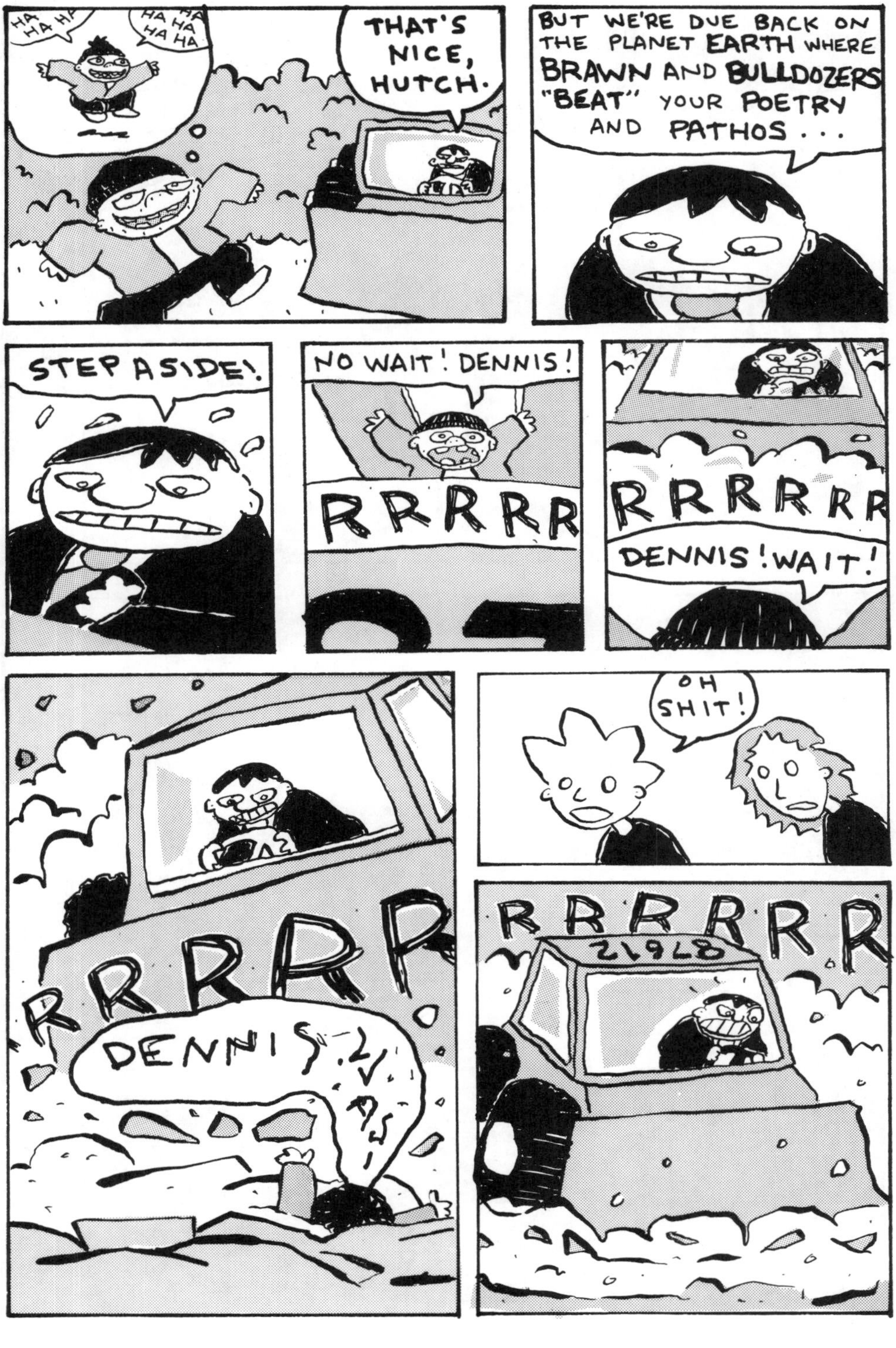
HA HA HA
HA HA HA HA HA
THAT'S NICE, HUTCH.
BUT WE'RE DUE BACK ON THE PLANET EARTH WHERE BRAWN AND BULLDOZERS "BEAT" YOUR POETRY AND PATHOS . . .
STEP ASIDE!
NO WAIT! DENNIS!
RRRRRR
RRRRRRR
DENNIS! WAIT!
RRRRR
DENNIS
OH SHIT!
RRRRRRR

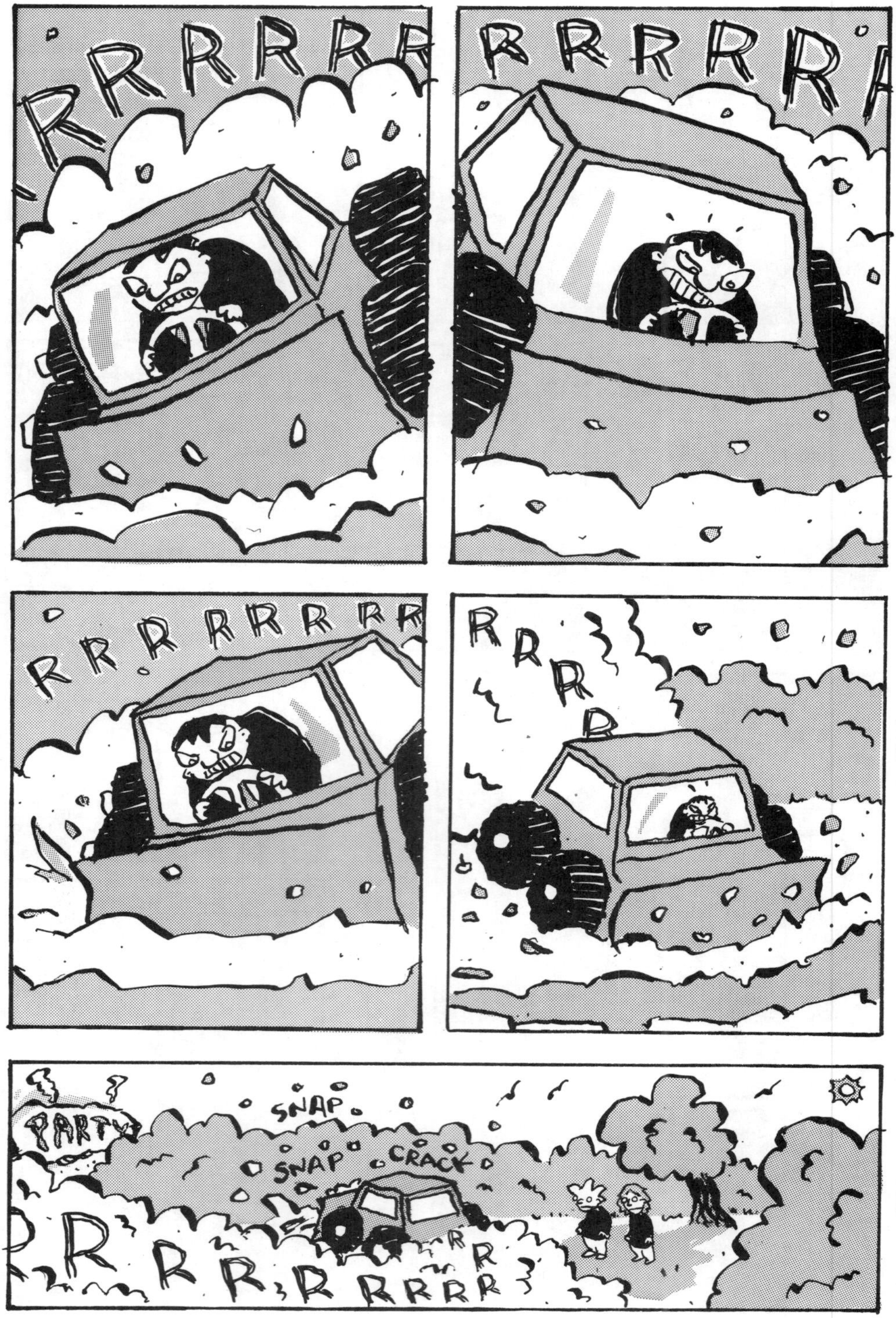
RRRRRRR
RRRRRRR
RRRRRRRR
RRRR
PARTY
SNAP
SNAP
CRACK
RRRRRRRRR

RRRRR
RRRRRR
RRRR
RRR
R

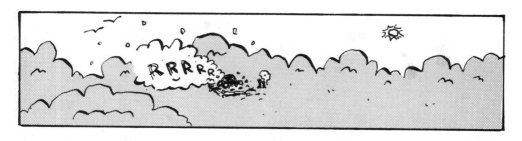

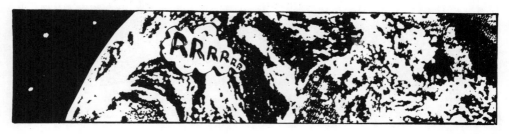

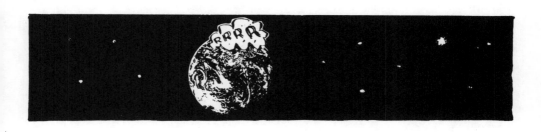

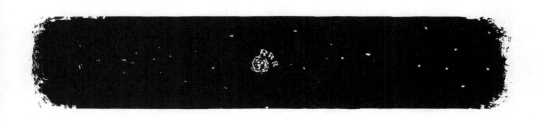

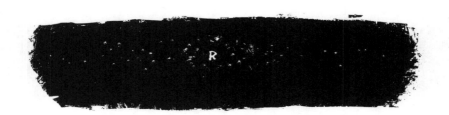

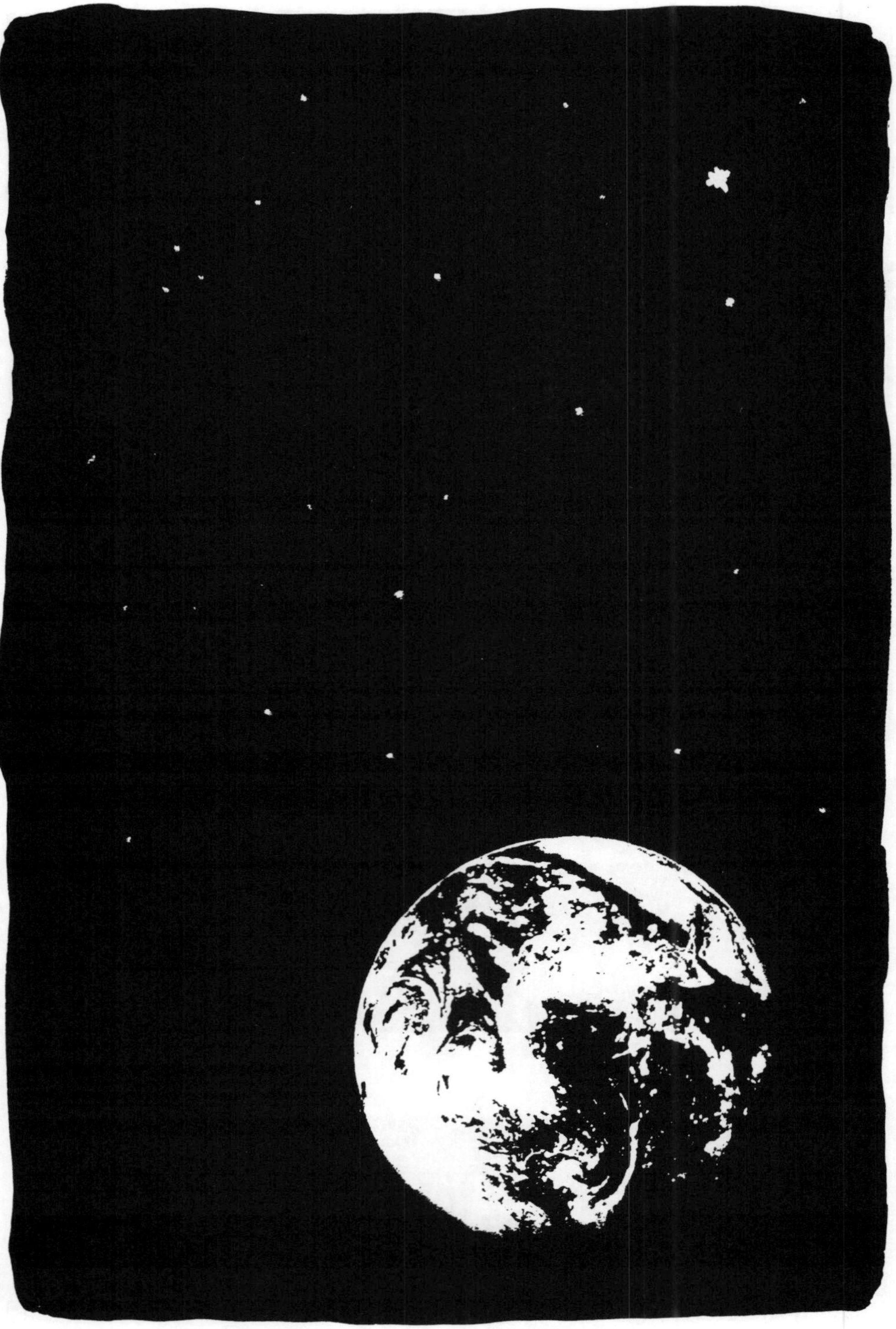

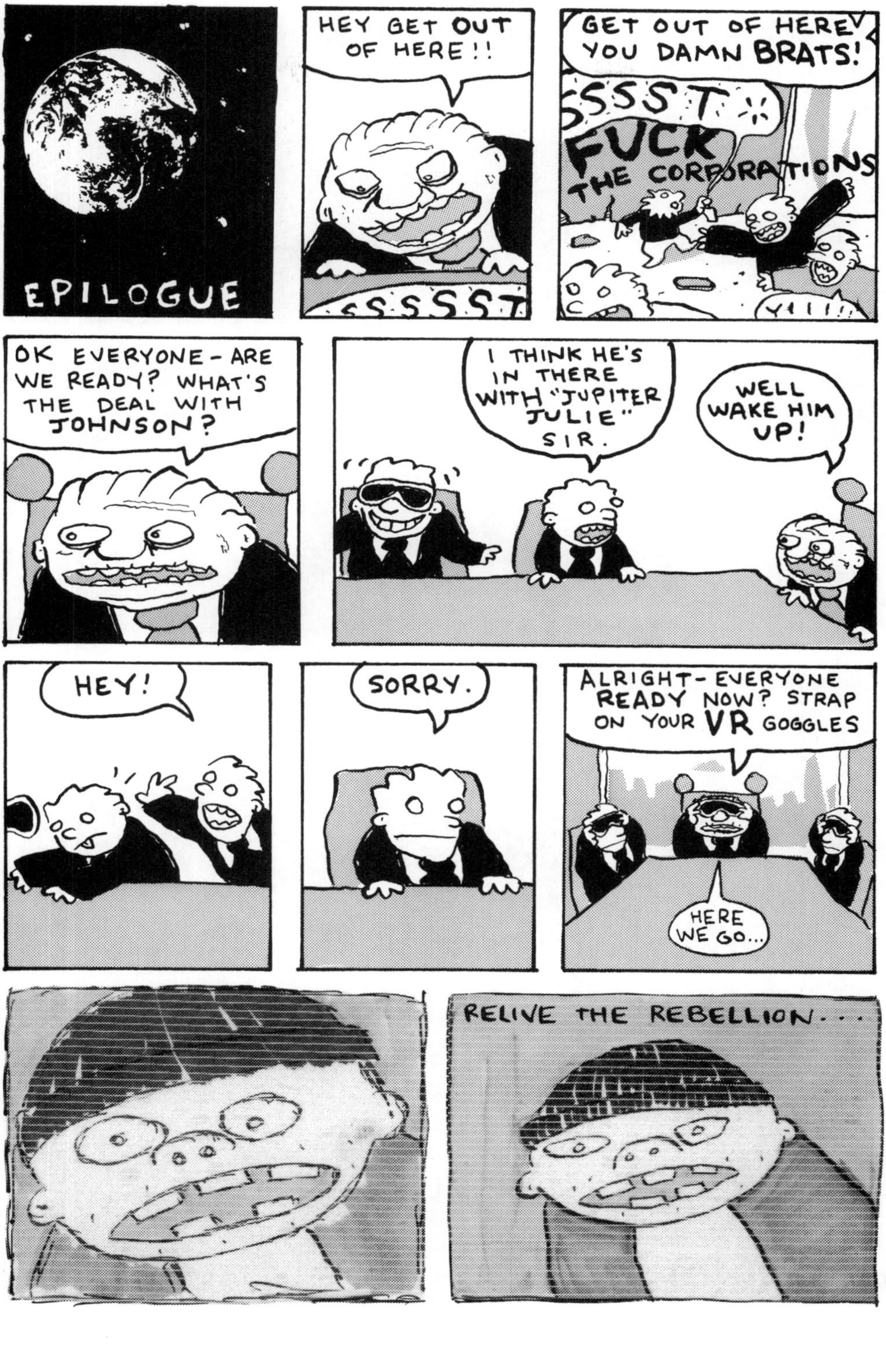
EPILOGUE
HEY GET OUT OF HERE!!
SSSSST
GET OUT OF HERE YOU DAMN BRATS!
SSSST
FUCK THE CORPORATIONS
YAAAH!!
OK EVERYONE - ARE WE READY? WHAT'S THE DEAL WITH JOHNSON?
I THINK HE'S IN THERE WITH "JUPITER JULIE" SIR.
WELL WAKE HIM UP!
HEY!
SORRY.
ALRIGHT - EVERYONE READY NOW? STRAP ON YOUR VR GOGGLES
HERE WE GO...
RELIVE THE REBELLION...

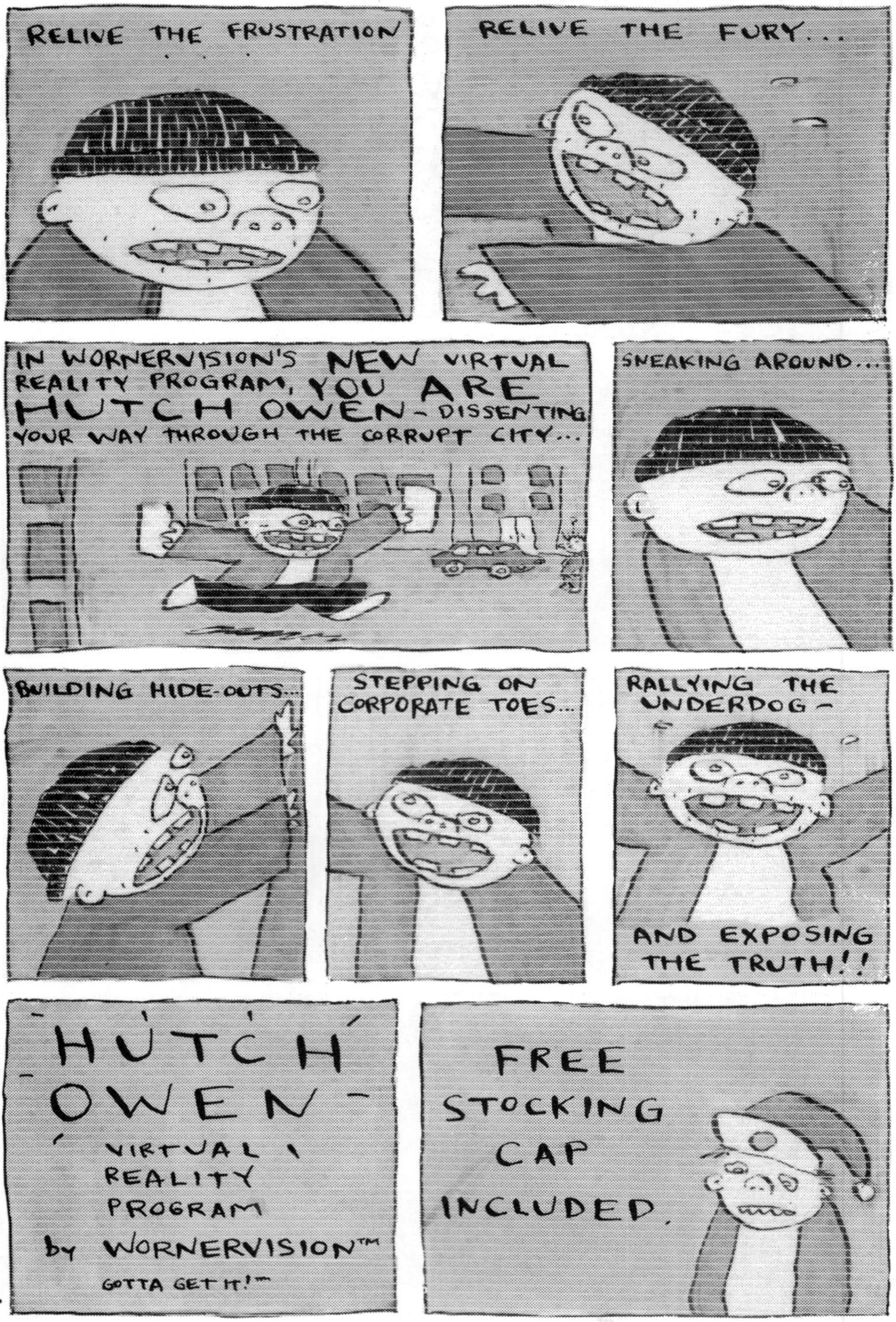
RELIVE THE FRUSTRATION...
RELIVE THE FURY...
IN WORNERVISION'S NEW VIRTUAL REALITY PROGRAM, YOU ARE HUTCH OWEN - DISSENTING YOUR WAY THROUGH THE CORRUPT CITY...
SNEAKING AROUND...
BUILDING HIDE-OUTS...
STEPPING ON CORPORATE TOES...
RALLYING THE UNDERDOG -
AND EXPOSING THE TRUTH!!
HUTCH OWEN
VIRTUAL REALITY PROGRAM
by WORNERVISION™
GOTTA GET IT!™
FREE STOCKING CAP INCLUDED.

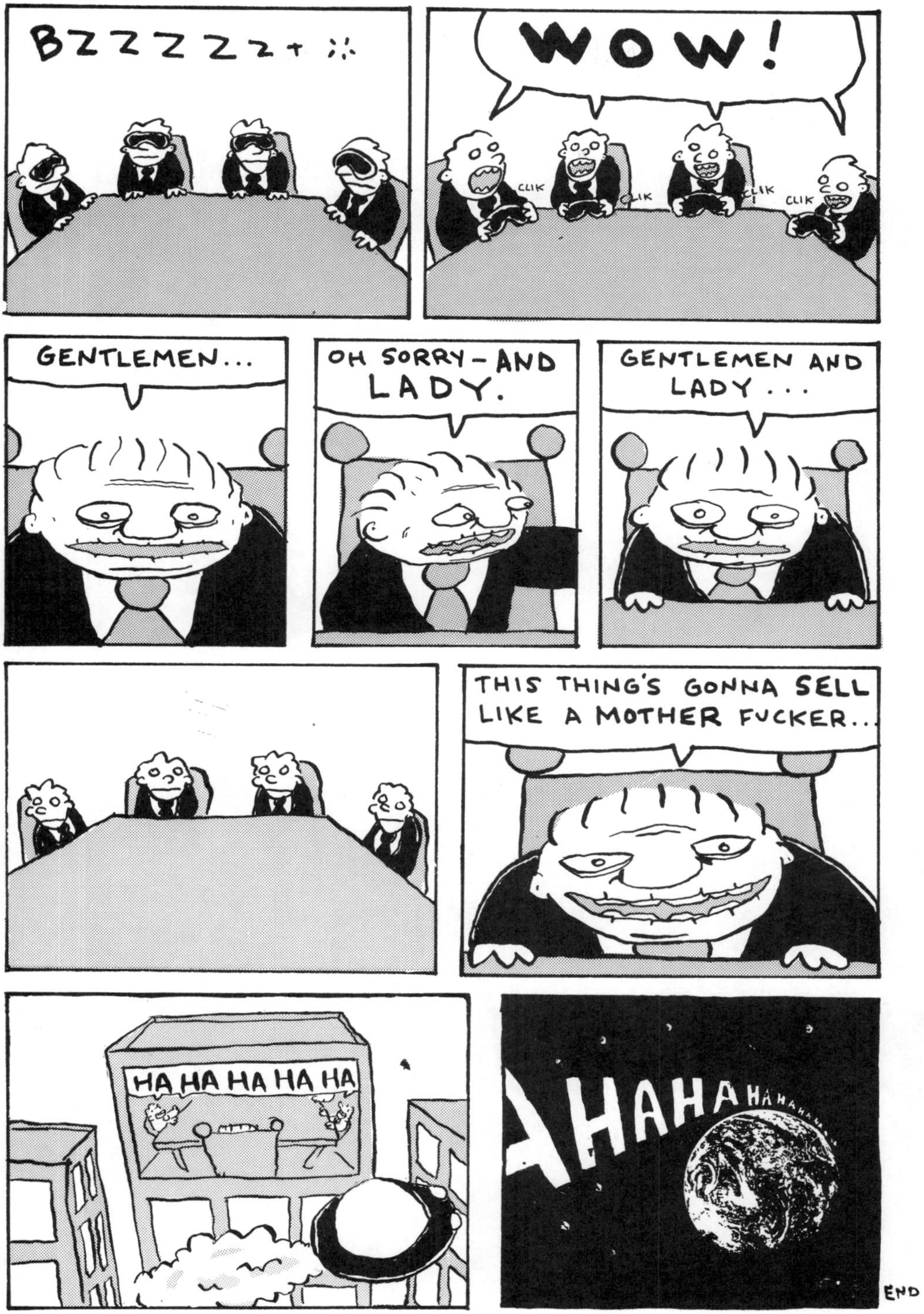
BZZZZZ+
WOW!
CLIK
CLIK
CLIK
CLIK
GENTLEMEN...
OH SORRY- AND LADY.
GENTLEMEN AND LADY...
THIS THING'S GONNA SELL LIKE A MOTHER FUCKER...
HA HA HA HA HA
HAHAHAHA
END

II. Emerging Markets

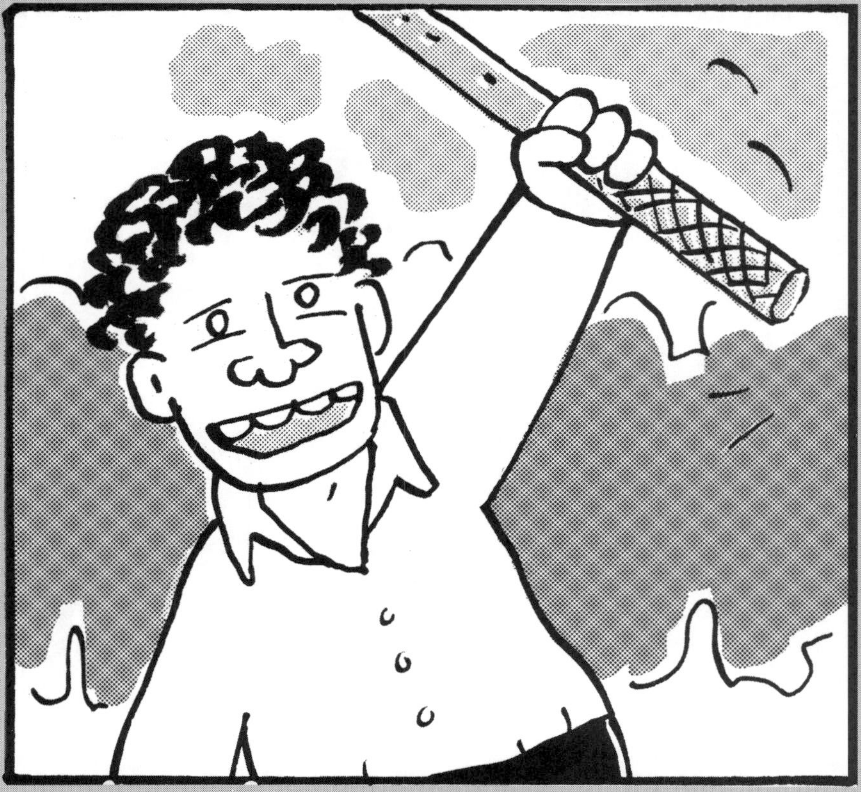

for the Wayward Council

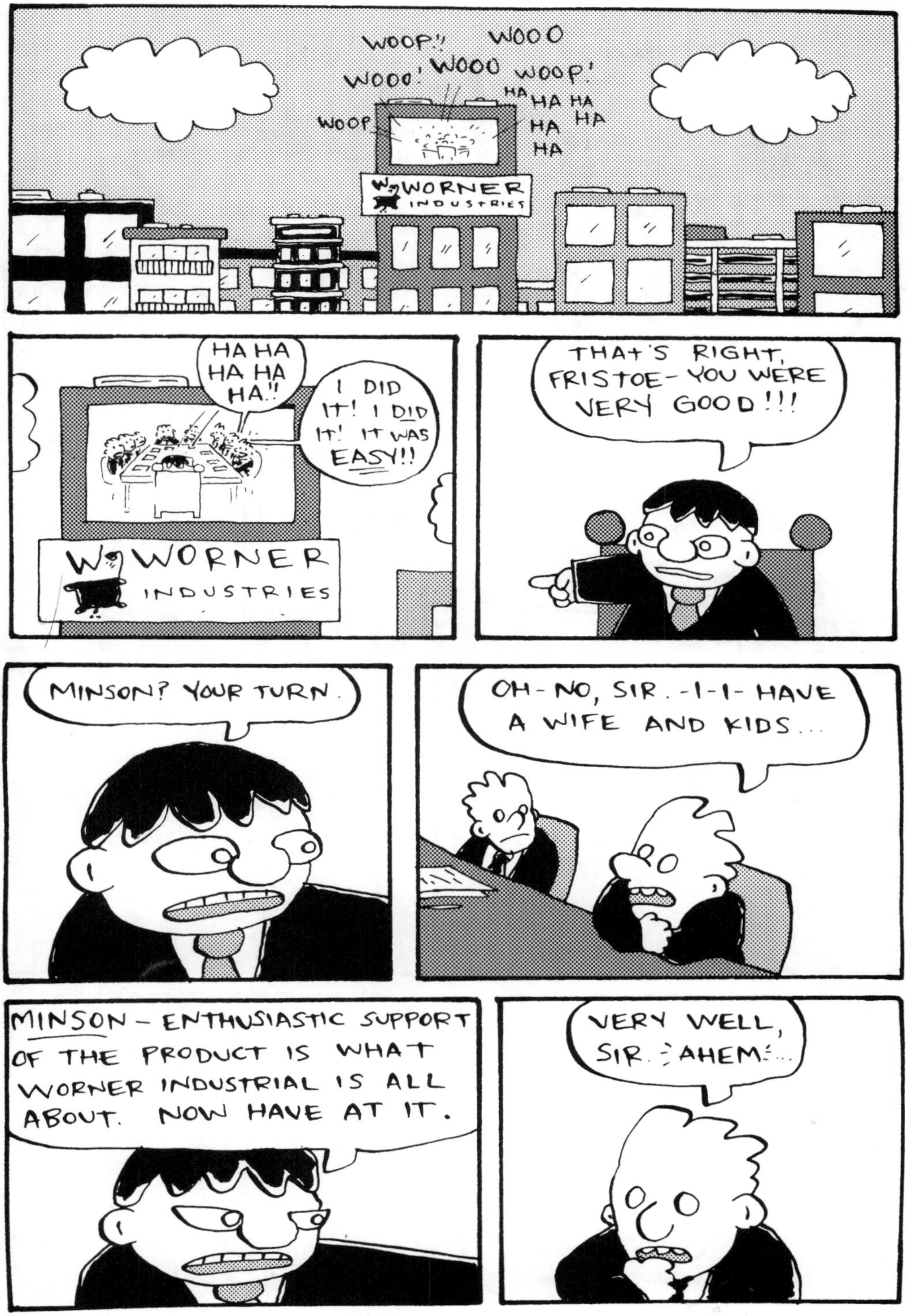
WOOP!! WOOO
WOOO! WOOO WOOP!
WOOP
HA HA HA HA HA HA HA
WORNER INDUSTRIES
HA HA HA HA HA!!
I DID IT! I DID IT! IT WAS EASY!!
WORNER INDUSTRIES
THAT'S RIGHT, FRISTOE- YOU WERE VERY GOOD!!!
MINSON? YOUR TURN.
OH- NO, SIR. -I-I- HAVE A WIFE AND KIDS...
MINSON- ENTHUSIASTIC SUPPORT OF THE PRODUCT IS WHAT WORNER INDUSTRIAL IS ALL ABOUT. NOW HAVE AT IT.
VERY WELL, SIR. AHEM...

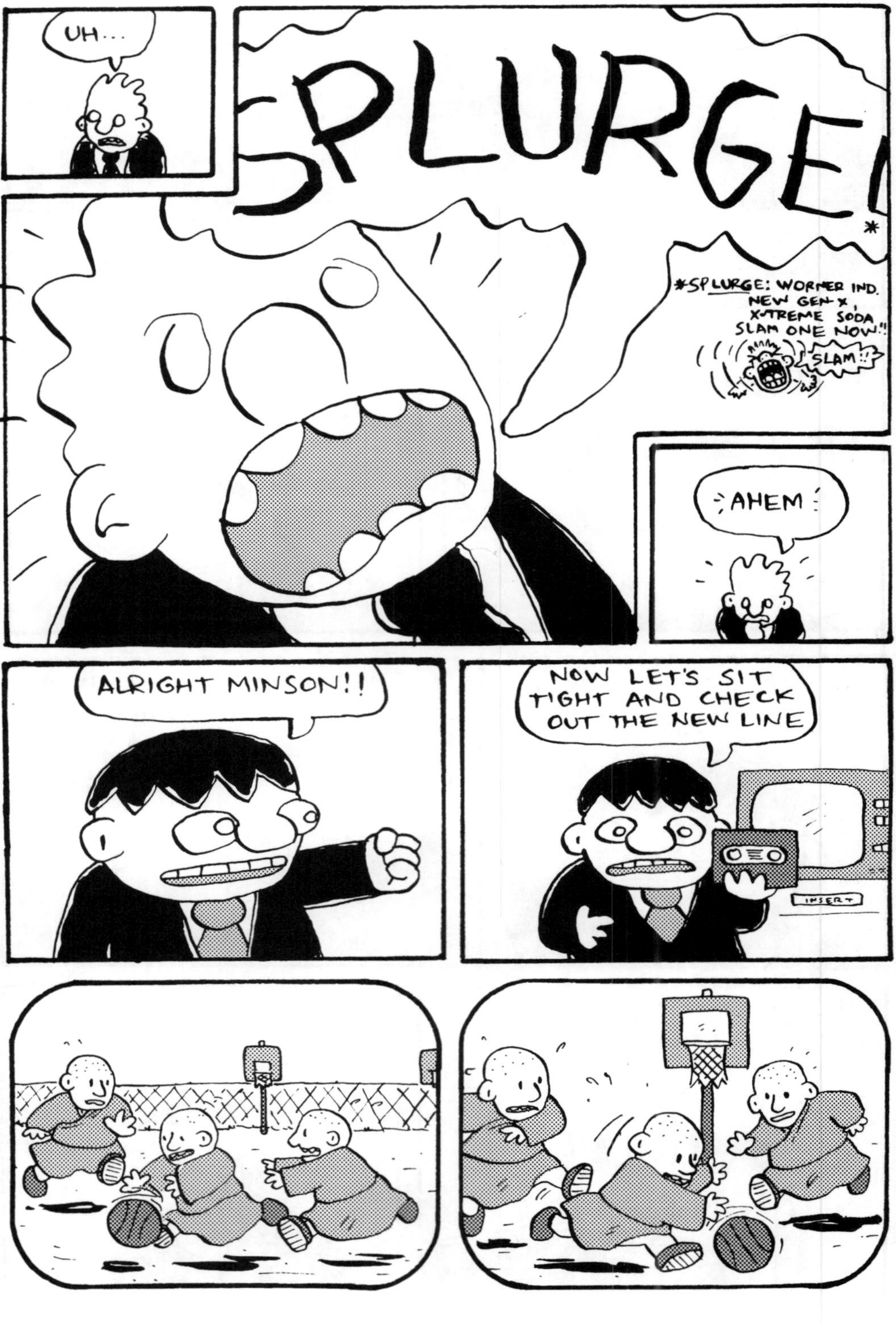
UH...
SPLURGE!*
*SPLURGE: WORNER IND. NEW GEN-X, X-TREME SODA SLAM ONE NOW!!
SLAM!!
AHEM
ALRIGHT MINSON!!
NOW LET'S SIT TIGHT AND CHECK OUT THE NEW LINE
INSERT

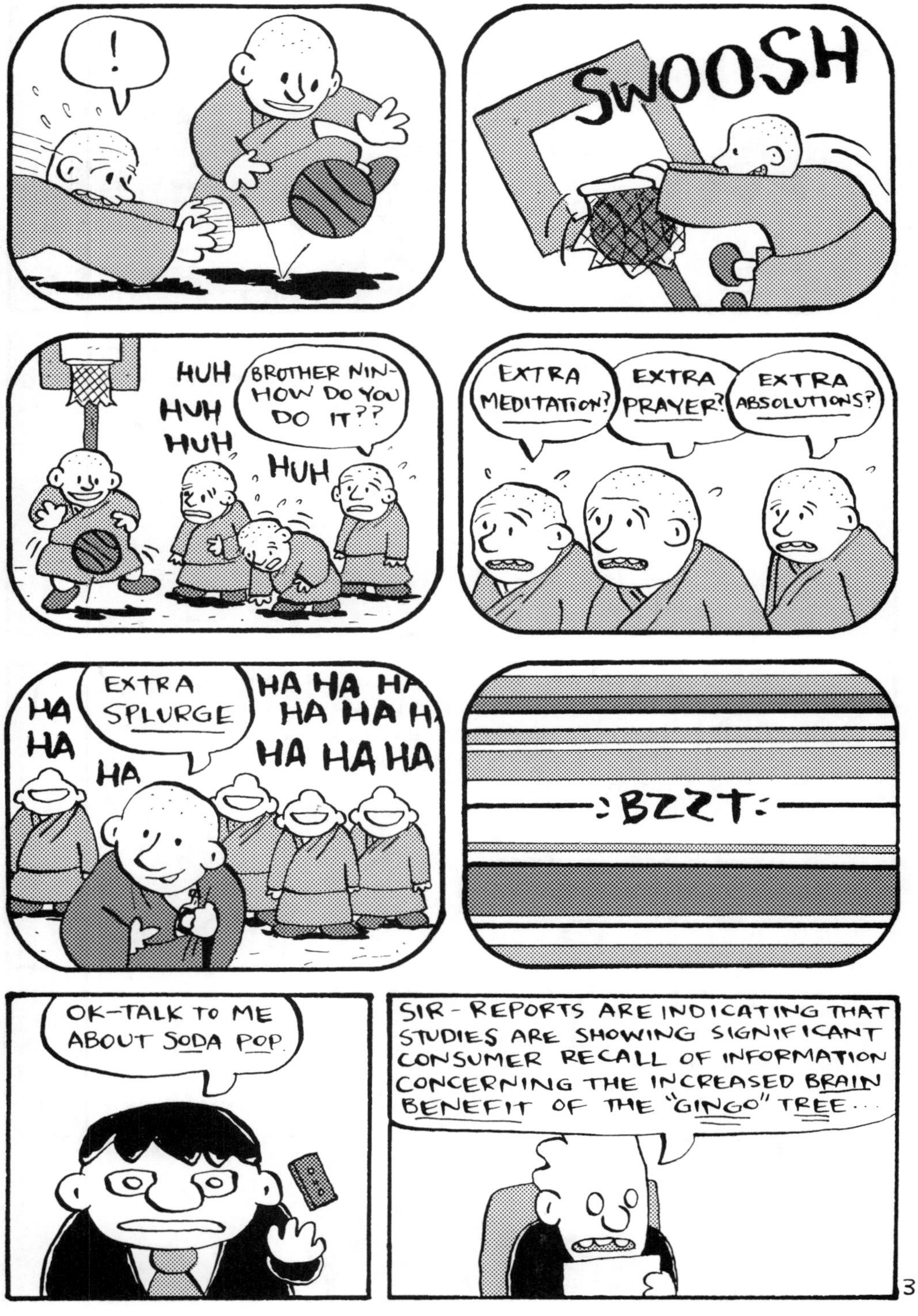
!
SWOOSH
HUH HUH HUH
BROTHER NIN- HOW DO YOU DO IT??
HUH
EXTRA MEDITATION?
EXTRA PRAYER?
EXTRA ABSOLUTIONS?
EXTRA SPLURGE
HA HA
HA
HA HA HA HA HA HA HA HA HA
BZZT
OK—TALK TO ME ABOUT SODA POP.
SIR - REPORTS ARE INDICATING THAT STUDIES ARE SHOWING SIGNIFICANT CONSUMER RECALL OF INFORMATION CONCERNING THE INCREASED BRAIN BENEFIT OF THE "GINGO" TREE...

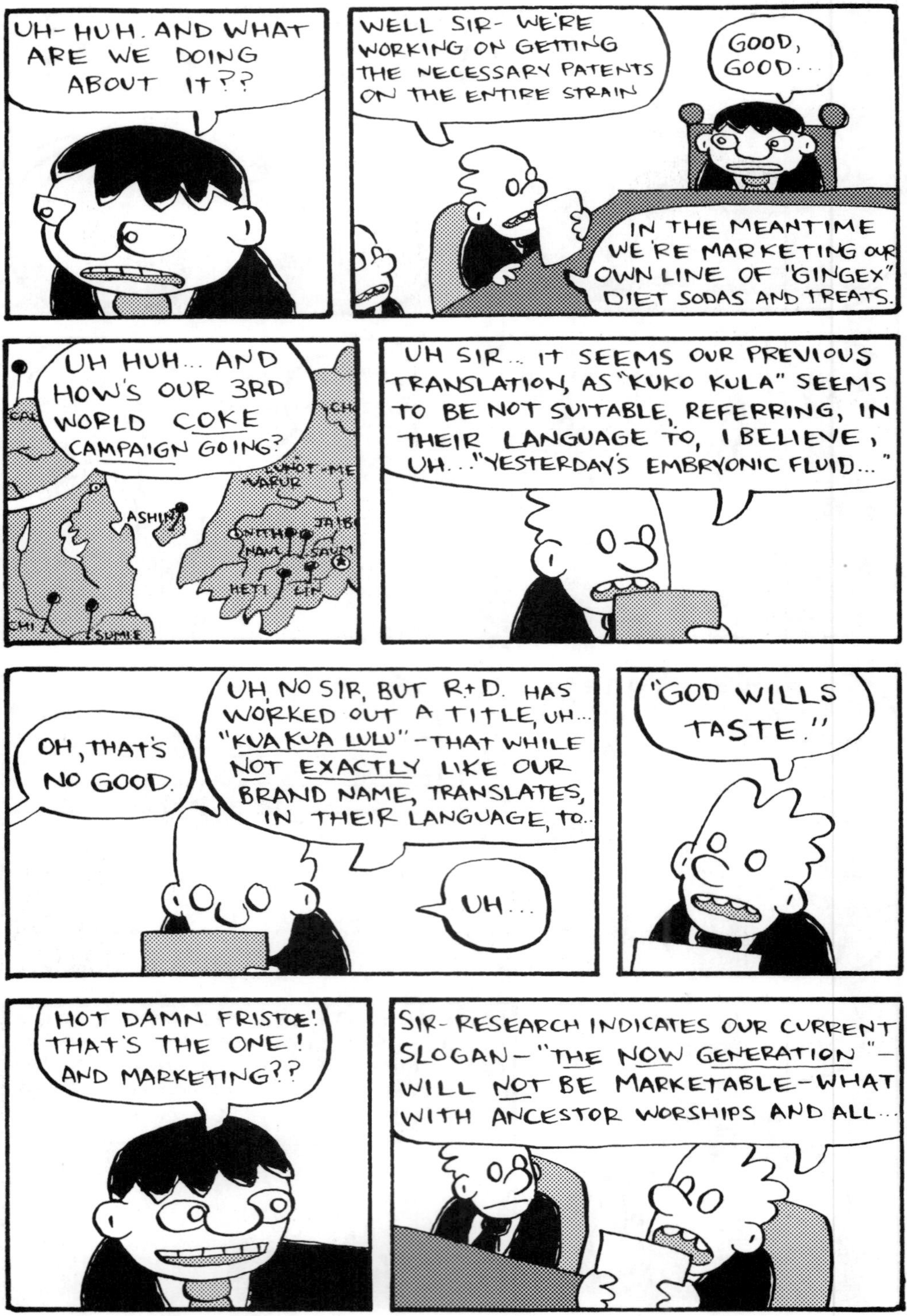
UH-HUH. AND WHAT ARE WE DOING ABOUT IT??
WELL SIR- WE'RE WORKING ON GETTING THE NECESSARY PATENTS ON THE ENTIRE STRAIN
GOOD, GOOD...
IN THE MEANTIME WE'RE MARKETING OUR OWN LINE OF "GINGEX" DIET SODAS AND TREATS.
UH HUH... AND HOW'S OUR 3RD WORLD COKE CAMPAIGN GOING?
ASHIN
UH SIR... IT SEEMS OUR PREVIOUS TRANSLATION, AS "KUKO KULA" SEEMS TO BE NOT SUITABLE, REFERRING, IN THEIR LANGUAGE TO, I BELIEVE, UH..."YESTERDAY'S EMBRYONIC FLUID..."
OH, THAT'S NO GOOD.
UH, NO SIR, BUT R+D. HAS WORKED OUT A TITLE, UH... "KUA KUA LULU" - THAT WHILE NOT EXACTLY LIKE OUR BRAND NAME, TRANSLATES, IN THEIR LANGUAGE, TO...
UH...
"GOD WILLS TASTE."
HOT DAMN FRISTOE! THAT'S THE ONE! AND MARKETING??
SIR- RESEARCH INDICATES OUR CURRENT SLOGAN - "THE NOW GENERATION" - WILL NOT BE MARKETABLE - WHAT WITH ANCESTOR WORSHIPS AND ALL...

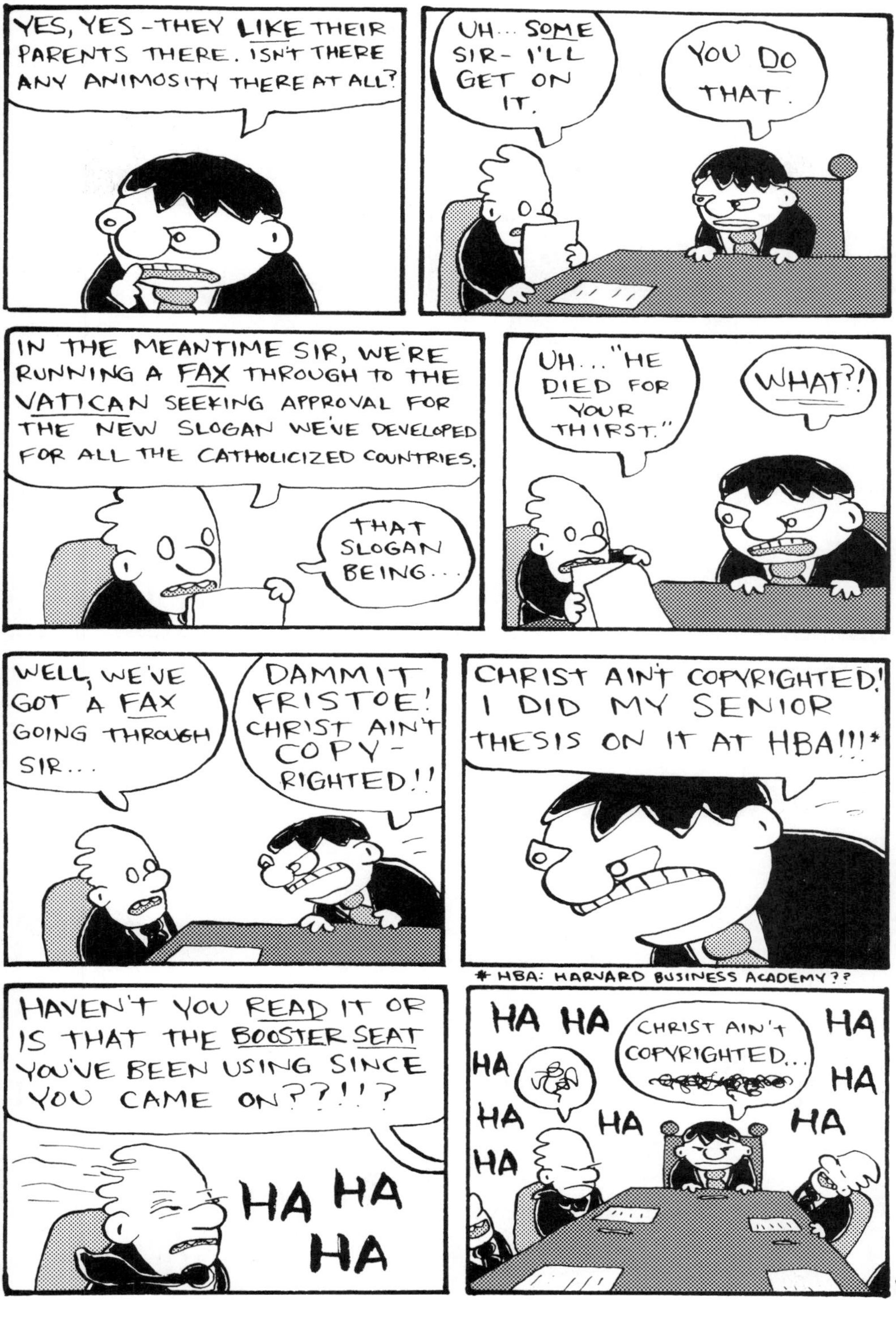
YES, YES - THEY LIKE THEIR PARENTS THERE. ISN'T THERE ANY ANIMOSITY THERE AT ALL?
UH... SOME SIR - I'LL GET ON IT.
YOU DO THAT.
IN THE MEANTIME SIR, WE'RE RUNNING A FAX THROUGH TO THE VATICAN SEEKING APPROVAL FOR THE NEW SLOGAN WE'VE DEVELOPED FOR ALL THE CATHOLICIZED COUNTRIES.
THAT SLOGAN BEING...
UH... "HE DIED FOR YOUR THIRST."
WHAT?!
WELL, WE'VE GOT A FAX GOING THROUGH SIR...
DAMMIT FRISTOE! CHRIST AIN'T COPY-RIGHTED!!
CHRIST AIN'T COPYRIGHTED! I DID MY SENIOR THESIS ON IT AT HBA!!!*
* HBA: HARVARD BUSINESS ACADEMY??
HAVEN'T YOU READ IT OR IS THAT THE BOOSTER SEAT YOU'VE BEEN USING SINCE YOU CAME ON??!!?
HA HA HA
HA HA
CHRIST AIN'T COPYRIGHTED...
HA HA HA HA HA HA HA HA

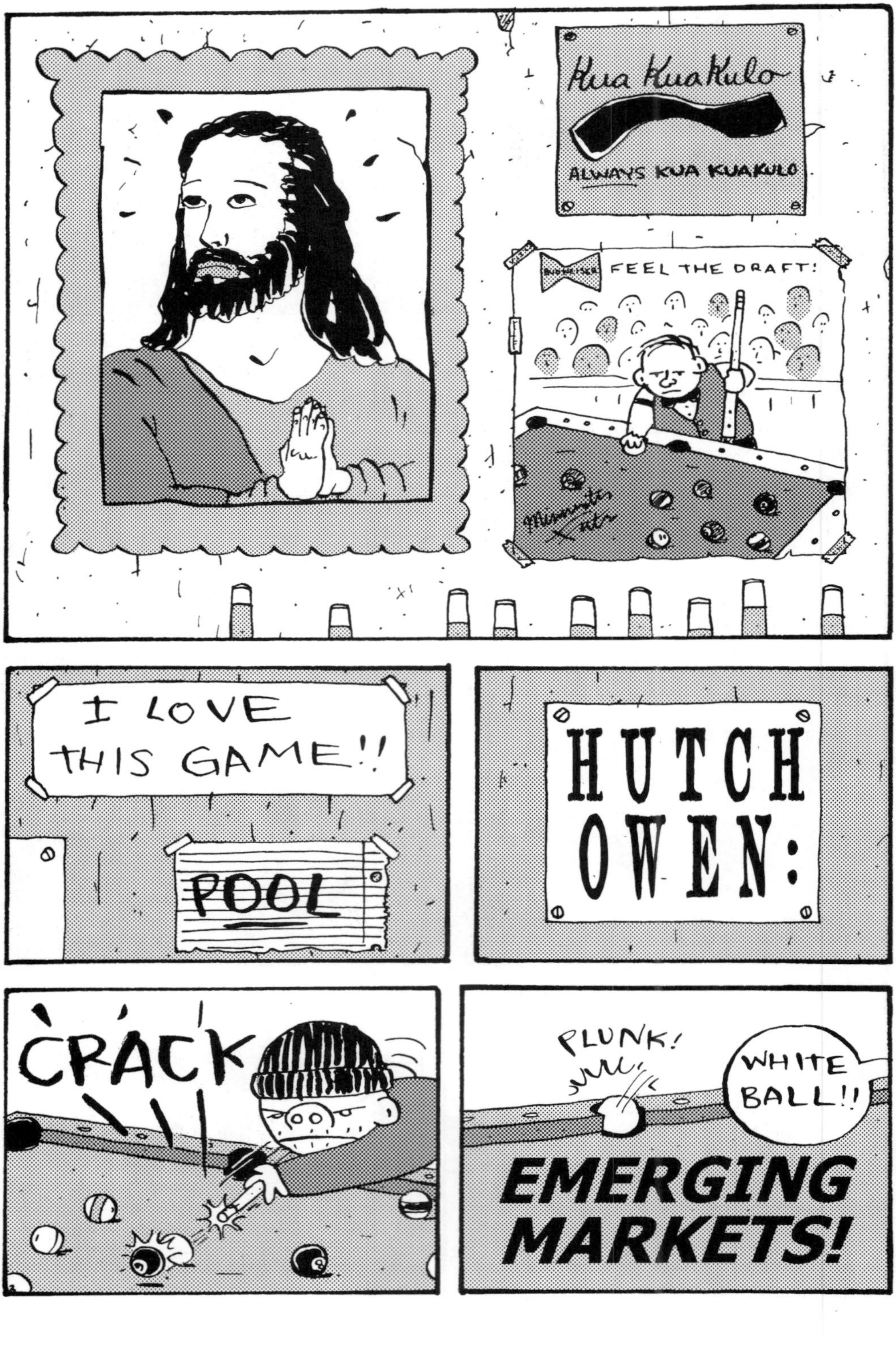
Kua KuaKulo
ALWAYS KUA KUAKULO
FEEL THE DRAFT!
I LOVE THIS GAME!!
POOL
HUTCH OWEN:
CRACK
PLUNK!
WHITE BALL!!
EMERGING MARKETS!

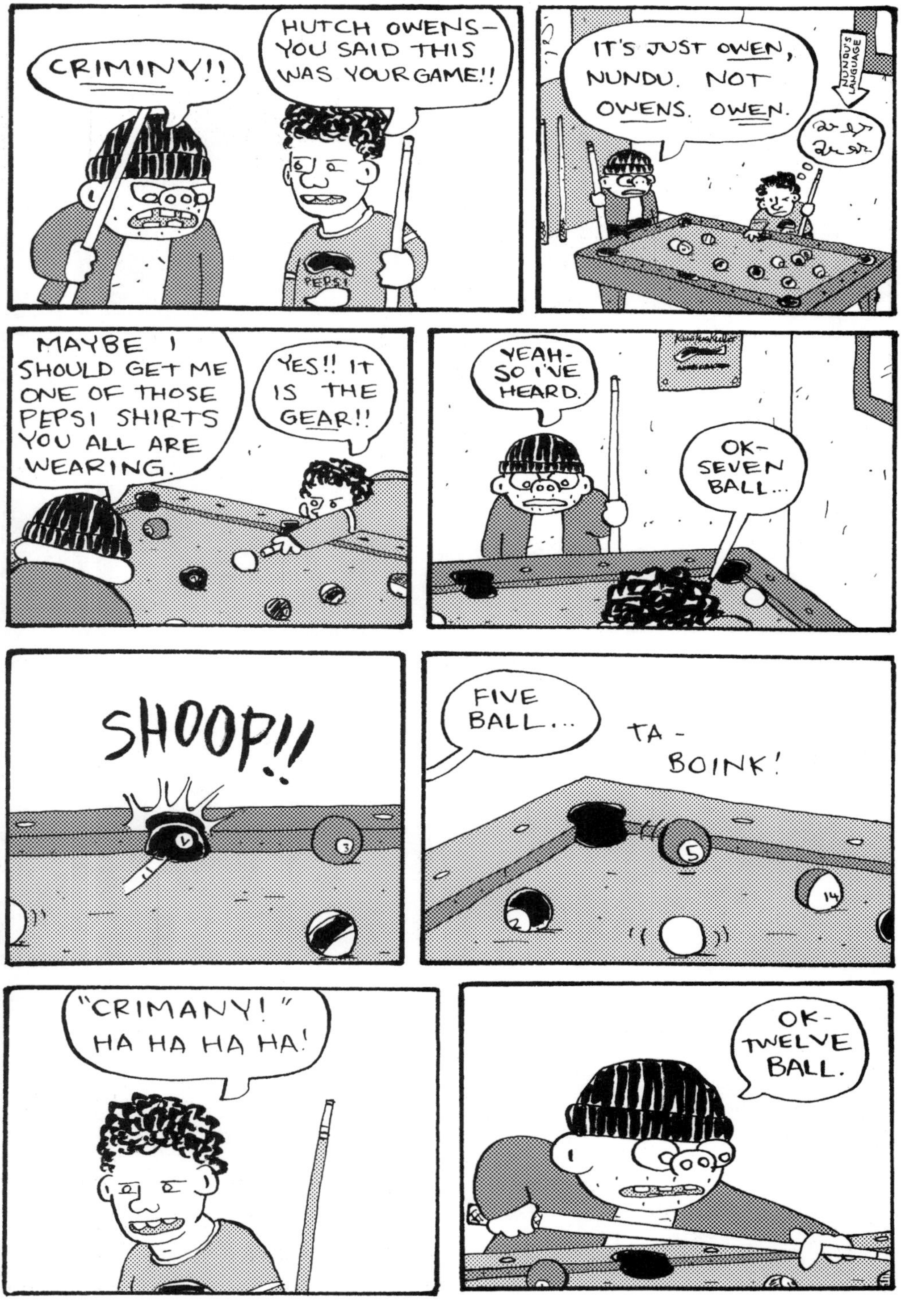
CRIMINY!!
HUTCH OWENS- YOU SAID THIS WAS YOUR GAME!!
IT'S JUST OWEN, NUNDU. NOT OWENS. OWEN.
NUNDU'S LANGUAGE
MAYBE I SHOULD GET ME ONE OF THOSE PEPSI SHIRTS YOU ALL ARE WEARING.
YES!! IT IS THE GEAR!!
YEAH- SO I'VE HEARD.
OK- SEVEN BALL...
SHOOP!!
FIVE BALL...
TA - BOINK!
"CRIMANY!" HA HA HA HA!
OK- TWELVE BALL.

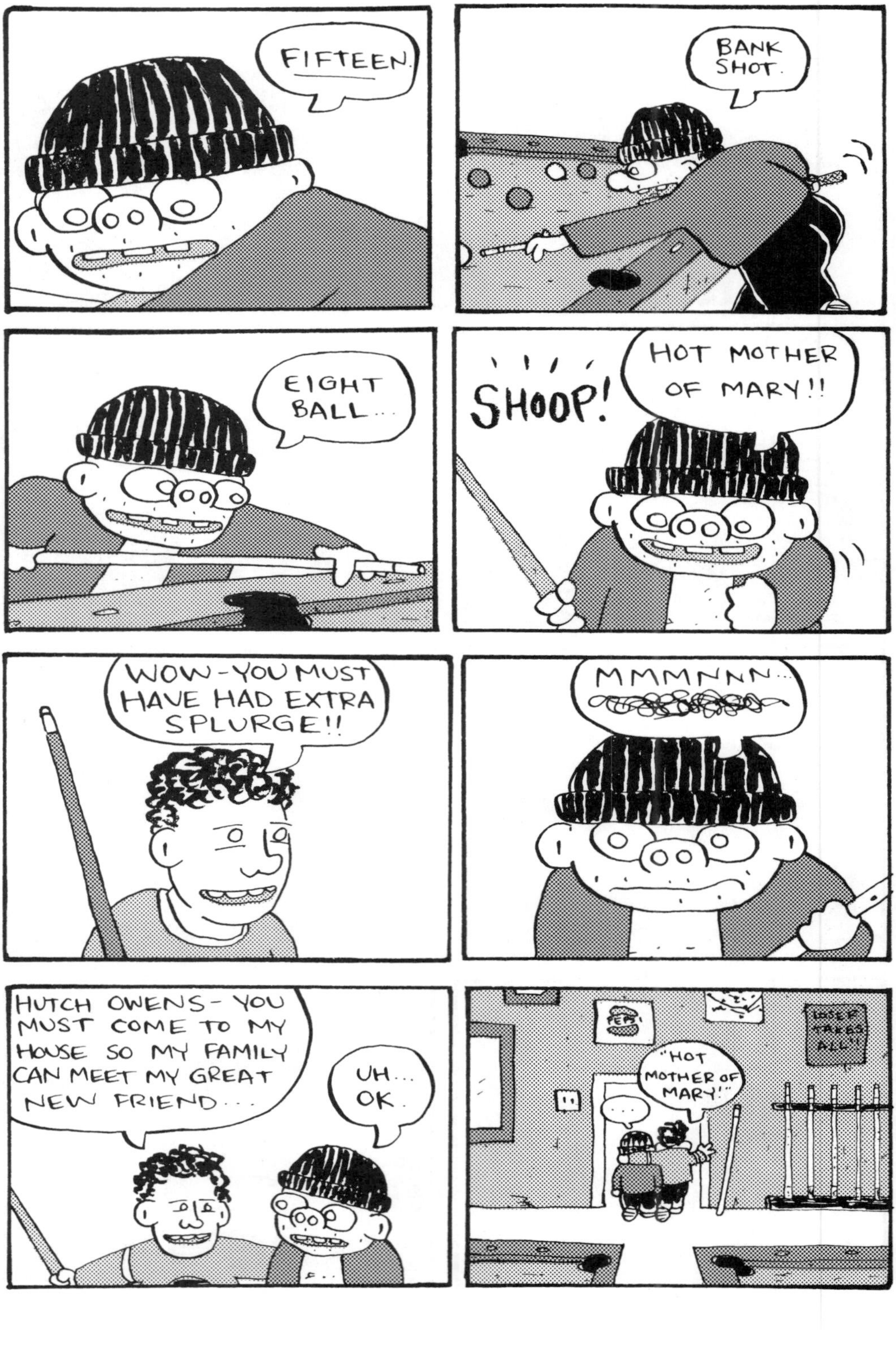
FIFTEEN.
BANK SHOT.
EIGHT BALL...
SHOOP!
HOT MOTHER OF MARY!!
WOW-YOU MUST HAVE HAD EXTRA SPLURGE!!
MMMNNN...
HUTCH OWENS- YOU MUST COME TO MY HOUSE SO MY FAMILY CAN MEET MY GREAT NEW FRIEND...
UH... OK.
LOSER TAKES ALL!!
"HOT MOTHER OF MARY!"
...

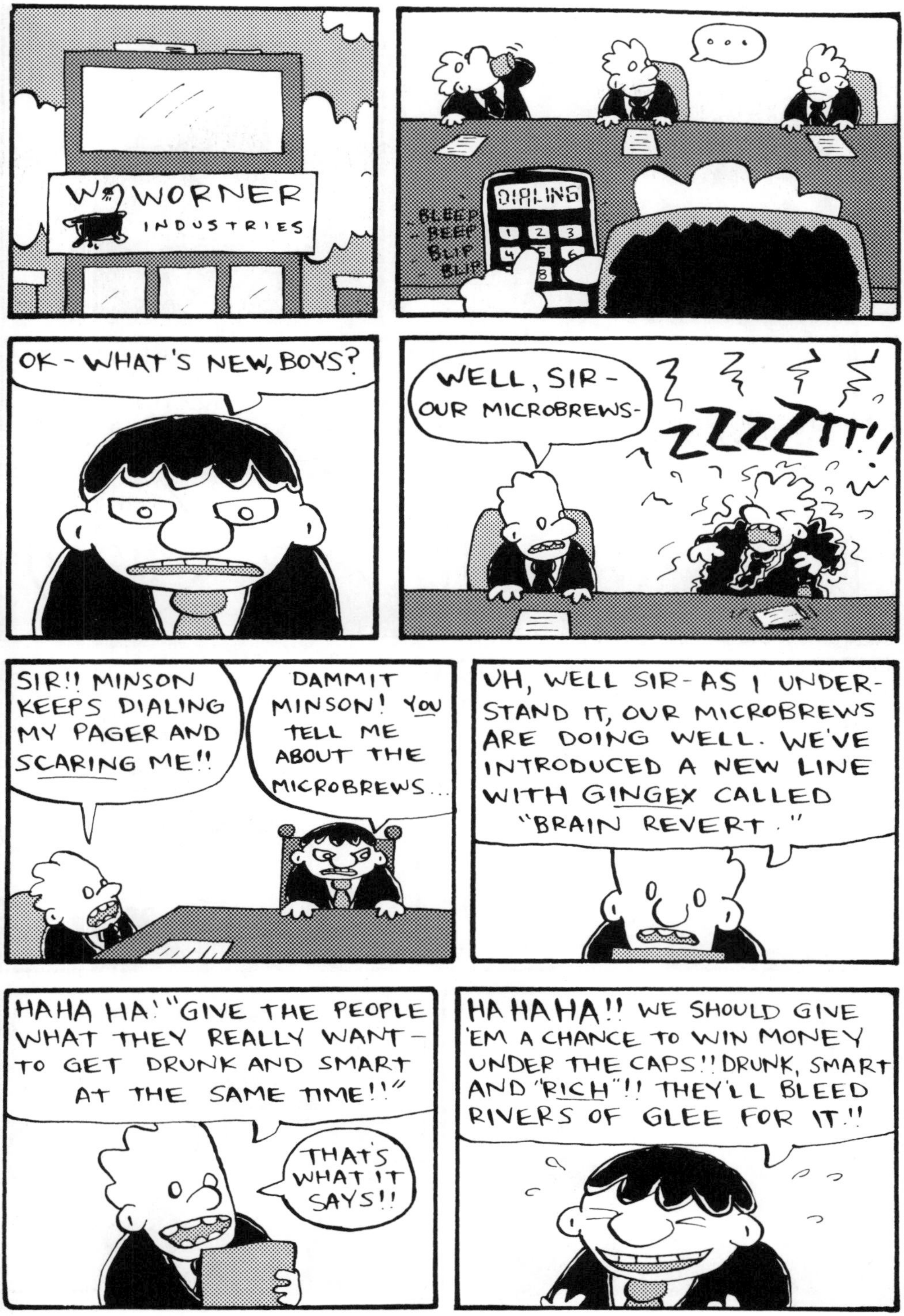
WORNER
INDUSTRIES
DIALING
BLEEP BEEP BLIP BLIP
...
OK - WHAT'S NEW, BOYS?
WELL, SIR - OUR MICROBREWS-
ZZZZTT!!
SIR!! MINSON KEEPS DIALING MY PAGER AND SCARING ME!!
DAMMIT MINSON! YOU TELL ME ABOUT THE MICROBREWS...
UH, WELL SIR - AS I UNDERSTAND IT, OUR MICROBREWS ARE DOING WELL. WE'VE INTRODUCED A NEW LINE WITH GINGEX CALLED "BRAIN REVERT."
HAHA HA! "GIVE THE PEOPLE WHAT THEY REALLY WANT - TO GET DRUNK AND SMART AT THE SAME TIME!!"
THAT'S WHAT IT SAYS!!
HA HA HA!! WE SHOULD GIVE 'EM A CHANCE TO WIN MONEY UNDER THE CAPS!! DRUNK, SMART AND "RICH"!! THEY'LL BLEED RIVERS OF GLEE FOR IT!!

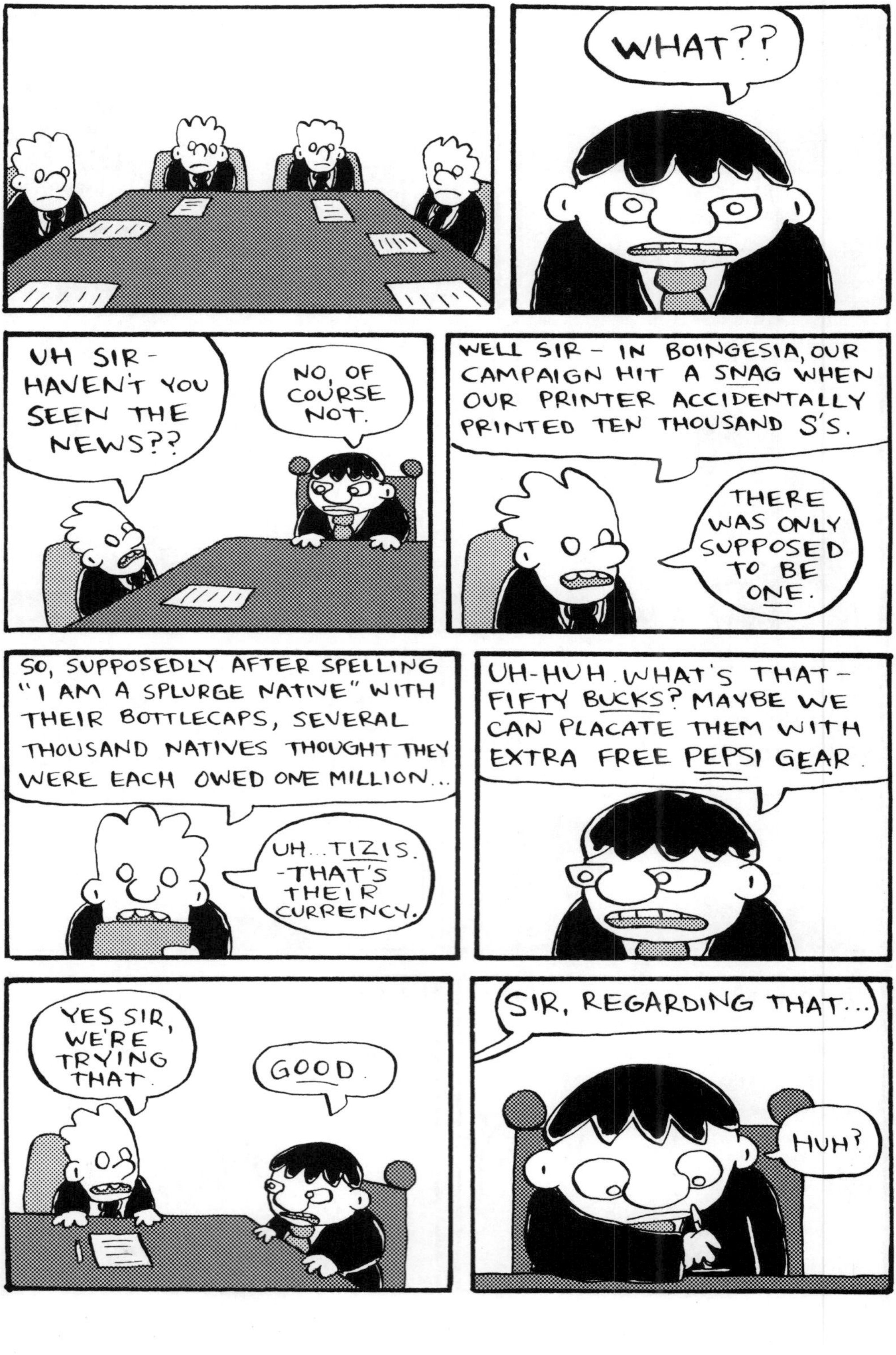
WHAT??
UH SIR - HAVEN'T YOU SEEN THE NEWS??
NO, OF COURSE NOT.
WELL SIR - IN BOINGESIA, OUR CAMPAIGN HIT A SNAG WHEN OUR PRINTER ACCIDENTALLY PRINTED TEN THOUSAND S'S.
THERE WAS ONLY SUPPOSED TO BE ONE.
SO, SUPPOSEDLY AFTER SPELLING "I AM A SPLURGE NATIVE" WITH THEIR BOTTLECAPS, SEVERAL THOUSAND NATIVES THOUGHT THEY WERE EACH OWED ONE MILLION...
UH... TIZIS. -THAT'S THEIR CURRENCY.
UH-HUH. WHAT'S THAT - FIFTY BUCKS? MAYBE WE CAN PLACATE THEM WITH EXTRA FREE PEPSI GEAR.
YES SIR, WE'RE TRYING THAT.
GOOD.
SIR, REGARDING THAT...
HUH?

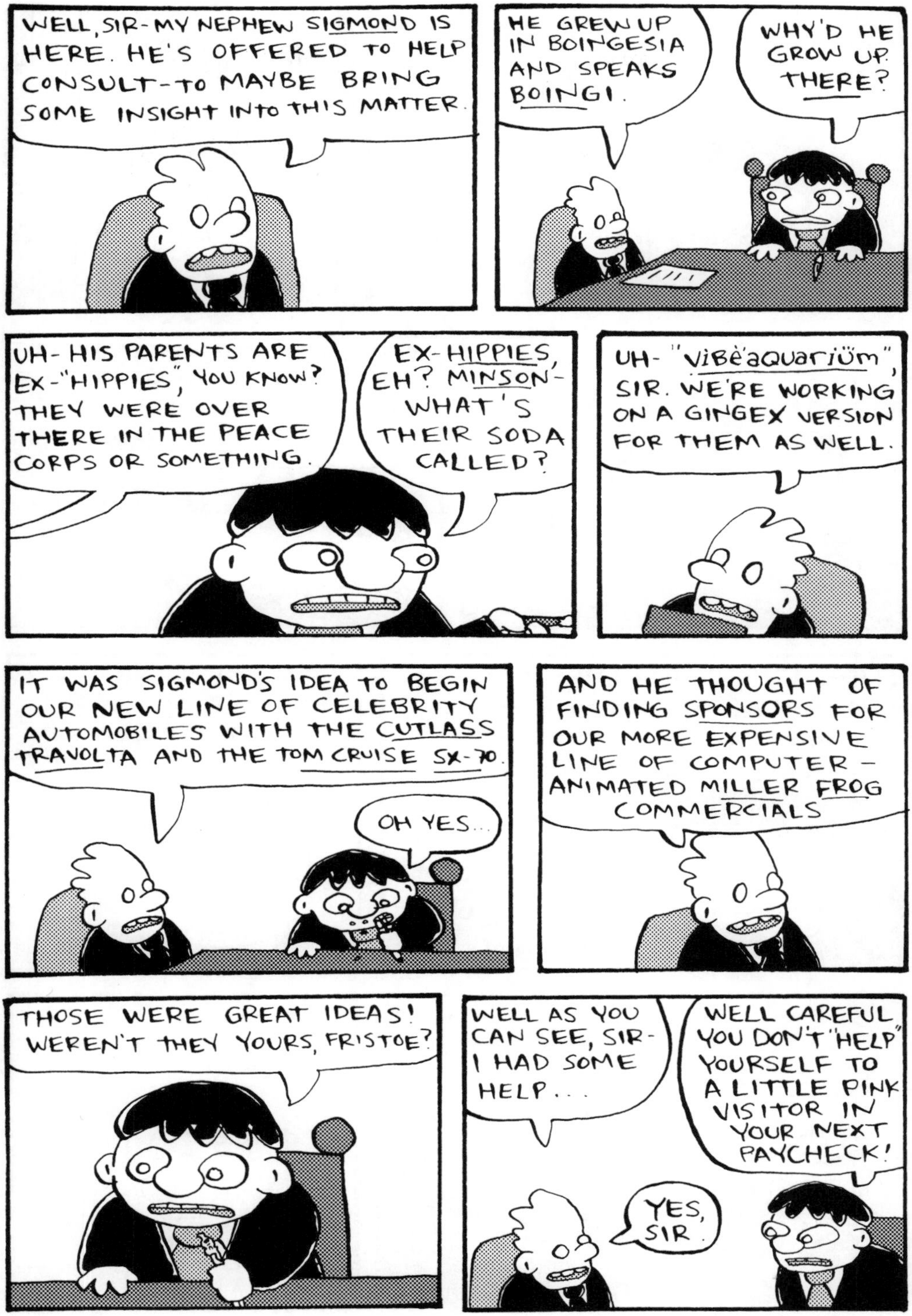
WELL, SIR- MY NEPHEW SIGMOND IS HERE. HE'S OFFERED TO HELP CONSULT- TO MAYBE BRING SOME INSIGHT INTO THIS MATTER.
HE GREW UP IN BOINGESIA AND SPEAKS BOINGI.
WHY'D HE GROW UP THERE?
UH- HIS PARENTS ARE EX-"HIPPIES", YOU KNOW? THEY WERE OVER THERE IN THE PEACE CORPS OR SOMETHING.
EX-HIPPIES, EH? MINSON- WHAT'S THEIR SODA CALLED?
UH- "ViBèaQuariüm", SIR. WE'RE WORKING ON A GINGEX VERSION FOR THEM AS WELL.
IT WAS SIGMOND'S IDEA TO BEGIN OUR NEW LINE OF CELEBRITY AUTOMOBILES WITH THE CUTLASS TRAVOLTA AND THE TOM CRUISE SX-70.
OH YES...
AND HE THOUGHT OF FINDING SPONSORS FOR OUR MORE EXPENSIVE LINE OF COMPUTER-ANIMATED MILLER FROG COMMERCIALS
THOSE WERE GREAT IDEAS! WEREN'T THEY YOURS, FRISTOE?
WELL AS YOU CAN SEE, SIR- I HAD SOME HELP...
WELL CAREFUL YOU DON'T "HELP" YOURSELF TO A LITTLE PINK VISITOR IN YOUR NEXT PAYCHECK!
YES, SIR.

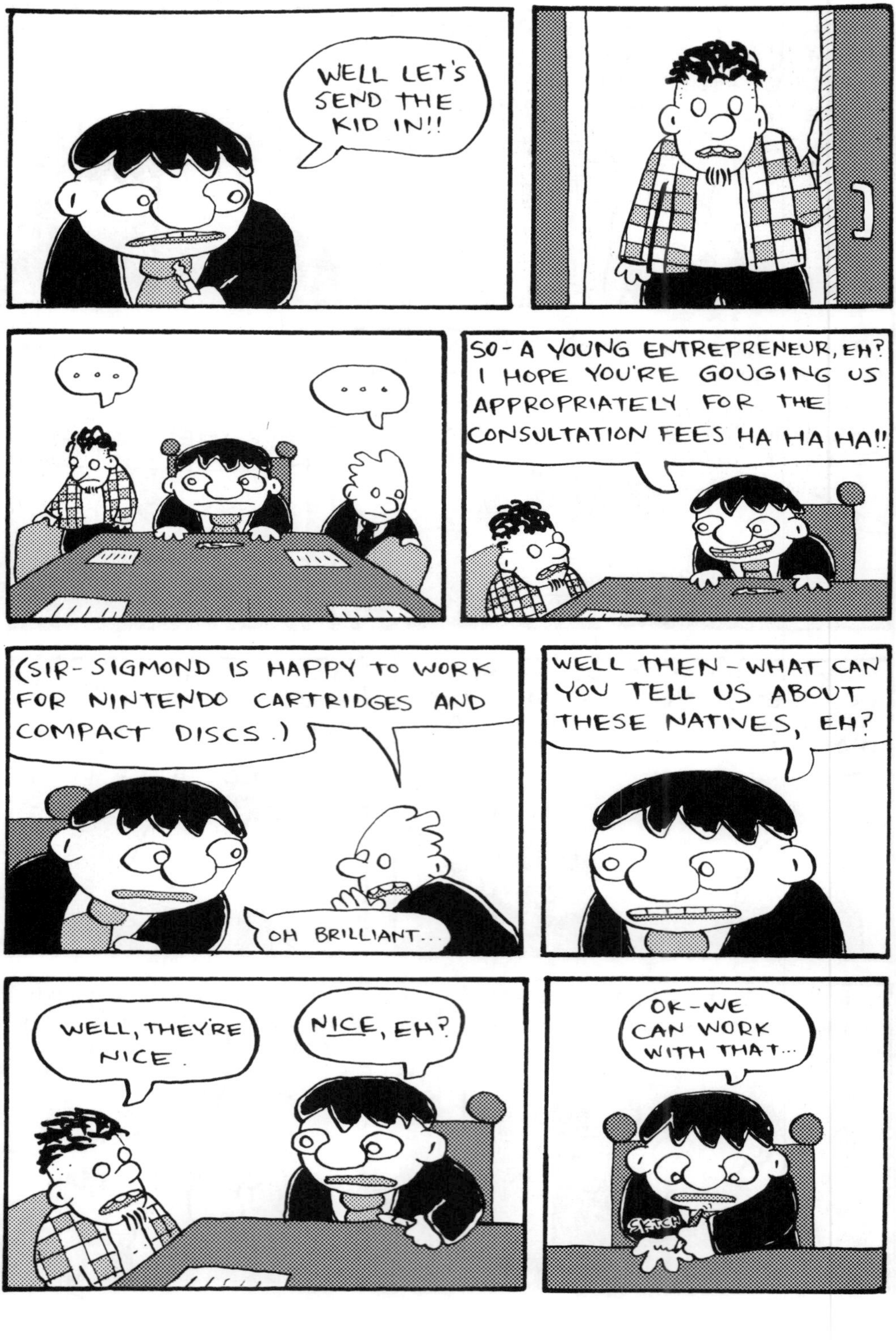
WELL LET'S SEND THE KID IN!!
...
...
SO- A YOUNG ENTREPRENEUR, EH? I HOPE YOU'RE GOUGING US APPROPRIATELY FOR THE CONSULTATION FEES HA HA HA!!
(SIR-SIGMOND IS HAPPY TO WORK FOR NINTENDO CARTRIDGES AND COMPACT DISCS.)
OH BRILLIANT...
WELL THEN - WHAT CAN YOU TELL US ABOUT THESE NATIVES, EH?
WELL, THEY'RE NICE.
NICE, EH?
OK - WE CAN WORK WITH THAT...
SKTCH

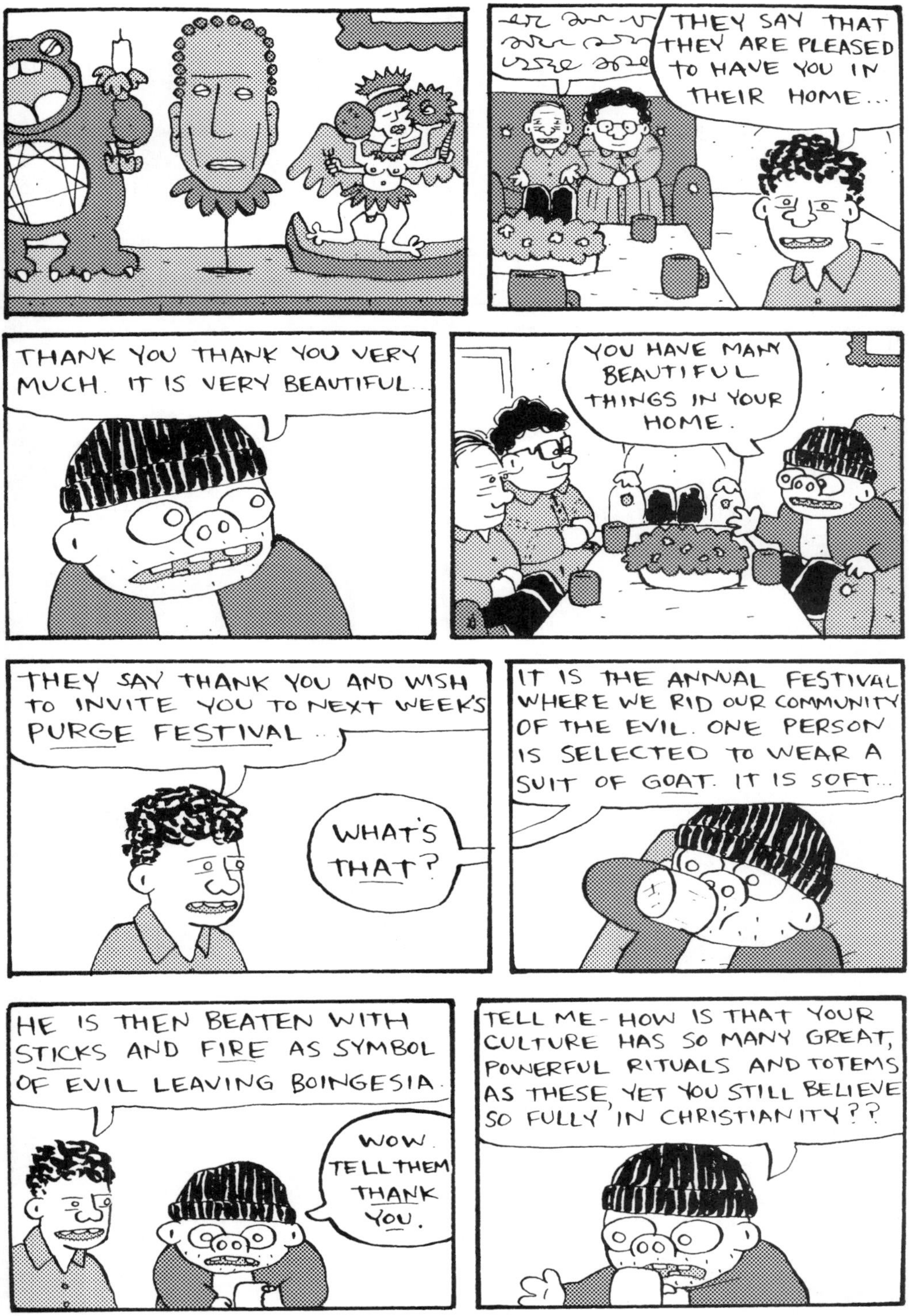
THEY SAY THAT THEY ARE PLEASED TO HAVE YOU IN THEIR HOME...
THANK YOU THANK YOU VERY MUCH. IT IS VERY BEAUTIFUL...
YOU HAVE MANY BEAUTIFUL THINGS IN YOUR HOME.
THEY SAY THANK YOU AND WISH TO INVITE YOU TO NEXT WEEK'S PURGE FESTIVAL...
WHAT'S THAT?
IT IS THE ANNUAL FESTIVAL WHERE WE RID OUR COMMUNITY OF THE EVIL. ONE PERSON IS SELECTED TO WEAR A SUIT OF GOAT. IT IS SOFT...
HE IS THEN BEATEN WITH STICKS AND FIRE AS SYMBOL OF EVIL LEAVING BOINGESIA.
WOW. TELL THEM THANK YOU.
TELL ME- HOW IS THAT YOUR CULTURE HAS SO MANY GREAT, POWERFUL RITUALS AND TOTEMS AS THESE, YET YOU STILL BELIEVE SO FULLY IN CHRISTIANITY??

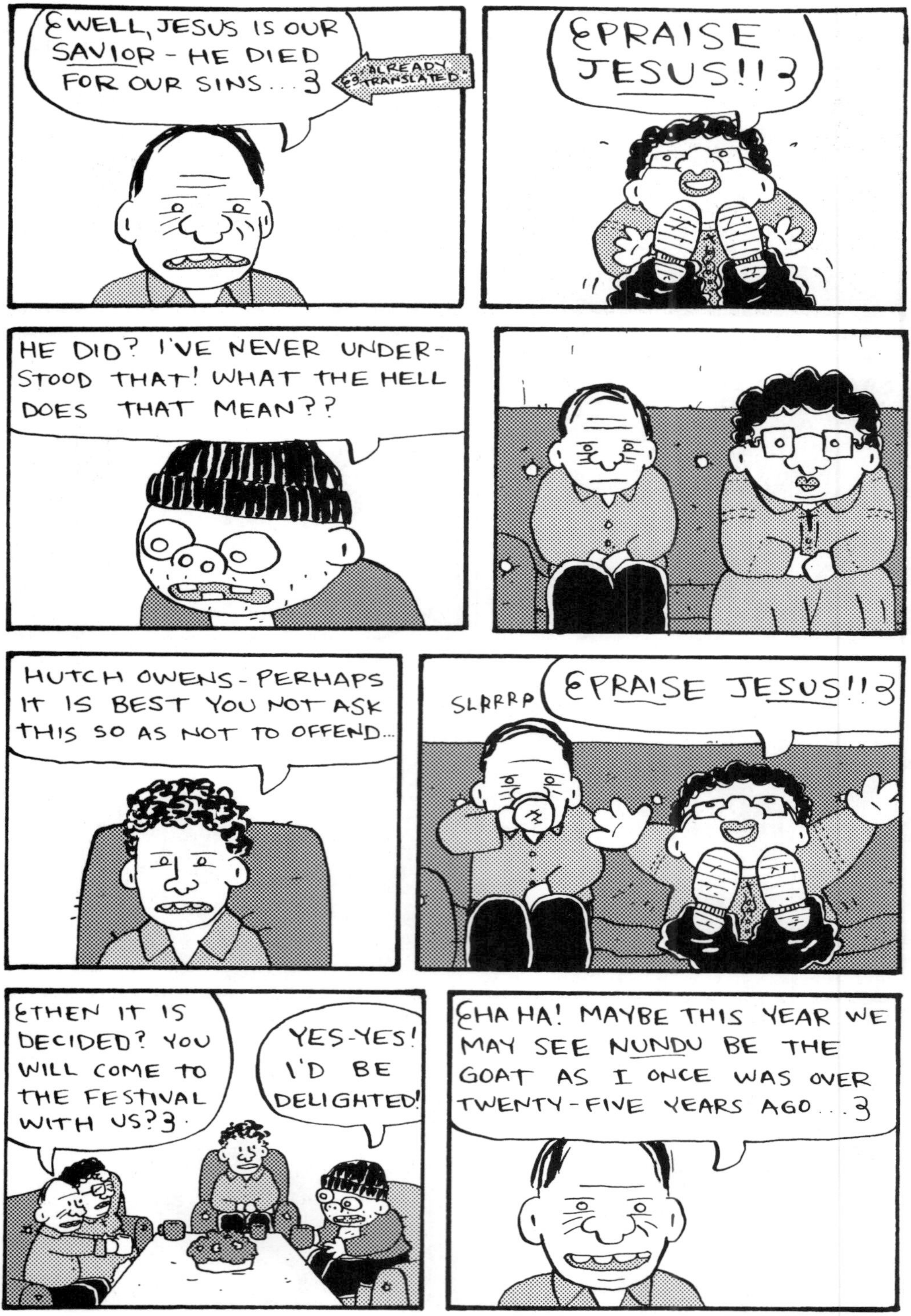
{WELL, JESUS IS OUR SAVIOR - HE DIED FOR OUR SINS... }
{}= ALREADY TRANSLATED*
{PRAISE JESUS!!}
HE DID? I'VE NEVER UNDERSTOOD THAT! WHAT THE HELL DOES THAT MEAN??
HUTCH OWENS - PERHAPS IT IS BEST YOU NOT ASK THIS SO AS NOT TO OFFEND...
SLRRRP
{PRAISE JESUS!!}
{THEN IT IS DECIDED? YOU WILL COME TO THE FESTIVAL WITH US?}
YES-YES! I'D BE DELIGHTED!
{HA HA! MAYBE THIS YEAR WE MAY SEE NUNDU BE THE GOAT AS I ONCE WAS OVER TWENTY-FIVE YEARS AGO...}

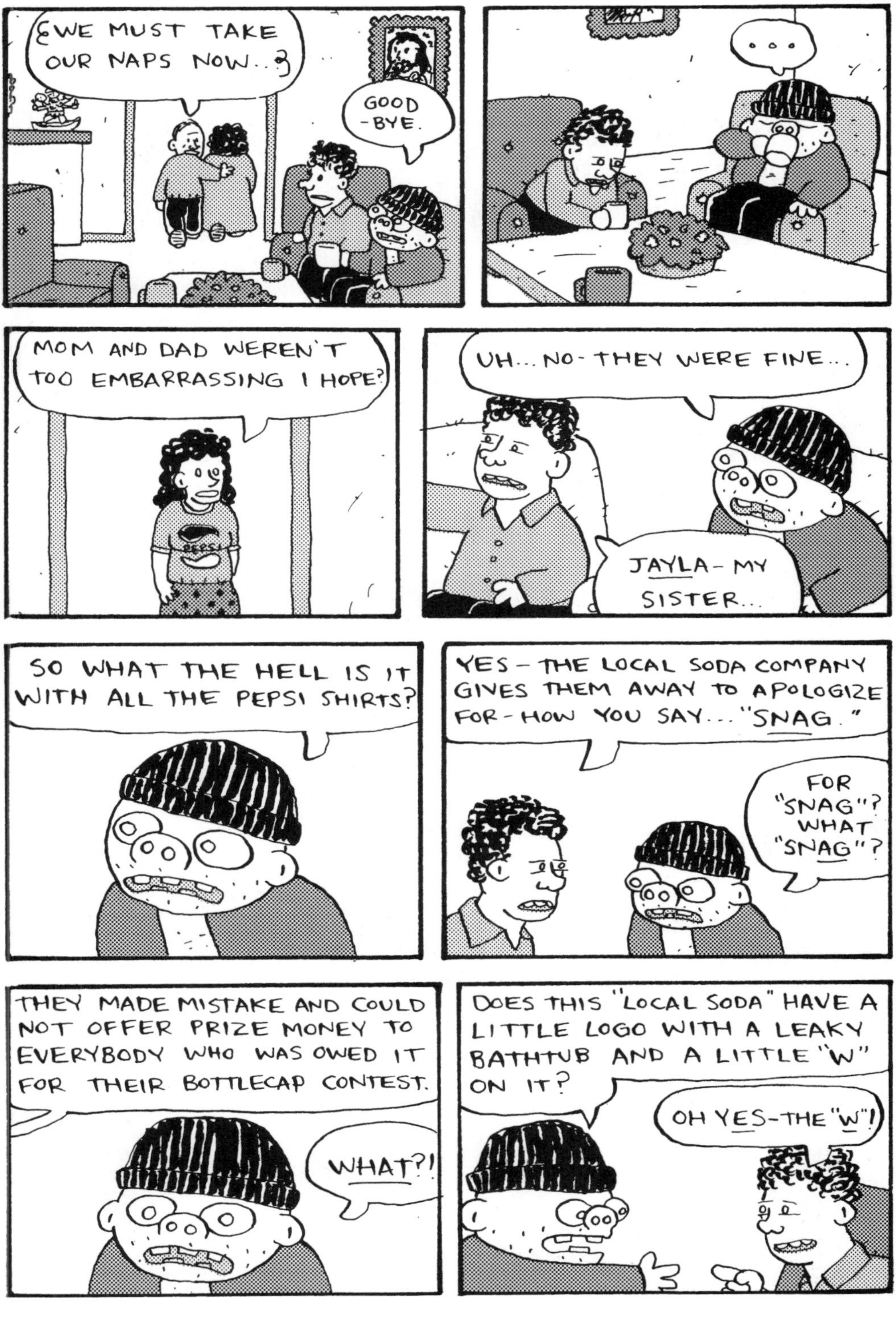

{WE MUST TAKE OUR NAPS NOW...}
GOOD-BYE.
...
MOM AND DAD WEREN'T TOO EMBARRASSING I HOPE?
UH... NO- THEY WERE FINE...
JAYLA- MY SISTER...
SO WHAT THE HELL IS IT WITH ALL THE PEPSI SHIRTS?
YES- THE LOCAL SODA COMPANY GIVES THEM AWAY TO APOLOGIZE FOR- HOW YOU SAY... "SNAG."
FOR "SNAG"? WHAT "SNAG"?
THEY MADE MISTAKE AND COULD NOT OFFER PRIZE MONEY TO EVERYBODY WHO WAS OWED IT FOR THEIR BOTTLECAP CONTEST.
WHAT?!
DOES THIS "LOCAL SODA" HAVE A LITTLE LOGO WITH A LEAKY BATHTUB AND A LITTLE "W" ON IT?
OH YES- THE "W"!

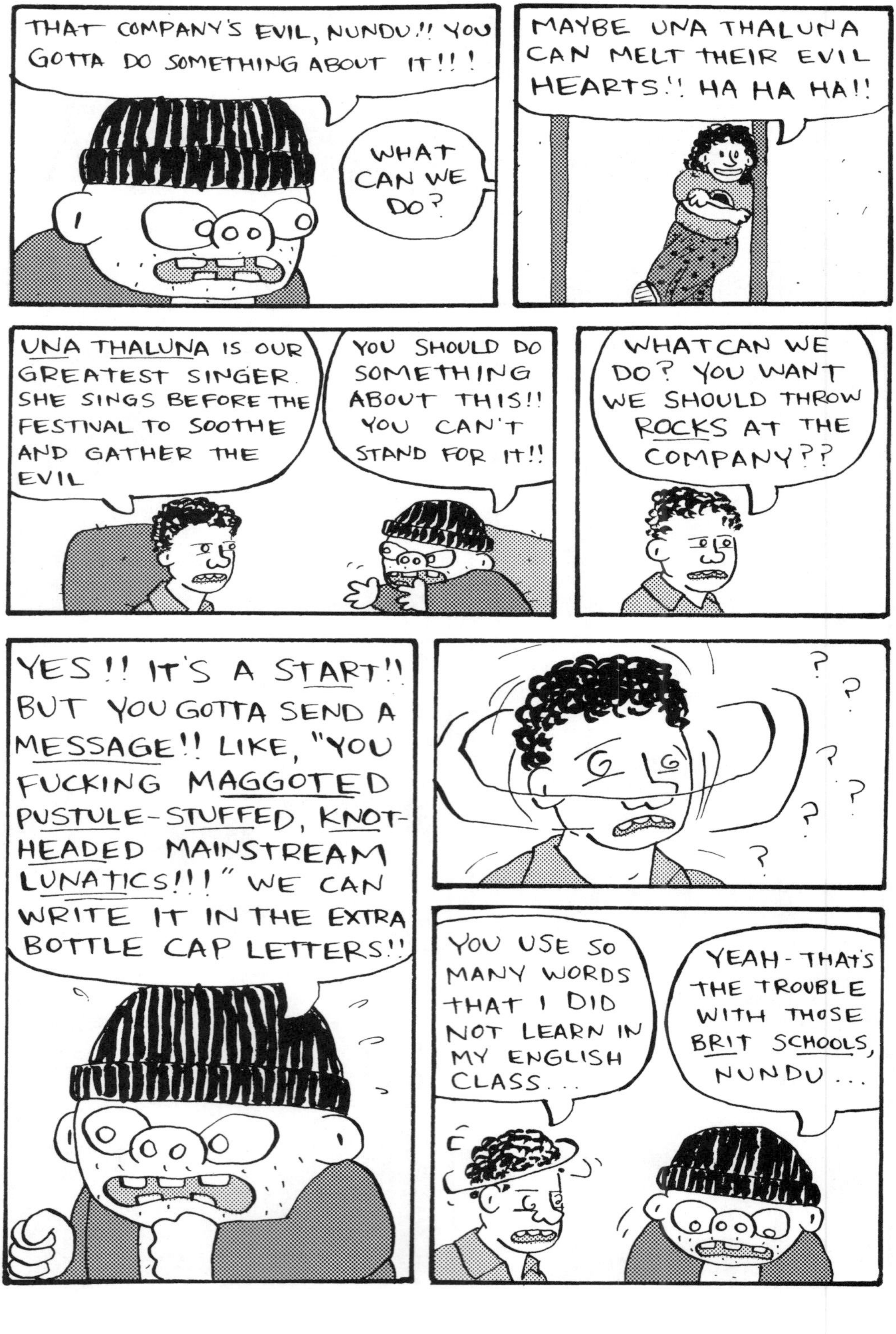
THAT COMPANY'S EVIL, NUNDU!! YOU GOTTA DO SOMETHING ABOUT IT!!!
WHAT CAN WE DO?
MAYBE UNA THALUNA CAN MELT THEIR EVIL HEARTS!! HA HA HA!!
UNA THALUNA IS OUR GREATEST SINGER. SHE SINGS BEFORE THE FESTIVAL TO SOOTHE AND GATHER THE EVIL
YOU SHOULD DO SOMETHING ABOUT THIS!! YOU CAN'T STAND FOR IT!!
WHAT CAN WE DO? YOU WANT WE SHOULD THROW ROCKS AT THE COMPANY??
YES!! IT'S A START!! BUT YOU GOTTA SEND A MESSAGE!! LIKE, "YOU FUCKING MAGGOTED PUSTULE-STUFFED, KNOT-HEADED MAINSTREAM LUNATICS!!!" WE CAN WRITE IT IN THE EXTRA BOTTLE CAP LETTERS!!
? ? ? ? ? ?
YOU USE SO MANY WORDS THAT I DID NOT LEARN IN MY ENGLISH CLASS...
YEAH- THAT'S THE TROUBLE WITH THOSE BRIT SCHOOLS, NUNDU...

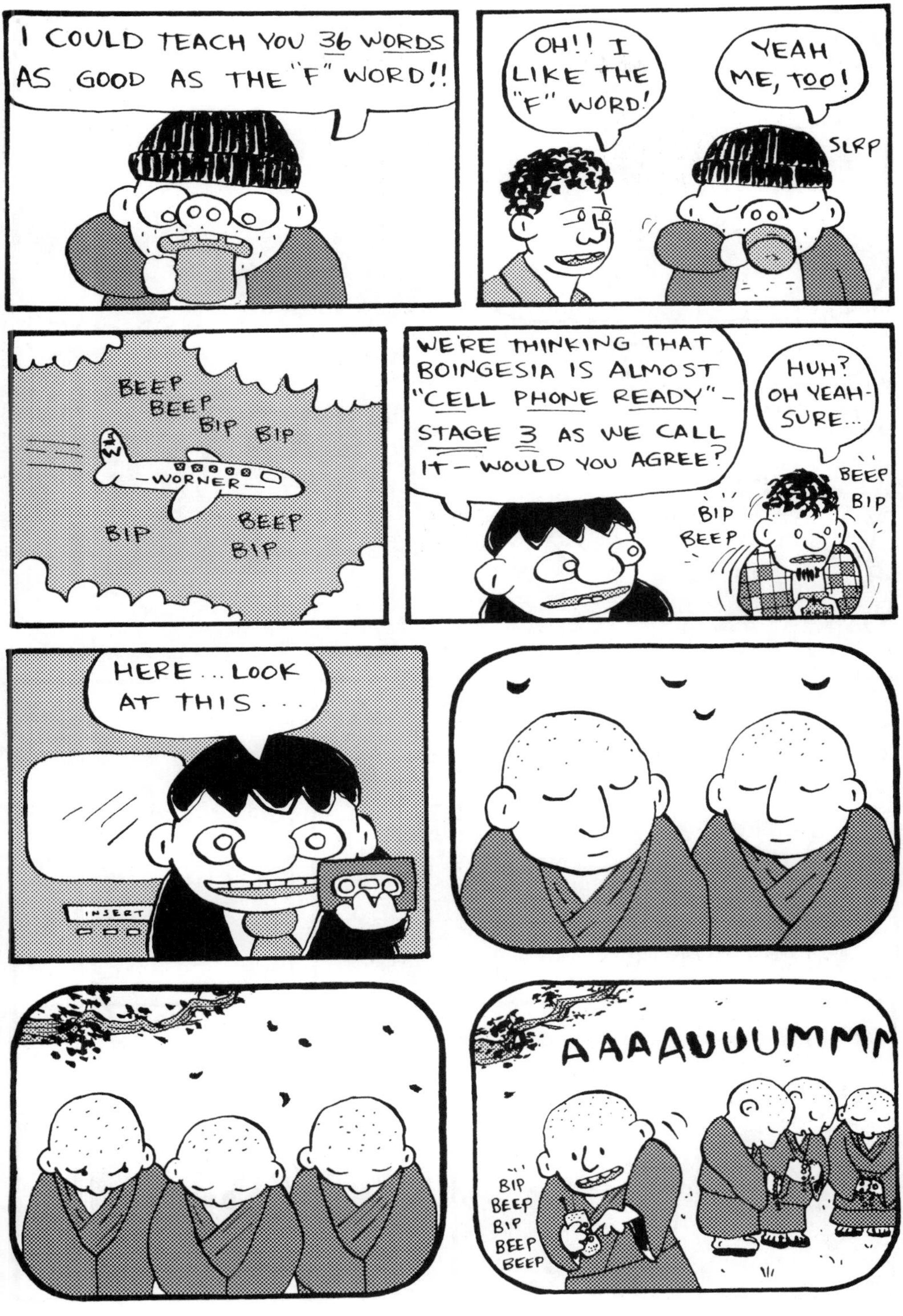
I COULD TEACH YOU 36 WORDS AS GOOD AS THE "F" WORD!!
OH!! I LIKE THE "F" WORD!
YEAH ME, TOO!
SLRP
BEEP BEEP BIP BIP
WORNER
BIP BEEP BIP
WE'RE THINKING THAT BOINGESIA IS ALMOST "CELL PHONE READY" - STAGE 3 AS WE CALL IT - WOULD YOU AGREE?
HUH? OH YEAH-SURE...
BIP BEEP
BEEP BIP
HERE... LOOK AT THIS...
INSERT
AAAAUUUMMM
BIP BEEP BIP BEEP BEEP

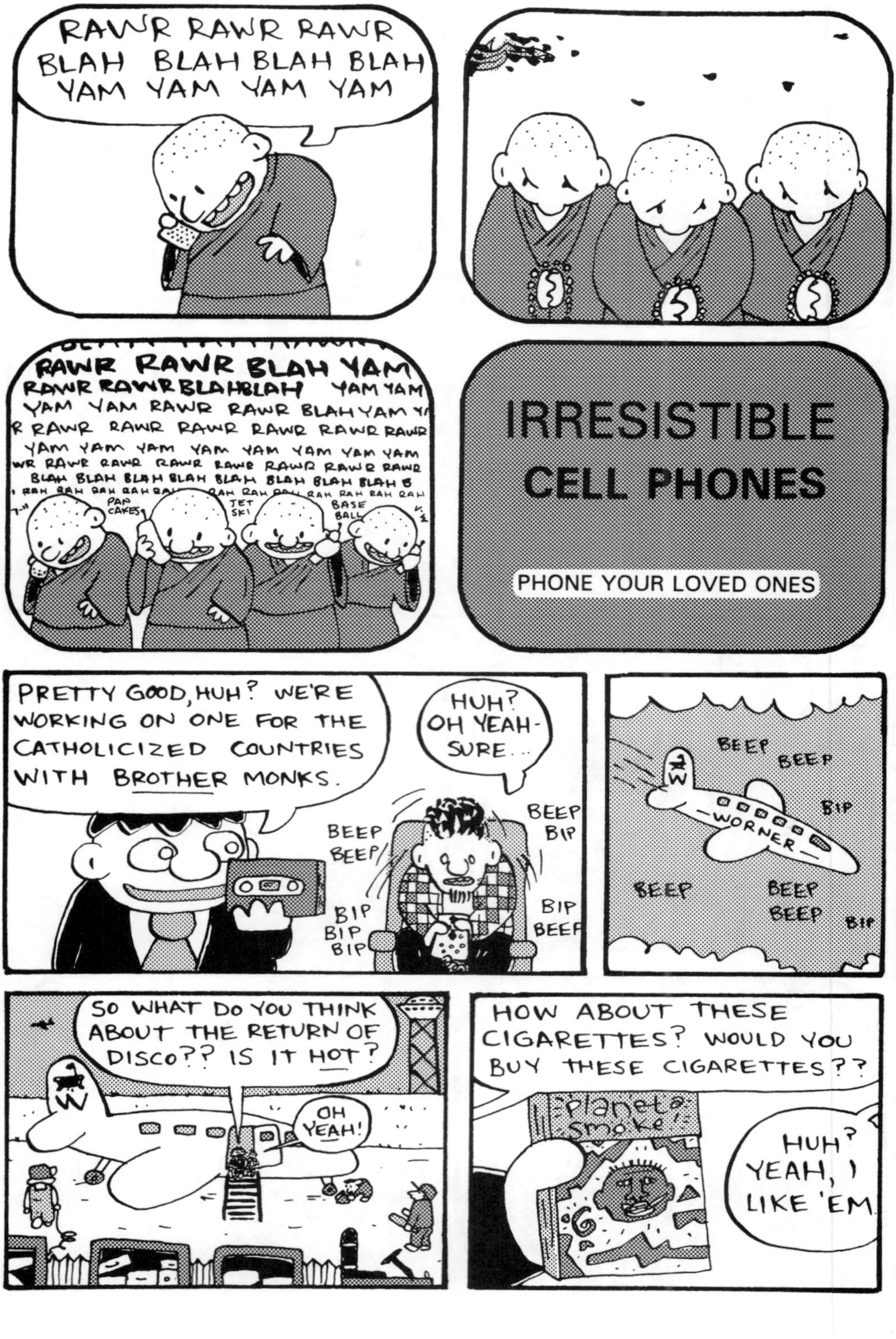

RAWR RAWR RAWR
BLAH BLAH BLAH BLAH
YAM YAM YAM YAM
RAWR RAWR BLAH YAM
RAWR RAWR BLAHBLAH YAM YAM
YAM YAM RAWR RAWR BLAH YAM
RAWR RAWR RAWR RAWR RAWR RAWR
YAM YAM YAM YAM YAM YAM YAM YAM
RAWR RAWR RAWR RAWR RAWR RAWR RAWR
BLAH BLAH BLAH BLAH BLAH BLAH BLAH BLAH
RAH RAH RAH RAH RAH RAH RAH RAH RAH RAH
7-11
PAN CAKES
JET SKI
BASE BALL
IRRESISTIBLE
CELL PHONES
PHONE YOUR LOVED ONES
PRETTY GOOD, HUH? WE'RE WORKING ON ONE FOR THE CATHOLICIZED COUNTRIES WITH BROTHER MONKS.
HUH? OH YEAH- SURE...
BEEP BEEP
BEEP BIP
BIP BIP BIP
BIP BEEP
BEEP BEEP
BIP
WORNER
BEEP
BEEP BEEP
BIP
SO WHAT DO YOU THINK ABOUT THE RETURN OF DISCO?? IS IT HOT?
OH YEAH!
HOW ABOUT THESE CIGARETTES? WOULD YOU BUY THESE CIGARETTES??
planeta smoke
HUH? YEAH, I LIKE 'EM.

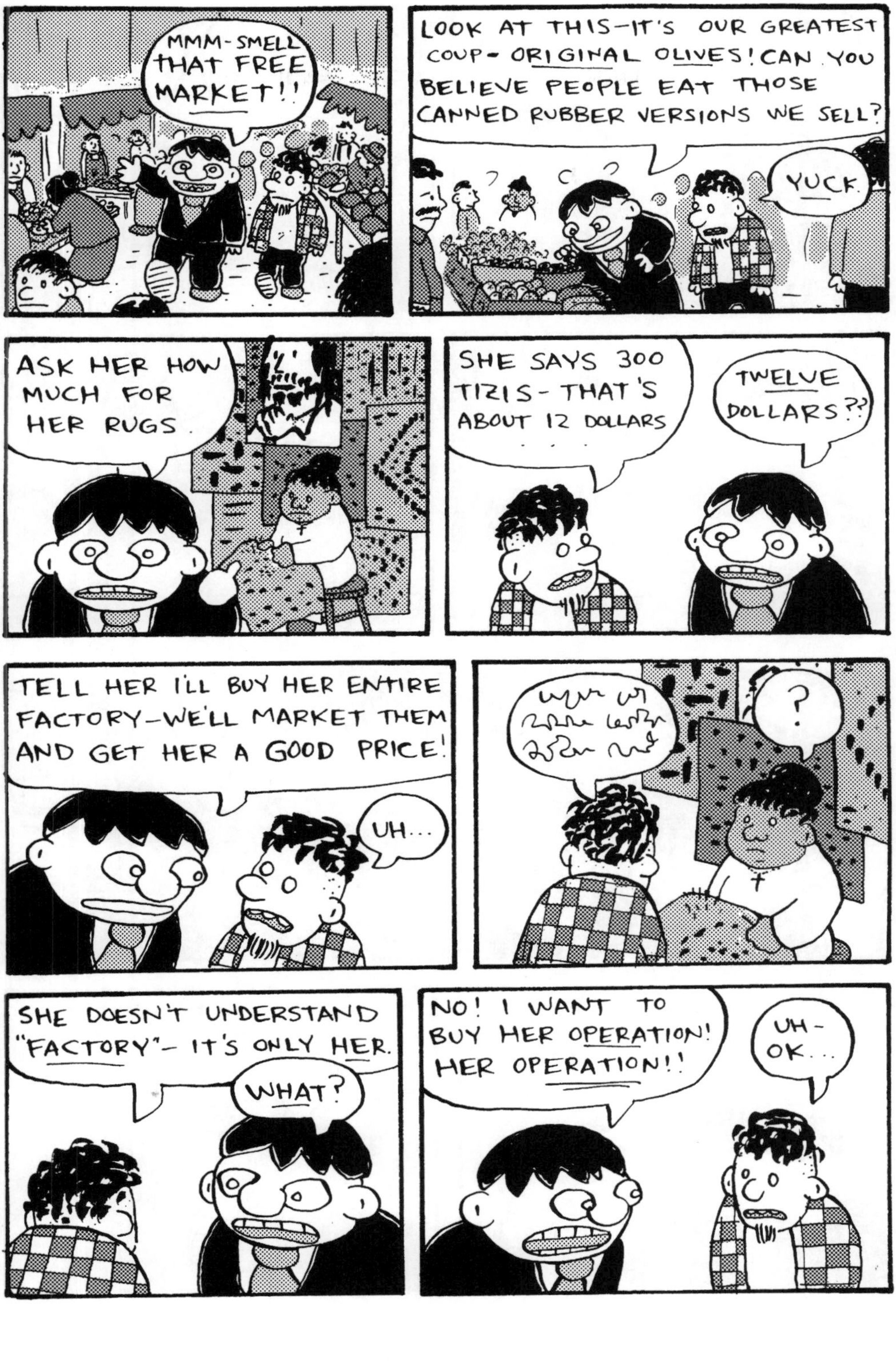
MMM-SMELL THAT FREE MARKET!!
LOOK AT THIS—IT'S OUR GREATEST COUP—ORIGINAL OLIVES! CAN YOU BELIEVE PEOPLE EAT THOSE CANNED RUBBER VERSIONS WE SELL?
YUCK
ASK HER HOW MUCH FOR HER RUGS.
SHE SAYS 300 TIZIS—THAT'S ABOUT 12 DOLLARS . . .
TWELVE DOLLARS??
TELL HER I'LL BUY HER ENTIRE FACTORY—WE'LL MARKET THEM AND GET HER A GOOD PRICE!
UH...
?
SHE DOESN'T UNDERSTAND "FACTORY"—IT'S ONLY HER.
WHAT?
NO! I WANT TO BUY HER OPERATION! HER OPERATION!!
UH-OK...

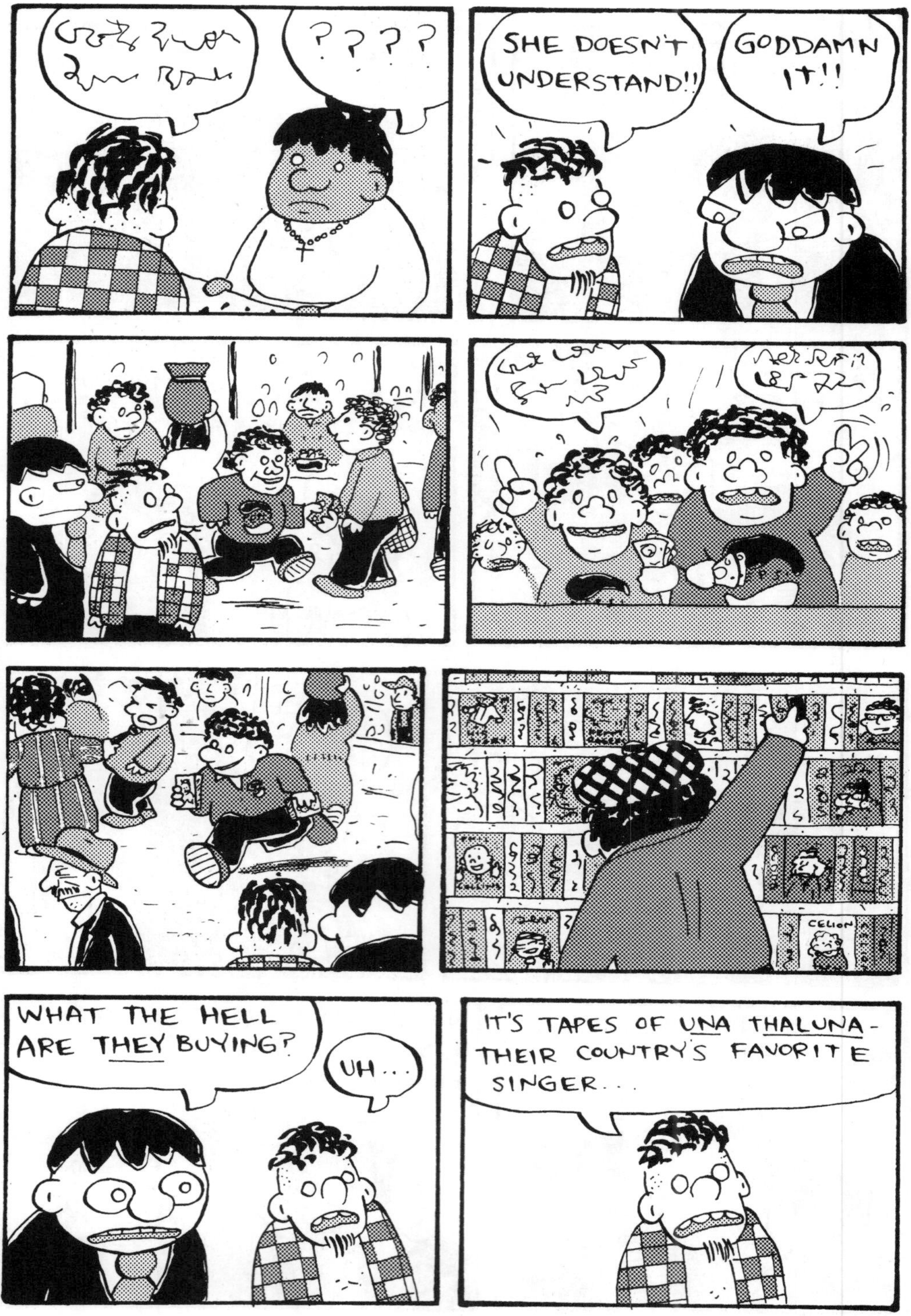
????
SHE DOESN'T UNDERSTAND!!
GODDAMN IT!!
CELION
WHAT THE HELL ARE THEY BUYING?
UH...
IT'S TAPES OF UNA THALUNA-THEIR COUNTRY'S FAVORITE SINGER...

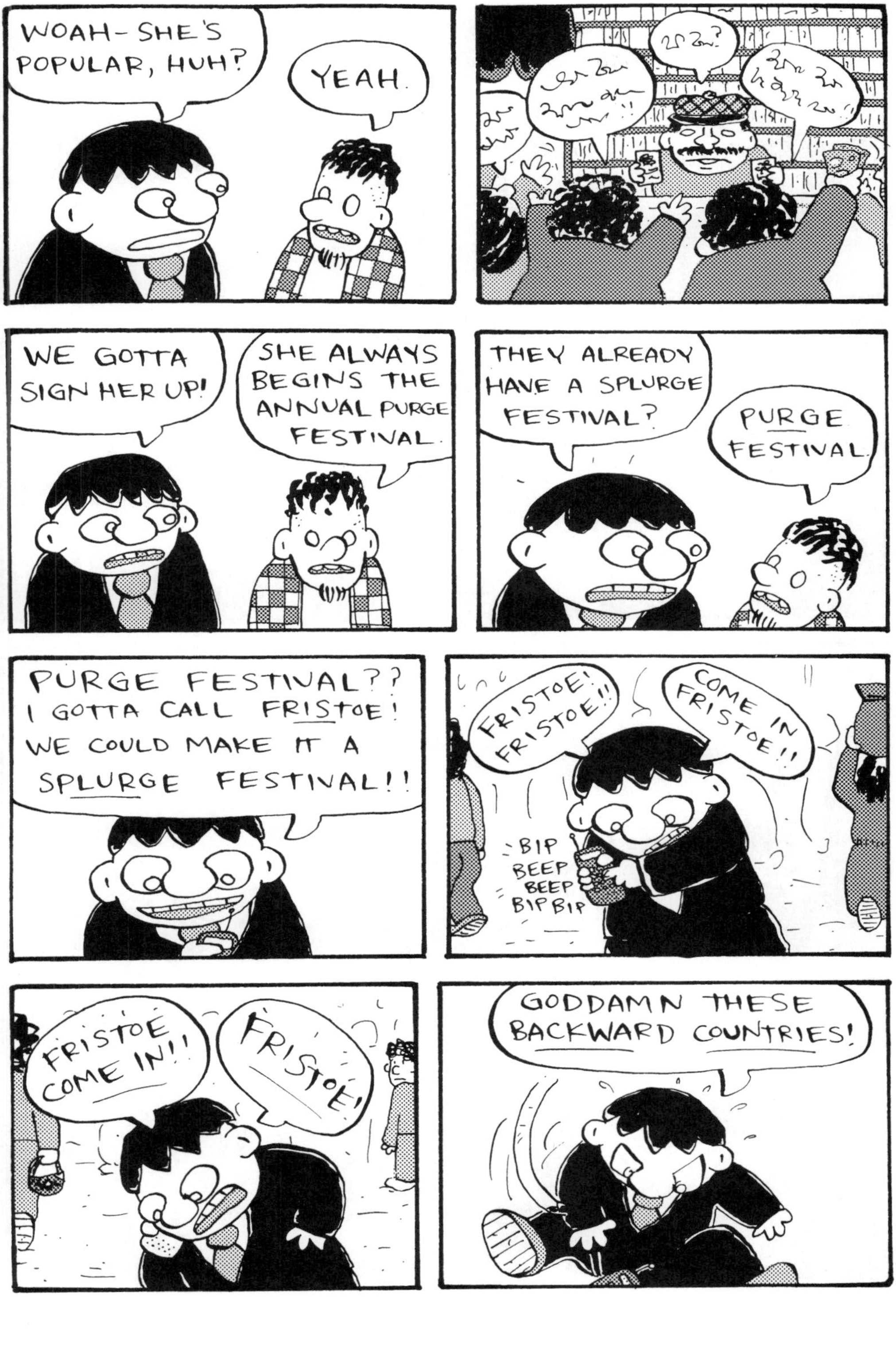
WOAH- SHE'S POPULAR, HUH?
YEAH.
WE GOTTA SIGN HER UP!
SHE ALWAYS BEGINS THE ANNUAL PURGE FESTIVAL.
THEY ALREADY HAVE A SPLURGE FESTIVAL?
PURGE FESTIVAL.
PURGE FESTIVAL?? I GOTTA CALL FRISTOE! WE COULD MAKE IT A SPLURGE FESTIVAL!!
FRISTOE! FRISTOE!!
COME IN FRISTOE!!
BIP BEEP BEEP BIP BIP
FRISTOE COME IN!!
FRISTOE!
GODDAMN THESE BACKWARD COUNTRIES!

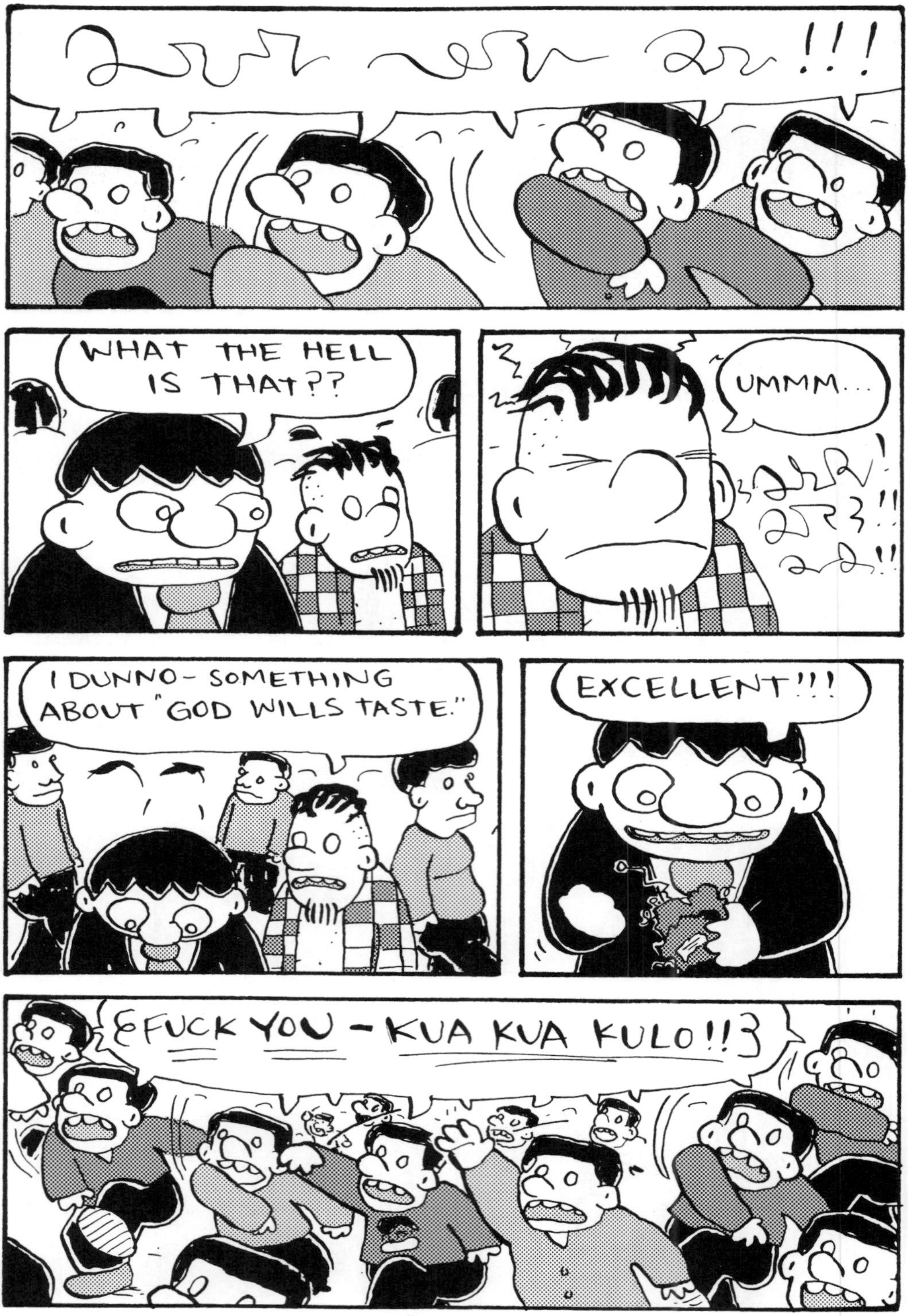

WHAT THE HELL IS THAT??
UMMM...
I DUNNO- SOMETHING ABOUT "GOD WILLS TASTE."
EXCELLENT!!!
FUCK YOU - KUA KUA KULO!!

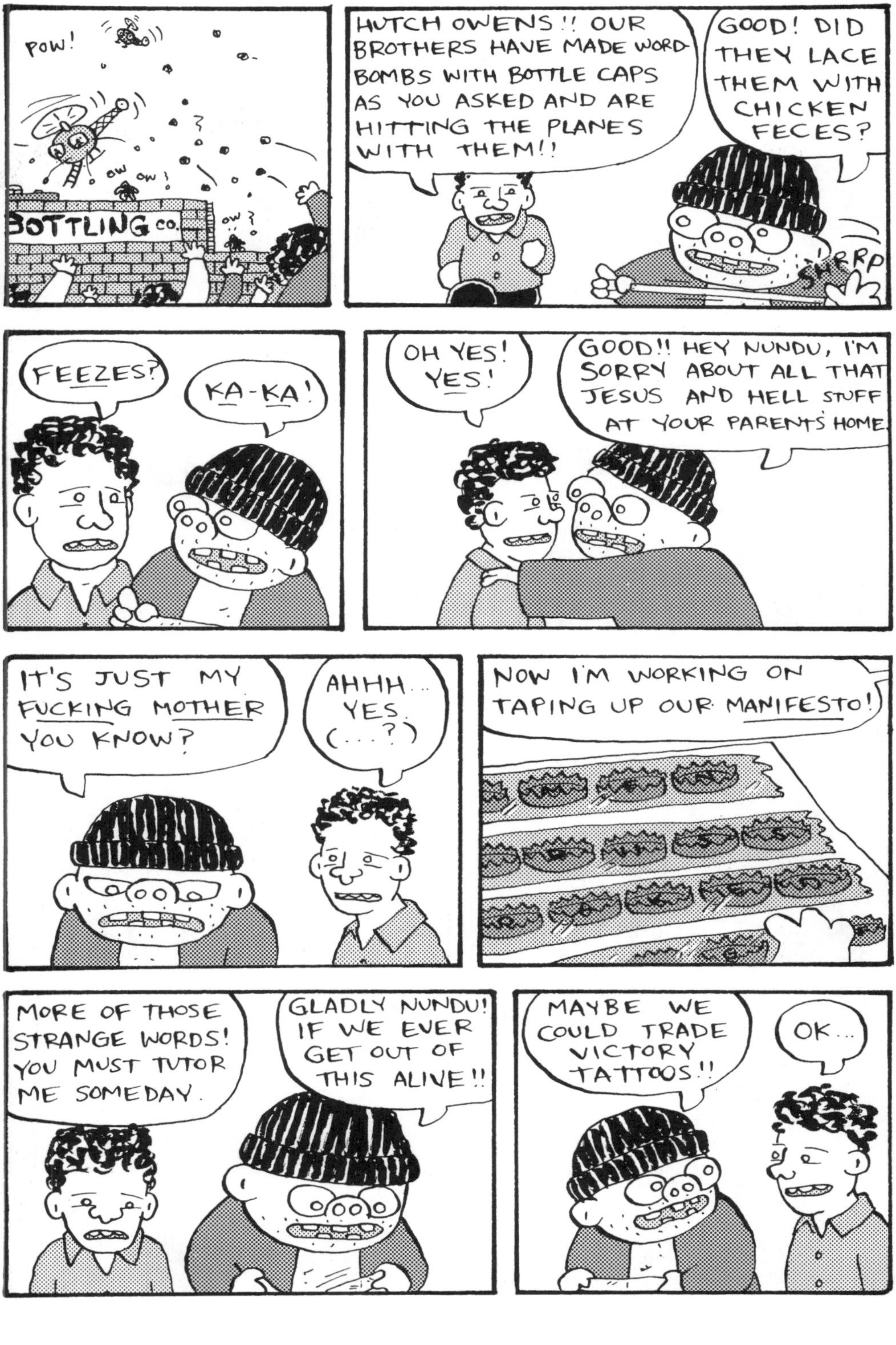
POW!
OW OW!
BOTTLING CO.
OW?
HUTCH OWENS!! OUR BROTHERS HAVE MADE WORD-BOMBS WITH BOTTLE CAPS AS YOU ASKED AND ARE HITTING THE PLANES WITH THEM!!
GOOD! DID THEY LACE THEM WITH CHICKEN FECES?
SHRRP
FEEZES?
KA-KA!
OH YES! YES!
GOOD!! HEY NUNDU, I'M SORRY ABOUT ALL THAT JESUS AND HELL STUFF AT YOUR PARENTS' HOME.
IT'S JUST MY FUCKING MOTHER YOU KNOW?
AHHH... YES (...?)
NOW I'M WORKING ON TAPING UP OUR MANIFESTO!
MORE OF THOSE STRANGE WORDS! YOU MUST TUTOR ME SOMEDAY.
GLADLY NUNDU! IF WE EVER GET OUT OF THIS ALIVE!!
MAYBE WE COULD TRADE VICTORY TATTOOS!!
OK...

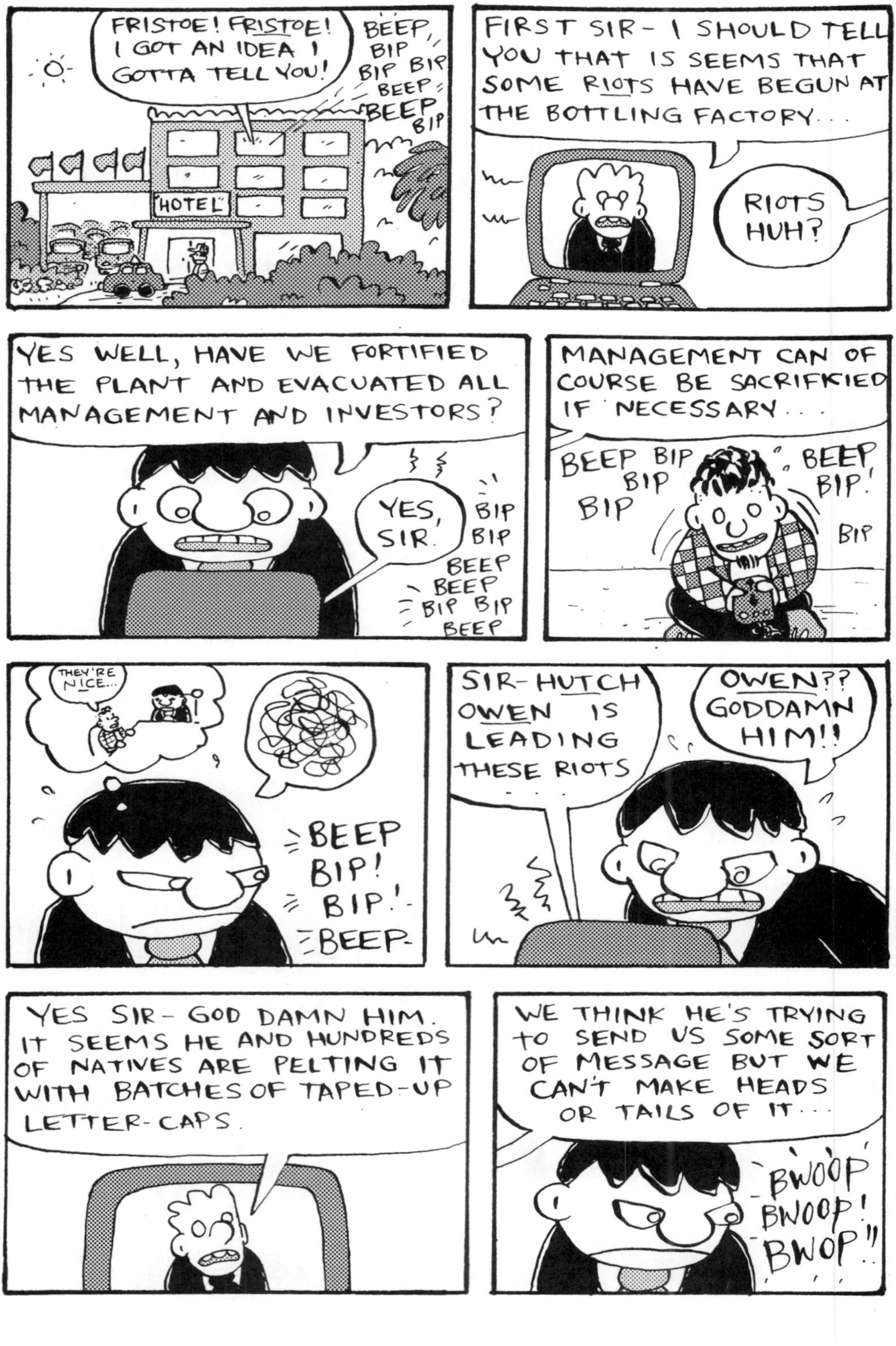
FRISTOE! FRISTOE! I GOT AN IDEA I GOTTA TELL YOU!
BEEP, BIP BIP BIP BEEP BEEP BIP
HOTEL
FIRST SIR- I SHOULD TELL YOU THAT IS SEEMS THAT SOME RIOTS HAVE BEGUN AT THE BOTTLING FACTORY...
RIOTS HUH?
YES WELL, HAVE WE FORTIFIED THE PLANT AND EVACUATED ALL MANAGEMENT AND INVESTORS?
YES, SIR.
BIP BIP BEEP BEEP BIP BIP BEEP
MANAGEMENT CAN OF COURSE BE SACRIFKIED IF NECESSARY...
BEEP BIP BIP BIP BEEP BIP! BIP
THEY'RE NICE...
BEEP BIP! BIP! BEEP
SIR- HUTCH OWEN IS LEADING THESE RIOTS
OWEN?? GODDAMN HIM!!
YES SIR- GOD DAMN HIM. IT SEEMS HE AND HUNDREDS OF NATIVES ARE PELTING IT WITH BATCHES OF TAPED-UP LETTER-CAPS.
WE THINK HE'S TRYING TO SEND US SOME SORT OF MESSAGE BUT WE CAN'T MAKE HEADS OR TAILS OF IT...
BWOOP BWOOP! BWOP!!

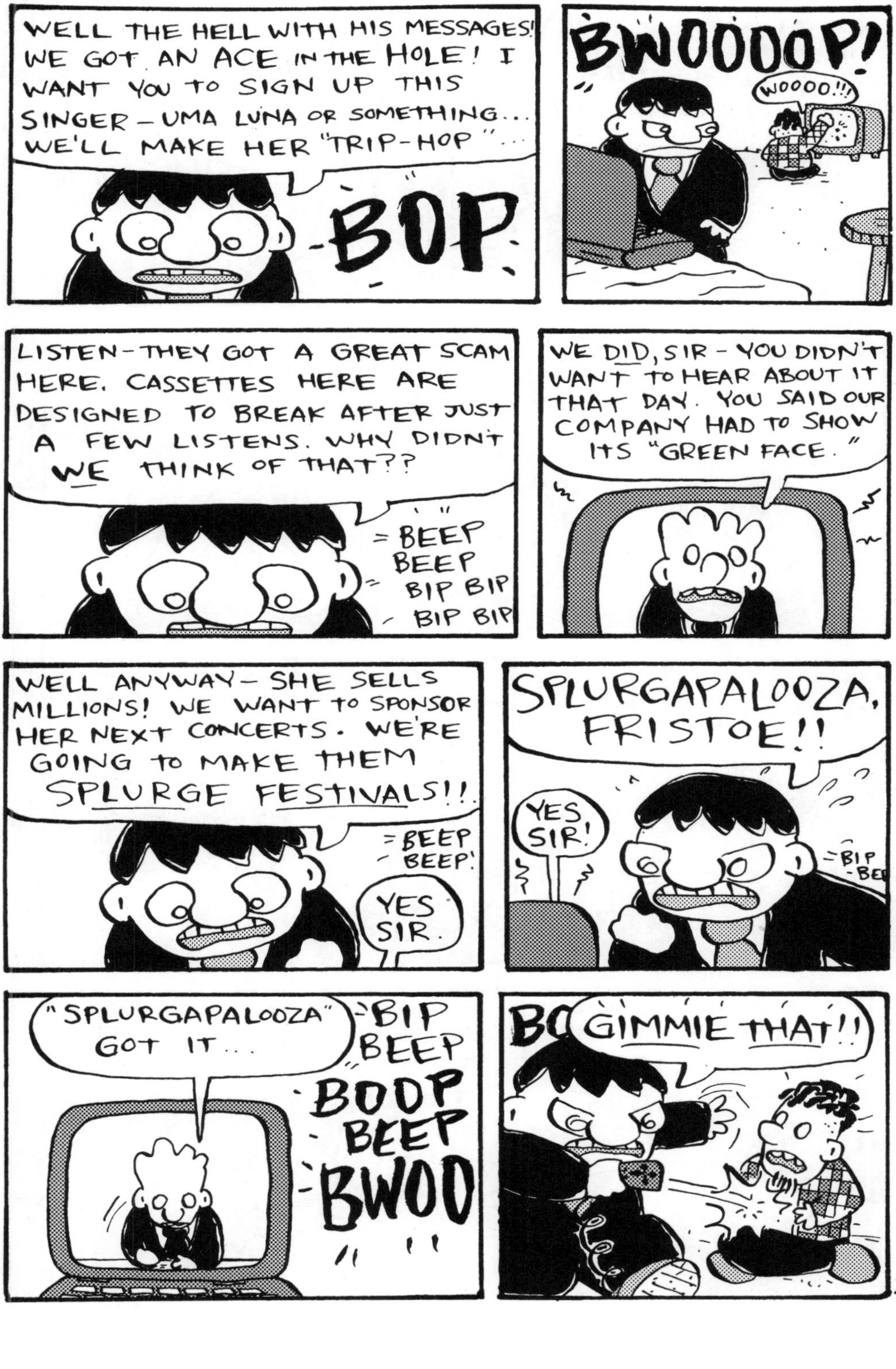

WELL THE HELL WITH HIS MESSAGES! WE GOT AN ACE IN THE HOLE! I WANT YOU TO SIGN UP THIS SINGER — UMA LUNA OR SOMETHING... WE'LL MAKE HER "TRIP-HOP"...
BOP
BWOOOOP!
WOOOO!!!
LISTEN — THEY GOT A GREAT SCAM HERE. CASSETTES HERE ARE DESIGNED TO BREAK AFTER JUST A FEW LISTENS. WHY DIDN'T WE THINK OF THAT??
BEEP BEEP BIP BIP BIP BIP
WE DID, SIR — YOU DIDN'T WANT TO HEAR ABOUT IT THAT DAY. YOU SAID OUR COMPANY HAD TO SHOW ITS "GREEN FACE."
WELL ANYWAY — SHE SELLS MILLIONS! WE WANT TO SPONSOR HER NEXT CONCERTS. WE'RE GOING TO MAKE THEM SPLURGE FESTIVALS!!
BEEP BEEP!
YES SIR.
SPLURGAPALOOZA, FRISTOE!!
YES SIR!
BIP BE
"SPLURGAPALOOZA" GOT IT...
BIP BEEP
BOOP BEEP BWOO
BO
GIMMIE THAT!!

HUTCH OWENS!! IT IS TIME TO GO TO THE PURGE FESTIVAL AND MS. THALUNA'S CONCERT!

OK— ONE MORE!

HA!!

IF THAT ONE EXPLODES RIGHT, IT WILL SAY "SUCK ON SULFER, VILE EVILTICIANS"...

HA HA HA HA HA...

SOON—MS. THALUNA WILL SING AND WHILE SHE IS SINGING, THE ELDERS WILL PICK WHO IS TO BE THE GOAT.

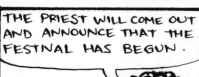

THE PRIEST WILL COME OUT AND ANNOUNCE THAT THE FESTIVAL HAS BEGUN.

AT WHICH POINT THE GOAT WILL APPEAR AND THEN WE CLOBBER HIM WITH STICKS AND ROCKS!!

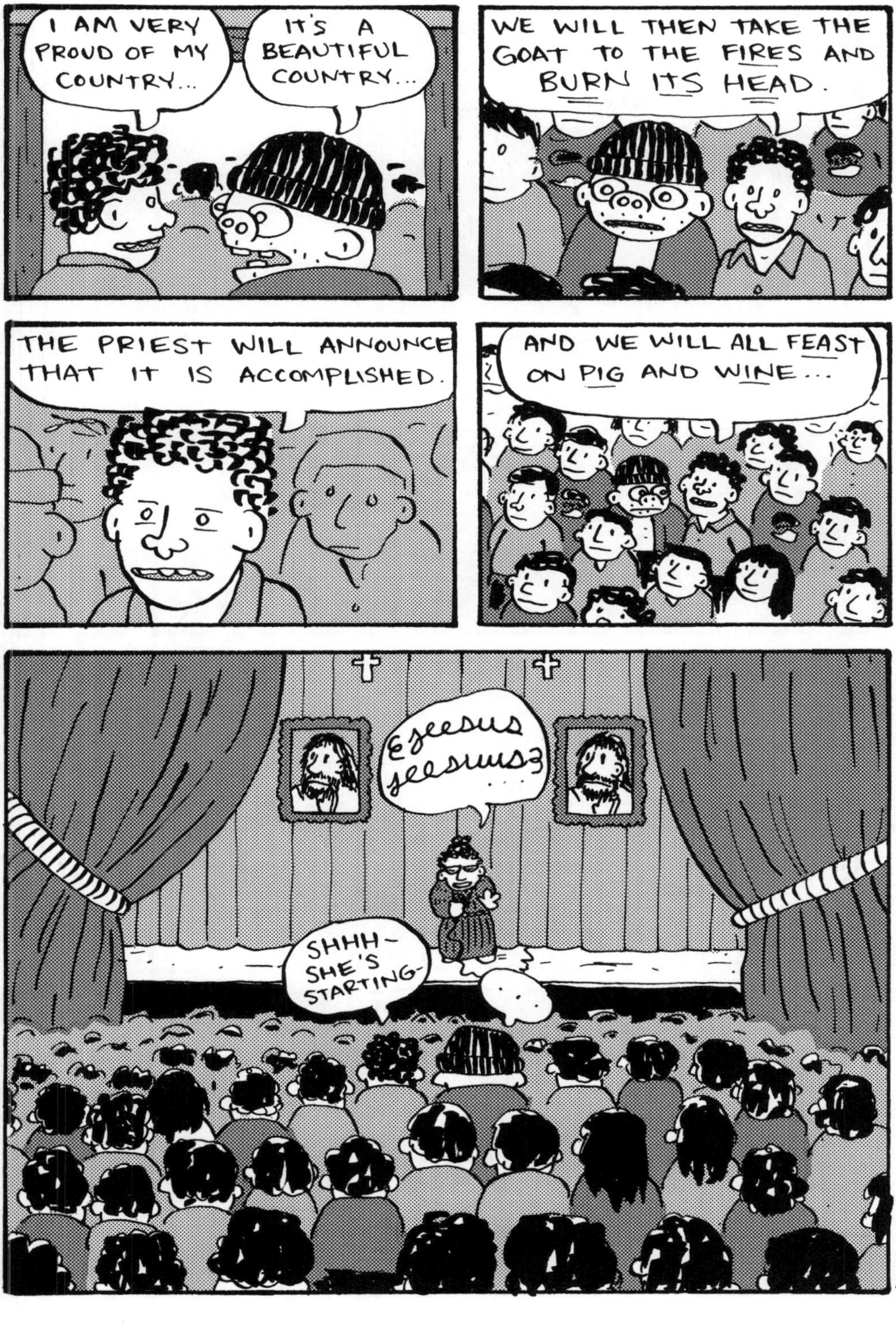
I AM VERY PROUD OF MY COUNTRY...
IT'S A BEAUTIFUL COUNTRY...
WE WILL THEN TAKE THE GOAT TO THE FIRES AND BURN ITS HEAD.
THE PRIEST WILL ANNOUNCE THAT IT IS ACCOMPLISHED.
AND WE WILL ALL FEAST ON PIG AND WINE...
jeesus jeesuus...
SHHH- SHE'S STARTING-

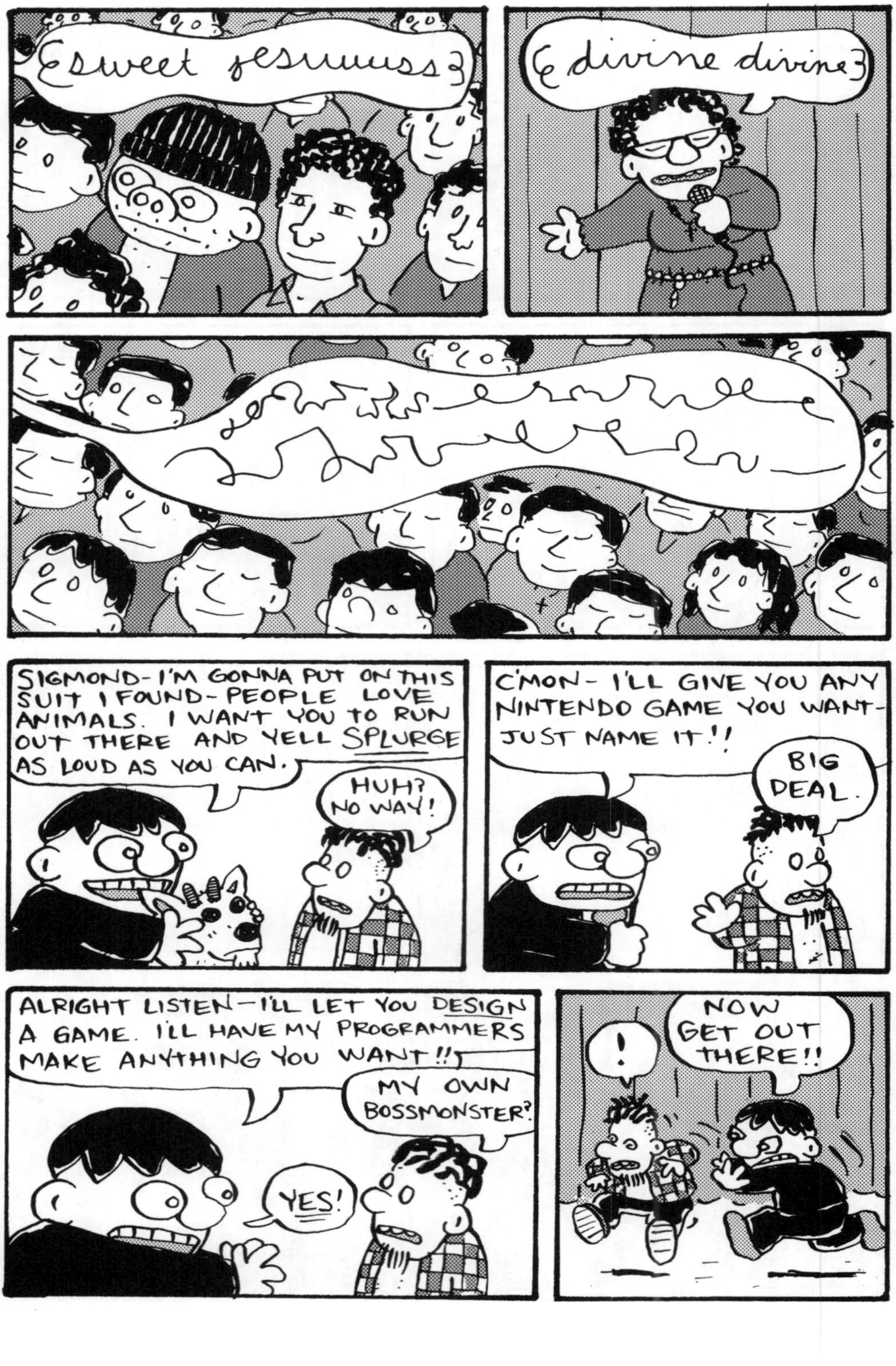
{sweet jesuuuss}
{divine divine}
SIGMOND- I'M GONNA PUT ON THIS SUIT I FOUND- PEOPLE LOVE ANIMALS. I WANT YOU TO RUN OUT THERE AND YELL SPLURGE AS LOUD AS YOU CAN.
HUH? NO WAY!
C'MON- I'LL GIVE YOU ANY NINTENDO GAME YOU WANT- JUST NAME IT!!
BIG DEAL.
ALRIGHT LISTEN- I'LL LET YOU DESIGN A GAME. I'LL HAVE MY PROGRAMMERS MAKE ANYTHING YOU WANT!!
MY OWN BOSSMONSTER?
YES!
!
NOW GET OUT THERE!!

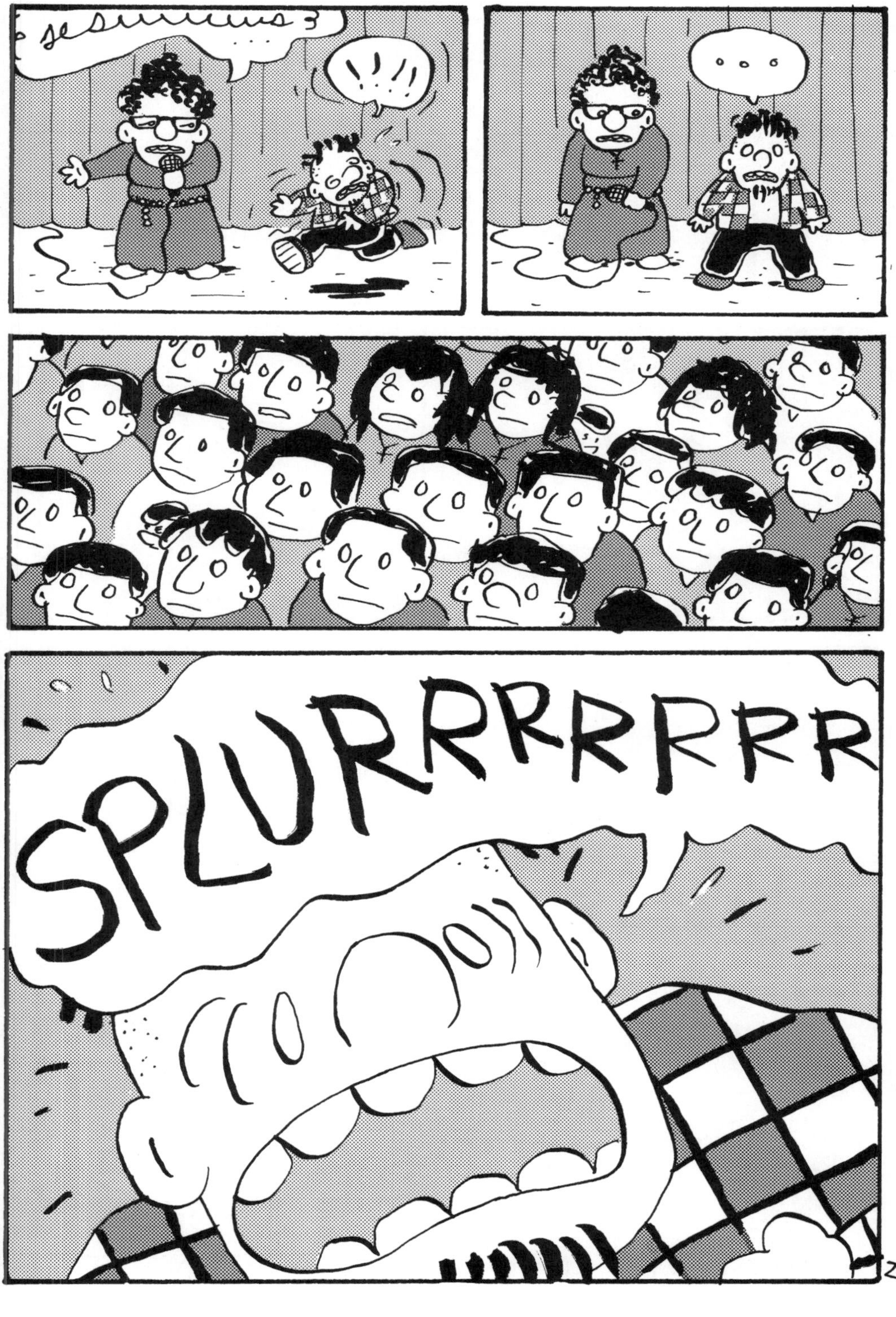

¿Jesuuuus? ...
!!!
...
SPLURRRRRRRR

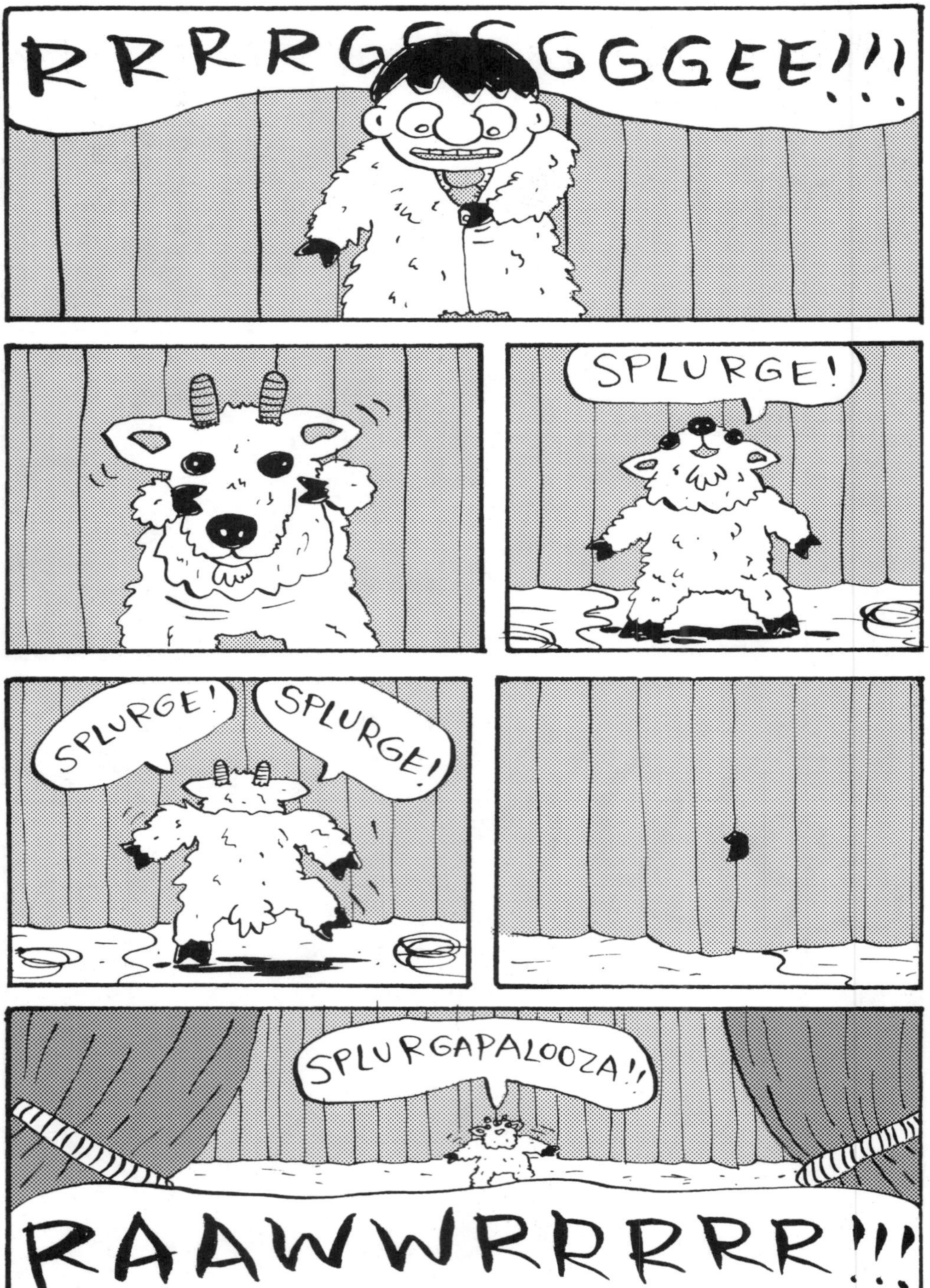
RRRRGEEGGGEE!!!
SPLURGE!
SPLURGE!
SPLURGE!
SPLURGAPALOOZA!!
RAAWWRRRRR!!!

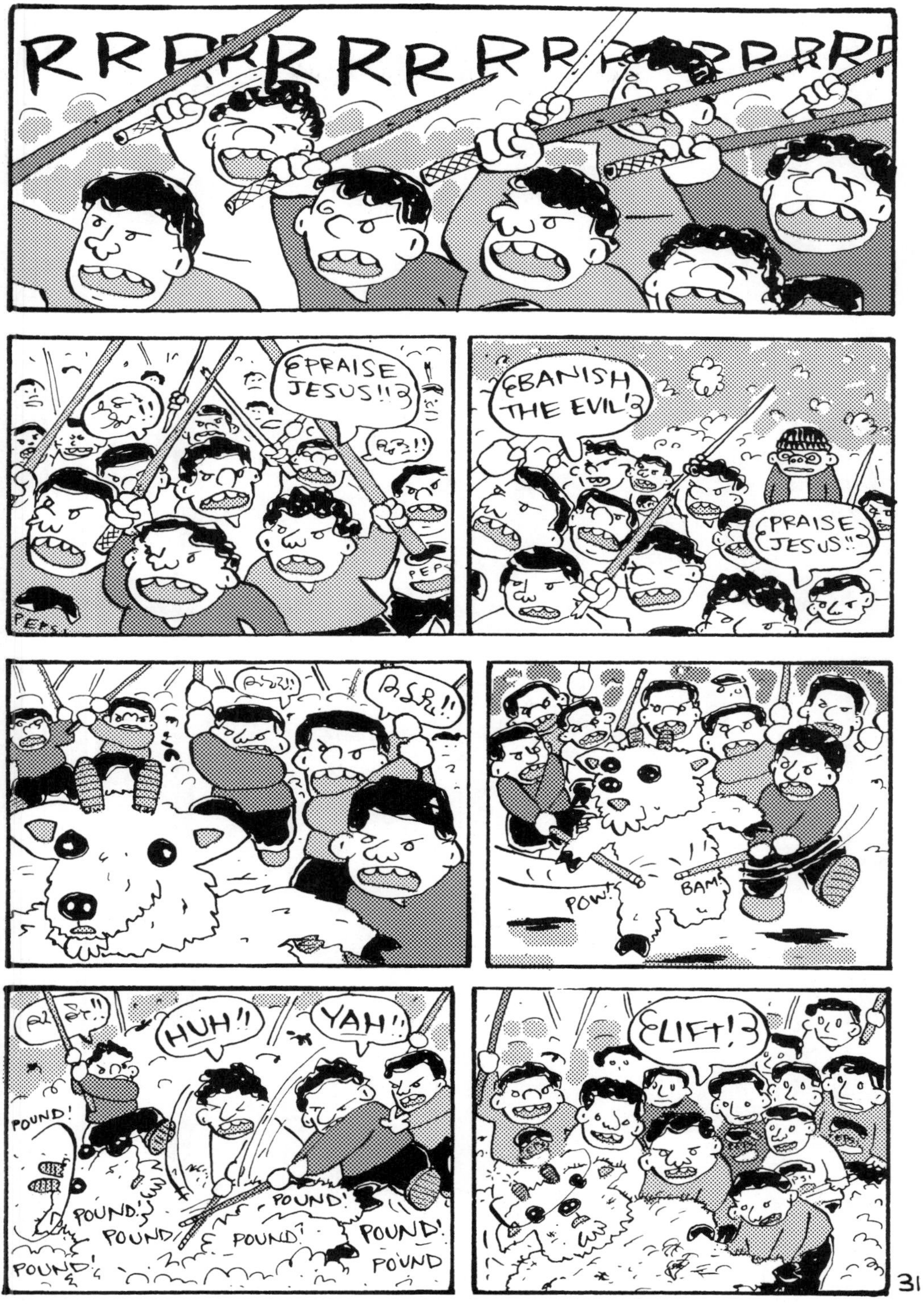
RRRRRRRRRRRRRRRR
PRAISE JESUS!!
BANISH THE EVIL!
PRAISE JESUS!!
POW!
BAM!
HUH!!
YAH!!
POUND!
LIFT!

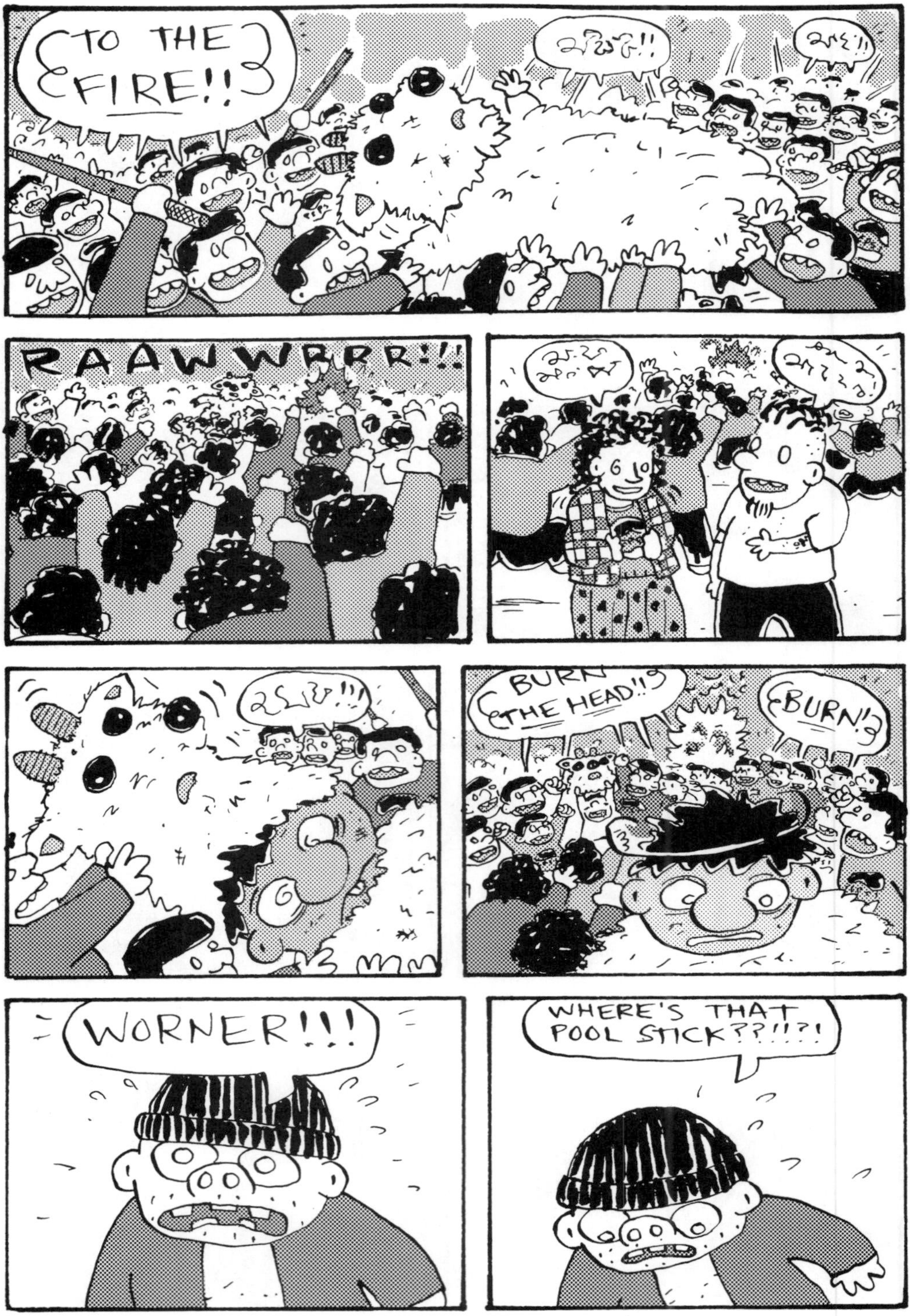
TO THE FIRE!!
RAAWWRRRR!!!
BURN THE HEAD!!
BURN!
WORNER!!!
WHERE'S THAT POOL STICK??!!?!

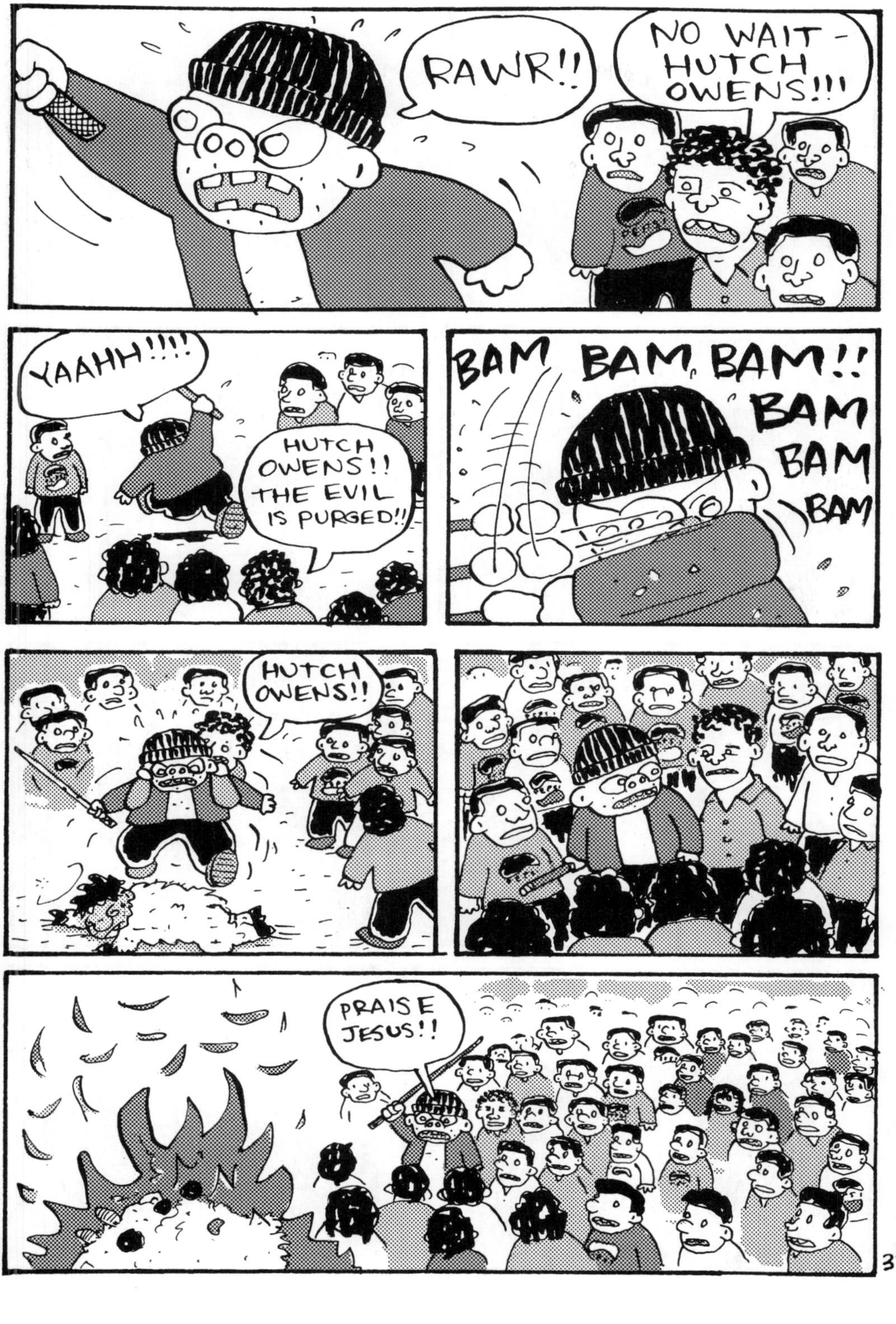

RAWR!!
NO WAIT - HUTCH OWENS!!!
YAAHH!!!!
HUTCH OWENS!! THE EVIL IS PURGED!!
BAM BAM BAM!! BAM BAM BAM
HUTCH OWENS!!
PRAISE JESUS!!

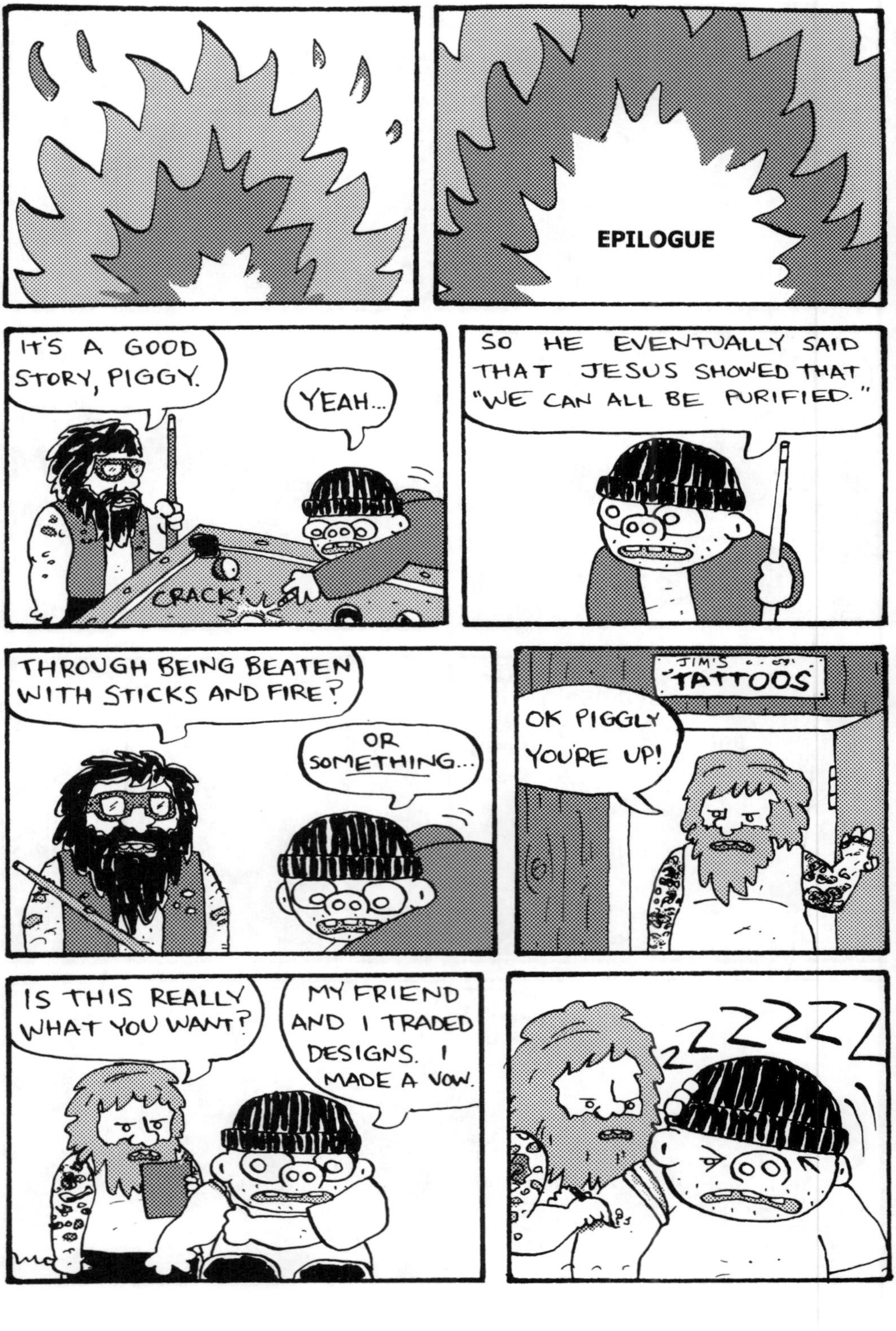

EPILOGUE
IT'S A GOOD STORY, PIGGY.
YEAH...
CRACK!
SO HE EVENTUALLY SAID THAT JESUS SHOWED THAT "WE CAN ALL BE PURIFIED."
THROUGH BEING BEATEN WITH STICKS AND FIRE?
OR SOMETHING...
JIM'S TATTOOS
OK PIGGLY YOU'RE UP!
IS THIS REALLY WHAT YOU WANT?
MY FRIEND AND I TRADED DESIGNS. I MADE A VOW.
zZZZZZ

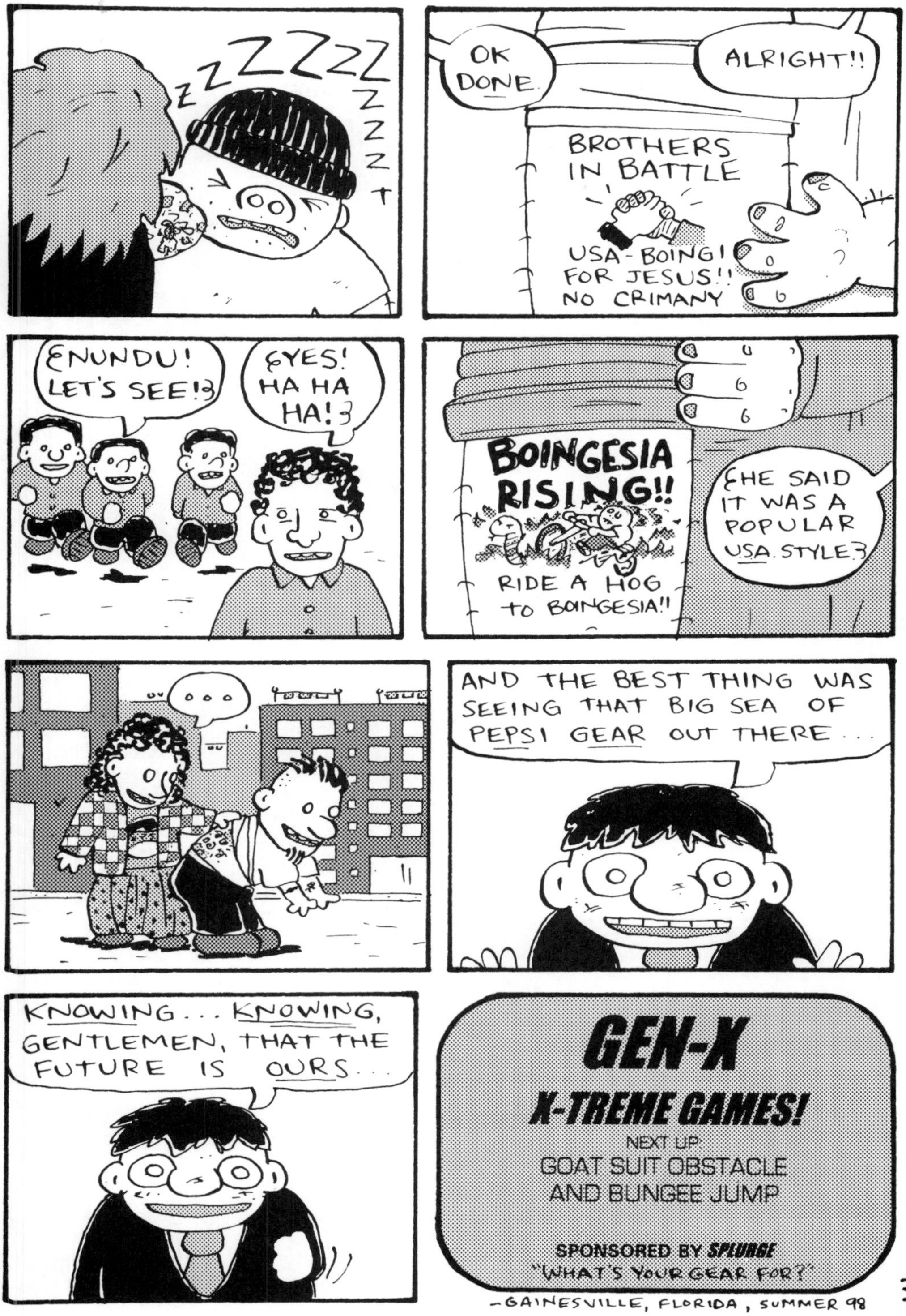

zZZZZZZ
Z
Z
Z
OK DONE
ALRIGHT!!
BROTHERS IN BATTLE
USA-BOING! FOR JESUS!! NO CRIMANY
ENUNDU! LET'S SEE!
YES! HA HA HA!
BOINGESIA RISING!!
RIDE A HOG TO BOINGESIA!!
HE SAID IT WAS A POPULAR USA STYLE
...
AND THE BEST THING WAS SEEING THAT BIG SEA OF PEPSI GEAR OUT THERE...
KNOWING... KNOWING, GENTLEMEN, THAT THE FUTURE IS OURS...
GEN-X
X-TREME GAMES!
NEXT UP:
GOAT SUIT OBSTACLE AND BUNGEE JUMP
SPONSORED BY SPLURGE
"WHAT'S YOUR GEAR FOR?"

-GAINESVILLE, FLORIDA, SUMMER 98

III . Stocks are Surging!

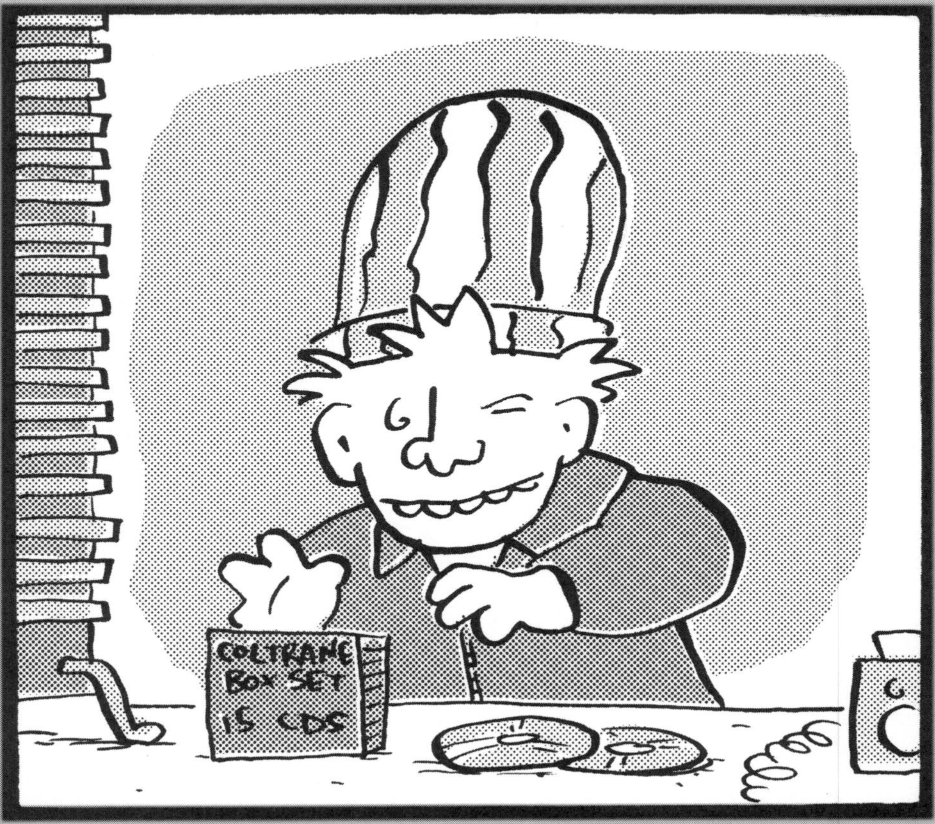
COLTRANE
BOX SET
15 CDS

for Dan Gervais and Craig Bostick

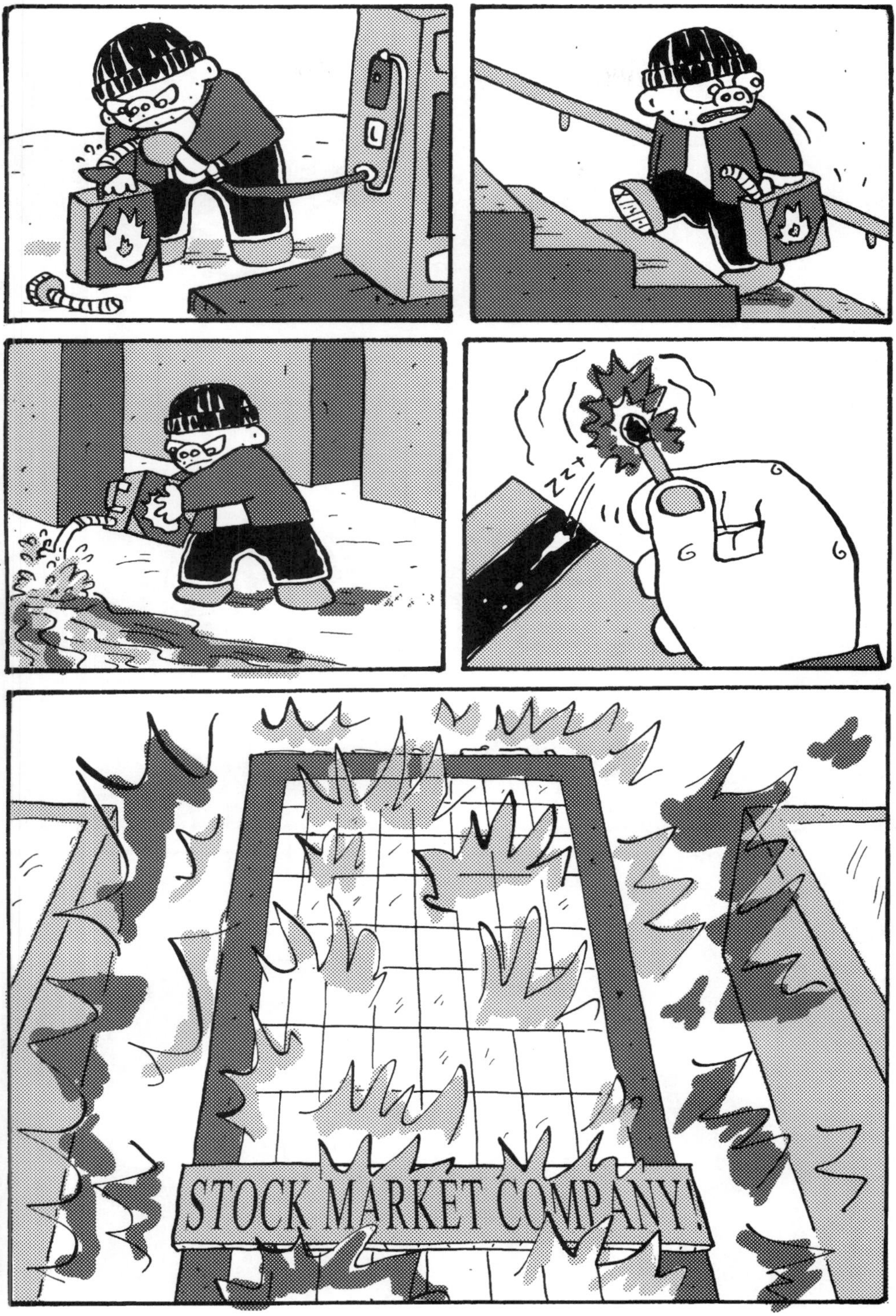

ZZZT
STOCK MARKET COMPANY!

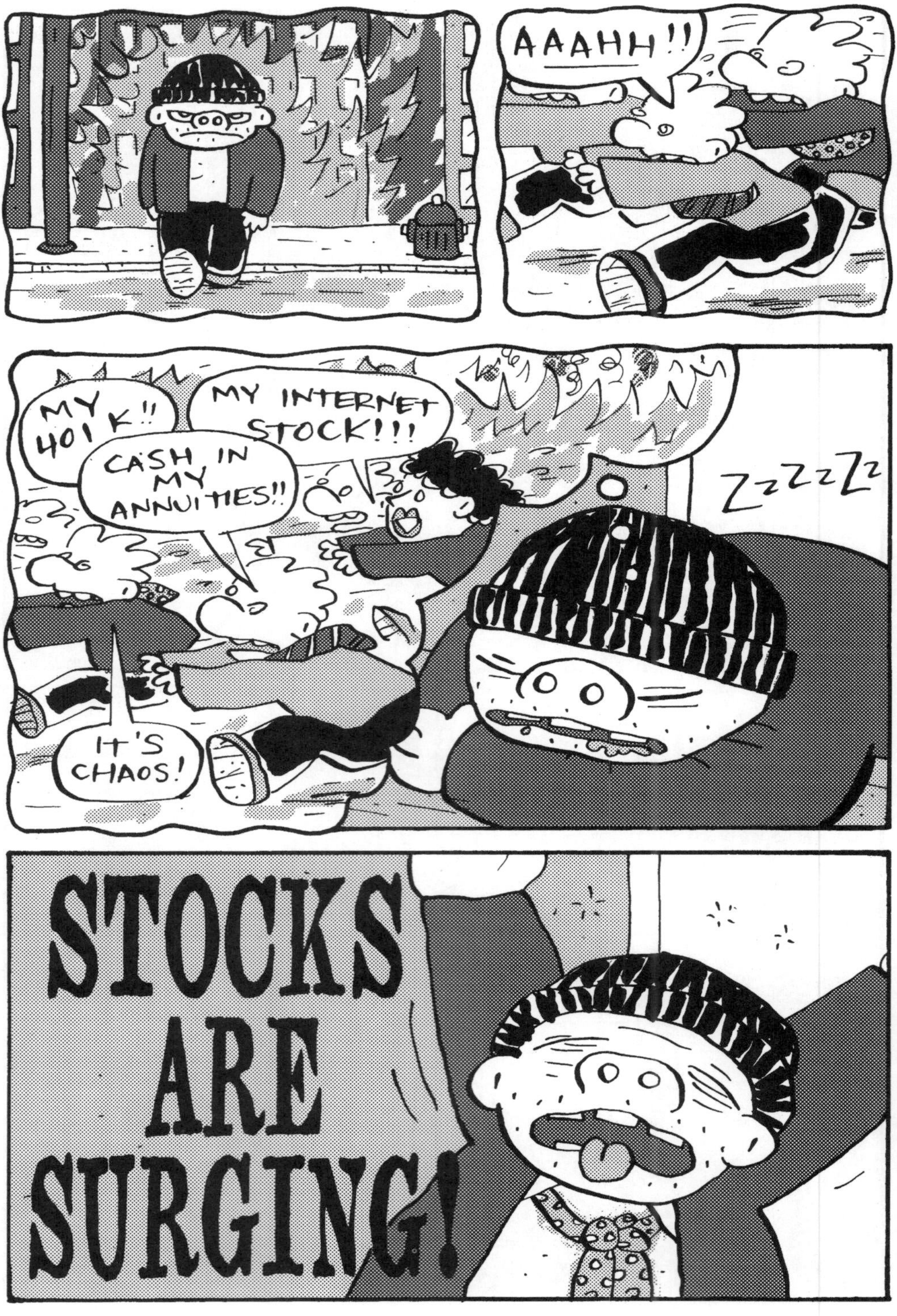
AAAHH!!
MY 401 K!!
MY INTERNET STOCK!!!
CASH IN MY ANNUITIES!!
ZzzzzZz
IT'S CHAOS!
STOCKS ARE SURGING!

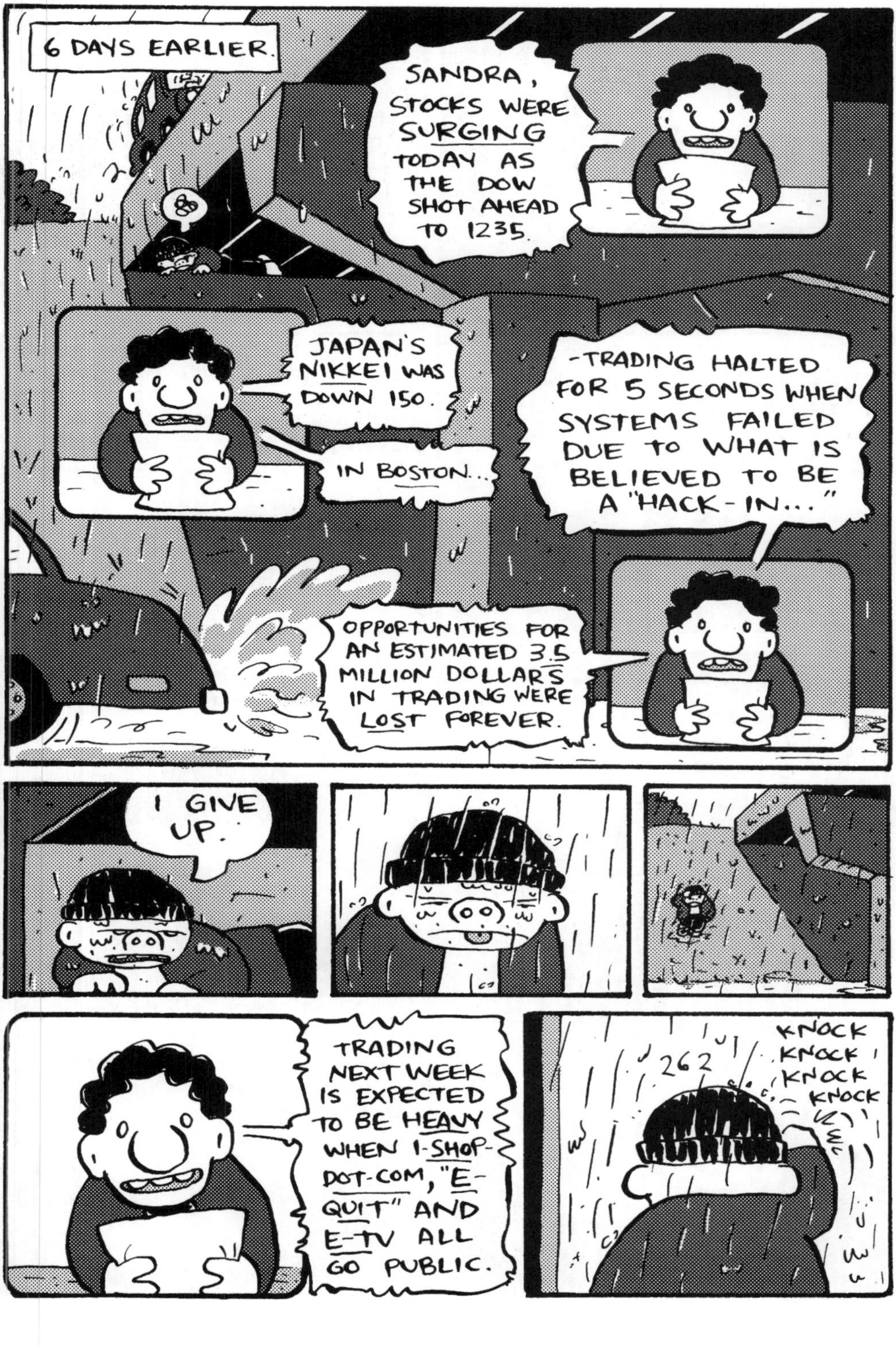
6 DAYS EARLIER.
SANDRA, STOCKS WERE SURGING TODAY AS THE DOW SHOT AHEAD TO 1235.
JAPAN'S NIKKEI WAS DOWN 150.
IN BOSTON...
-TRADING HALTED FOR 5 SECONDS WHEN SYSTEMS FAILED DUE TO WHAT IS BELIEVED TO BE A "HACK-IN..."
OPPORTUNITIES FOR AN ESTIMATED 3.5 MILLION DOLLARS IN TRADING WERE LOST FOREVER.
I GIVE UP.
TRADING NEXT WEEK IS EXPECTED TO BE HEAVY WHEN I-SHOP-DOT-COM, "E-QUIT" AND E-TV ALL GO PUBLIC.
262
KNOCK KNOCK KNOCK KNOCK

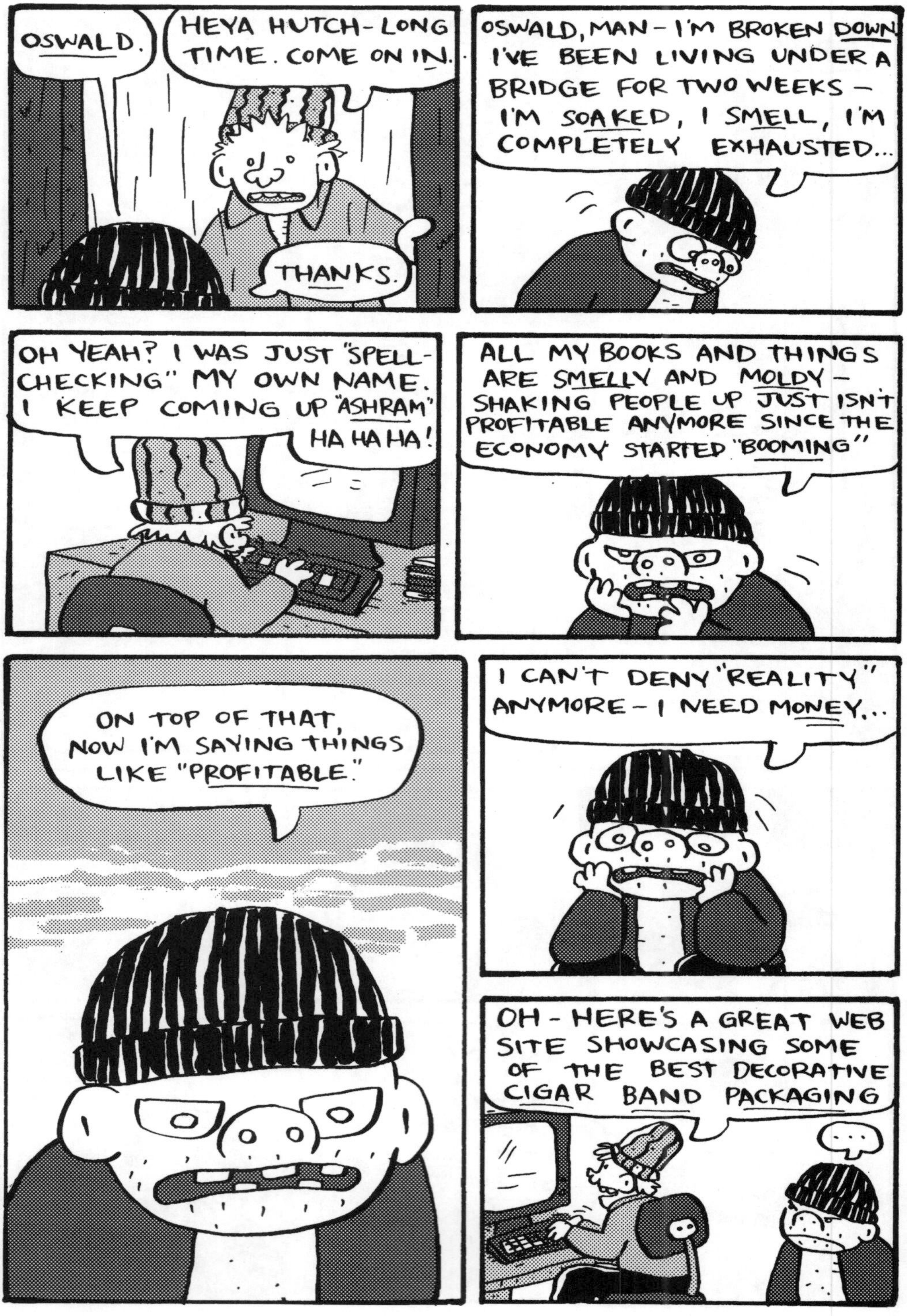

OSWALD.
HEYA HUTCH - LONG TIME. COME ON IN.
THANKS.
OSWALD, MAN - I'M BROKEN DOWN! I'VE BEEN LIVING UNDER A BRIDGE FOR TWO WEEKS - I'M SOAKED, I SMELL, I'M COMPLETELY EXHAUSTED...
OH YEAH? I WAS JUST "SPELL-CHECKING" MY OWN NAME. I KEEP COMING UP "ASHRAM" HA HA HA!
ALL MY BOOKS AND THINGS ARE SMELLY AND MOLDY - SHAKING PEOPLE UP JUST ISN'T PROFITABLE ANYMORE SINCE THE ECONOMY STARTED "BOOMING"
ON TOP OF THAT, NOW I'M SAYING THINGS LIKE "PROFITABLE."
I CAN'T DENY "REALITY" ANYMORE - I NEED MONEY...
OH - HERE'S A GREAT WEB SITE SHOWCASING SOME OF THE BEST DECORATIVE CIGAR BAND PACKAGING

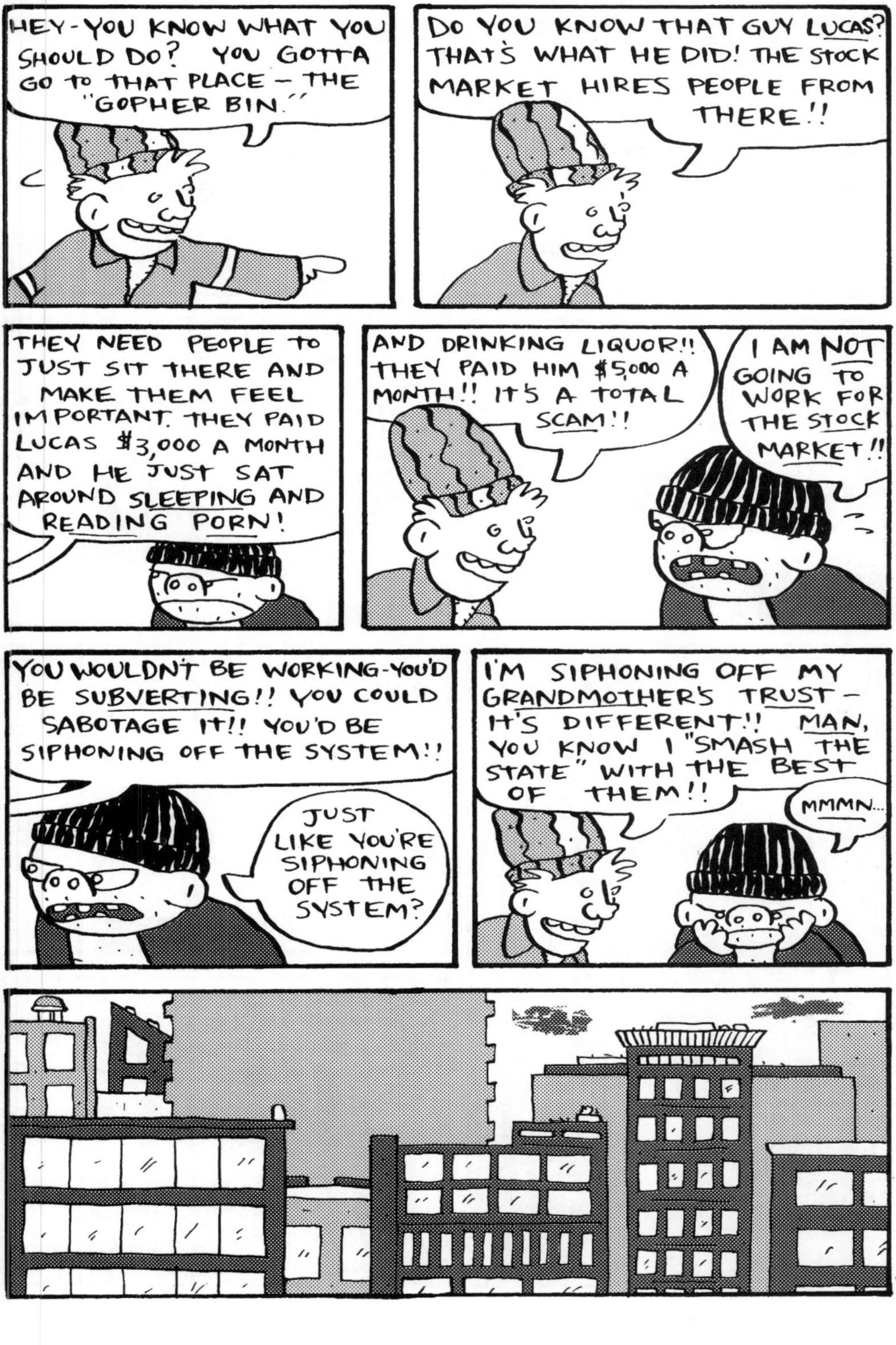
HEY - YOU KNOW WHAT YOU SHOULD DO? YOU GOTTA GO TO THAT PLACE - THE "GOPHER BIN."
DO YOU KNOW THAT GUY LUCAS? THAT'S WHAT HE DID! THE STOCK MARKET HIRES PEOPLE FROM THERE!!
THEY NEED PEOPLE TO JUST SIT THERE AND MAKE THEM FEEL IMPORTANT. THEY PAID LUCAS $3,000 A MONTH AND HE JUST SAT AROUND SLEEPING AND READING PORN!
AND DRINKING LIQUOR!! THEY PAID HIM $5,000 A MONTH!! IT'S A TOTAL SCAM!!
I AM NOT GOING TO WORK FOR THE STOCK MARKET!!
YOU WOULDN'T BE WORKING - YOU'D BE SUBVERTING!! YOU COULD SABOTAGE IT!! YOU'D BE SIPHONING OFF THE SYSTEM!!
JUST LIKE YOU'RE SIPHONING OFF THE SYSTEM?
I'M SIPHONING OFF MY GRANDMOTHER'S TRUST - IT'S DIFFERENT!! MAN, YOU KNOW I "SMASH THE STATE" WITH THE BEST OF THEM!!
MMMN...

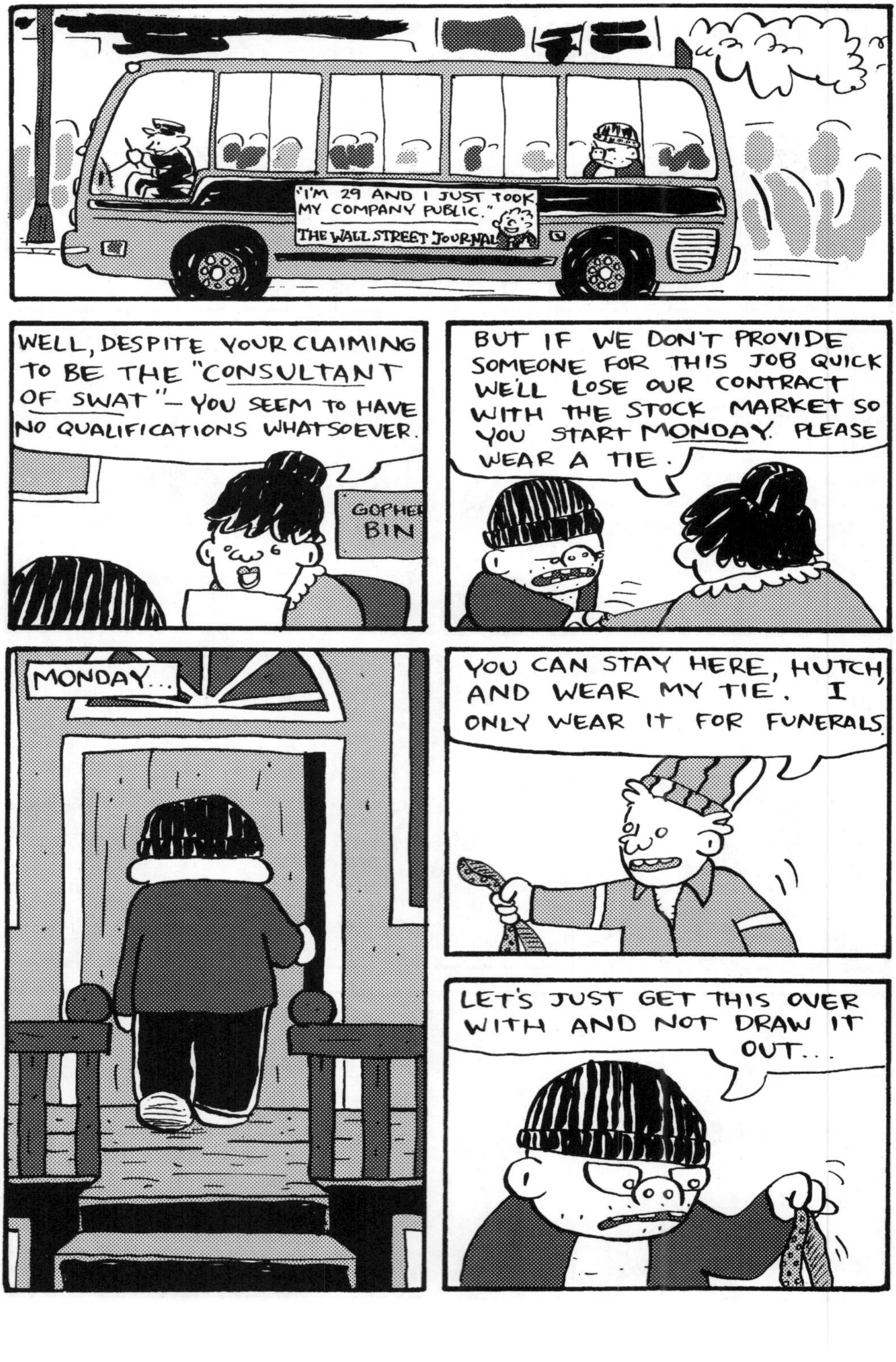
"I'M 29 AND I JUST TOOK MY COMPANY PUBLIC."
THE WALL STREET JOURNAL
WELL, DESPITE YOUR CLAIMING TO BE THE "CONSULTANT OF SWAT" — YOU SEEM TO HAVE NO QUALIFICATIONS WHATSOEVER.
GOPHER BIN
BUT IF WE DON'T PROVIDE SOMEONE FOR THIS JOB QUICK WE'LL LOSE OUR CONTRACT WITH THE STOCK MARKET SO YOU START MONDAY. PLEASE WEAR A TIE.
MONDAY...
YOU CAN STAY HERE, HUTCH, AND WEAR MY TIE. I ONLY WEAR IT FOR FUNERALS.
LET'S JUST GET THIS OVER WITH AND NOT DRAW IT OUT...

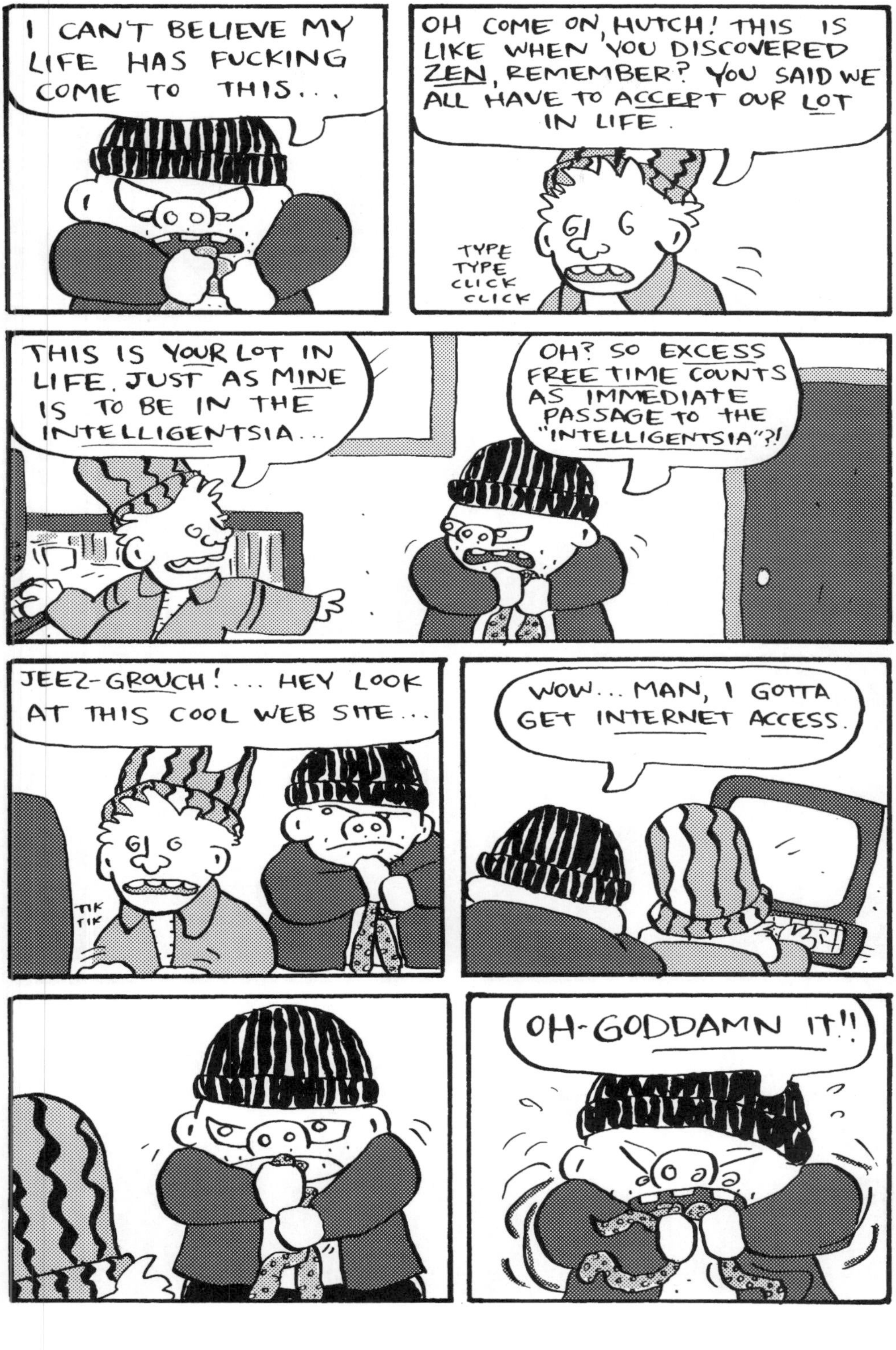
I CAN'T BELIEVE MY LIFE HAS FUCKING COME TO THIS...
OH COME ON, HUTCH! THIS IS LIKE WHEN YOU DISCOVERED ZEN, REMEMBER? YOU SAID WE ALL HAVE TO ACCEPT OUR LOT IN LIFE.
TYPE TYPE CLICK CLICK
THIS IS YOUR LOT IN LIFE. JUST AS MINE IS TO BE IN THE INTELLIGENTSIA...
OH? SO EXCESS FREE TIME COUNTS AS IMMEDIATE PASSAGE TO THE "INTELLIGENTSIA"?!
JEEZ-GROUCH! ... HEY LOOK AT THIS COOL WEB SITE...
TIK TIK
WOW... MAN, I GOTTA GET INTERNET ACCESS.
OH-GODDAMN IT!!

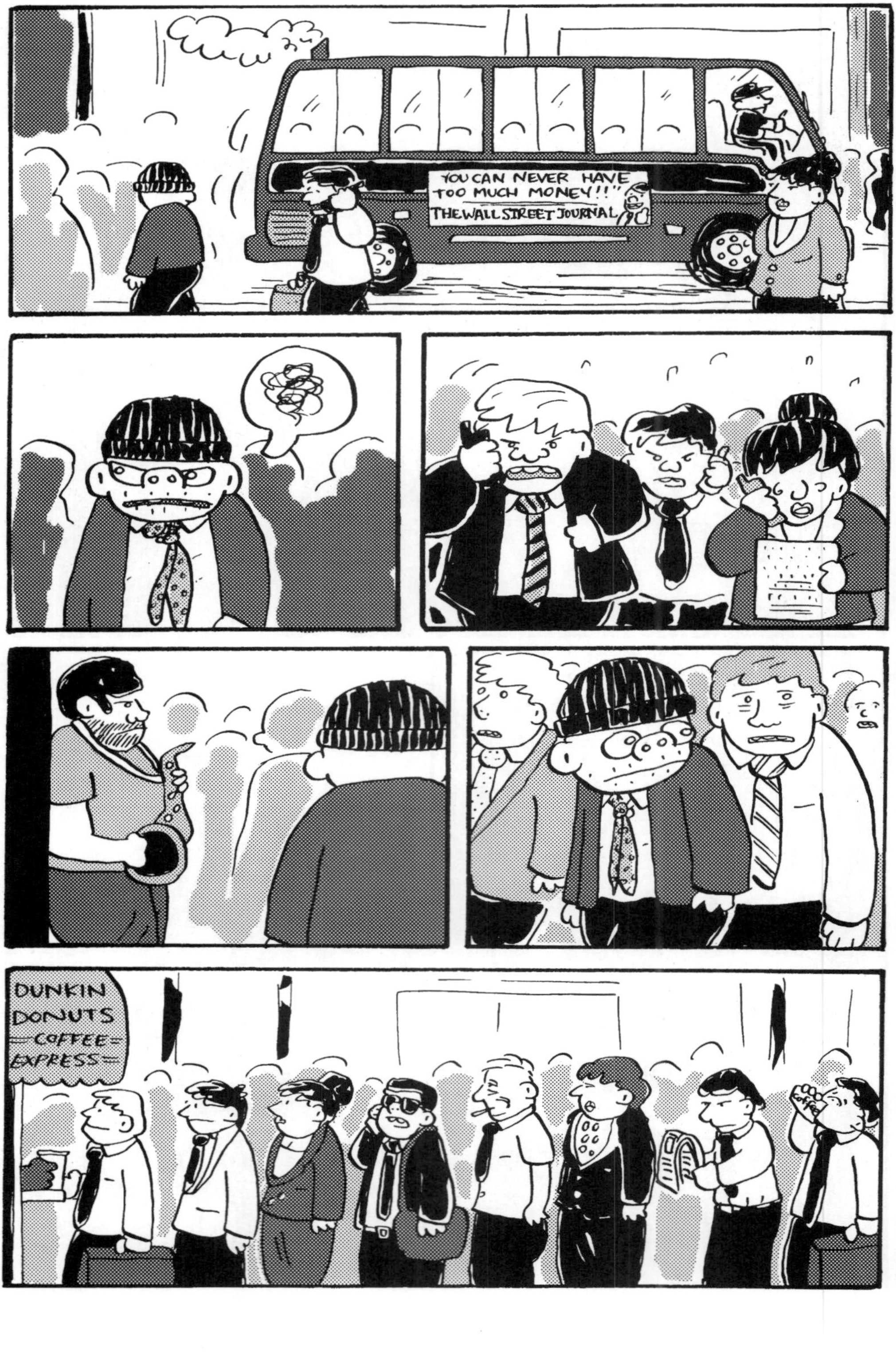
"YOU CAN NEVER HAVE TOO MUCH MONEY!!"
THE WALL STREET JOURNAL
DUNKIN DONUTS
=COFFEE=
EXPRESS=

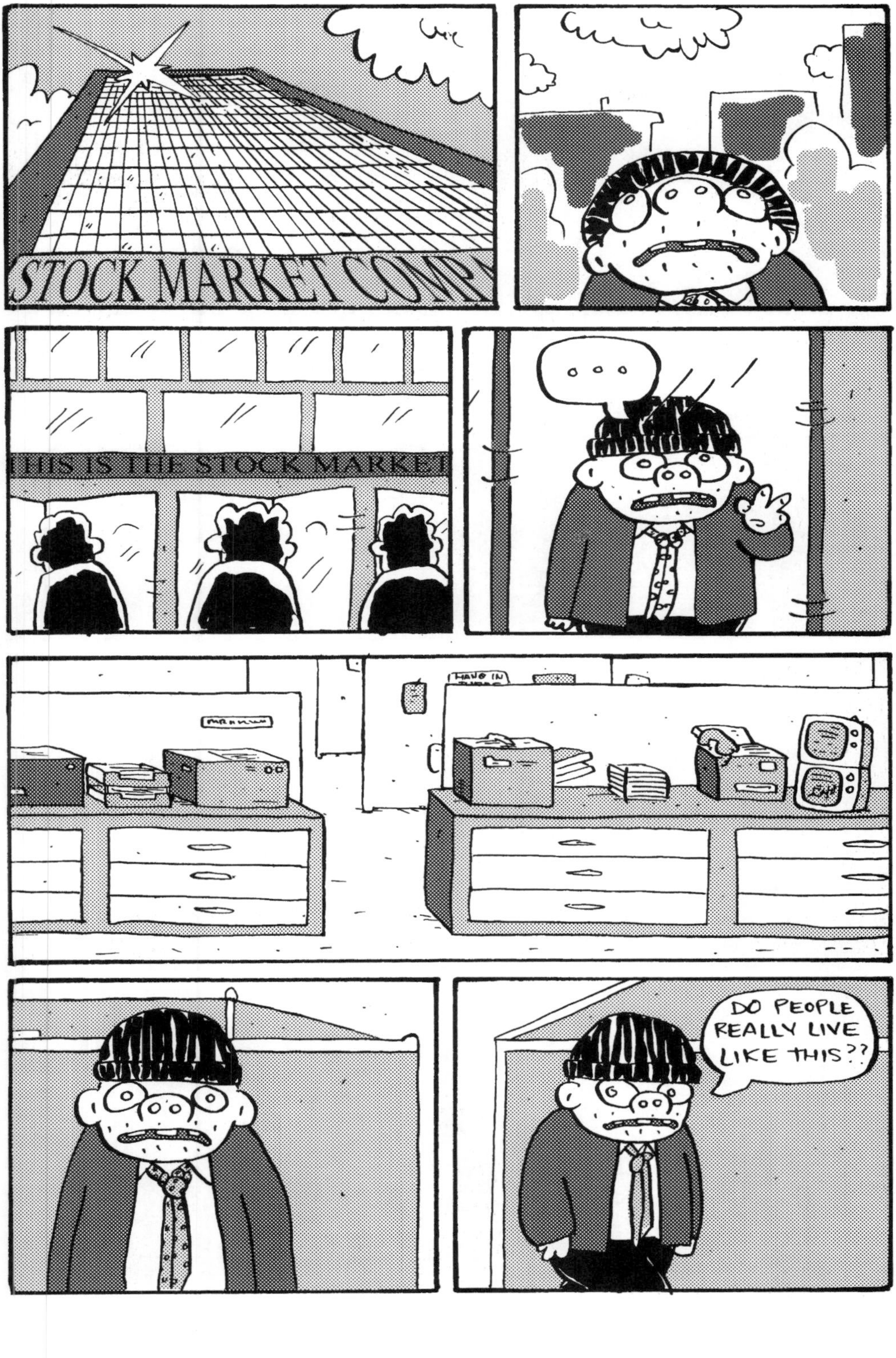
STOCK MARKET COMP
HIS IS THE STOCK MARKE
DO PEOPLE REALLY LIVE LIKE THIS??

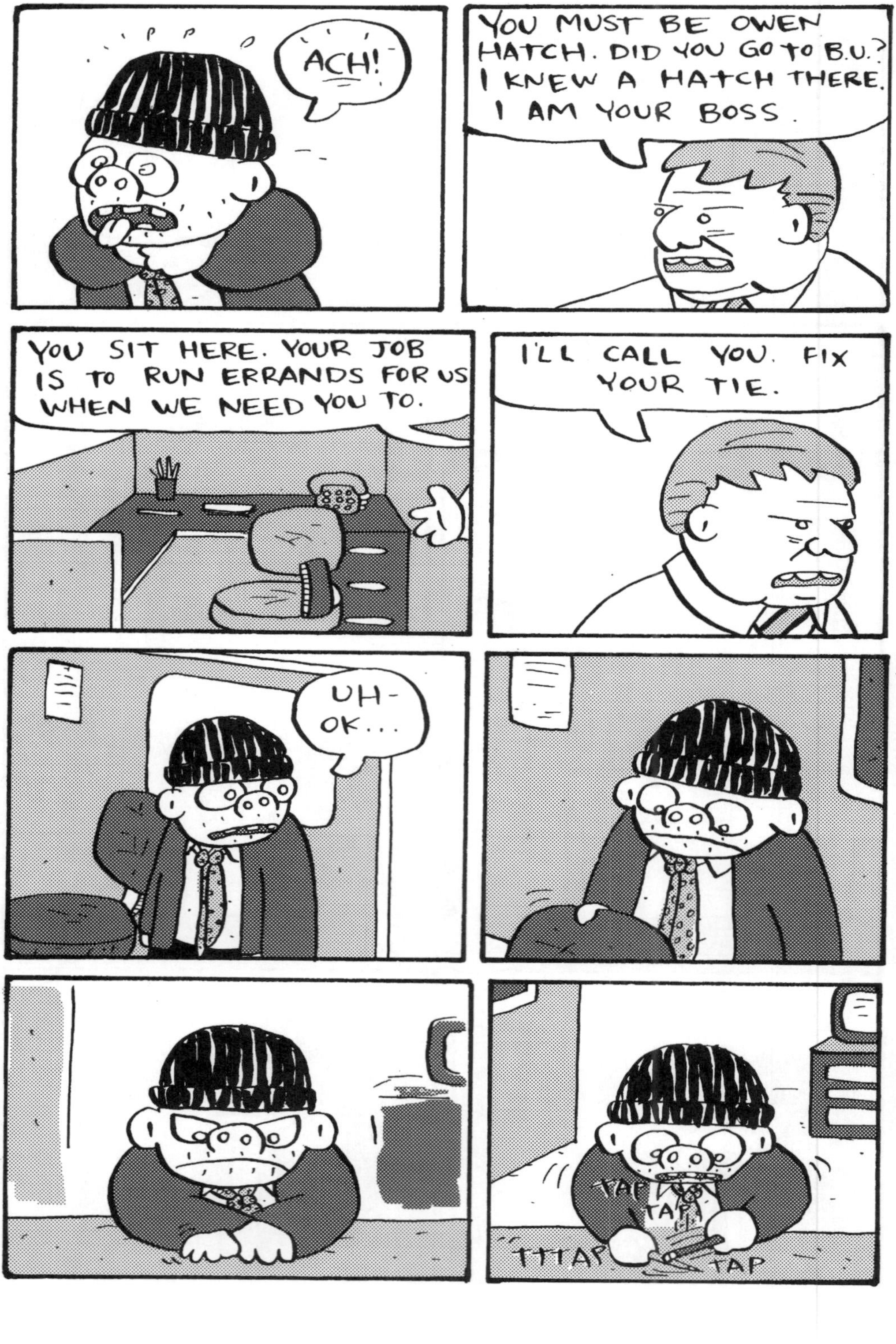
ACH!
YOU MUST BE OWEN HATCH. DID YOU GO TO B.U.? I KNEW A HATCH THERE. I AM YOUR BOSS.
YOU SIT HERE. YOUR JOB IS TO RUN ERRANDS FOR US WHEN WE NEED YOU TO.
I'LL CALL YOU. FIX YOUR TIE.
UH- OK...
TAP
TAP
TTTAP
TAP

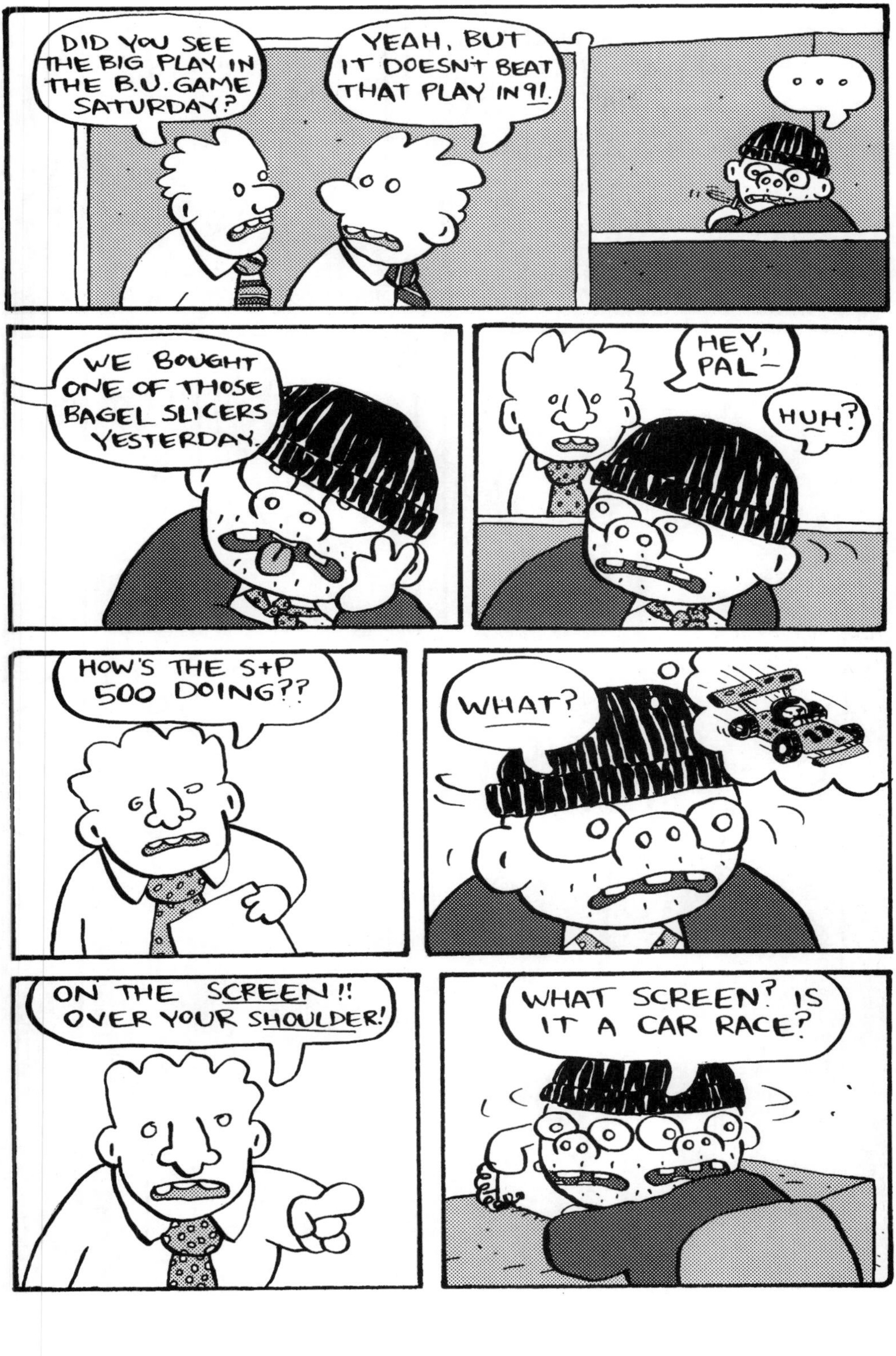
DID YOU SEE THE BIG PLAY IN THE B.U. GAME SATURDAY?
YEAH, BUT IT DOESN'T BEAT THAT PLAY IN 91.
. . .
WE BOUGHT ONE OF THOSE BAGEL SLICERS YESTERDAY.
HEY, PAL—
HUH?
HOW'S THE S+P 500 DOING??
WHAT?
ON THE SCREEN!! OVER YOUR SHOULDER!
WHAT SCREEN? IS IT A CAR RACE?

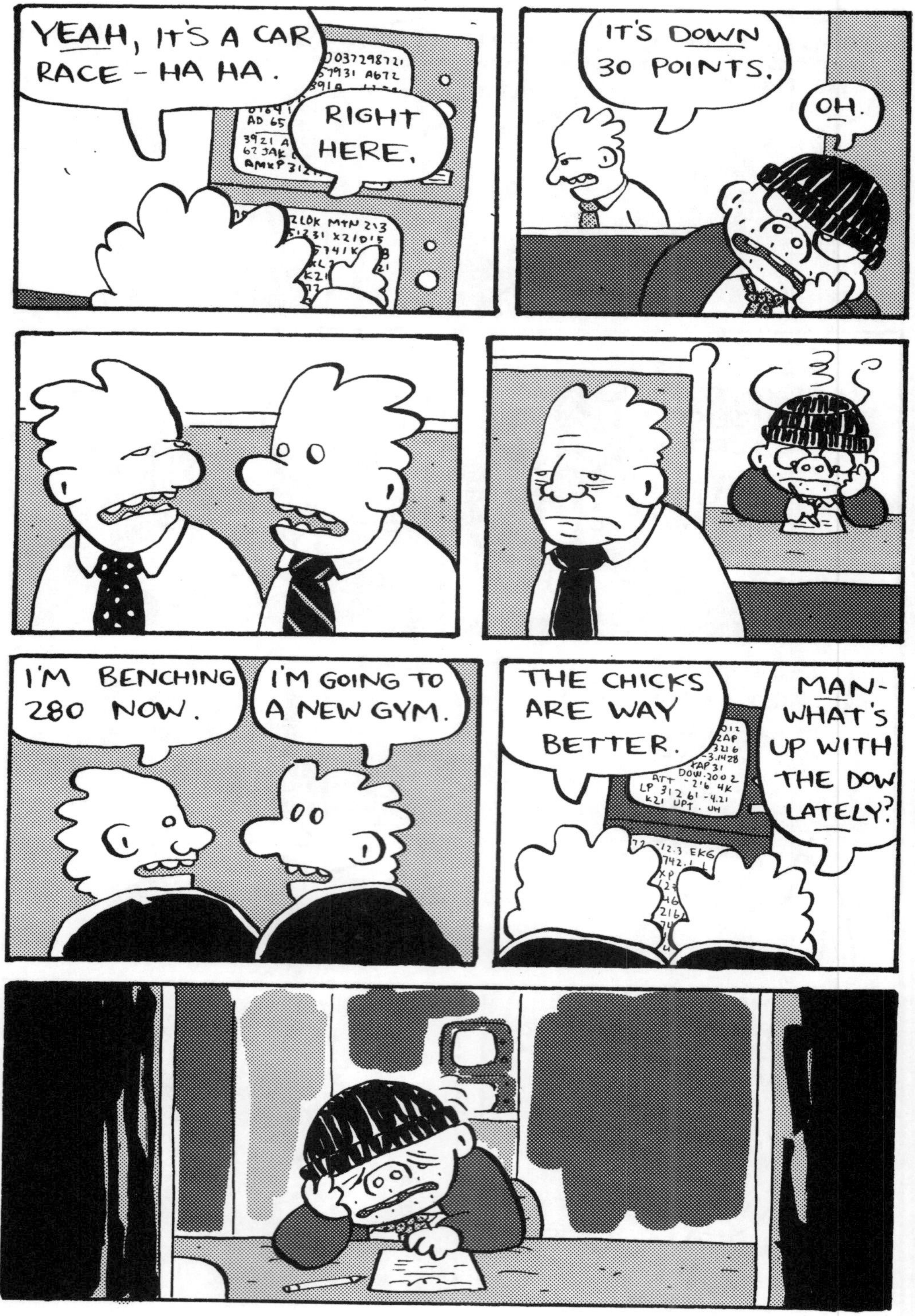
YEAH, IT'S A CAR RACE - HA HA.
RIGHT HERE.
IT'S DOWN 30 POINTS.
OH.
I'M BENCHING 280 NOW.
I'M GOING TO A NEW GYM.
THE CHICKS ARE WAY BETTER.
MAN- WHAT'S UP WITH THE DOW LATELY?

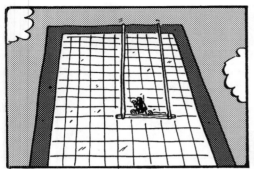

WELL-AM I ALLOWED TO PEE OR DO I JUST HAVE TO SIT HERE?

FORGET IT!!

I FEEL LIKE I'M IN FUCKING HIGH SCHOOL!

LIKE I NEED A HALL PASS!!

HEY PAL-WHERE'S THE NURSE'S OFFICE? HA HA!

IT'S ON 7. YOU NEED A PASS.

13

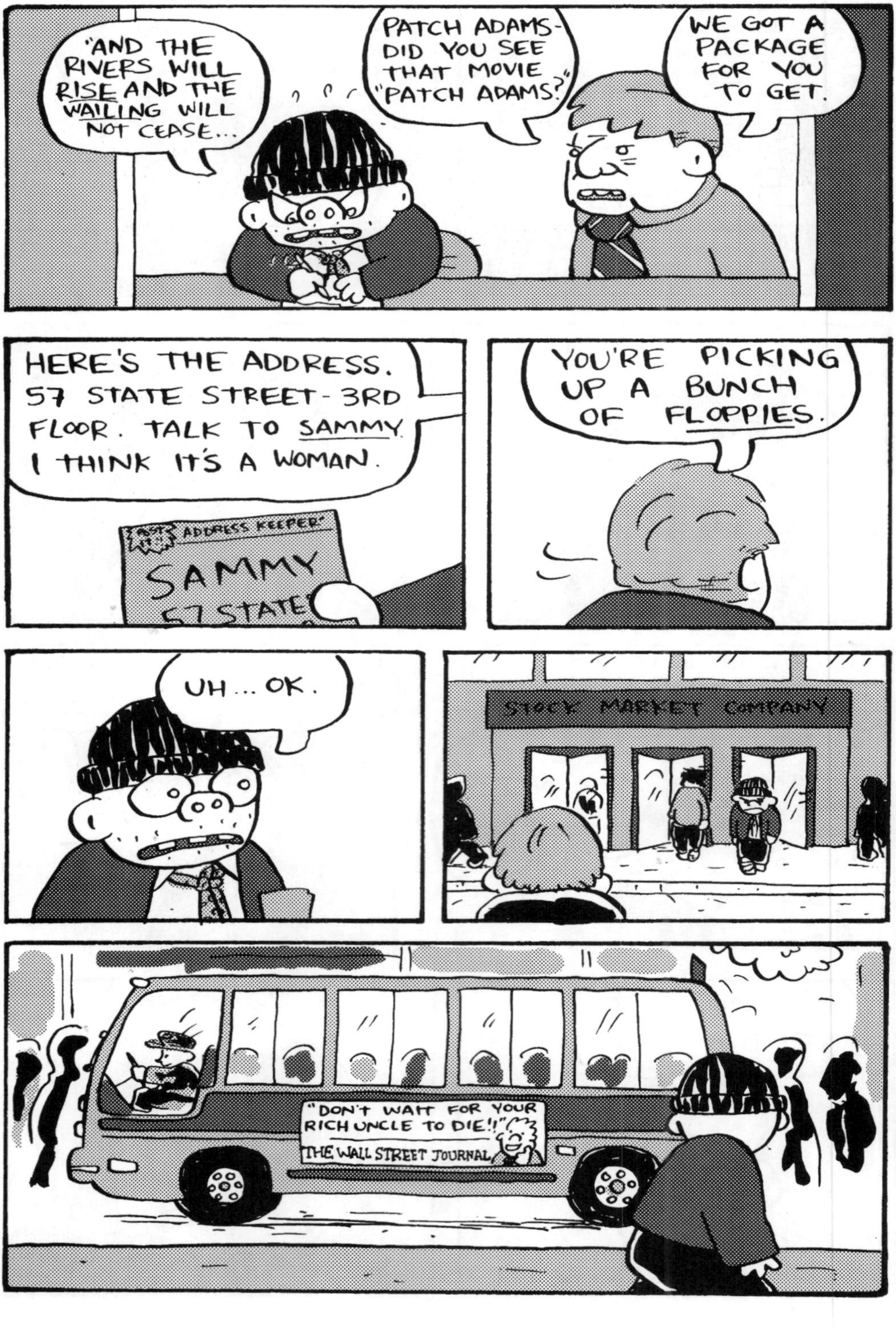
"AND THE RIVERS WILL RISE AND THE WAILING WILL NOT CEASE...
PATCH ADAMS- DID YOU SEE THAT MOVIE "PATCH ADAMS?"
WE GOT A PACKAGE FOR YOU TO GET.
HERE'S THE ADDRESS. 57 STATE STREET- 3RD FLOOR. TALK TO SAMMY. I THINK IT'S A WOMAN.
ADDRESS KEEPER
SAMMY
57 STATE
YOU'RE PICKING UP A BUNCH OF FLOPPIES.
UH... OK.
STOCK MARKET COMPANY
"DON'T WAIT FOR YOUR RICH UNCLE TO DIE!!"
THE WALL STREET JOURNAL

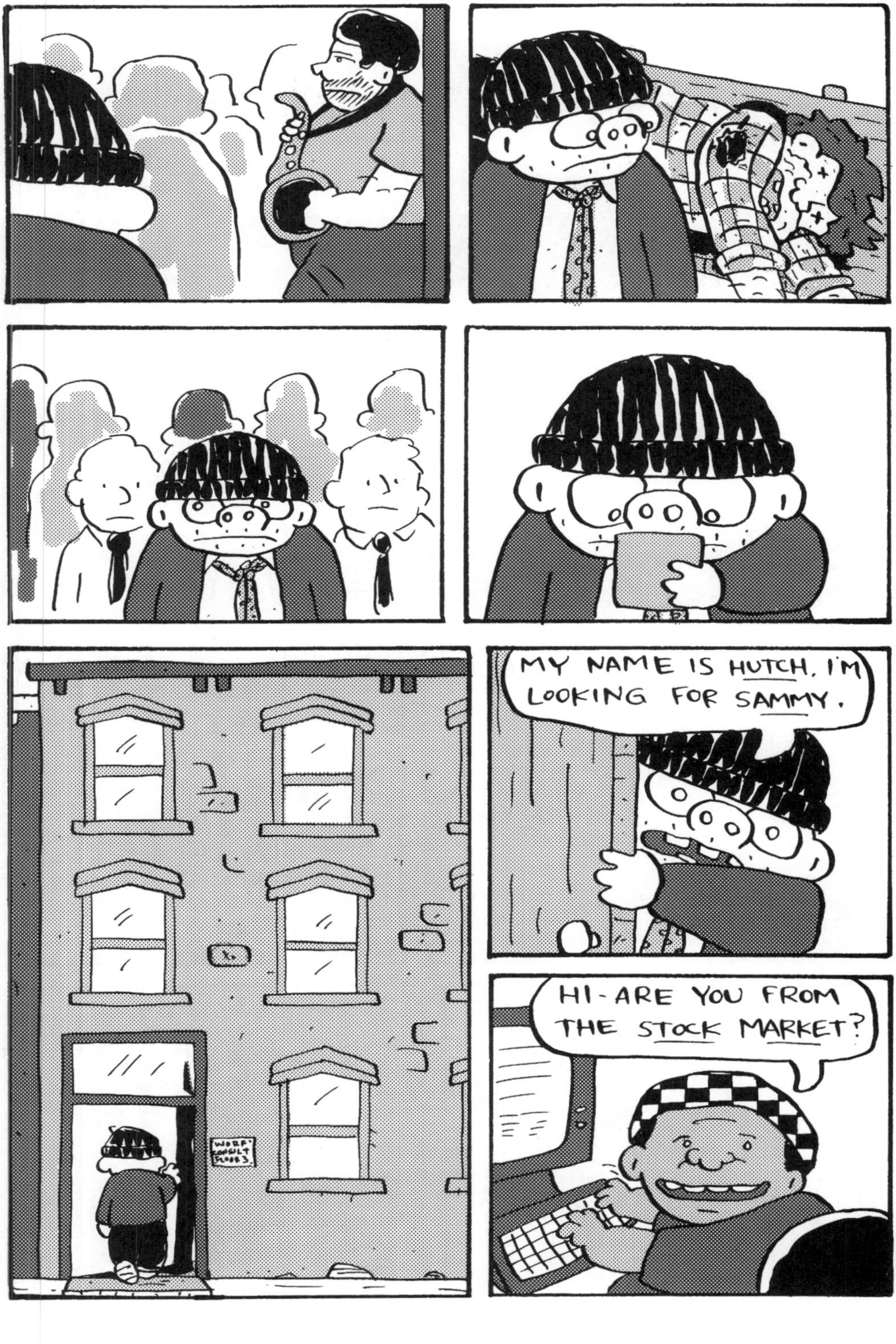
WORF CONSULT FLOOR 3
MY NAME IS HUTCH. I'M LOOKING FOR SAMMY.
HI - ARE YOU FROM THE STOCK MARKET?

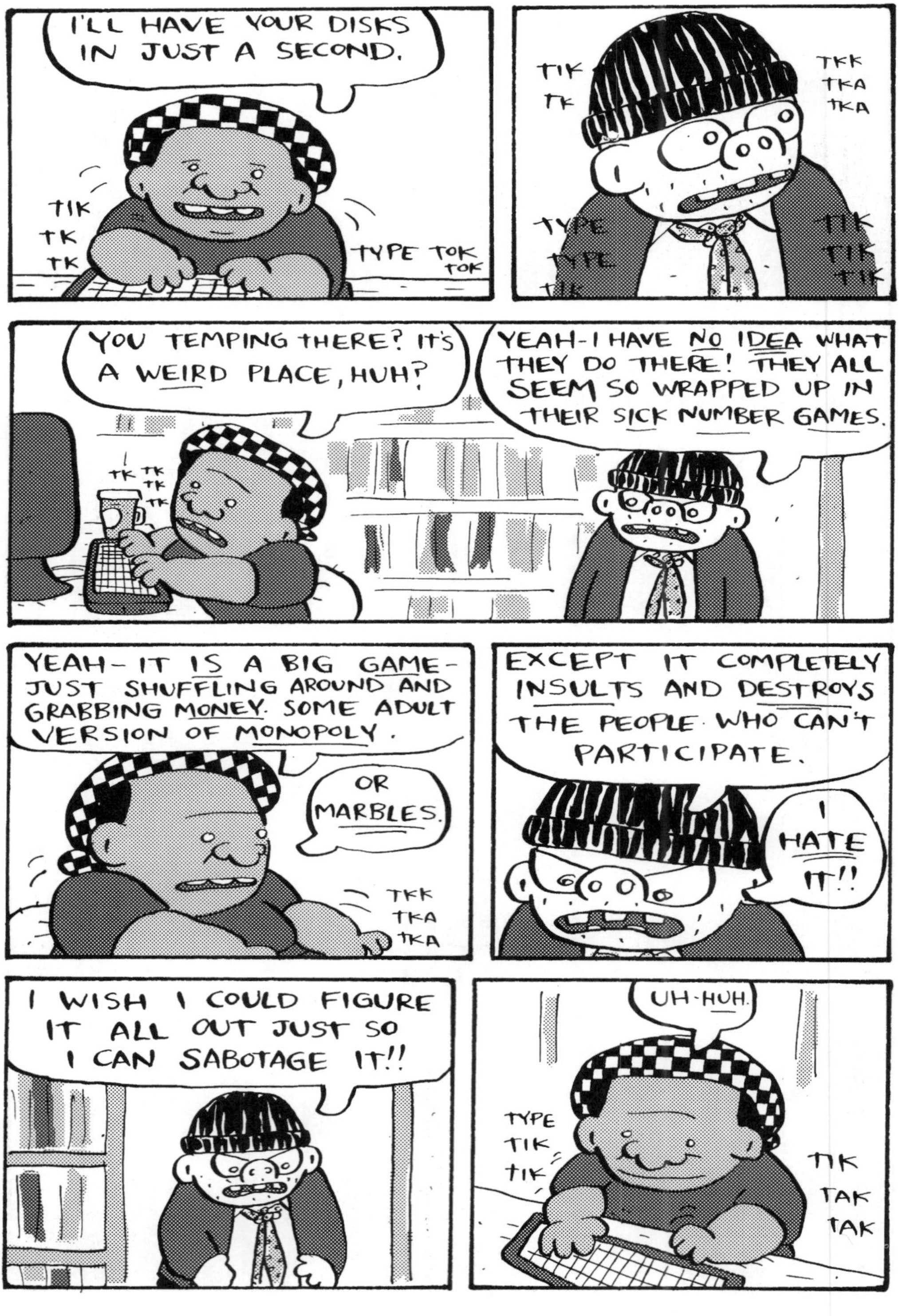
I'LL HAVE YOUR DISKS IN JUST A SECOND.
TIK TK TK
TYPE TOK TOK
TIK TK
TKK TKA TKA
TYPE TYPE
TIK TIK TIK
YOU TEMPING THERE? IT'S A WEIRD PLACE, HUH?
YEAH-I HAVE NO IDEA WHAT THEY DO THERE! THEY ALL SEEM SO WRAPPED UP IN THEIR SICK NUMBER GAMES.
TK TK TK TK
YEAH- IT IS A BIG GAME- JUST SHUFFLING AROUND AND GRABBING MONEY. SOME ADULT VERSION OF MONOPOLY.
OR MARBLES.
TKK TKA TKA
EXCEPT IT COMPLETELY INSULTS AND DESTROYS THE PEOPLE WHO CAN'T PARTICIPATE.
I HATE IT!!
I WISH I COULD FIGURE IT ALL OUT JUST SO I CAN SABOTAGE IT!!
UH-HUH.
TYPE TIK TIK
TIK TAK TAK

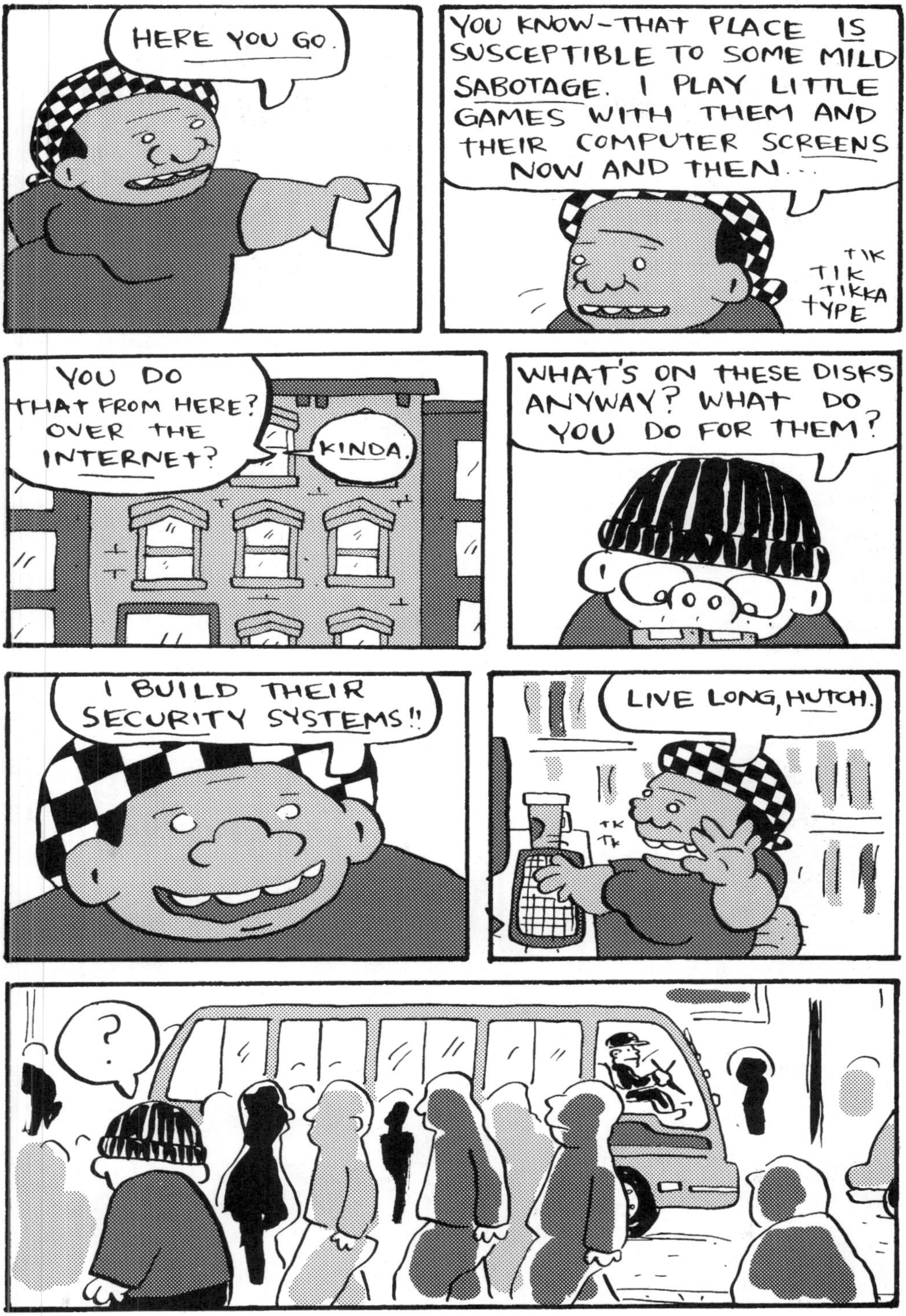
HERE YOU GO.
YOU KNOW-THAT PLACE IS SUSCEPTIBLE TO SOME MILD SABOTAGE. I PLAY LITTLE GAMES WITH THEM AND THEIR COMPUTER SCREENS NOW AND THEN...
TIK TIK TIKKA TYPE
YOU DO THAT FROM HERE? OVER THE INTERNET?
KINDA.
WHAT'S ON THESE DISKS ANYWAY? WHAT DO YOU DO FOR THEM?
I BUILD THEIR SECURITY SYSTEMS!!
LIVE LONG, HUTCH.
TK TK
?

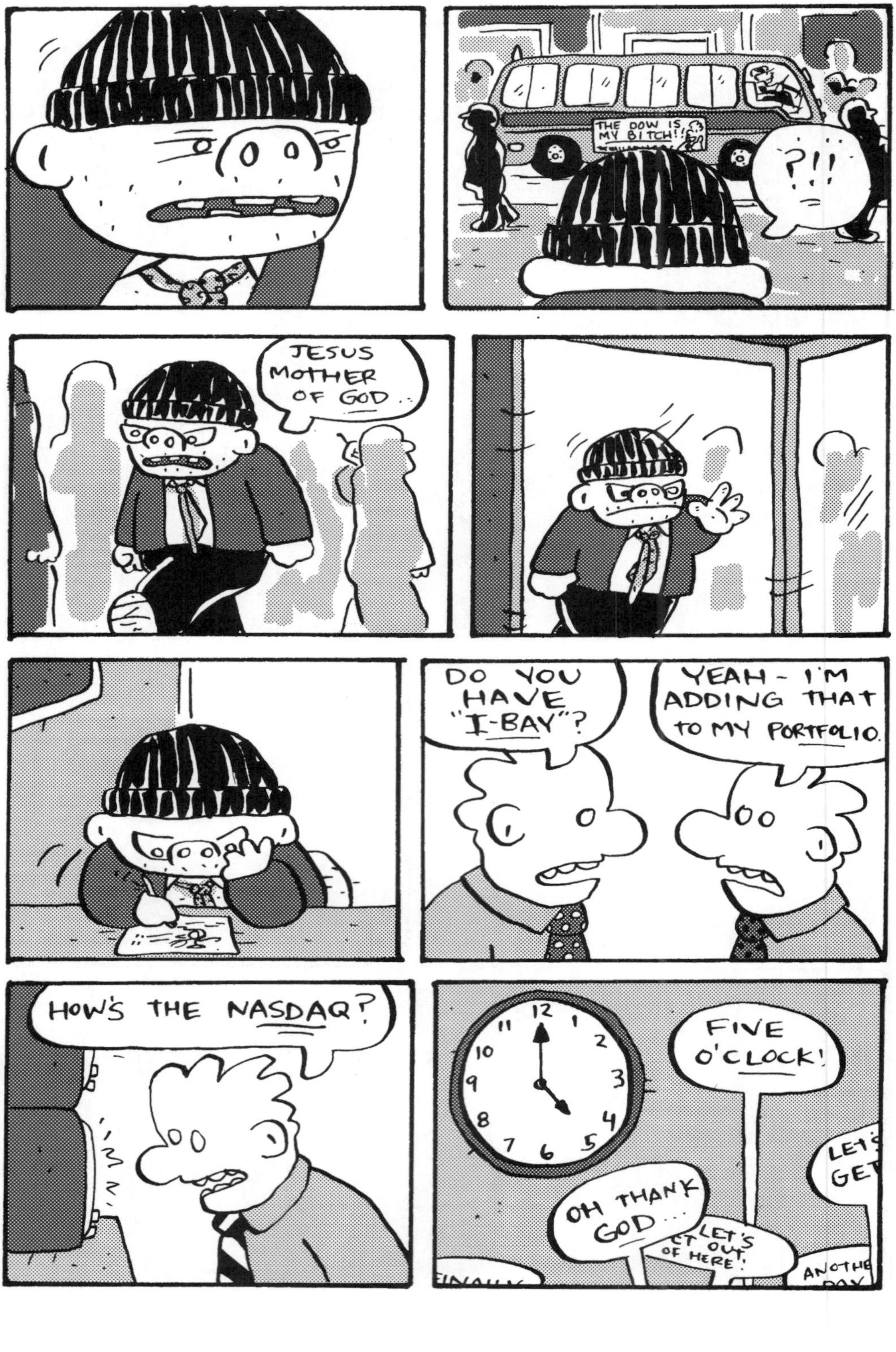
THE DOW IS MY BITCH!!
?!!
JESUS MOTHER OF GOD...
DO YOU HAVE "I-BAY"?
YEAH - I'M ADDING THAT TO MY PORTFOLIO.
HOW'S THE NASDAQ?
FIVE O'CLOCK!
OH THANK GOD...
OF HERE!

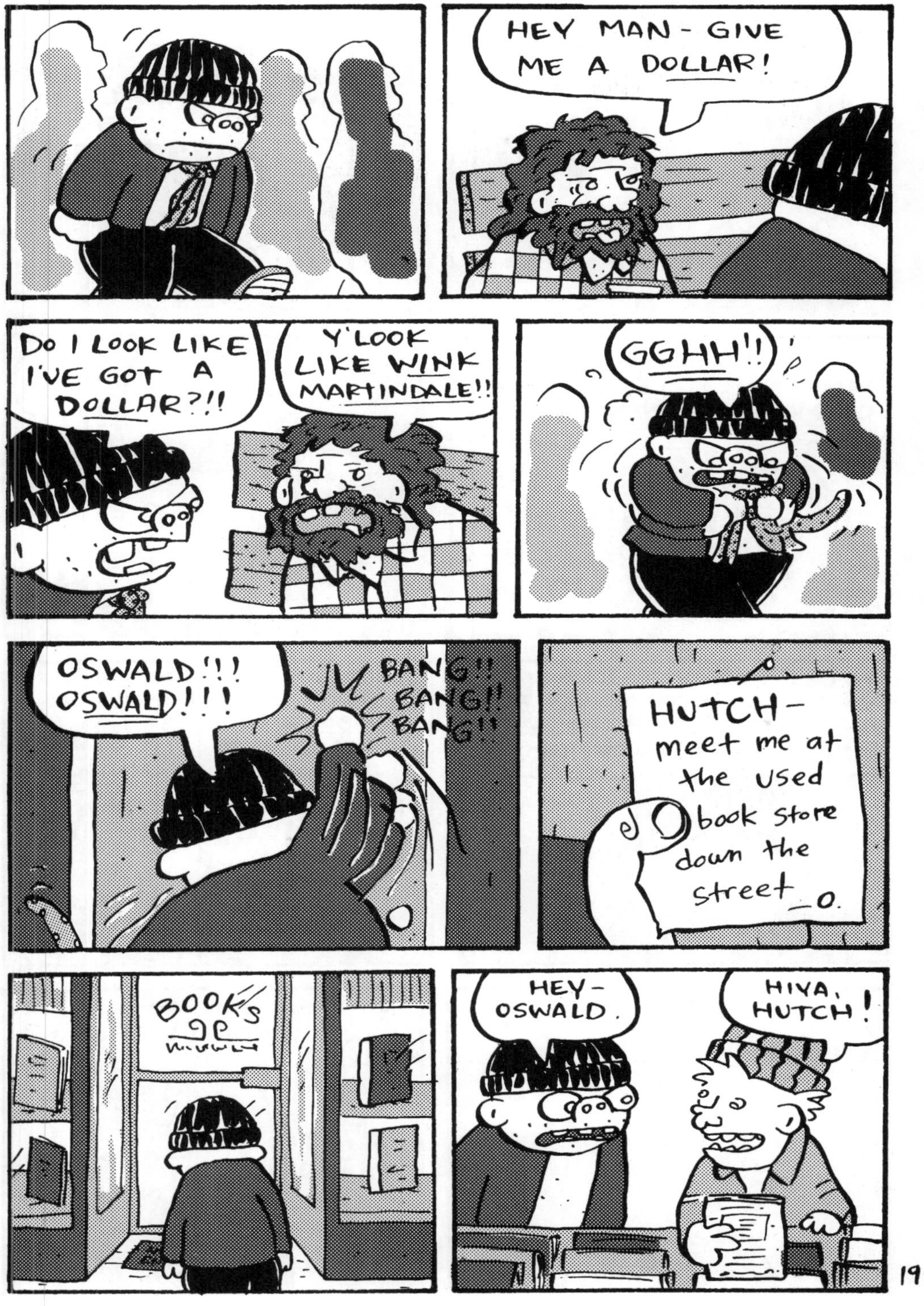
HEY MAN - GIVE ME A DOLLAR!
DO I LOOK LIKE I'VE GOT A DOLLAR?!!
Y'LOOK LIKE WINK MARTINDALE!!
GGHH!!
OSWALD!!! OSWALD!!!
BANG!! BANG!! BANG!!
HUTCH - meet me at the used book store down the street _o.
BOOKS
HEY - OSWALD.
HIYA, HUTCH!

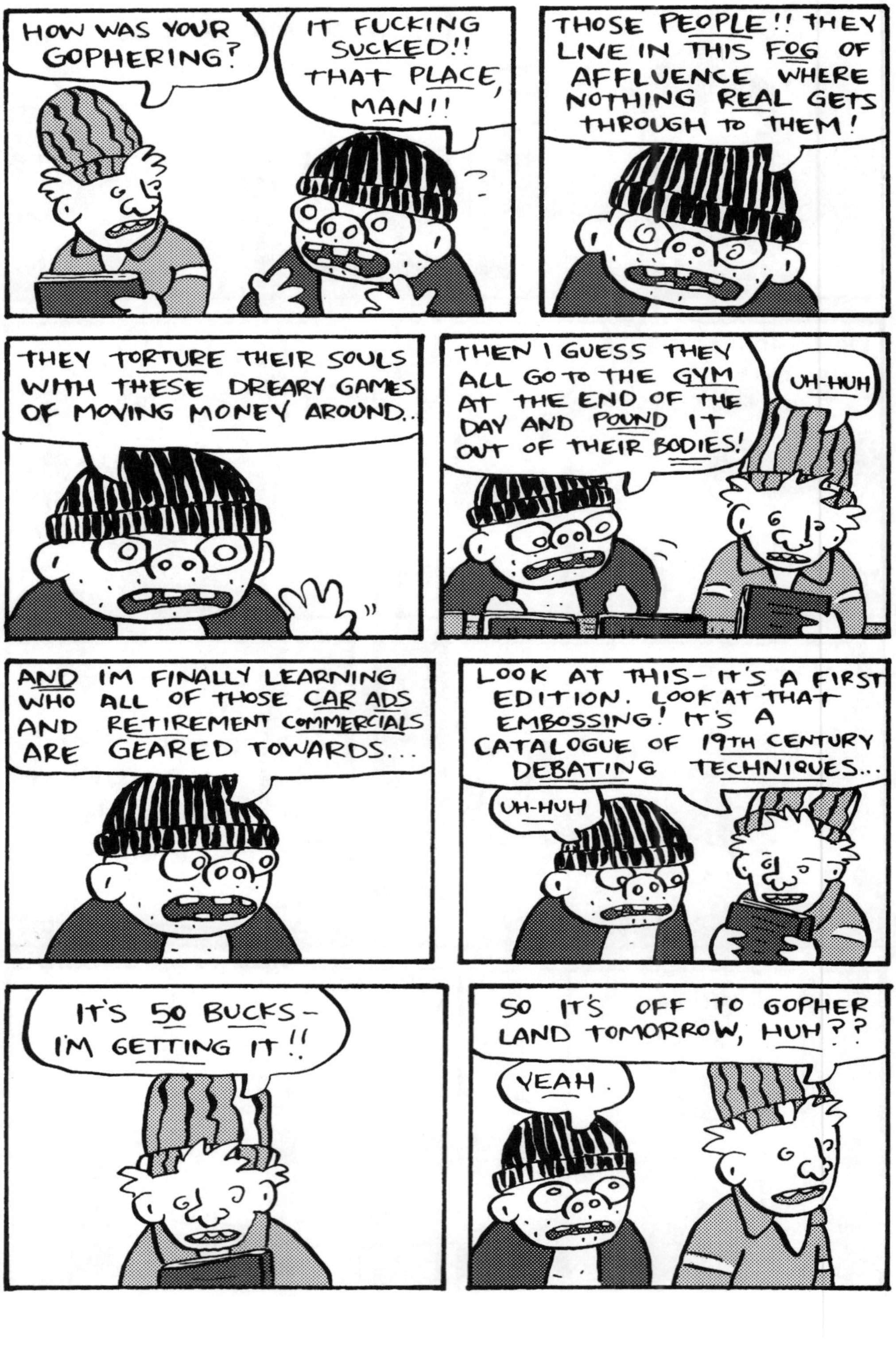
HOW WAS YOUR GOPHERING?
IT FUCKING SUCKED!! THAT PLACE, MAN!!
THOSE PEOPLE!! THEY LIVE IN THIS FOG OF AFFLUENCE WHERE NOTHING REAL GETS THROUGH TO THEM!
THEY TORTURE THEIR SOULS WITH THESE DREARY GAMES OF MOVING MONEY AROUND..
THEN I GUESS THEY ALL GO TO THE GYM AT THE END OF THE DAY AND POUND IT OUT OF THEIR BODIES!
UH-HUH
AND I'M FINALLY LEARNING WHO ALL OF THOSE CAR ADS AND RETIREMENT COMMERCIALS ARE GEARED TOWARDS...
LOOK AT THIS- IT'S A FIRST EDITION. LOOK AT THAT EMBOSSING! IT'S A CATALOGUE OF 19TH CENTURY DEBATING TECHNIQUES...
UH-HUH
IT'S 50 BUCKS- I'M GETTING IT!!
SO IT'S OFF TO GOPHER LAND TOMORROW, HUH??
YEAH.

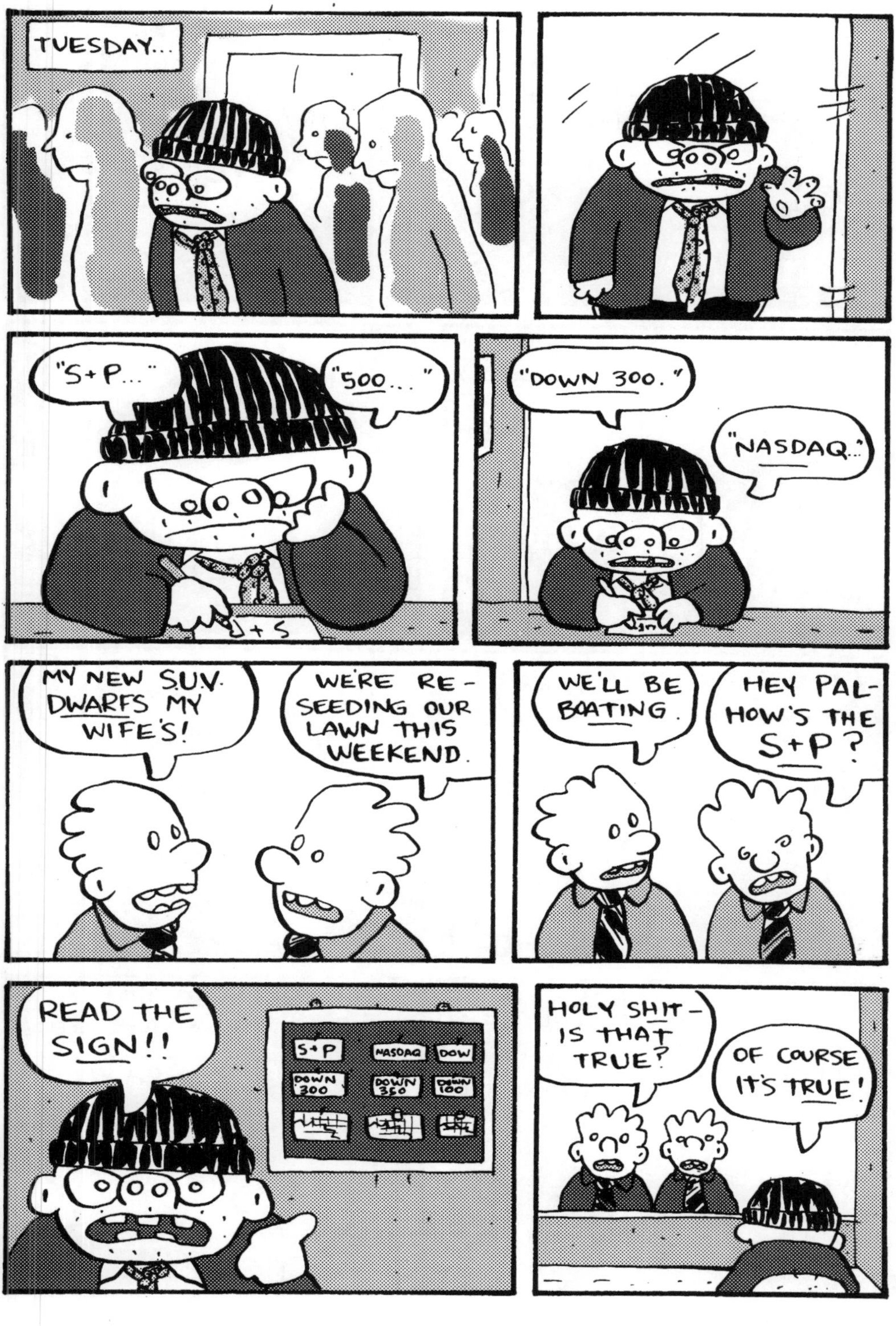

TUESDAY...
"S+P..."
"500..."
"DOWN 300."
"NASDAQ..."
MY NEW S.U.V. DWARFS MY WIFE'S!
WE'RE RE-SEEDING OUR LAWN THIS WEEKEND.
WE'LL BE BOATING.
HEY PAL-HOW'S THE S+P?
READ THE SIGN!!
S+P
NASDAQ
DOW
DOWN 300
DOWN 350
DOWN 100
HOLY SHIT-IS THAT TRUE?
OF COURSE IT'S TRUE!

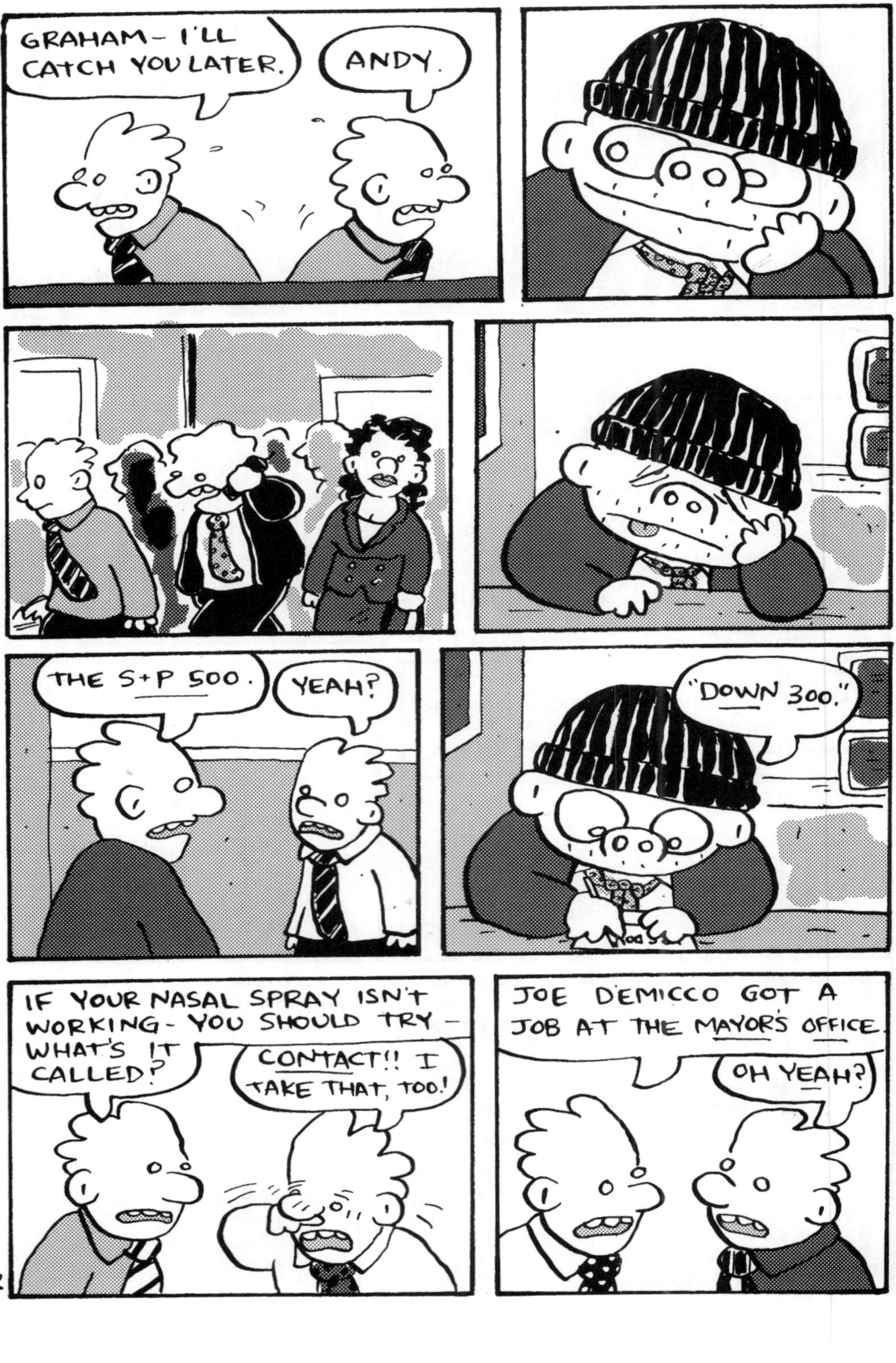

GRAHAM- I'LL CATCH YOU LATER.
ANDY.
THE S+P 500.
YEAH?
"DOWN 300."
IF YOUR NASAL SPRAY ISN'T WORKING- YOU SHOULD TRY- WHAT'S IT CALLED?
CONTACT!! I TAKE THAT, TOO!
JOE DEMICCO GOT A JOB AT THE MAYOR'S OFFICE.
OH YEAH?

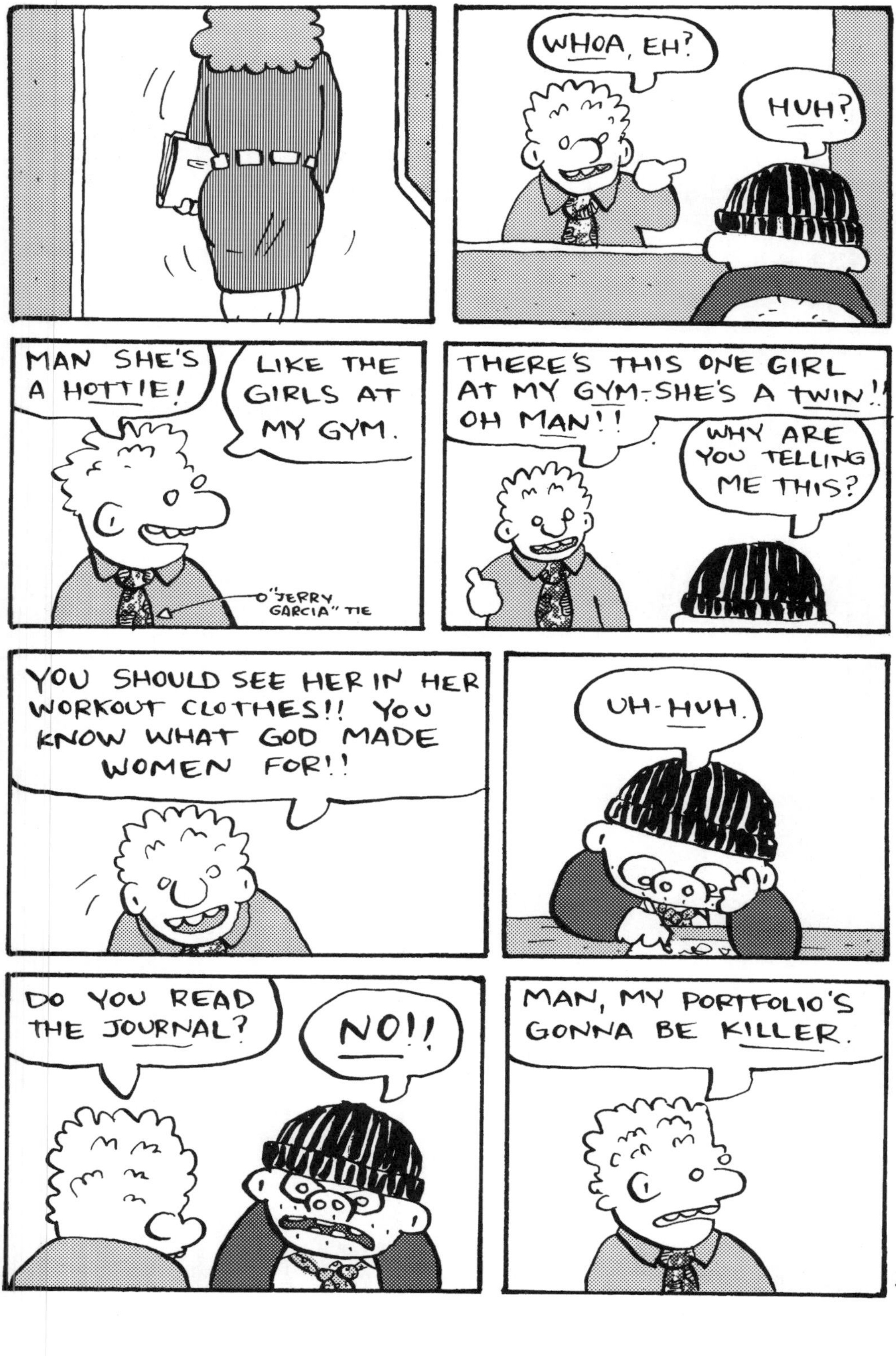
WHOA, EH?
HUH?
MAN SHE'S A HOTTIE!
LIKE THE GIRLS AT MY GYM.
"JERRY GARCIA" TIE
THERE'S THIS ONE GIRL AT MY GYM-SHE'S A TWIN!! OH MAN!!
WHY ARE YOU TELLING ME THIS?
YOU SHOULD SEE HER IN HER WORKOUT CLOTHES!! YOU KNOW WHAT GOD MADE WOMEN FOR!!
UH-HUH.
DO YOU READ THE JOURNAL?
NO!!
MAN, MY PORTFOLIO'S GONNA BE KILLER.

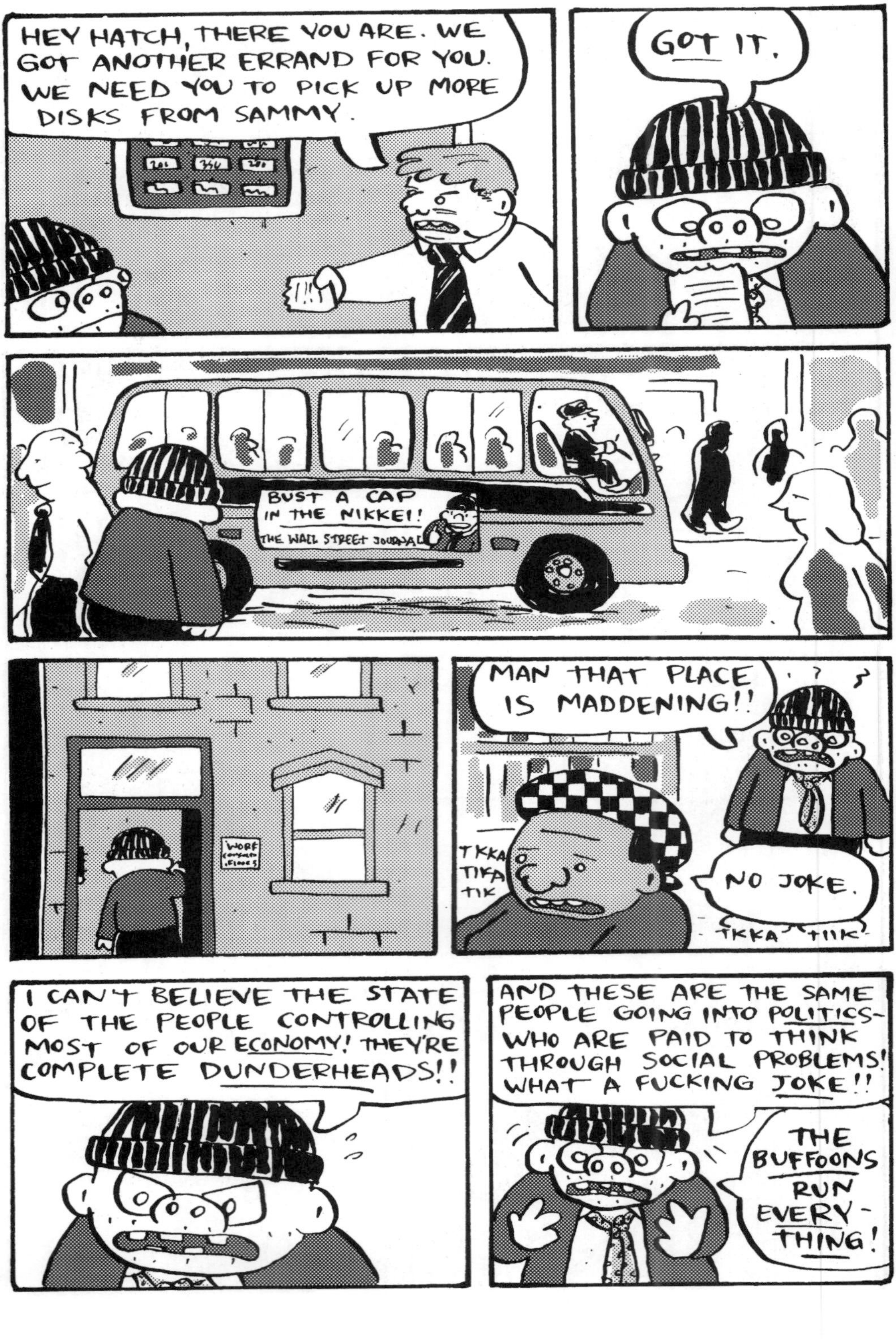
HEY HATCH, THERE YOU ARE. WE GOT ANOTHER ERRAND FOR YOU. WE NEED YOU TO PICK UP MORE DISKS FROM SAMMY.
GOT IT.
BUST A CAP IN THE NIKKEI!
THE WALL STREET JOURNAL
MAN THAT PLACE IS MADDENING!!
TKKA TIKA TIK
NO JOKE.
TKKA TIIK
I CAN'T BELIEVE THE STATE OF THE PEOPLE CONTROLLING MOST OF OUR ECONOMY! THEY'RE COMPLETE DUNDERHEADS!!
AND THESE ARE THE SAME PEOPLE GOING INTO POLITICS- WHO ARE PAID TO THINK THROUGH SOCIAL PROBLEMS! WHAT A FUCKING JOKE!!
THE BUFFOONS RUN EVERY-THING!

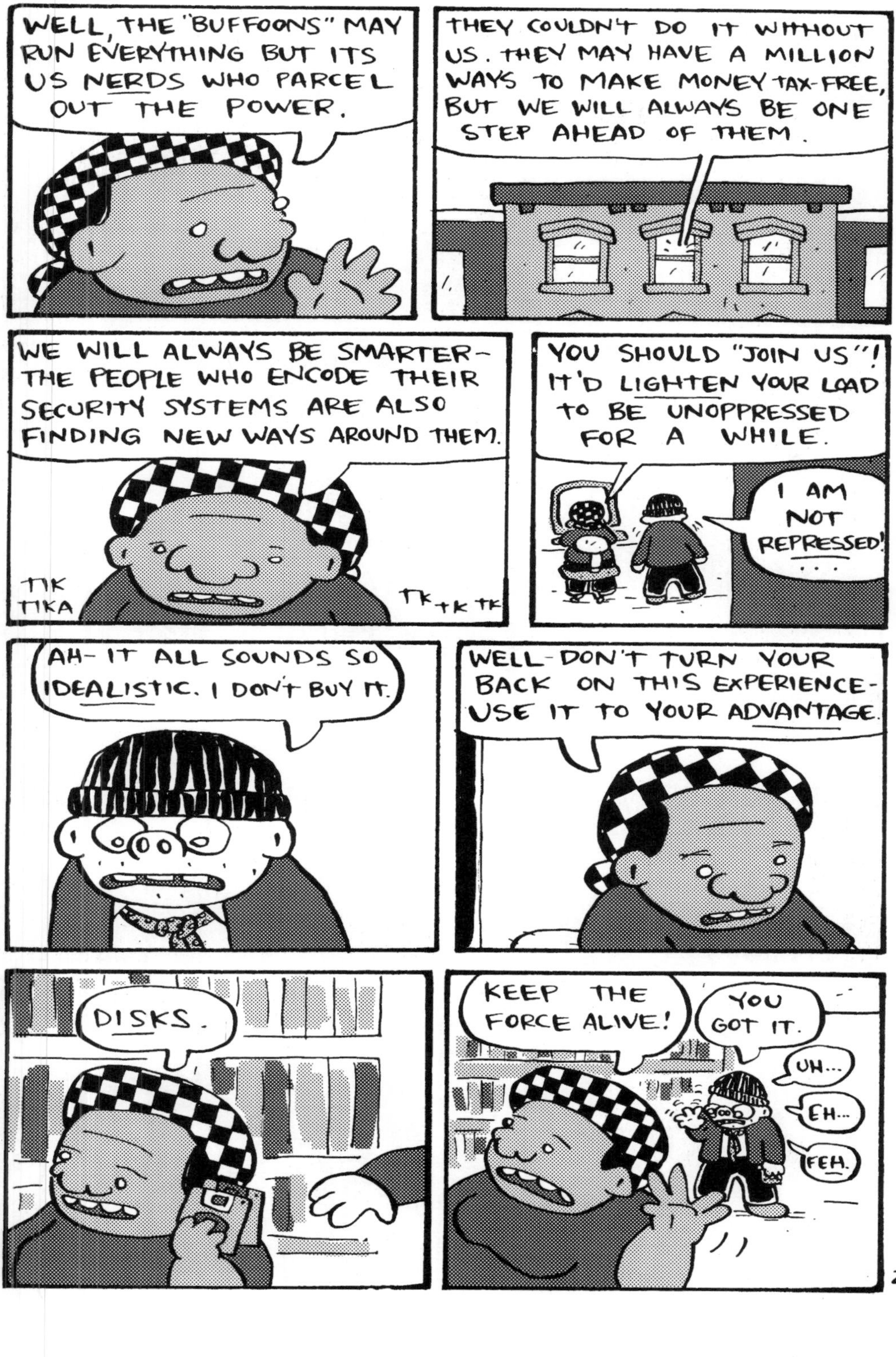

WELL, THE "BUFFOONS" MAY RUN EVERYTHING BUT ITS US NERDS WHO PARCEL OUT THE POWER.
THEY COULDN'T DO IT WITHOUT US. THEY MAY HAVE A MILLION WAYS TO MAKE MONEY TAX-FREE, BUT WE WILL ALWAYS BE ONE STEP AHEAD OF THEM.
WE WILL ALWAYS BE SMARTER- THE PEOPLE WHO ENCODE THEIR SECURITY SYSTEMS ARE ALSO FINDING NEW WAYS AROUND THEM.
TIK TIKA
TK TK TK
YOU SHOULD "JOIN US"! IT'D LIGHTEN YOUR LOAD TO BE UNOPPRESSED FOR A WHILE.
I AM NOT REPRESSED! ...
AH- IT ALL SOUNDS SO IDEALISTIC. I DON'T BUY IT.
WELL- DON'T TURN YOUR BACK ON THIS EXPERIENCE- USE IT TO YOUR ADVANTAGE.
DISKS.
KEEP THE FORCE ALIVE!
YOU GOT IT.
UH...
EH...
FEH.

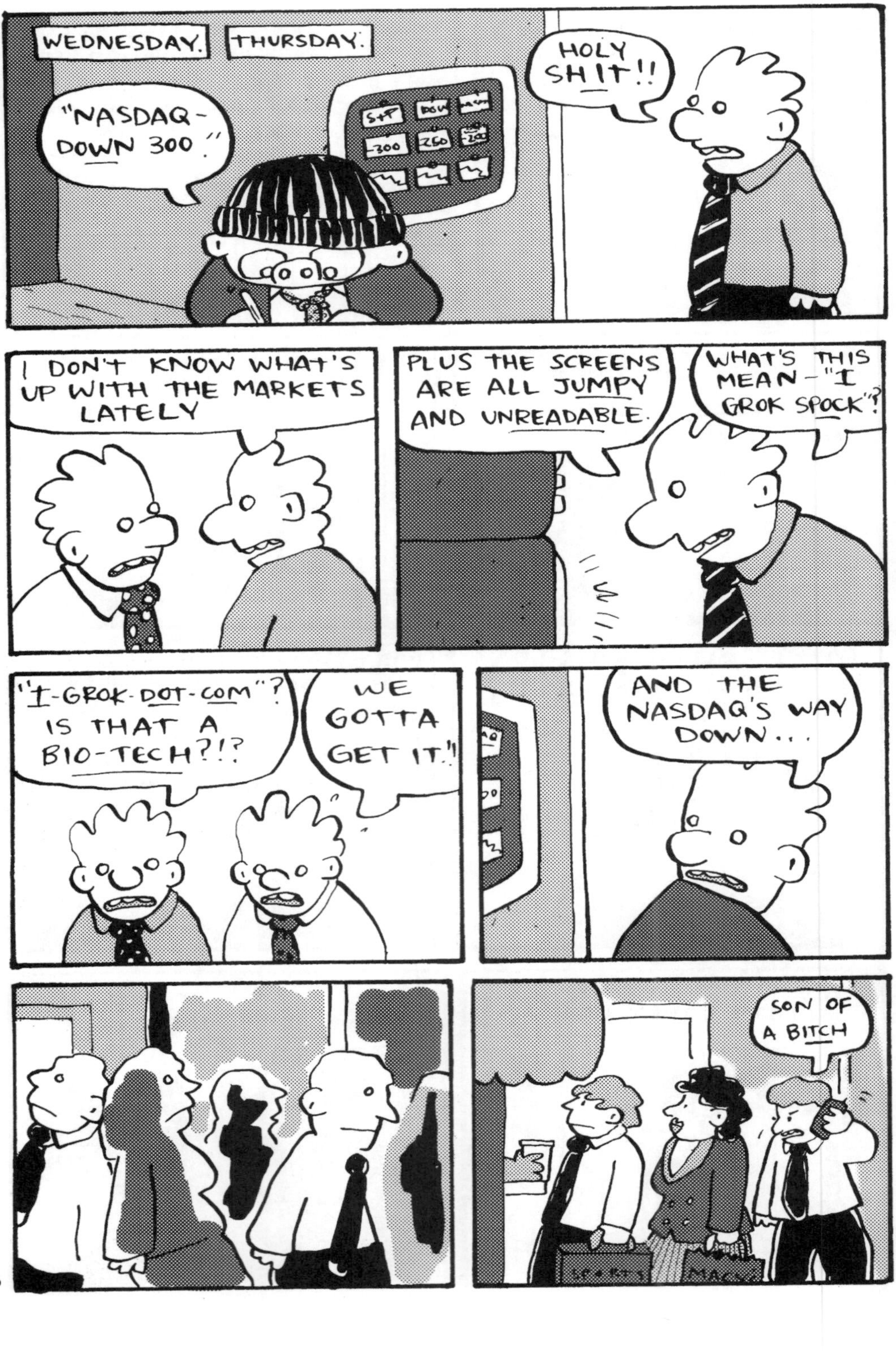
WEDNESDAY.
THURSDAY.
"NASDAQ-DOWN 300."
HOLY SHIT!!
S+P
DOW
-300
250
I DON'T KNOW WHAT'S UP WITH THE MARKETS LATELY
PLUS THE SCREENS ARE ALL JUMPY AND UNREADABLE.
WHAT'S THIS MEAN - "I GROK SPOCK"?
"I-GROK-DOT-COM"? IS THAT A BIO-TECH?!?
WE GOTTA GET IT!
AND THE NASDAQ'S WAY DOWN...
SON OF A BITCH

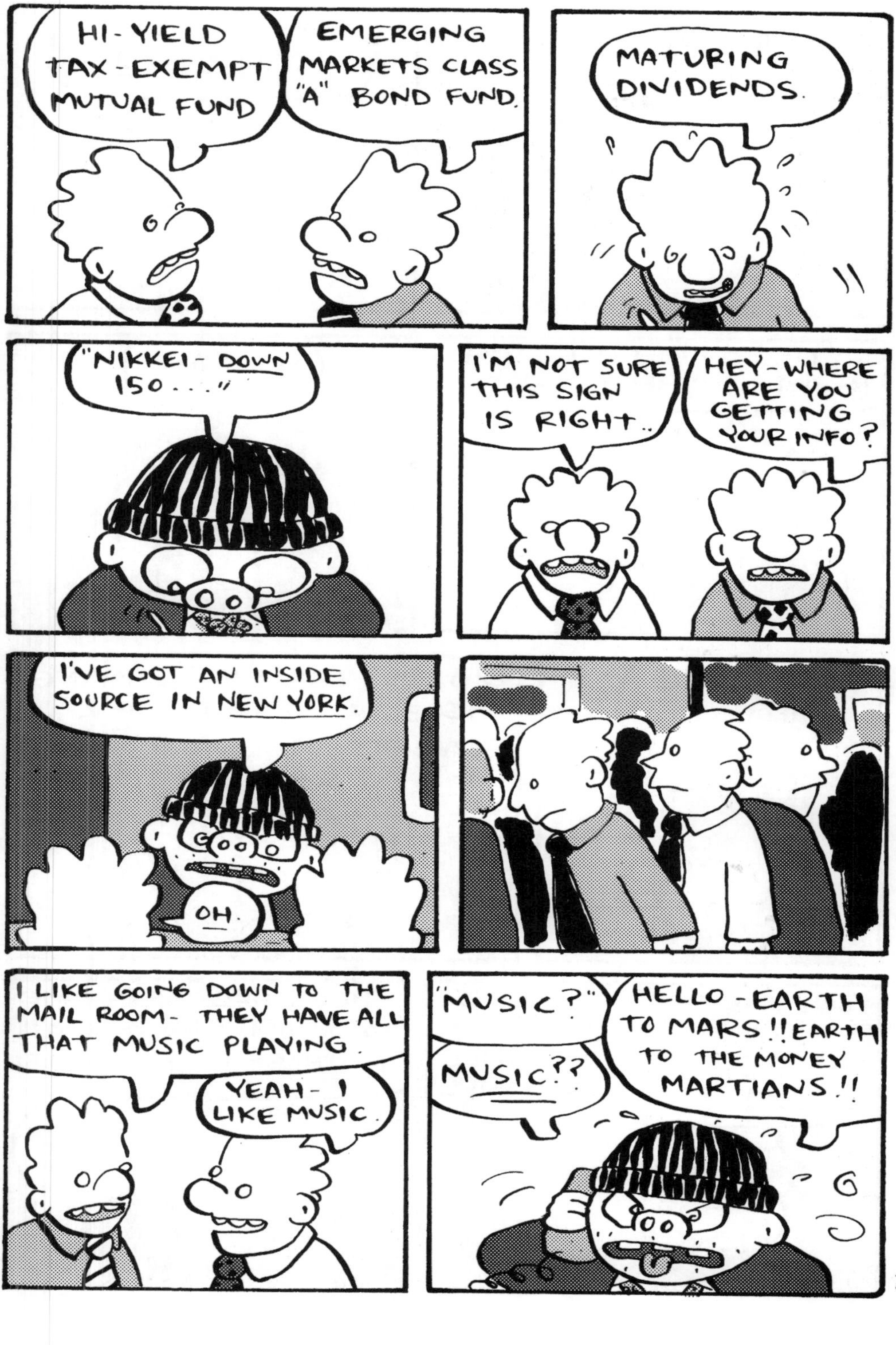
HI-YIELD TAX-EXEMPT MUTUAL FUND
EMERGING MARKETS CLASS "A" BOND FUND.
MATURING DIVIDENDS.
"NIKKEI- DOWN 150...."
I'M NOT SURE THIS SIGN IS RIGHT..
HEY- WHERE ARE YOU GETTING YOUR INFO?
I'VE GOT AN INSIDE SOURCE IN NEW YORK.
OH.
I LIKE GOING DOWN TO THE MAIL ROOM- THEY HAVE ALL THAT MUSIC PLAYING.
YEAH- I LIKE MUSIC.
"MUSIC?"
MUSIC??
HELLO-EARTH TO MARS!! EARTH TO THE MONEY MARTIANS!!

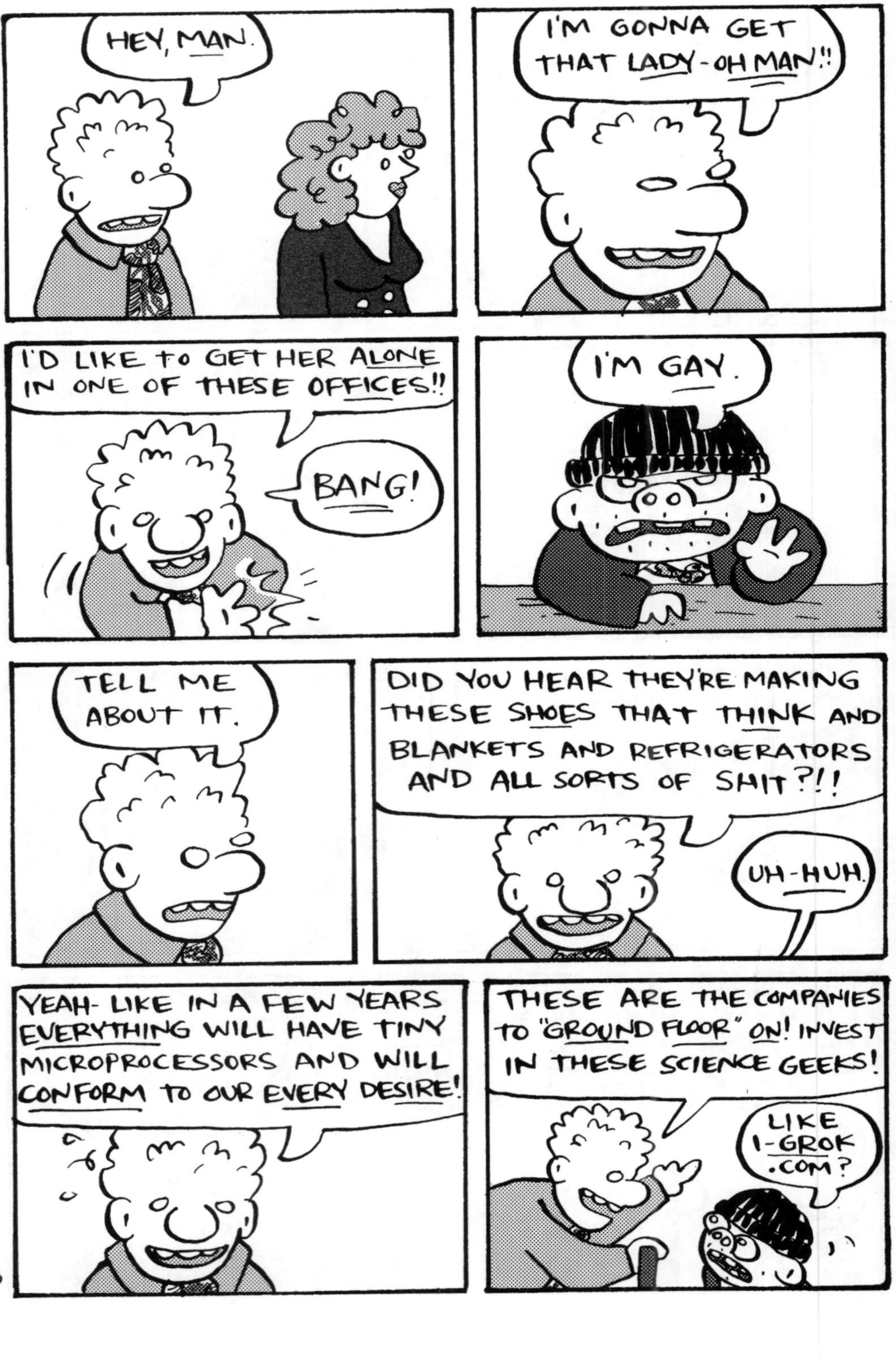
HEY, MAN.
I'M GONNA GET THAT LADY - OH MAN!!
I'D LIKE TO GET HER ALONE IN ONE OF THESE OFFICES!!
BANG!
I'M GAY.
TELL ME ABOUT IT.
DID YOU HEAR THEY'RE MAKING THESE SHOES THAT THINK AND BLANKETS AND REFRIGERATORS AND ALL SORTS OF SHIT?!!
UH-HUH.
YEAH- LIKE IN A FEW YEARS EVERYTHING WILL HAVE TINY MICROPROCESSORS AND WILL CONFORM TO OUR EVERY DESIRE!
THESE ARE THE COMPANIES TO "GROUND FLOOR" ON! INVEST IN THESE SCIENCE GEEKS!
LIKE I-GROK .COM?

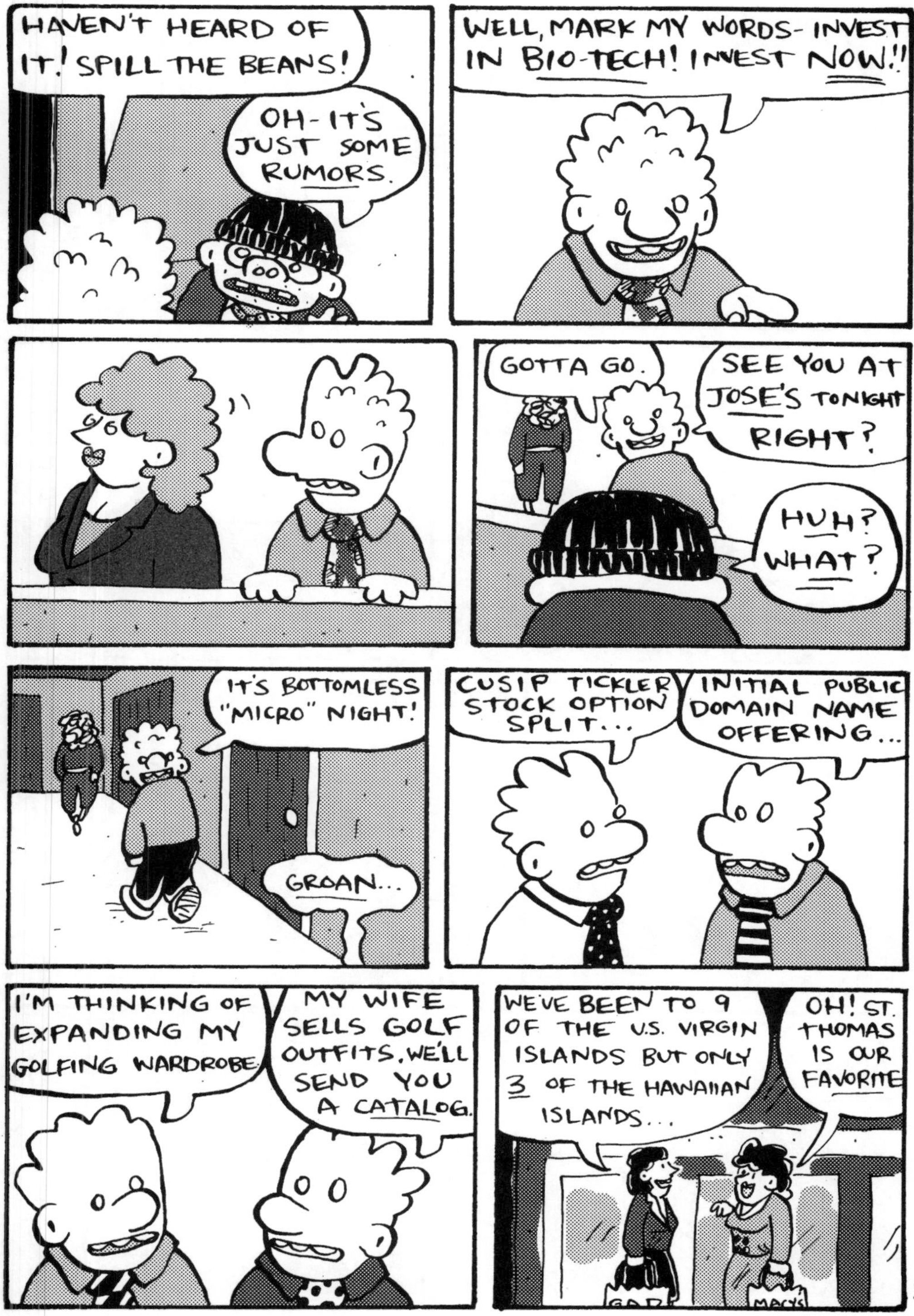
HAVEN'T HEARD OF IT! SPILL THE BEANS!
OH- IT'S JUST SOME RUMORS.
WELL, MARK MY WORDS- INVEST IN BIO-TECH! INVEST NOW!!
GOTTA GO.
SEE YOU AT JOSE'S TONIGHT RIGHT?
HUH? WHAT?
IT'S BOTTOMLESS "MICRO" NIGHT!
GROAN...
CUSIP TICKLER STOCK OPTION SPLIT...
INITIAL PUBLIC DOMAIN NAME OFFERING...
I'M THINKING OF EXPANDING MY GOLFING WARDROBE.
MY WIFE SELLS GOLF OUTFITS. WE'LL SEND YOU A CATALOG.
WE'VE BEEN TO 9 OF THE U.S. VIRGIN ISLANDS BUT ONLY 3 OF THE HAWAIIAN ISLANDS...
OH! ST. THOMAS IS OUR FAVORITE
MACY'S

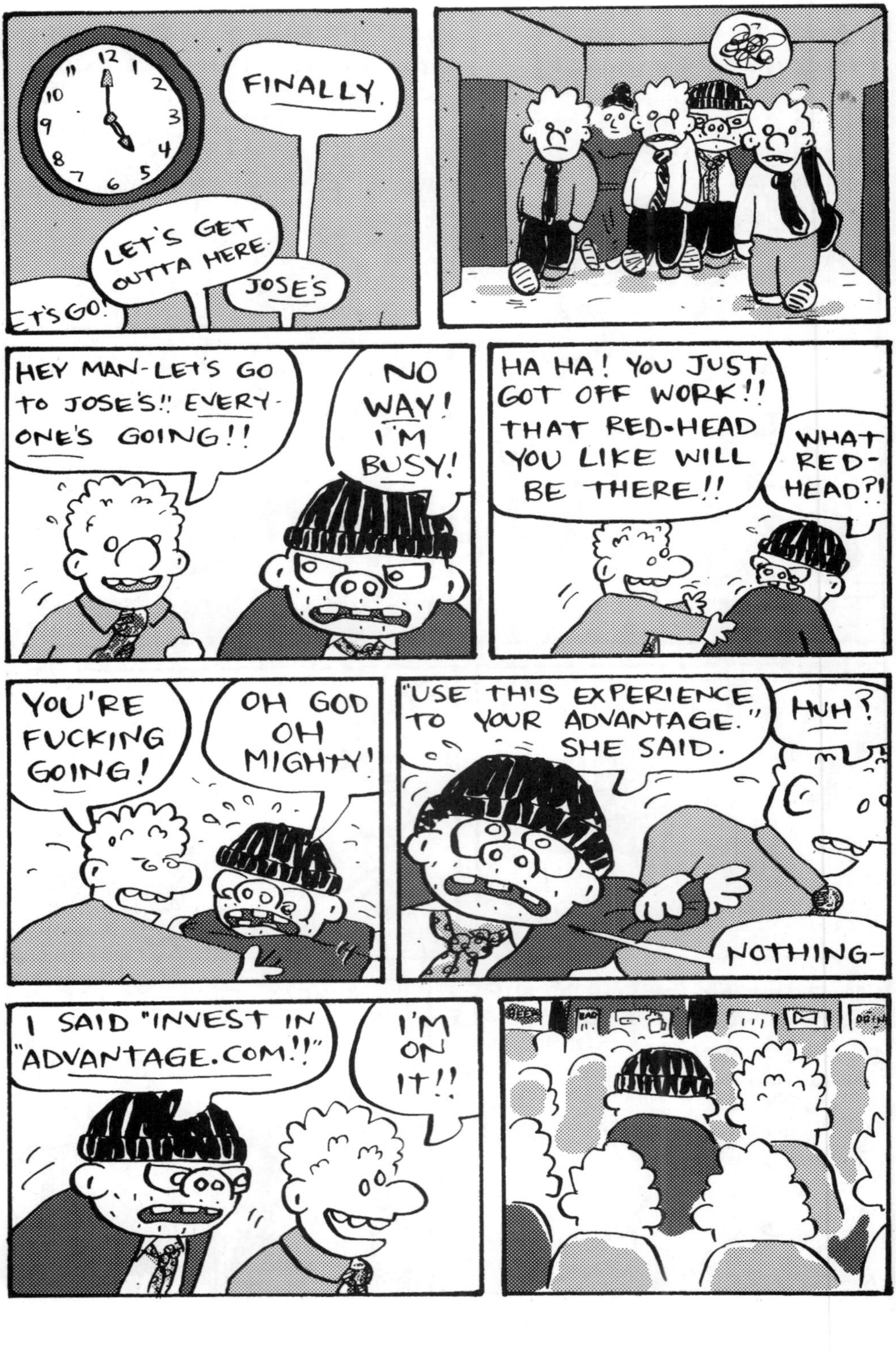

12 1 2 3 4 5 6 7 8 9 10 11
FINALLY.
LET'S GET OUTTA HERE.
JOSE'S
ET'S GO!
HEY MAN-LET'S GO TO JOSE'S!! EVERY-ONE'S GOING!!
NO WAY! I'M BUSY!
HA HA! YOU JUST GOT OFF WORK!! THAT RED-HEAD YOU LIKE WILL BE THERE!!
WHAT RED-HEAD?!
YOU'RE FUCKING GOING!
OH GOD OH MIGHTY!
"USE THIS EXPERIENCE TO YOUR ADVANTAGE." SHE SAID.
HUH?
NOTHING-
I SAID "INVEST IN "ADVANTAGE.COM!!"
I'M ON IT!!

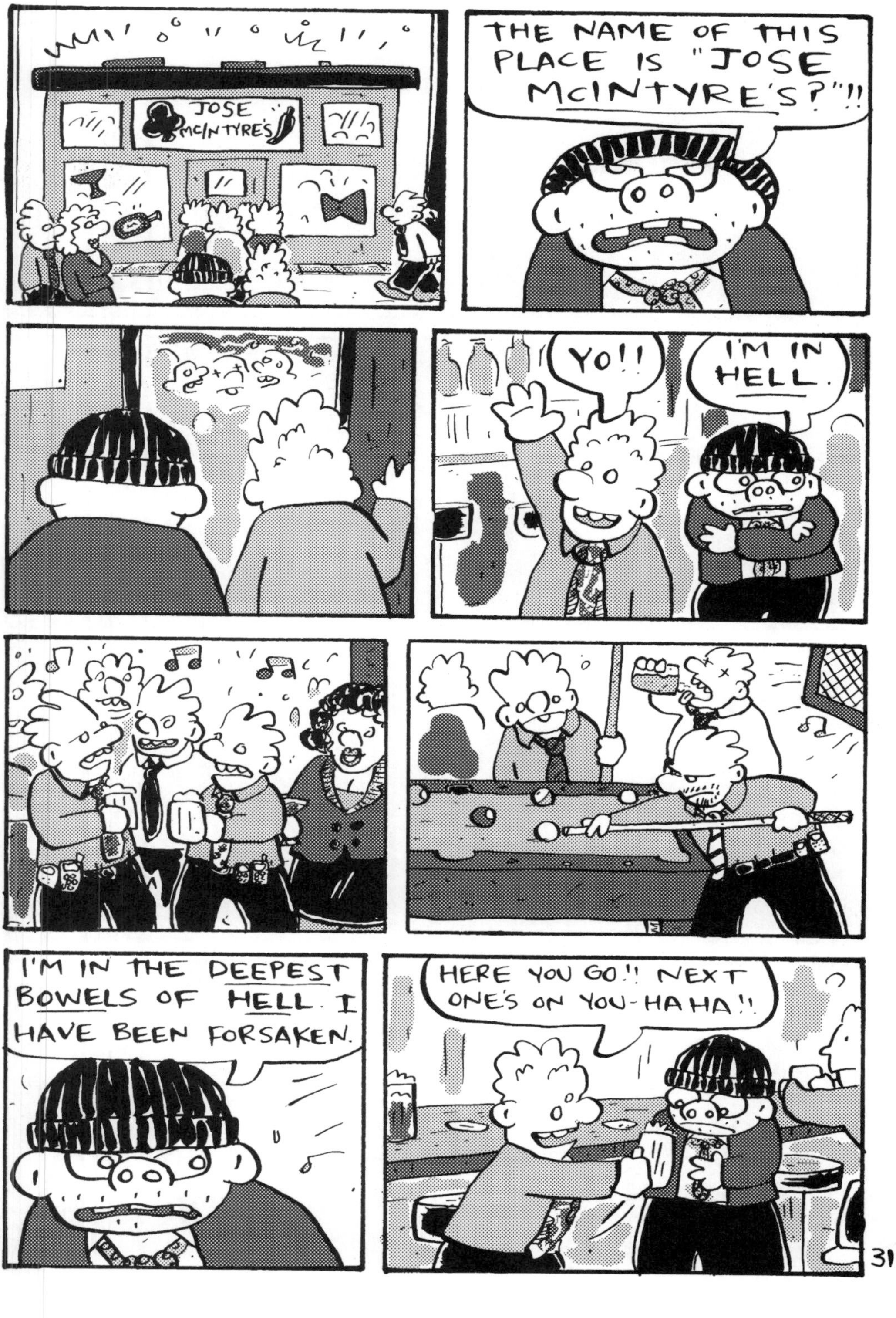
JOSE McINTYRE'S
THE NAME OF THIS PLACE IS "JOSE McINTYRE'S?"!!
YO!!
I'M IN HELL.
I'M IN THE DEEPEST BOWELS OF HELL. I HAVE BEEN FORSAKEN.
HERE YOU GO!! NEXT ONE'S ON YOU-HAHA!!

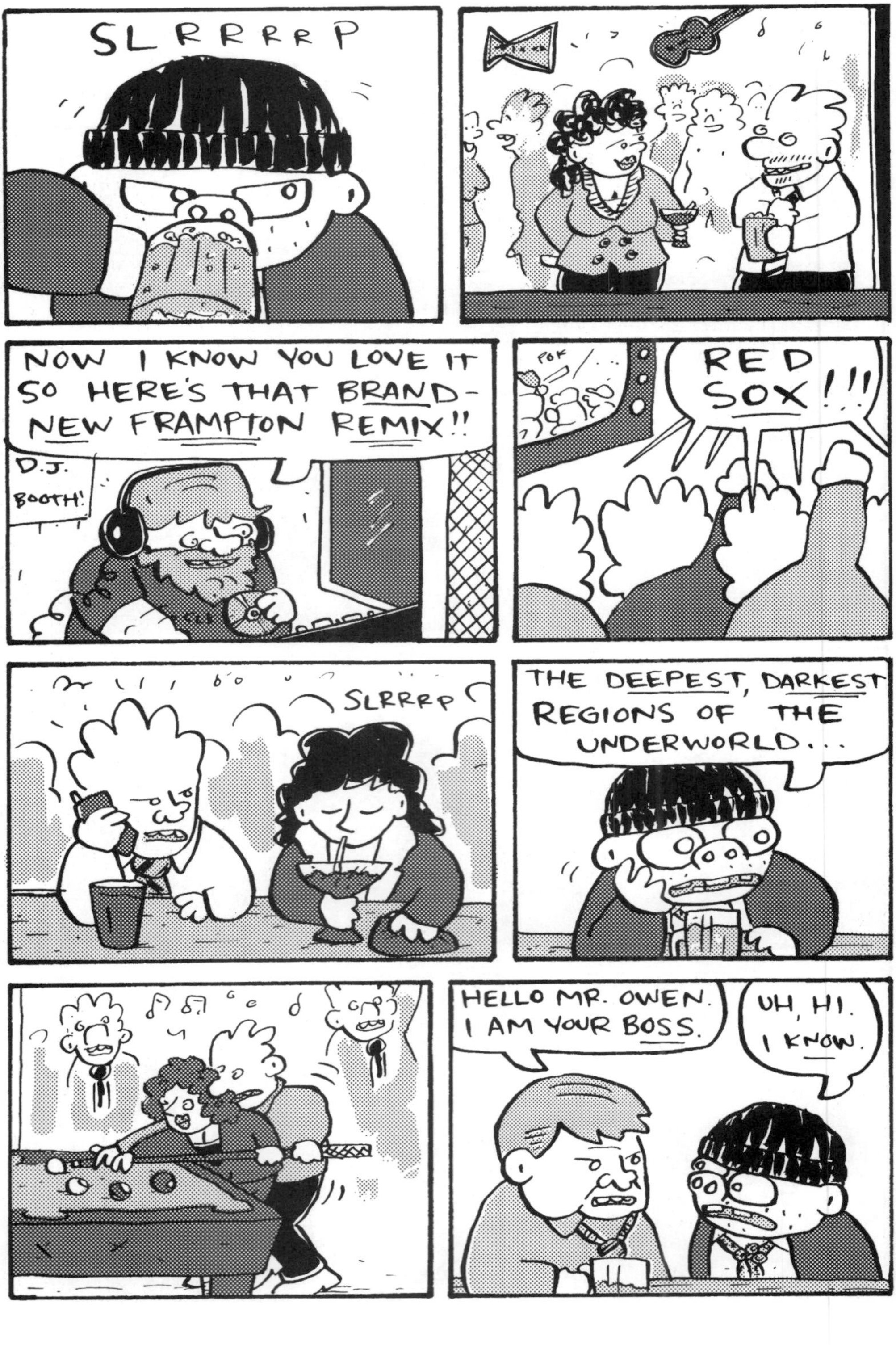
SLRRRRP
NOW I KNOW YOU LOVE IT SO HERE'S THAT BRAND-NEW FRAMPTON REMIX!!
D.J. BOOTH!
RED SOX!!!
SLRRRP
THE DEEPEST, DARKEST REGIONS OF THE UNDERWORLD...
HELLO MR. OWEN. I AM YOUR BOSS.
UH, HI. I KNOW.

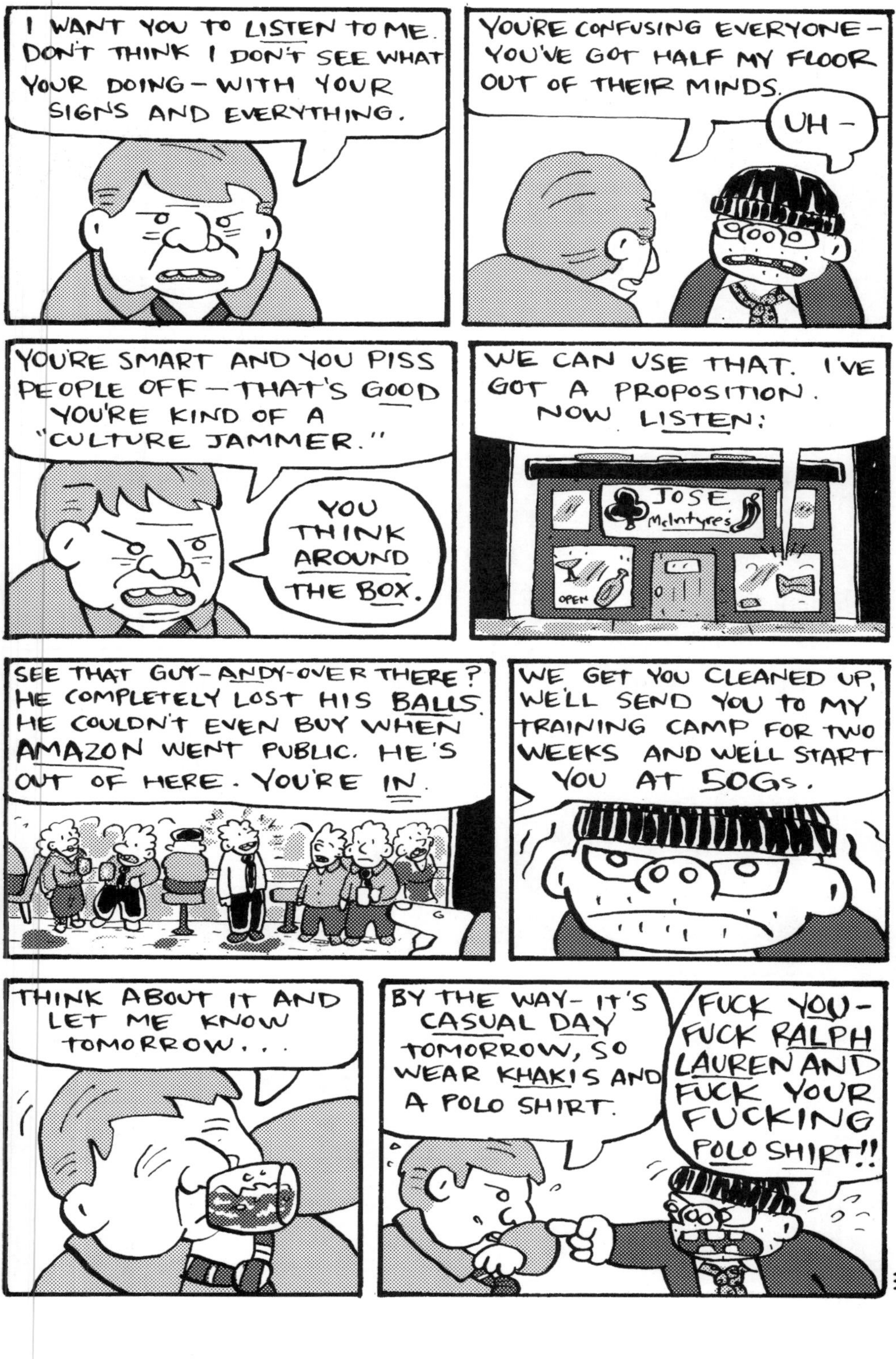
I WANT YOU TO LISTEN TO ME. DON'T THINK I DON'T SEE WHAT YOUR DOING – WITH YOUR SIGNS AND EVERYTHING.
YOU'RE CONFUSING EVERYONE – YOU'VE GOT HALF MY FLOOR OUT OF THEIR MINDS.
UH –
YOU'RE SMART AND YOU PISS PEOPLE OFF – THAT'S GOOD YOU'RE KIND OF A "CULTURE JAMMER."
YOU THINK AROUND THE BOX.
WE CAN USE THAT. I'VE GOT A PROPOSITION. NOW LISTEN:
JOSE McIntyres
OPEN
SEE THAT GUY – ANDY – OVER THERE? HE COMPLETELY LOST HIS BALLS. HE COULDN'T EVEN BUY WHEN AMAZON WENT PUBLIC. HE'S OUT OF HERE. YOU'RE IN.
WE GET YOU CLEANED UP, WE'LL SEND YOU TO MY TRAINING CAMP FOR TWO WEEKS AND WE'LL START YOU AT 50Gs.
THINK ABOUT IT AND LET ME KNOW TOMORROW...
BY THE WAY – IT'S CASUAL DAY TOMORROW, SO WEAR KHAKIS AND A POLO SHIRT.
FUCK YOU – FUCK RALPH LAUREN AND FUCK YOUR FUCKING POLO SHIRT!!

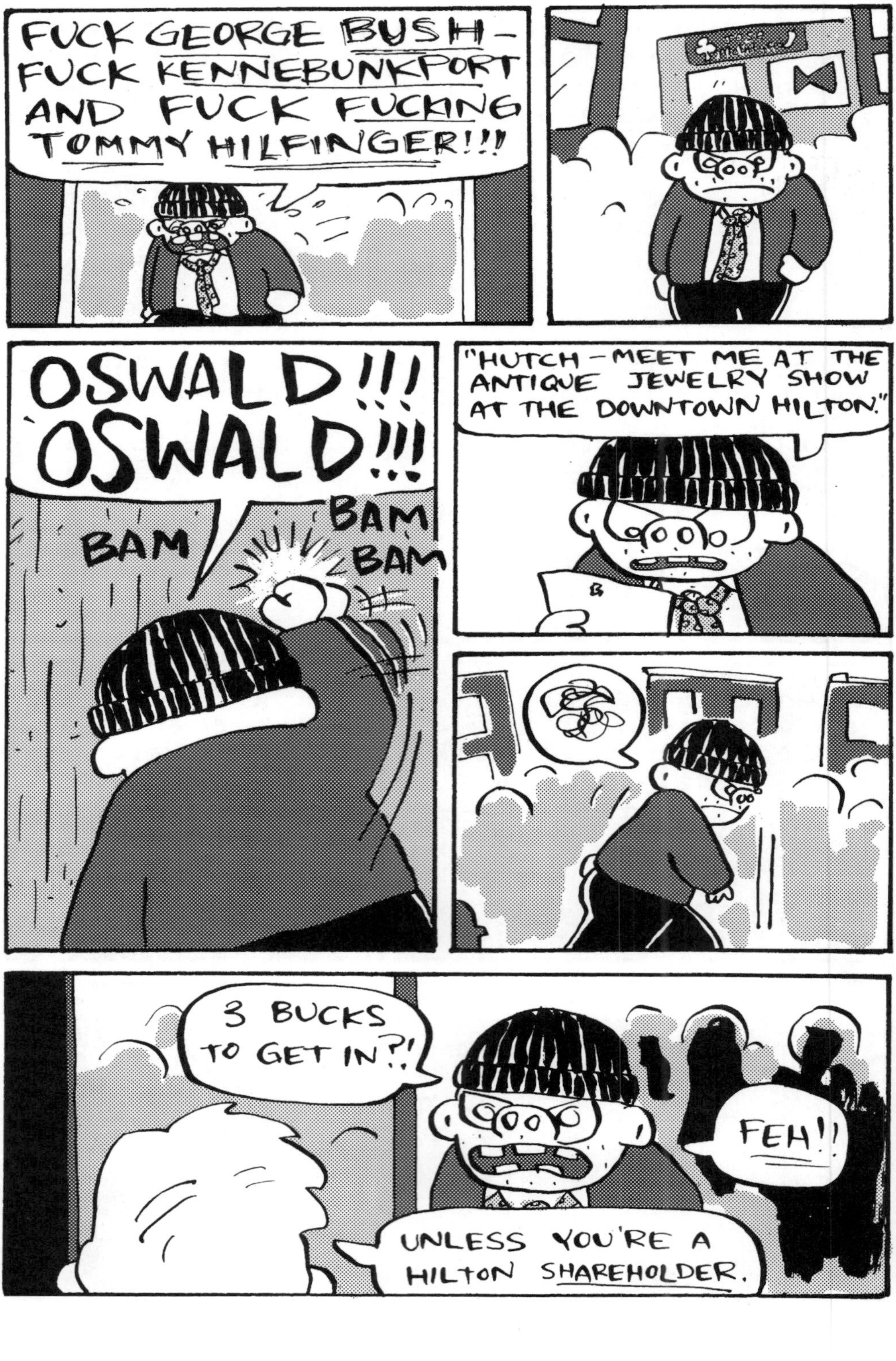
FUCK GEORGE BUSH - FUCK KENNEBUNKPORT AND FUCK FUCKING TOMMY HILFINGER!!!
OSWALD!!! OSWALD!!!
BAM
BAM BAM
"HUTCH - MEET ME AT THE ANTIQUE JEWELRY SHOW AT THE DOWNTOWN HILTON."
3 BUCKS TO GET IN?!
FEH!!
UNLESS YOU'RE A HILTON SHAREHOLDER.

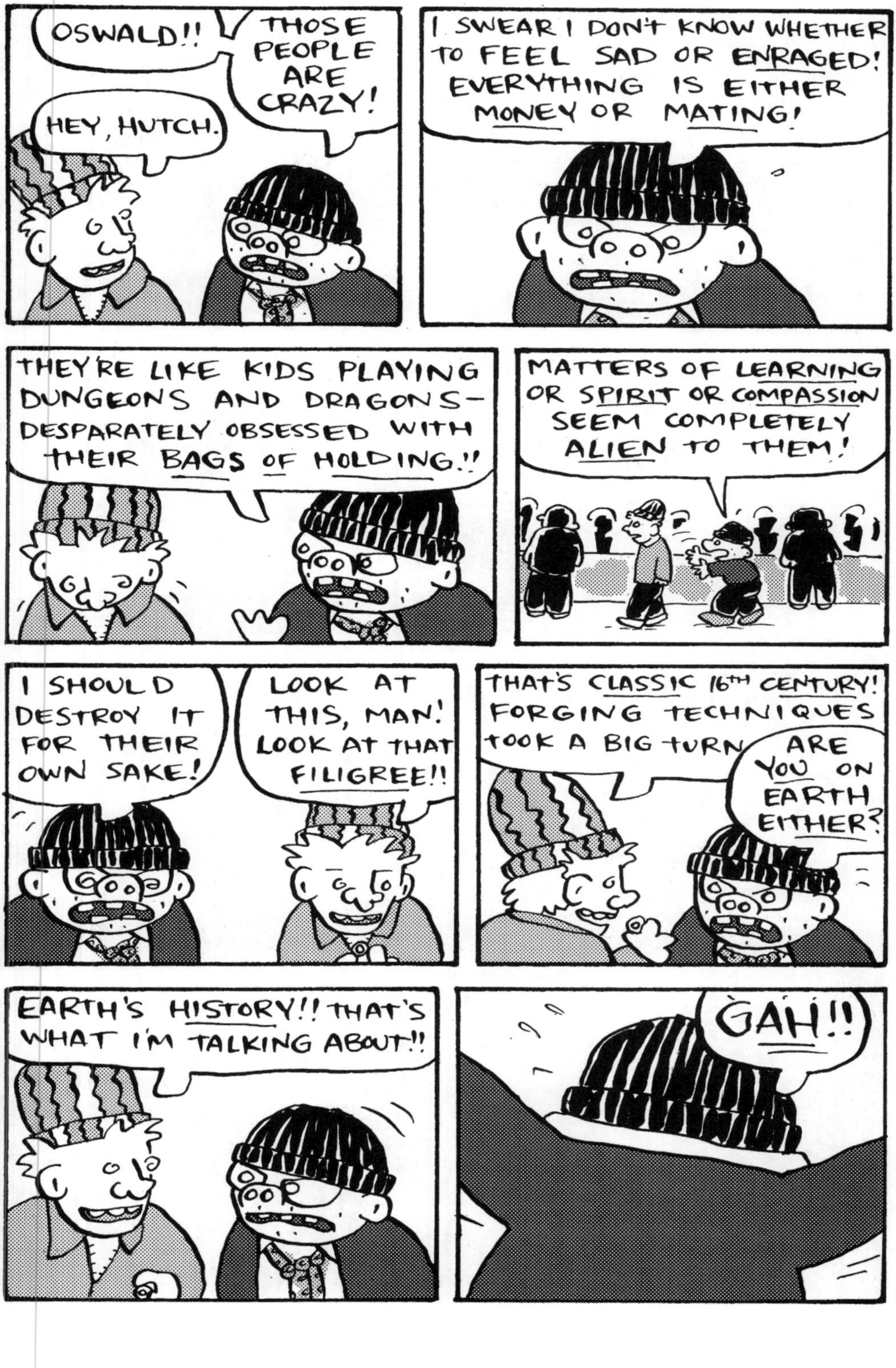
OSWALD!!
HEY, HUTCH.
THOSE PEOPLE ARE CRAZY!
I SWEAR I DON'T KNOW WHETHER TO FEEL SAD OR ENRAGED! EVERYTHING IS EITHER MONEY OR MATING!
THEY'RE LIKE KIDS PLAYING DUNGEONS AND DRAGONS- DESPARATELY OBSESSED WITH THEIR BAGS OF HOLDING!!
MATTERS OF LEARNING OR SPIRIT OR COMPASSION SEEM COMPLETELY ALIEN TO THEM!
I SHOULD DESTROY IT FOR THEIR OWN SAKE!
LOOK AT THIS, MAN! LOOK AT THAT FILIGREE!!
THAT'S CLASSIC 16TH CENTURY! FORGING TECHNIQUES TOOK A BIG TURN
ARE YOU ON EARTH EITHER?
EARTH'S HISTORY!! THAT'S WHAT I'M TALKING ABOUT!!
GAH!!

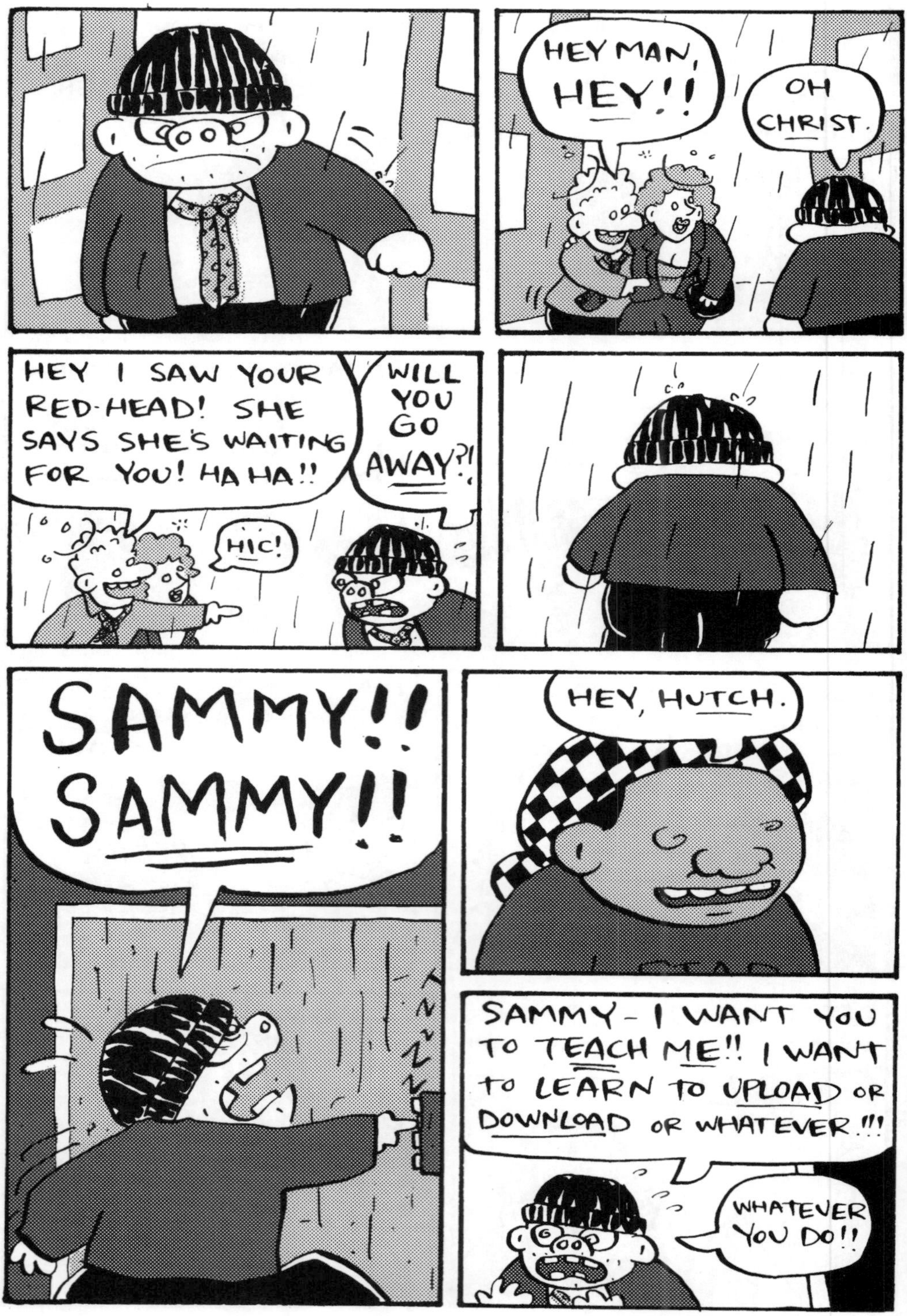

HEY MAN, HEY!!
OH CHRIST.
HEY I SAW YOUR RED-HEAD! SHE SAYS SHE'S WAITING FOR YOU! HA HA!!
WILL YOU GO AWAY?!
HIC!
SAMMY!! SAMMY!!
HEY, HUTCH.
SAMMY - I WANT YOU TO TEACH ME!! I WANT TO LEARN TO UPLOAD OR DOWNLOAD OR WHATEVER!!!
WHATEVER YOU DO!!

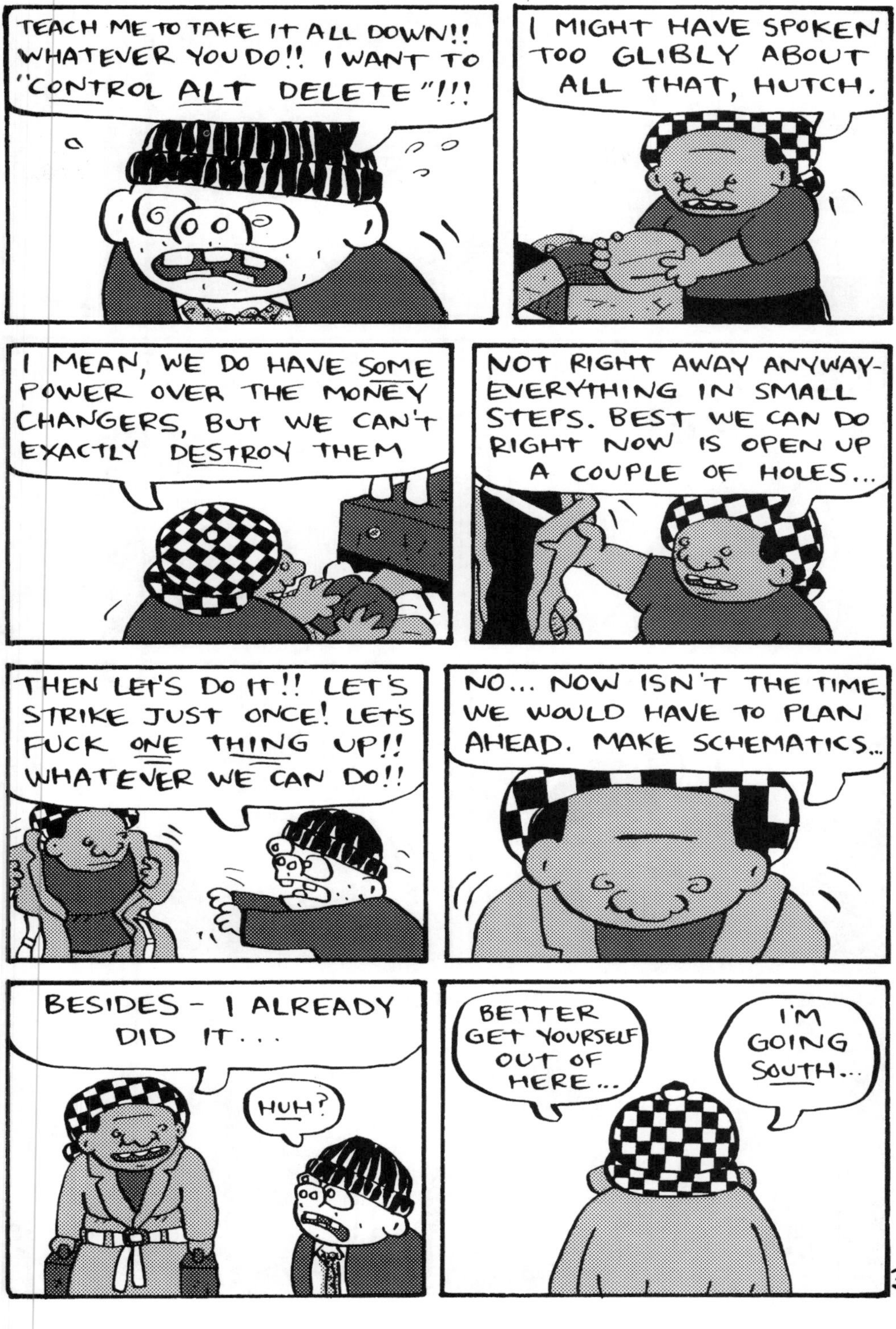
TEACH ME TO TAKE IT ALL DOWN!! WHATEVER YOU DO!! I WANT TO "CONTROL ALT DELETE"!!!
I MIGHT HAVE SPOKEN TOO GLIBLY ABOUT ALL THAT, HUTCH.
I MEAN, WE DO HAVE SOME POWER OVER THE MONEY CHANGERS, BUT WE CAN'T EXACTLY DESTROY THEM
NOT RIGHT AWAY ANYWAY- EVERYTHING IN SMALL STEPS. BEST WE CAN DO RIGHT NOW IS OPEN UP A COUPLE OF HOLES...
THEN LET'S DO IT!! LET'S STRIKE JUST ONCE! LET'S FUCK ONE THING UP!! WHATEVER WE CAN DO!!
NO... NOW ISN'T THE TIME. WE WOULD HAVE TO PLAN AHEAD. MAKE SCHEMATICS...
BESIDES - I ALREADY DID IT...
HUH?
BETTER GET YOURSELF OUT OF HERE...
I'M GOING SOUTH...

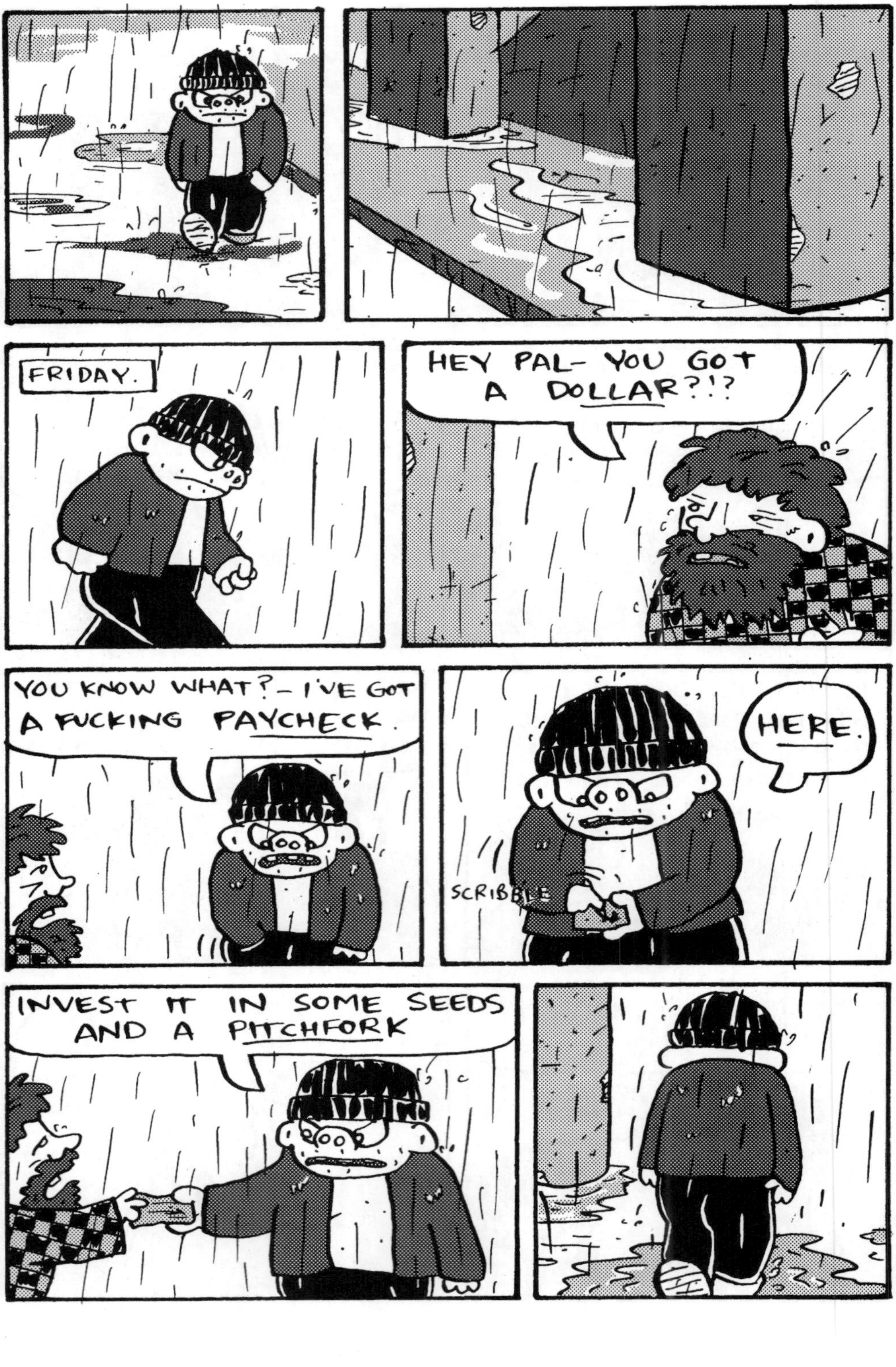
FRIDAY.
HEY PAL- YOU GOT A DOLLAR?!?
YOU KNOW WHAT?- I'VE GOT A FUCKING PAYCHECK.
HERE.
SCRIBBLE
INVEST IT IN SOME SEEDS AND A PITCHFORK

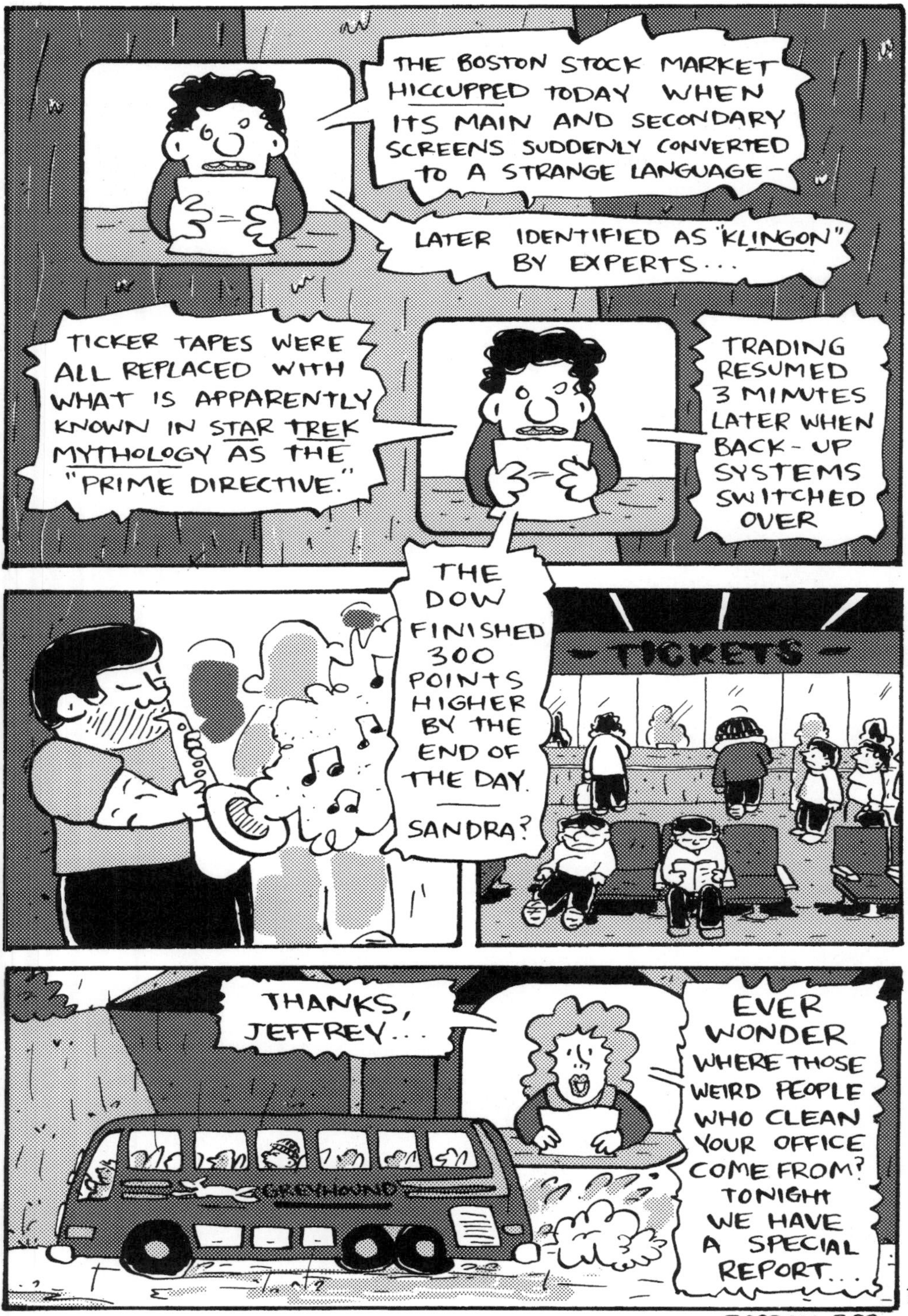
THE BOSTON STOCK MARKET HICCUPPED TODAY WHEN ITS MAIN AND SECONDARY SCREENS SUDDENLY CONVERTED TO A STRANGE LANGUAGE—
LATER IDENTIFIED AS "KLINGON" BY EXPERTS...
TICKER TAPES WERE ALL REPLACED WITH WHAT IS APPARENTLY KNOWN IN STAR TREK MYTHOLOGY AS THE "PRIME DIRECTIVE."
TRADING RESUMED 3 MINUTES LATER WHEN BACK-UP SYSTEMS SWITCHED OVER
THE DOW FINISHED 300 POINTS HIGHER BY THE END OF THE DAY.
SANDRA?
TICKETS
THANKS, JEFFREY...
EVER WONDER WHERE THOSE WEIRD PEOPLE WHO CLEAN YOUR OFFICE COME FROM? TONIGHT WE HAVE A SPECIAL REPORT...
GREYHOUND

-BOSTON 8.99-

IV . The Road to Self

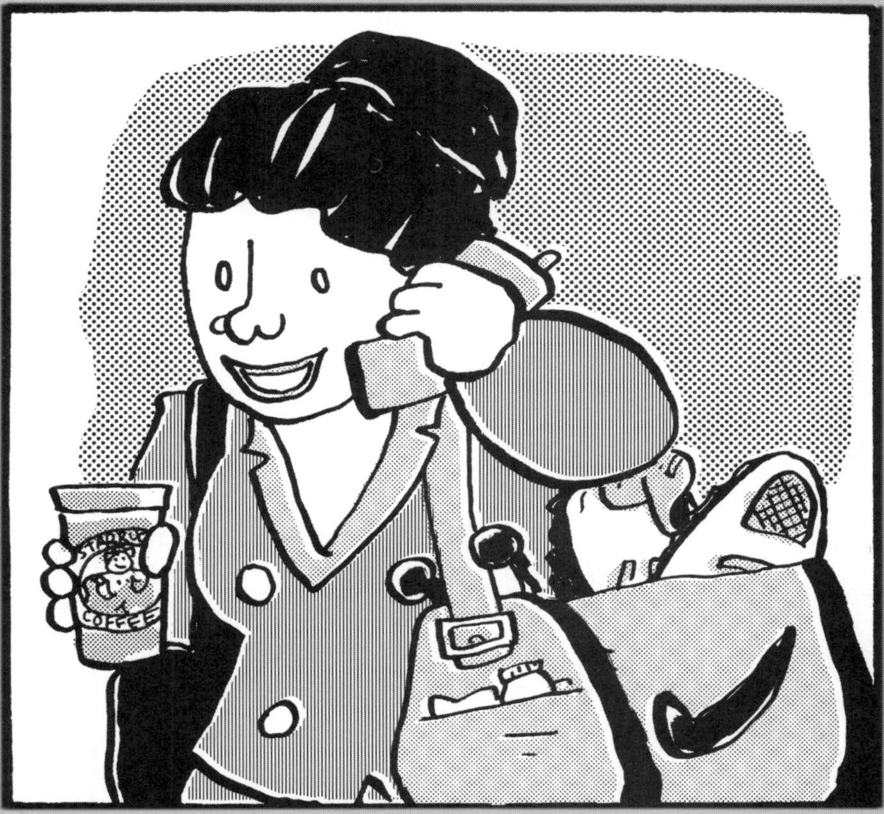
STARBUCKS
COFFEE

for Lee

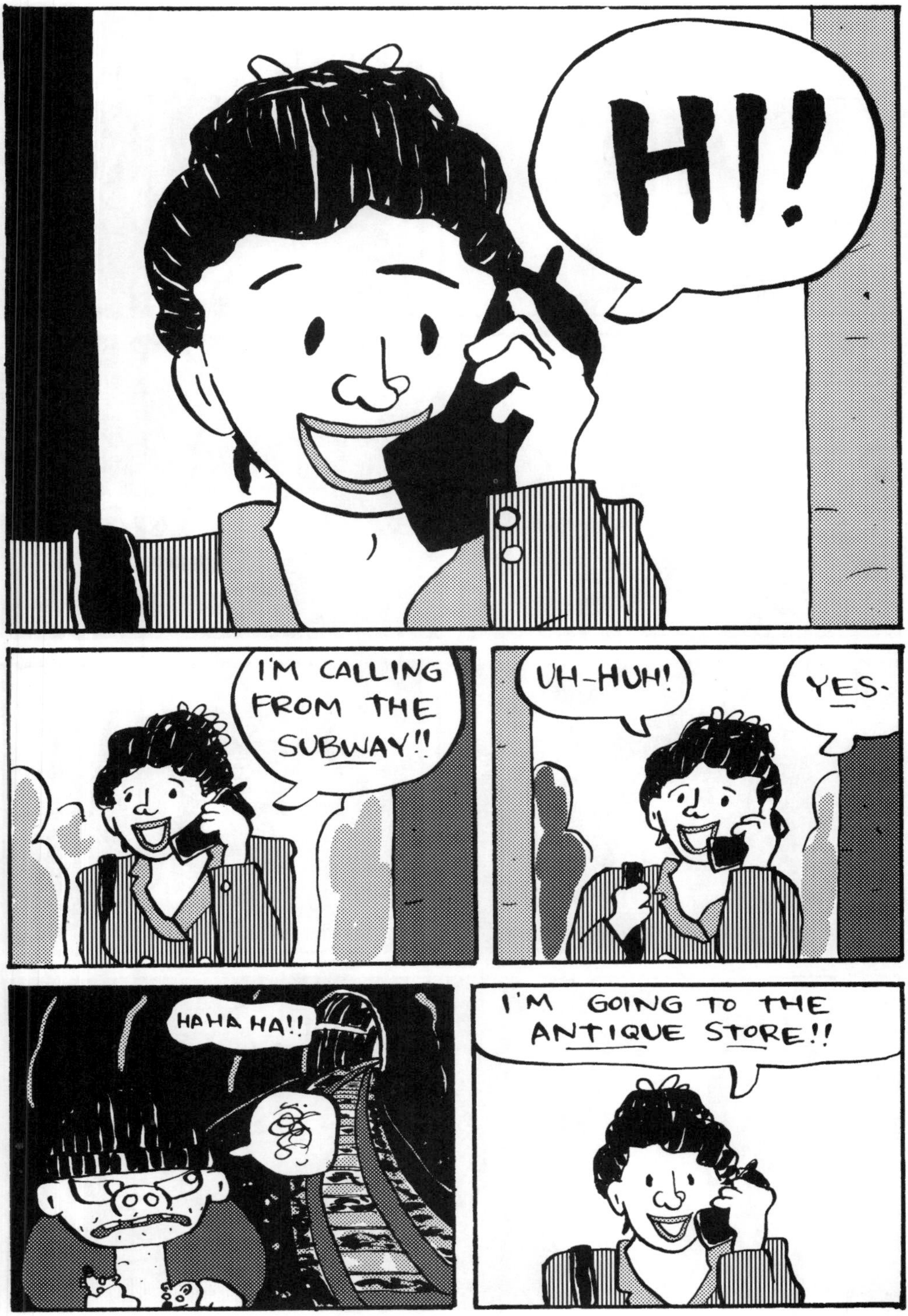
HI!
I'M CALLING FROM THE SUBWAY!!
UH-HUH!
YES-
HAHA HA!!
I'M GOING TO THE ANTIQUE STORE!!

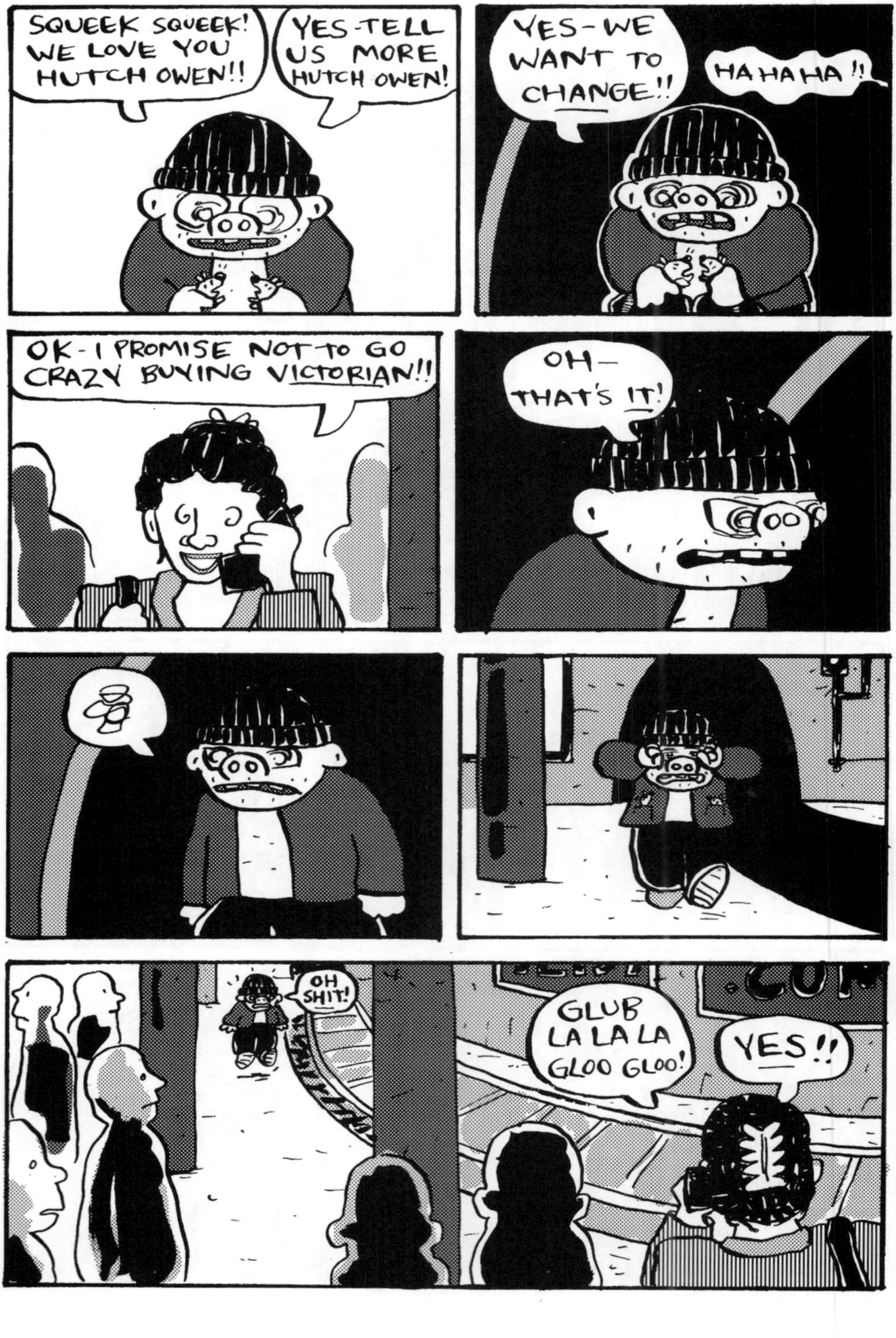
SQUEEK SQUEEK! WE LOVE YOU HUTCH OWEN!!
YES-TELL US MORE HUTCH OWEN!
YES- WE WANT TO CHANGE!!
HA HA HA !!
OK - I PROMISE NOT TO GO CRAZY BUYING VICTORIAN!!
OH- THAT'S IT!
OH SHIT!
GLUB LA LA LA GLOO GLOO!
YES!!

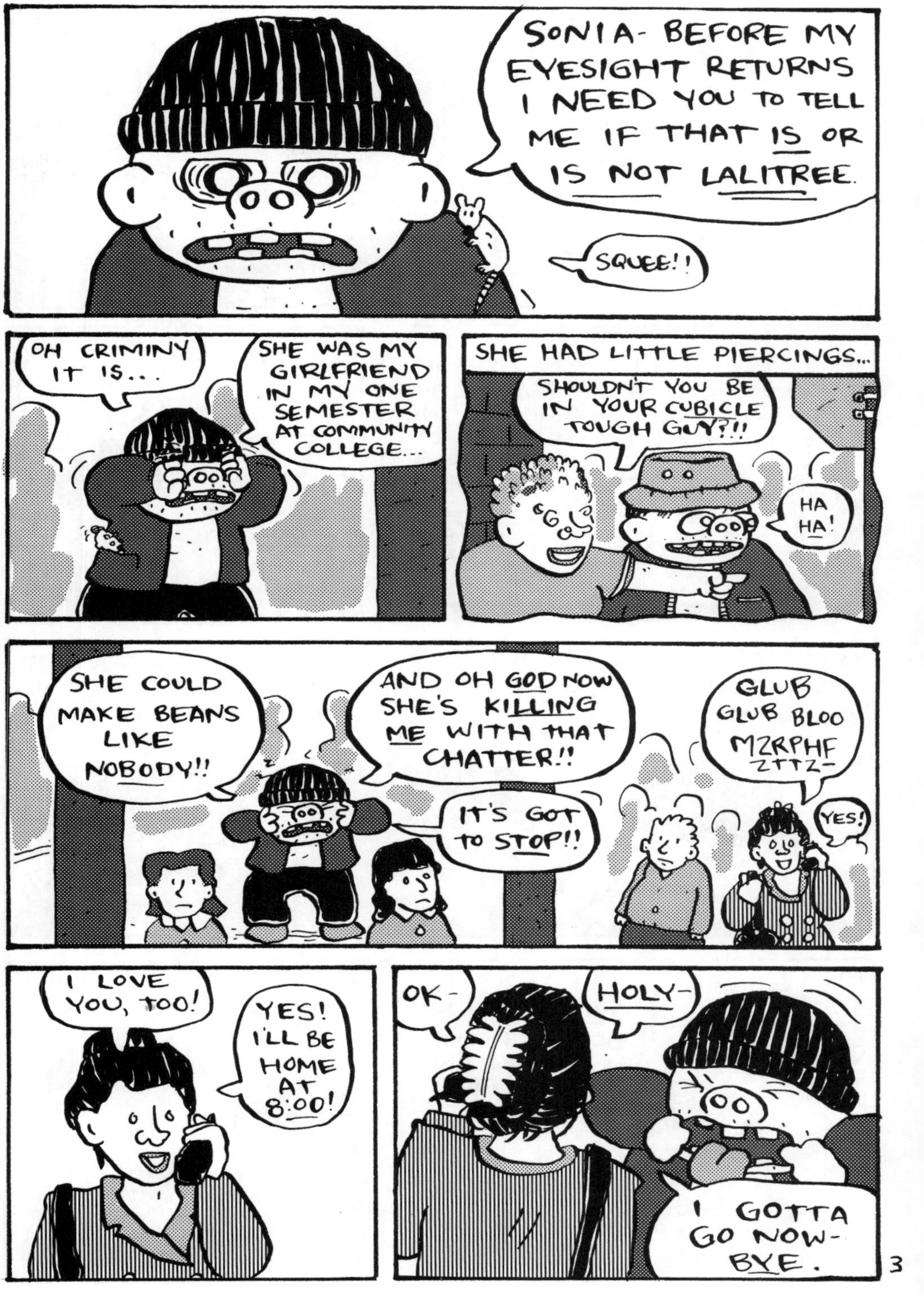
SONIA- BEFORE MY EYESIGHT RETURNS I NEED YOU TO TELL ME IF THAT IS OR IS NOT LALITREE.
SQUEE!!
OH CRIMINY IT IS...
SHE WAS MY GIRLFRIEND IN MY ONE SEMESTER AT COMMUNITY COLLEGE...
SHE HAD LITTLE PIERCINGS...
SHOULDN'T YOU BE IN YOUR CUBICLE TOUGH GUY?!!
HA HA!
SHE COULD MAKE BEANS LIKE NOBODY!!
AND OH GOD NOW SHE'S KILLING ME WITH THAT CHATTER!!
IT'S GOT TO STOP!!
GLUB GLUB BLOO MZRPHF ZTTZ-
YES!
I LOVE YOU, TOO!
YES! I'LL BE HOME AT 8:00!
OK-
HOLY-
I GOTTA GO NOW- BYE.

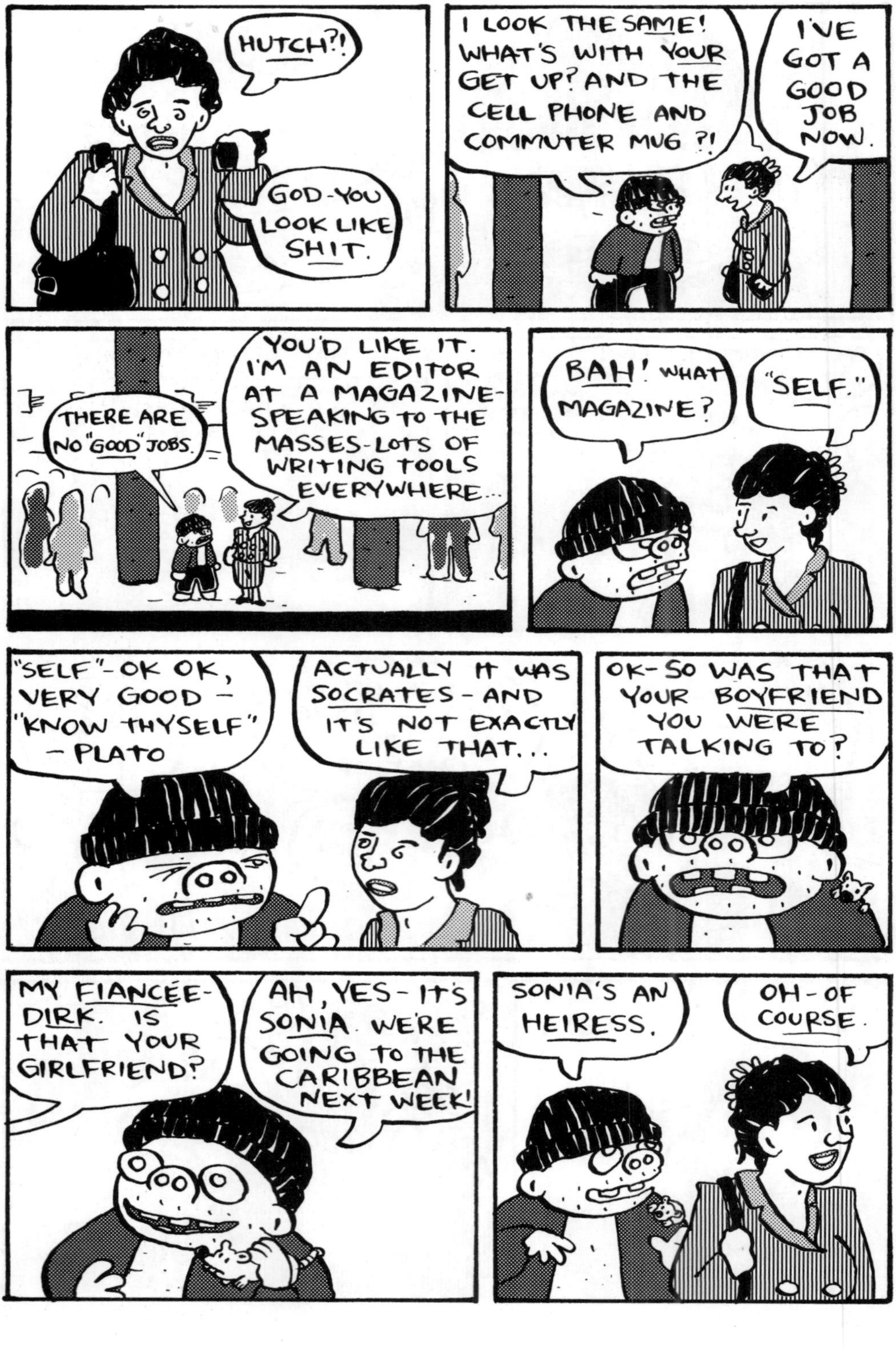
HUTCH?!
GOD-YOU LOOK LIKE SHIT.
I LOOK THE SAME! WHAT'S WITH YOUR GET UP? AND THE CELL PHONE AND COMMUTER MUG?!
I'VE GOT A GOOD JOB NOW.
THERE ARE NO "GOOD" JOBS.
YOU'D LIKE IT. I'M AN EDITOR AT A MAGAZINE-SPEAKING TO THE MASSES-LOTS OF WRITING TOOLS EVERYWHERE...
BAH! WHAT MAGAZINE?
"SELF."
"SELF"-OK OK, VERY GOOD - "KNOW THYSELF" - PLATO
ACTUALLY IT WAS SOCRATES - AND IT'S NOT EXACTLY LIKE THAT...
OK-SO WAS THAT YOUR BOYFRIEND YOU WERE TALKING TO?
MY FIANCÉE-DIRK. IS THAT YOUR GIRLFRIEND?
AH, YES - IT'S SONIA. WE'RE GOING TO THE CARIBBEAN NEXT WEEK!
SONIA'S AN HEIRESS.
OH-OF COURSE.

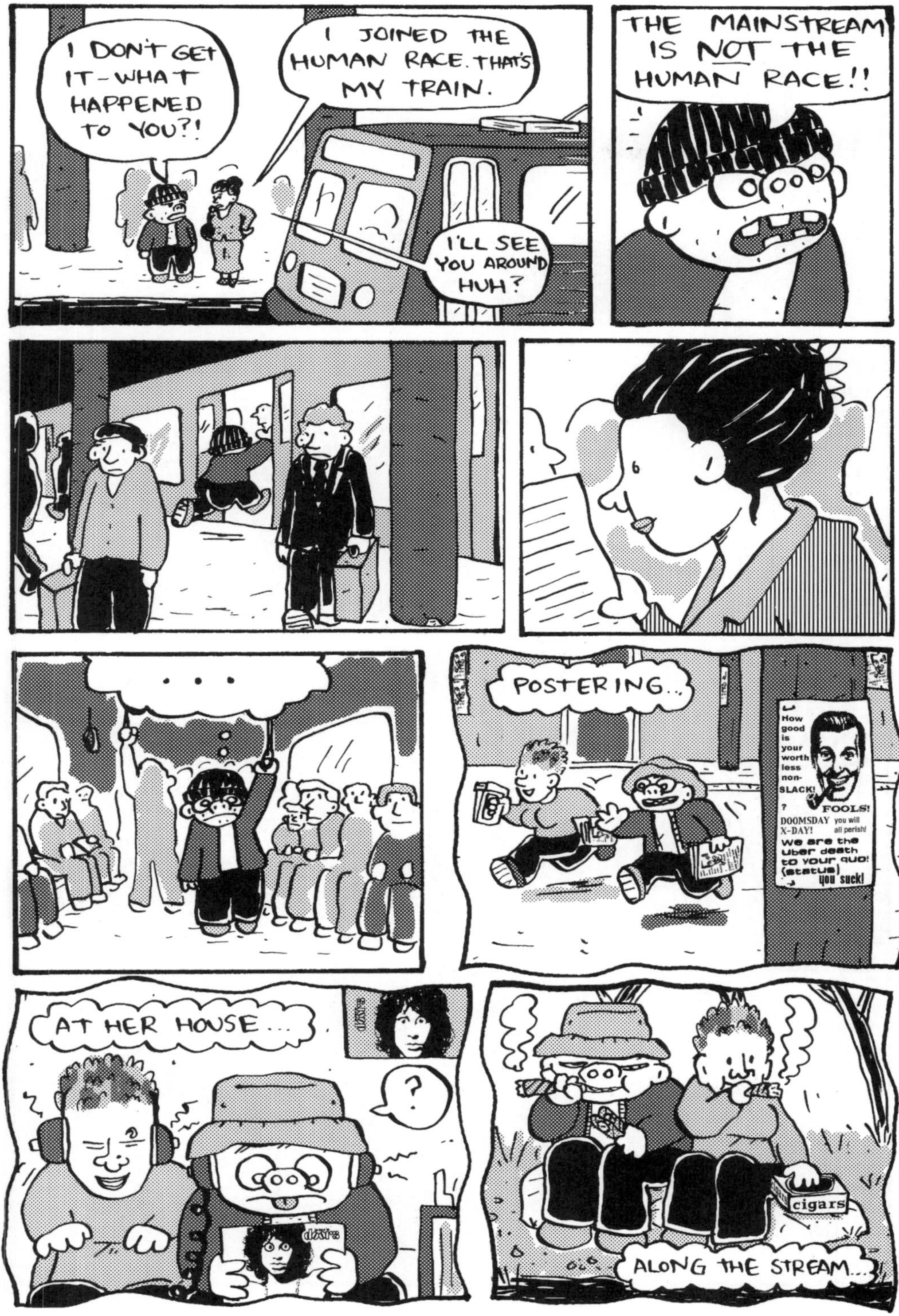

I DON'T GET IT-WHAT HAPPENED TO YOU?!
I JOINED THE HUMAN RACE. THAT'S MY TRAIN.
I'LL SEE YOU AROUND HUH?
THE MAINSTREAM IS NOT THE HUMAN RACE!!
. . .
POSTERING...
How good is your worth less non-SLACK!
? FOOLS!
DOOMSDAY X-DAY! you will all perish!
we are the uber death to your quo! (status)
you suck!
AT HER HOUSE...
?
doors
cigars
ALONG THE STREAM...

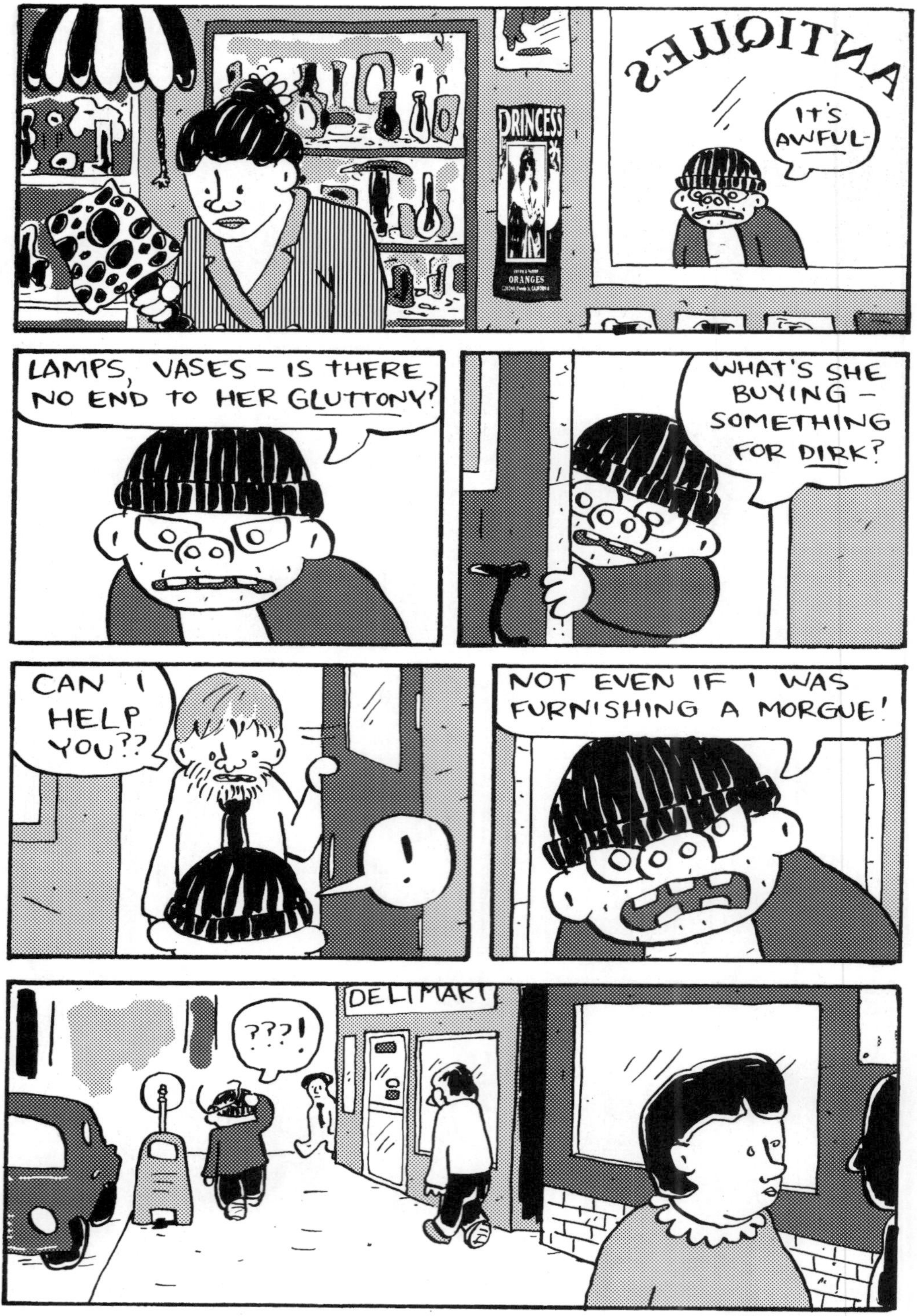
ANTIQUES
DRINCESS
ORANGES
IT'S AWFUL-
LAMPS, VASES - IS THERE NO END TO HER GLUTTONY?
WHAT'S SHE BUYING - SOMETHING FOR DIRK?
CAN I HELP YOU??
!
NOT EVEN IF I WAS FURNISHING A MORGUE!
DELIMART
???!

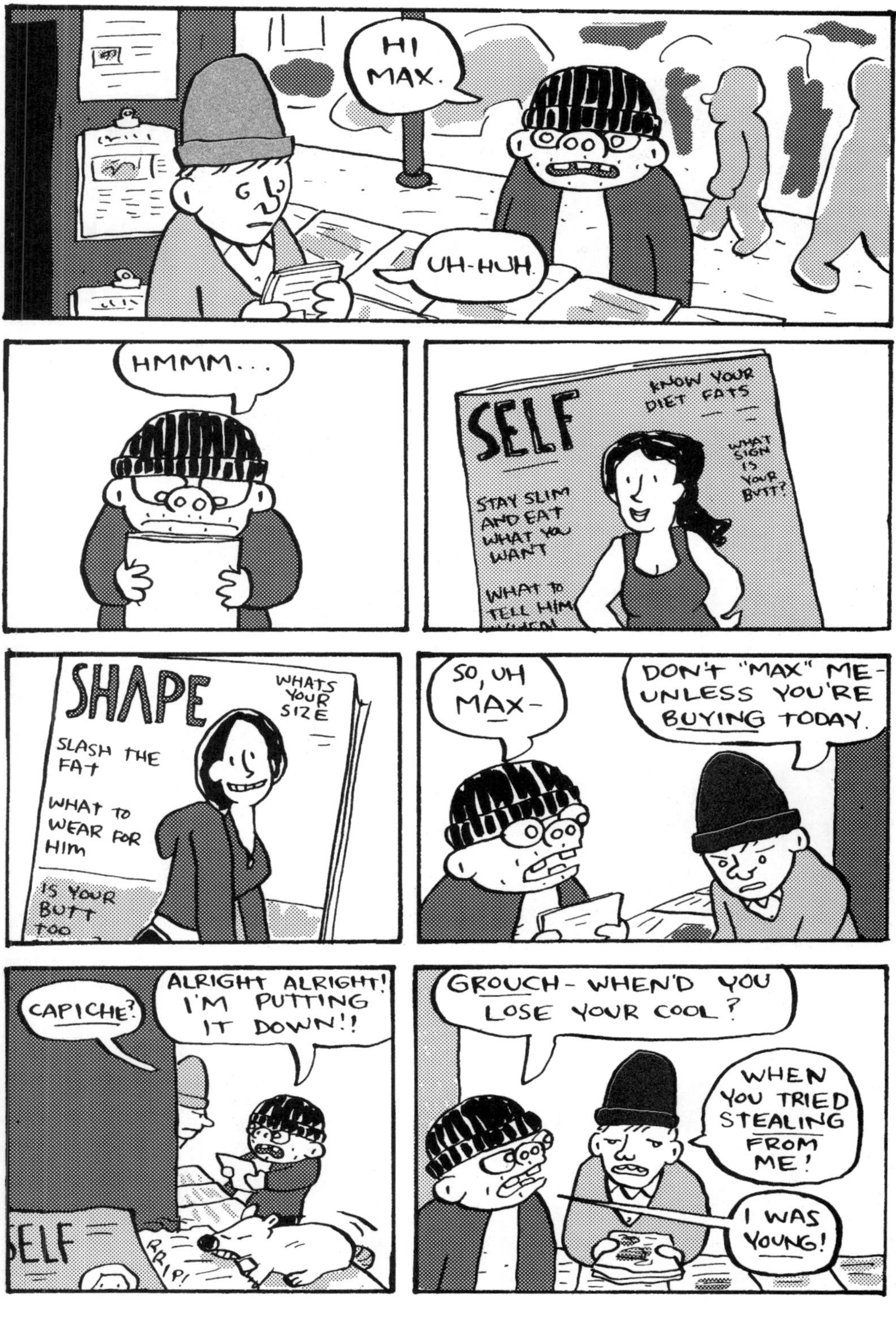
HI MAX.
UH-HUH.
HMMM...
SELF
KNOW YOUR DIET FATS
WHAT SIGN IS YOUR BUTT?
STAY SLIM AND EAT WHAT YOU WANT
WHAT TO TELL HIM
SHAPE
WHATS YOUR SIZE
SLASH THE FAT
WHAT TO WEAR FOR HIM
IS YOUR BUTT TOO
SO, UH MAX-
DON'T "MAX" ME- UNLESS YOU'RE BUYING TODAY.
CAPICHE?
ALRIGHT ALRIGHT! I'M PUTTING IT DOWN!!
SELF
RRIP!
GROUCH- WHEN'D YOU LOSE YOUR COOL?
WHEN YOU TRIED STEALING FROM ME!
I WAS YOUNG!

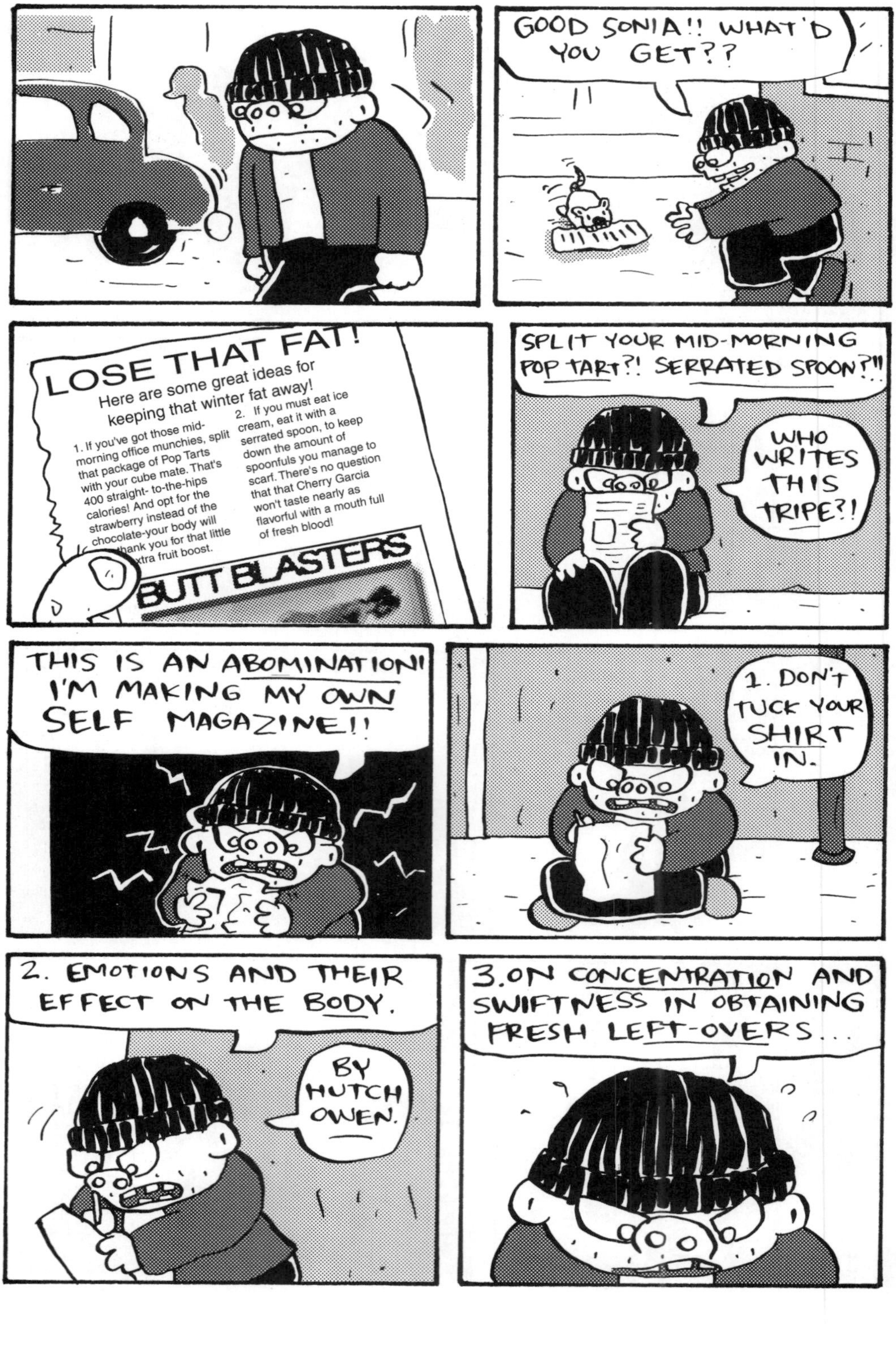
GOOD SONIA!! WHAT'D YOU GET??
LOSE THAT FAT!
Here are some great ideas for keeping that winter fat away!
1. If you've got those mid-morning office munchies, split that package of Pop Tarts with your cube mate. That's 400 straight- to-the-hips calories! And opt for the strawberry instead of the chocolate-your body will thank you for that little xtra fruit boost.
2. If you must eat ice cream, eat it with a serrated spoon, to keep down the amount of spoonfuls you manage to scarf. There's no question that that Cherry Garcia won't taste nearly as flavorful with a mouth full of fresh blood!
BUTT BLASTERS
SPLIT YOUR MID-MORNING POP TART?! SERRATED SPOON?!!
WHO WRITES THIS TRIPE?!
THIS IS AN ABOMINATION! I'M MAKING MY OWN SELF MAGAZINE!!
1. DON'T TUCK YOUR SHIRT IN.
2. EMOTIONS AND THEIR EFFECT ON THE BODY.
BY HUTCH OWEN.
3. ON CONCENTRATION AND SWIFTNESS IN OBTAINING FRESH LEFT-OVERS...

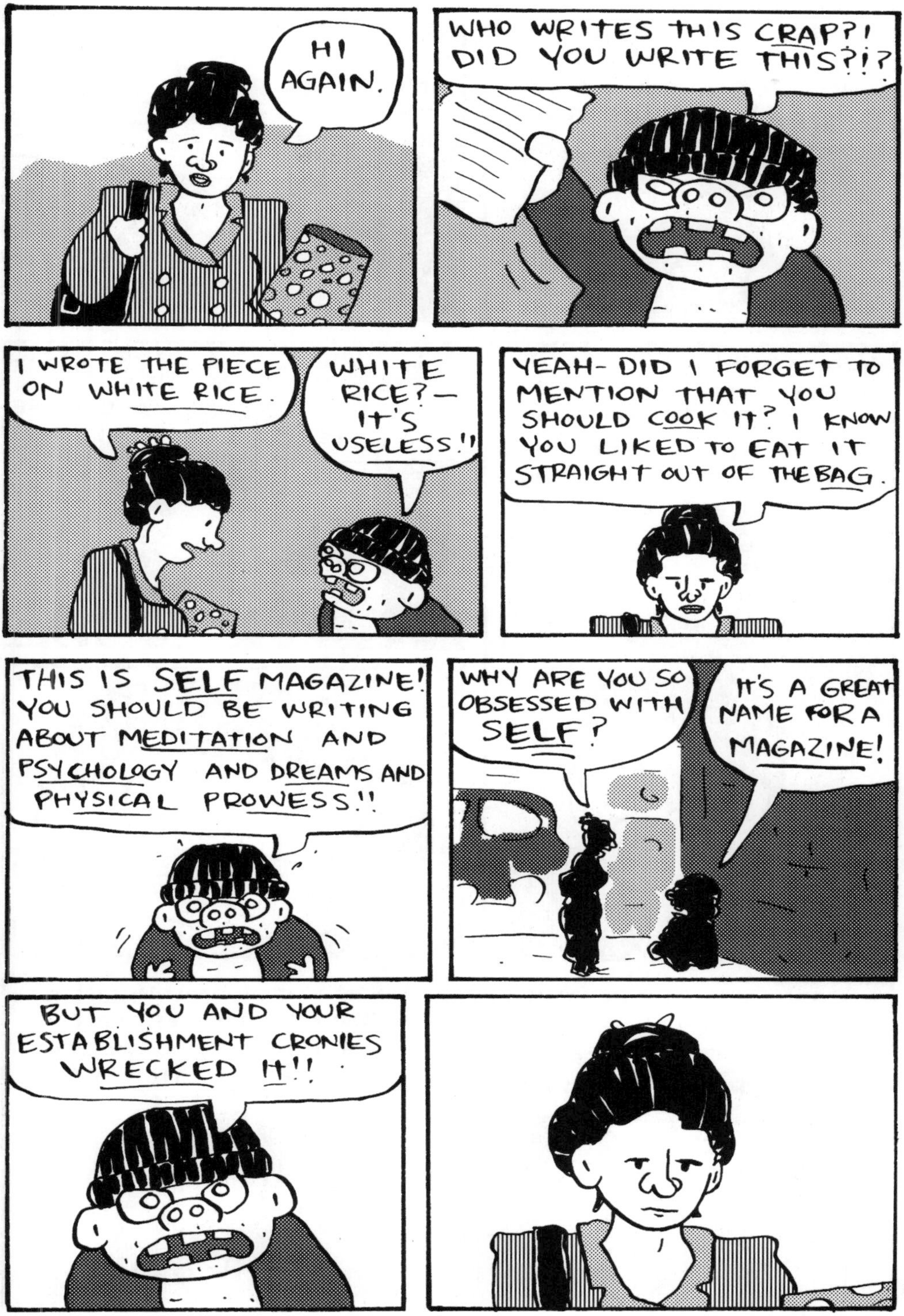
HI AGAIN.
WHO WRITES THIS CRAP?! DID YOU WRITE THIS?!?
I WROTE THE PIECE ON WHITE RICE.
WHITE RICE?— IT'S USELESS!!
YEAH- DID I FORGET TO MENTION THAT YOU SHOULD COOK IT? I KNOW YOU LIKED TO EAT IT STRAIGHT OUT OF THE BAG.
THIS IS SELF MAGAZINE! YOU SHOULD BE WRITING ABOUT MEDITATION AND PSYCHOLOGY AND DREAMS AND PHYSICAL PROWESS!!
WHY ARE YOU SO OBSESSED WITH SELF?
IT'S A GREAT NAME FOR A MAGAZINE!
BUT YOU AND YOUR ESTABLISHMENT CRONIES WRECKED IT!!

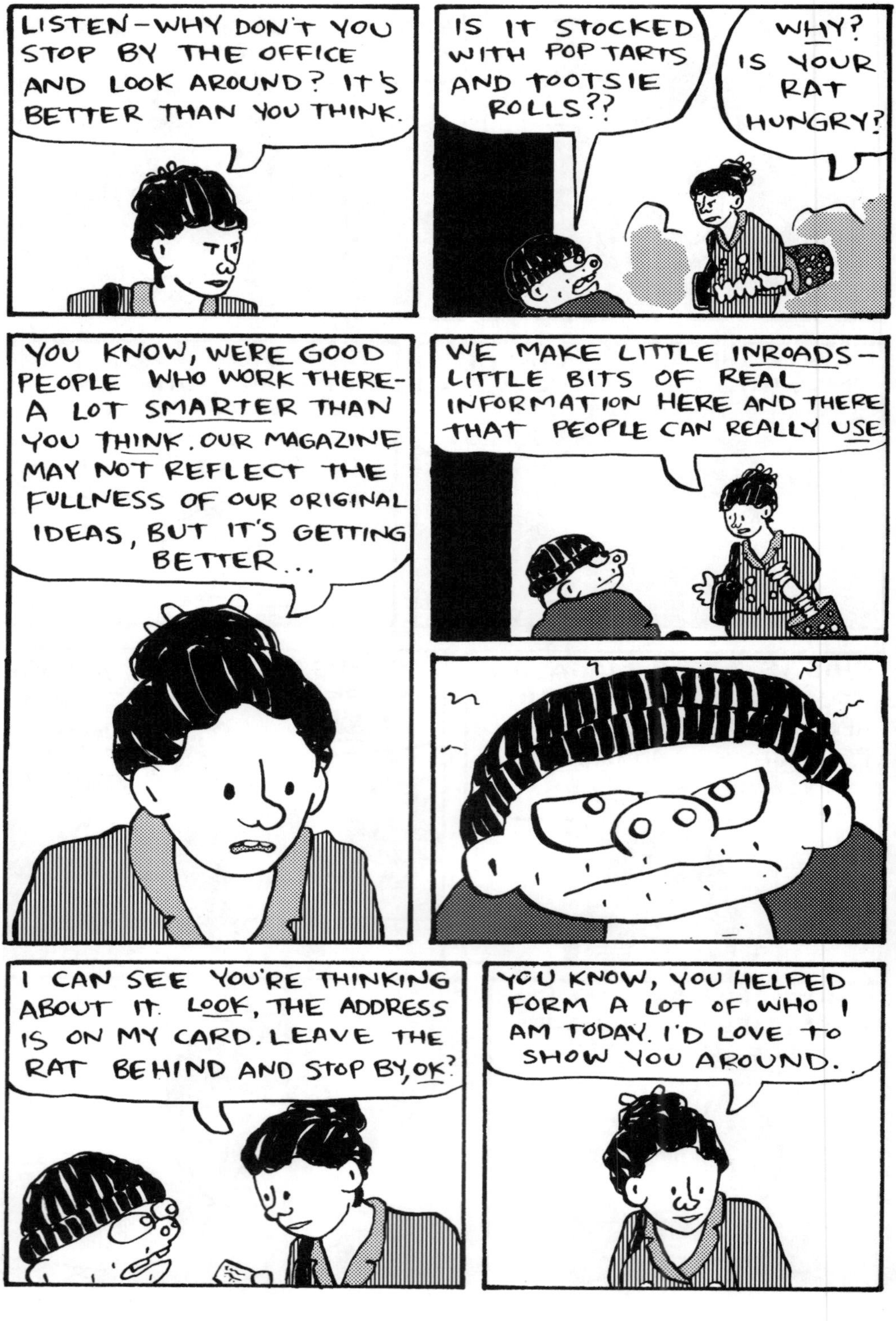
LISTEN—WHY DON'T YOU STOP BY THE OFFICE AND LOOK AROUND? IT'S BETTER THAN YOU THINK.
IS IT STOCKED WITH POP TARTS AND TOOTSIE ROLLS??
WHY? IS YOUR RAT HUNGRY?
YOU KNOW, WE'RE GOOD PEOPLE WHO WORK THERE—A LOT SMARTER THAN YOU THINK. OUR MAGAZINE MAY NOT REFLECT THE FULLNESS OF OUR ORIGINAL IDEAS, BUT IT'S GETTING BETTER...
WE MAKE LITTLE INROADS—LITTLE BITS OF REAL INFORMATION HERE AND THERE THAT PEOPLE CAN REALLY USE.
I CAN SEE YOU'RE THINKING ABOUT IT. LOOK, THE ADDRESS IS ON MY CARD. LEAVE THE RAT BEHIND AND STOP BY, OK?
YOU KNOW, YOU HELPED FORM A LOT OF WHO I AM TODAY. I'D LOVE TO SHOW YOU AROUND.

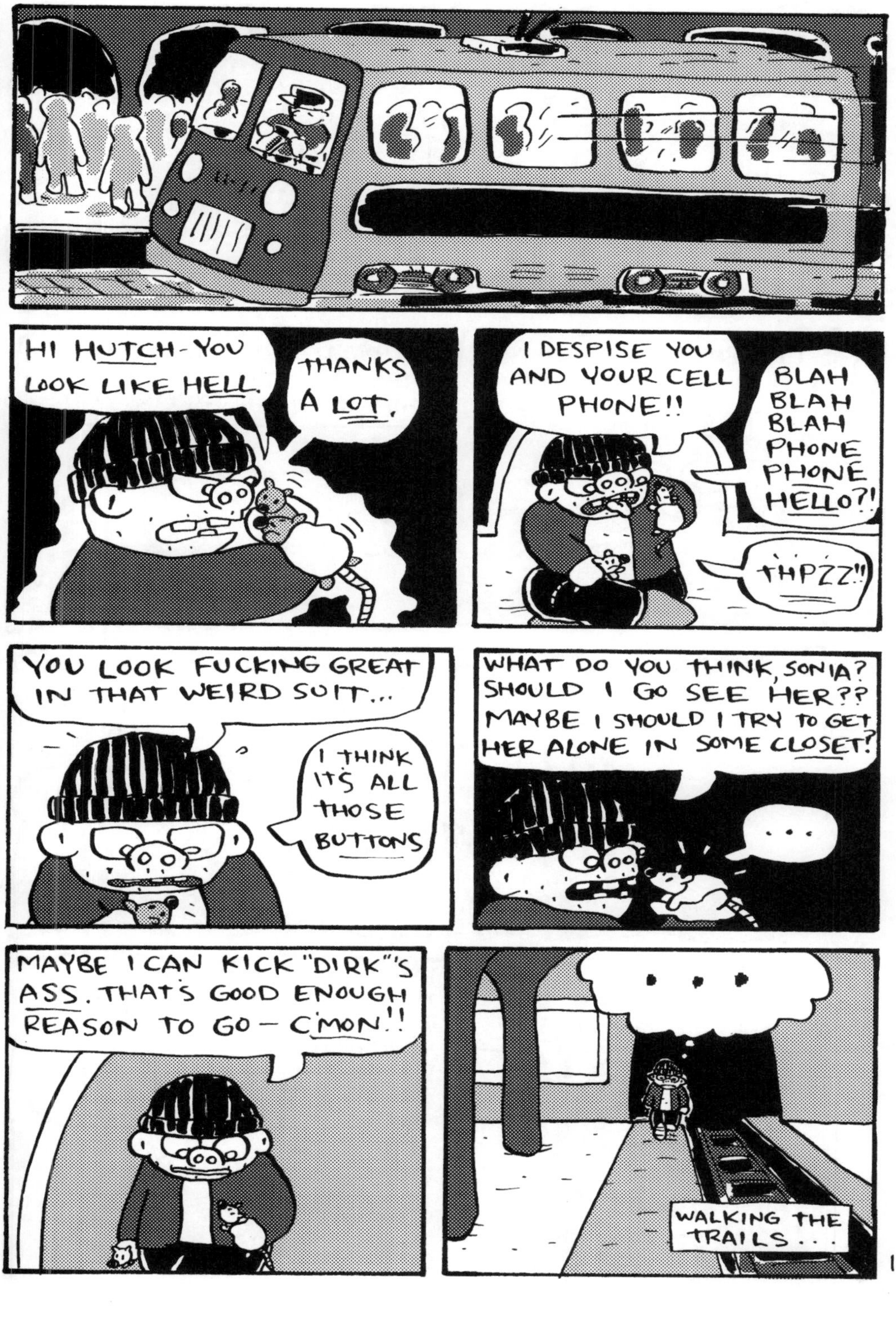

HI HUTCH - YOU LOOK LIKE HELL.
THANKS A LOT.
I DESPISE YOU AND YOUR CELL PHONE!!
BLAH BLAH BLAH PHONE PHONE HELLO?!
THPZZ!!
YOU LOOK FUCKING GREAT IN THAT WEIRD SUIT...
I THINK IT'S ALL THOSE BUTTONS
WHAT DO YOU THINK, SONIA? SHOULD I GO SEE HER?? MAYBE I SHOULD I TRY TO GET HER ALONE IN SOME CLOSET!
...
MAYBE I CAN KICK "DIRK"'S ASS. THAT'S GOOD ENOUGH REASON TO GO - C'MON!!
...
WALKING THE TRAILS...

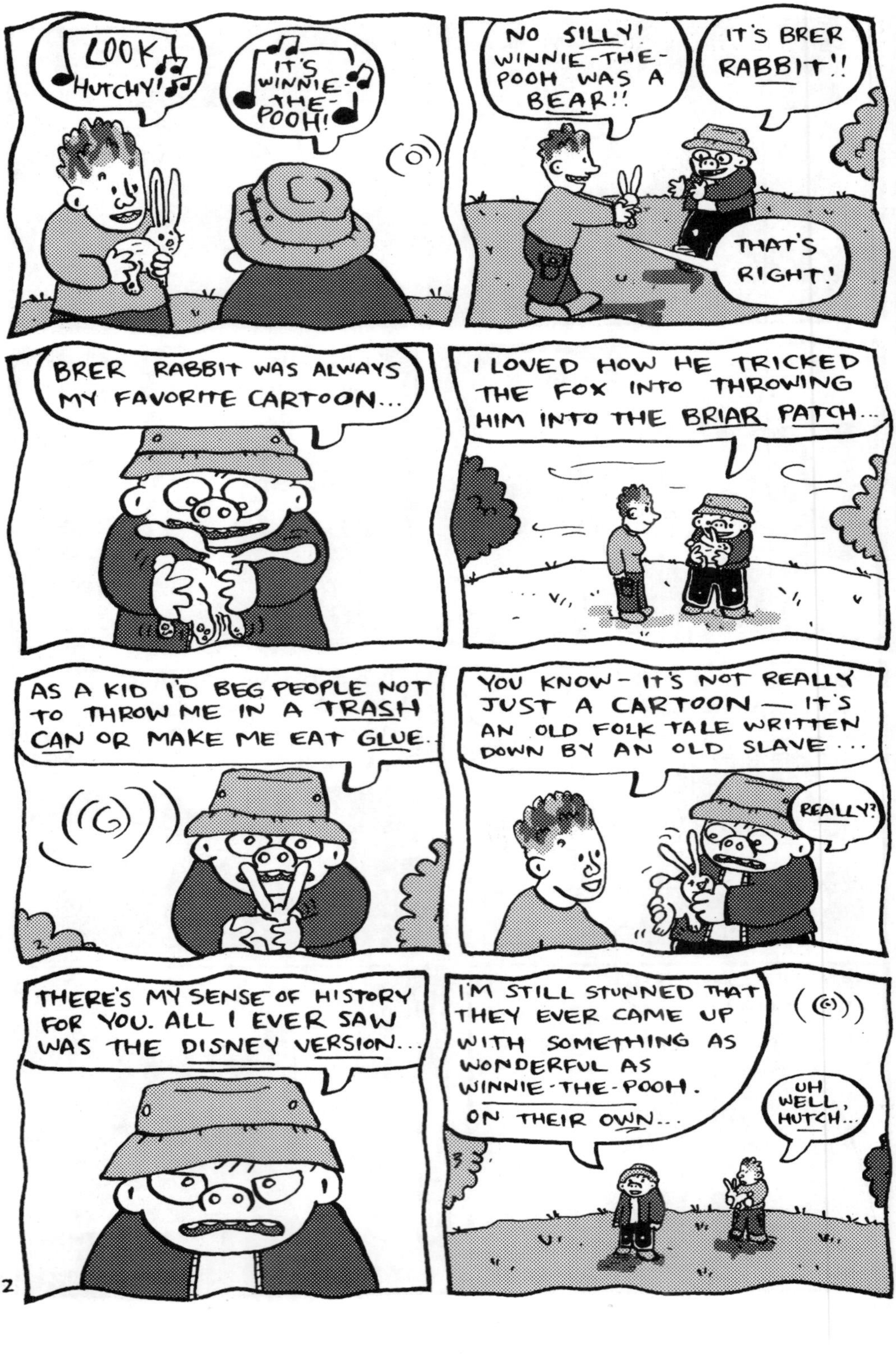
LOOK HUTCHY!
IT'S WINNIE-THE-POOH!
NO SILLY! WINNIE-THE-POOH WAS A BEAR!!
IT'S BRER RABBIT!!
THAT'S RIGHT!
BRER RABBIT WAS ALWAYS MY FAVORITE CARTOON...
I LOVED HOW HE TRICKED THE FOX INTO THROWING HIM INTO THE BRIAR PATCH...
AS A KID I'D BEG PEOPLE NOT TO THROW ME IN A TRASH CAN OR MAKE ME EAT GLUE...
YOU KNOW - IT'S NOT REALLY JUST A CARTOON - IT'S AN OLD FOLK TALE WRITTEN DOWN BY AN OLD SLAVE...
REALLY?
THERE'S MY SENSE OF HISTORY FOR YOU. ALL I EVER SAW WAS THE DISNEY VERSION...
I'M STILL STUNNED THAT THEY EVER CAME UP WITH SOMETHING AS WONDERFUL AS WINNIE-THE-POOH.
ON THEIR OWN...
UH WELL, HUTCH...

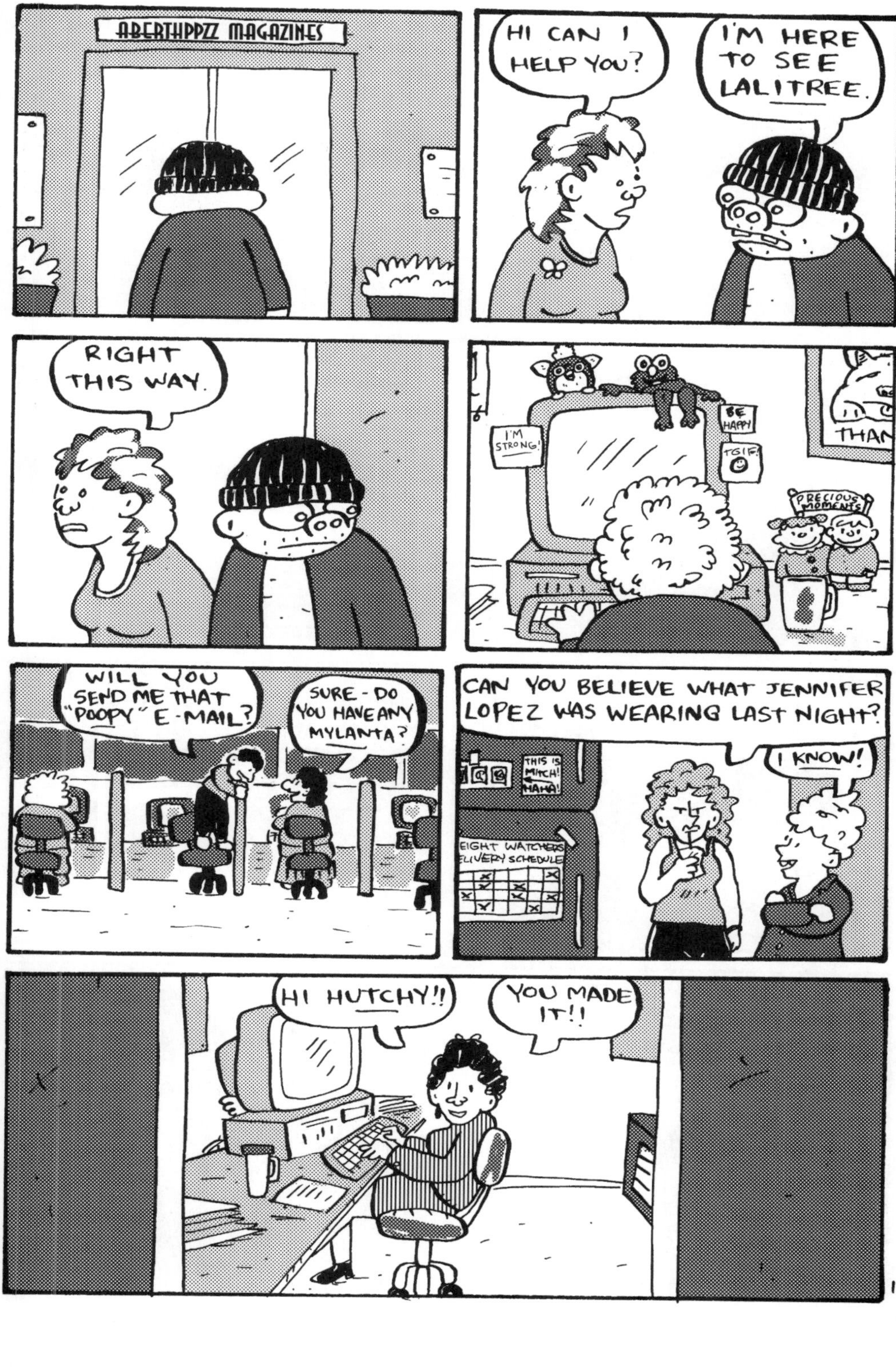
ABERTHPPZZ MAGAZINES
HI CAN I HELP YOU?
I'M HERE TO SEE LALITREE.
RIGHT THIS WAY.
I'M STRONG!
BE HAPPY
TGIF!
THAN
PRECIOUS MOMENTS
WILL YOU SEND ME THAT "POOPY" E-MAIL?
SURE - DO YOU HAVE ANY MYLANTA?
CAN YOU BELIEVE WHAT JENNIFER LOPEZ WAS WEARING LAST NIGHT?
I KNOW!
THIS IS MITCH! HAHA!
EIGHT WATCHERS
ELIVERY SCHEDULE
HI HUTCHY!!
YOU MADE IT!!

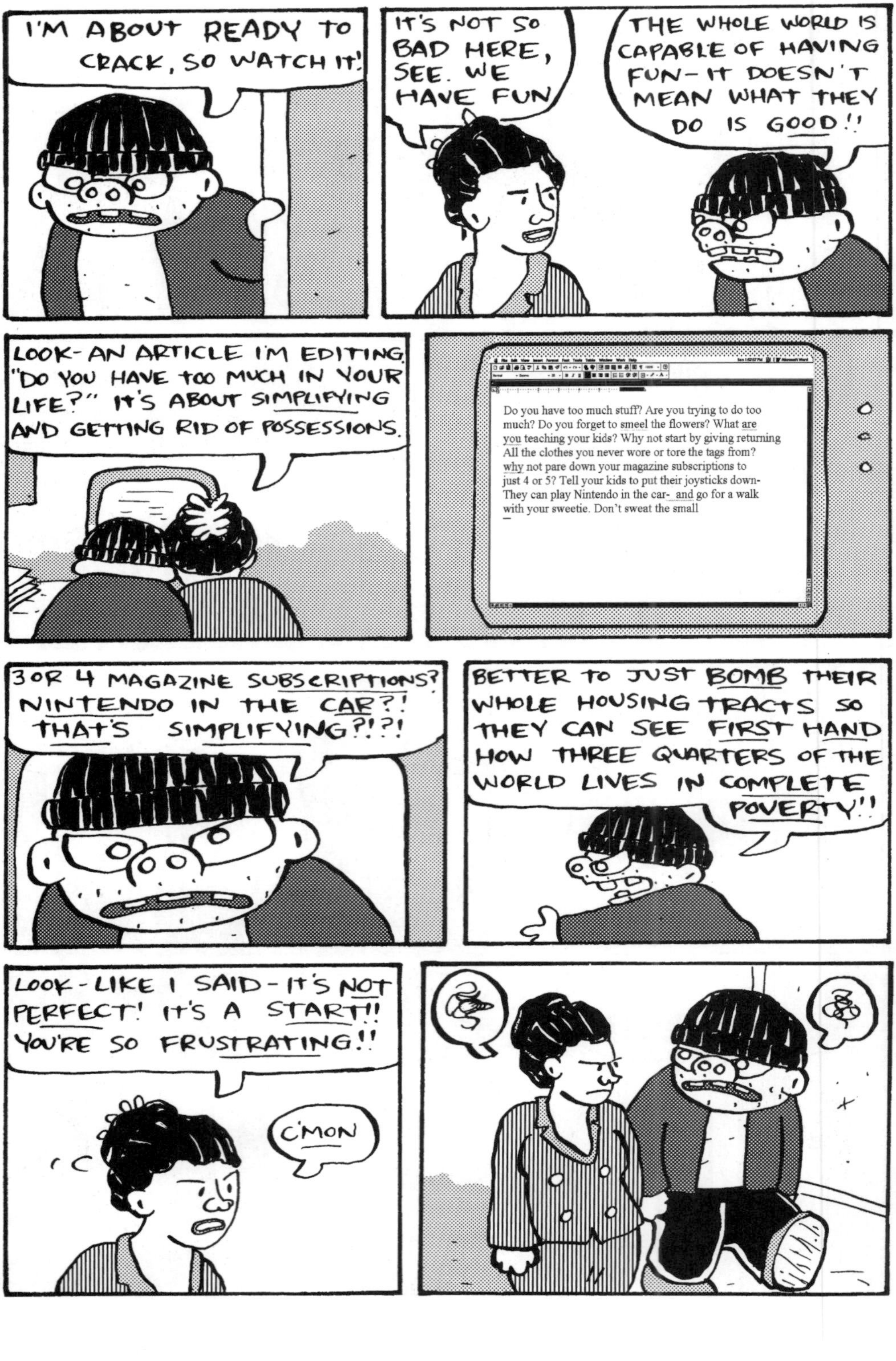
I'M ABOUT READY TO CRACK, SO WATCH IT!
IT'S NOT SO BAD HERE, SEE. WE HAVE FUN
THE WHOLE WORLD IS CAPABLE OF HAVING FUN- IT DOESN'T MEAN WHAT THEY DO IS GOOD!!
LOOK- AN ARTICLE I'M EDITING. "DO YOU HAVE TOO MUCH IN YOUR LIFE?" IT'S ABOUT SIMPLIFYING AND GETTING RID OF POSSESSIONS.
Do you have too much stuff? Are you trying to do too much? Do you forget to smeel the flowers? What are you teaching your kids? Why not start by giving returning All the clothes you never wore or tore the tags from? why not pare down your magazine subscriptions to just 4 or 5? Tell your kids to put their joysticks down- They can play Nintendo in the car- and go for a walk with your sweetie. Don't sweat the small
3 OR 4 MAGAZINE SUBSCRIPTIONS? NINTENDO IN THE CAR?! THAT'S SIMPLIFYING?!?!
BETTER TO JUST BOMB THEIR WHOLE HOUSING TRACTS SO THEY CAN SEE FIRST HAND HOW THREE QUARTERS OF THE WORLD LIVES IN COMPLETE POVERTY!!
LOOK- LIKE I SAID- IT'S NOT PERFECT! IT'S A START!! YOU'RE SO FRUSTRATING!!
C'MON

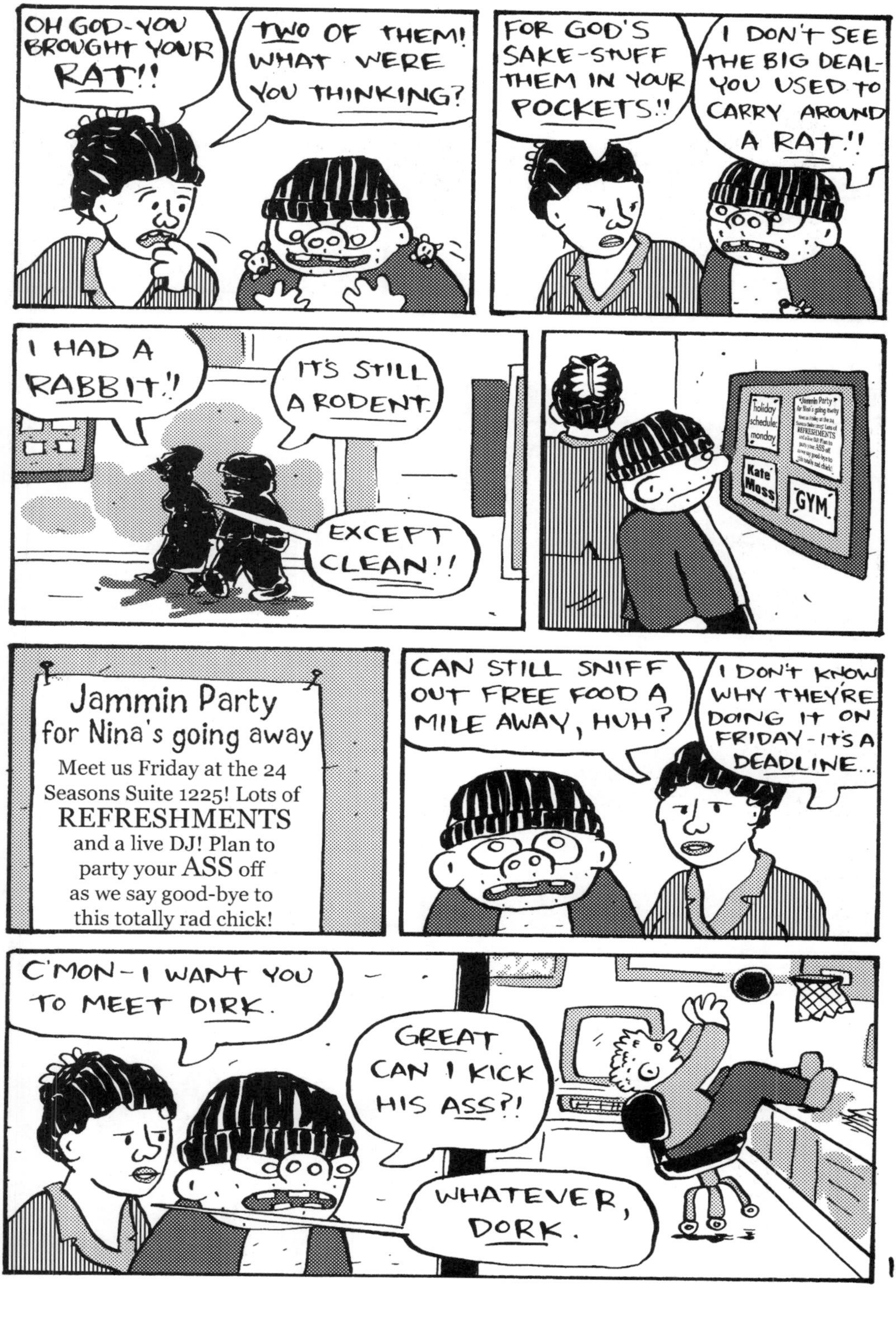
OH GOD-YOU BROUGHT YOUR RAT!!
TWO OF THEM! WHAT WERE YOU THINKING?
FOR GOD'S SAKE-STUFF THEM IN YOUR POCKETS!!
I DON'T SEE THE BIG DEAL-YOU USED TO CARRY AROUND A RAT!!
I HAD A RABBIT!!
IT'S STILL A RODENT.
EXCEPT CLEAN!!
holiday schedule: monday
Kate Moss
GYM
Jammin Party
for Nina's going away
Meet us Friday at the 24 Seasons Suite 1225! Lots of
REFRESHMENTS
and a live DJ! Plan to party your ASS off as we say good-bye to this totally rad chick!
CAN STILL SNIFF OUT FREE FOOD A MILE AWAY, HUH?
I DON'T KNOW WHY THEY'RE DOING IT ON FRIDAY-IT'S A DEADLINE...
C'MON-I WANT YOU TO MEET DIRK.
GREAT CAN I KICK HIS ASS?!
WHATEVER, DORK.

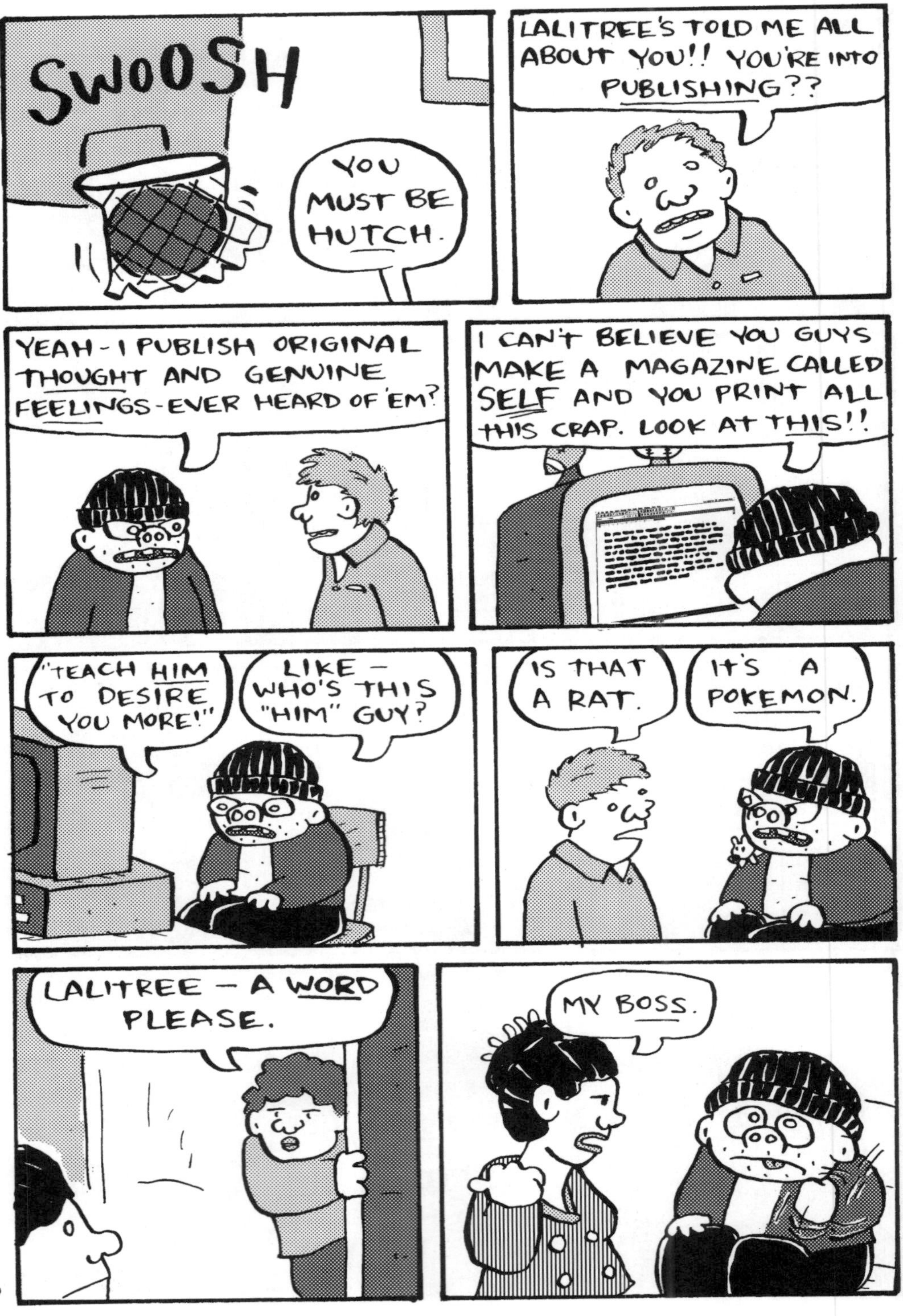
SWOOSH
YOU MUST BE HUTCH.
LALITREE'S TOLD ME ALL ABOUT YOU!! YOU'RE INTO PUBLISHING??
YEAH - I PUBLISH ORIGINAL THOUGHT AND GENUINE FEELINGS - EVER HEARD OF 'EM?
I CAN'T BELIEVE YOU GUYS MAKE A MAGAZINE CALLED SELF AND YOU PRINT ALL THIS CRAP. LOOK AT THIS!!
"TEACH HIM TO DESIRE YOU MORE!"
LIKE - WHO'S THIS "HIM" GUY?
IS THAT A RAT.
IT'S A POKEMON.
LALITREE - A WORD PLEASE.
MY BOSS.

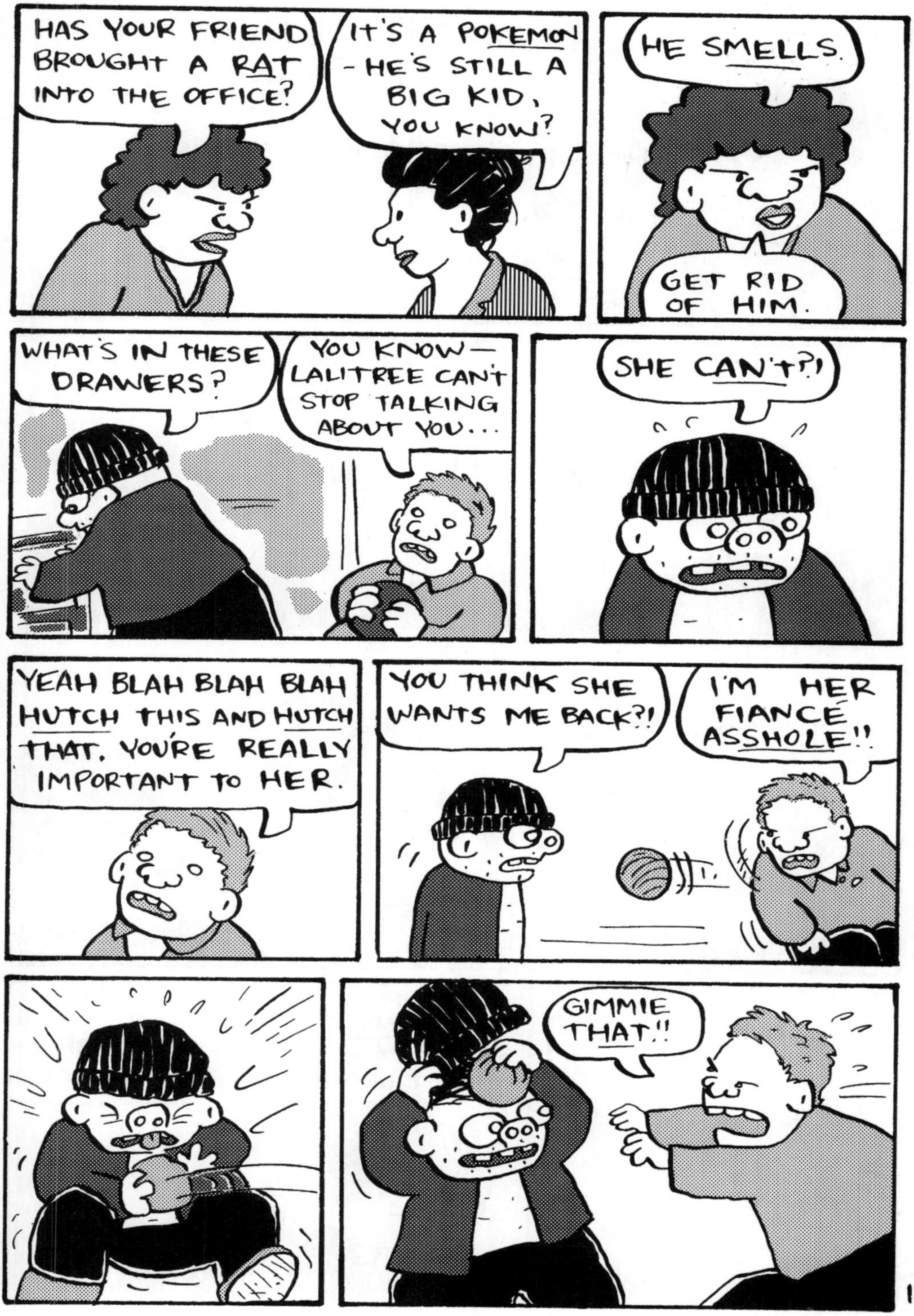
HAS YOUR FRIEND BROUGHT A RAT INTO THE OFFICE?
IT'S A POKEMON - HE'S STILL A BIG KID, YOU KNOW?
HE SMELLS.
GET RID OF HIM.
WHAT'S IN THESE DRAWERS?
YOU KNOW— LALITREE CAN'T STOP TALKING ABOUT YOU...
SHE CAN'T?!
YEAH BLAH BLAH BLAH HUTCH THIS AND HUTCH THAT. YOU'RE REALLY IMPORTANT TO HER.
YOU THINK SHE WANTS ME BACK?!
I'M HER FIANCE ASSHOLE!!
GIMMIE THAT!!

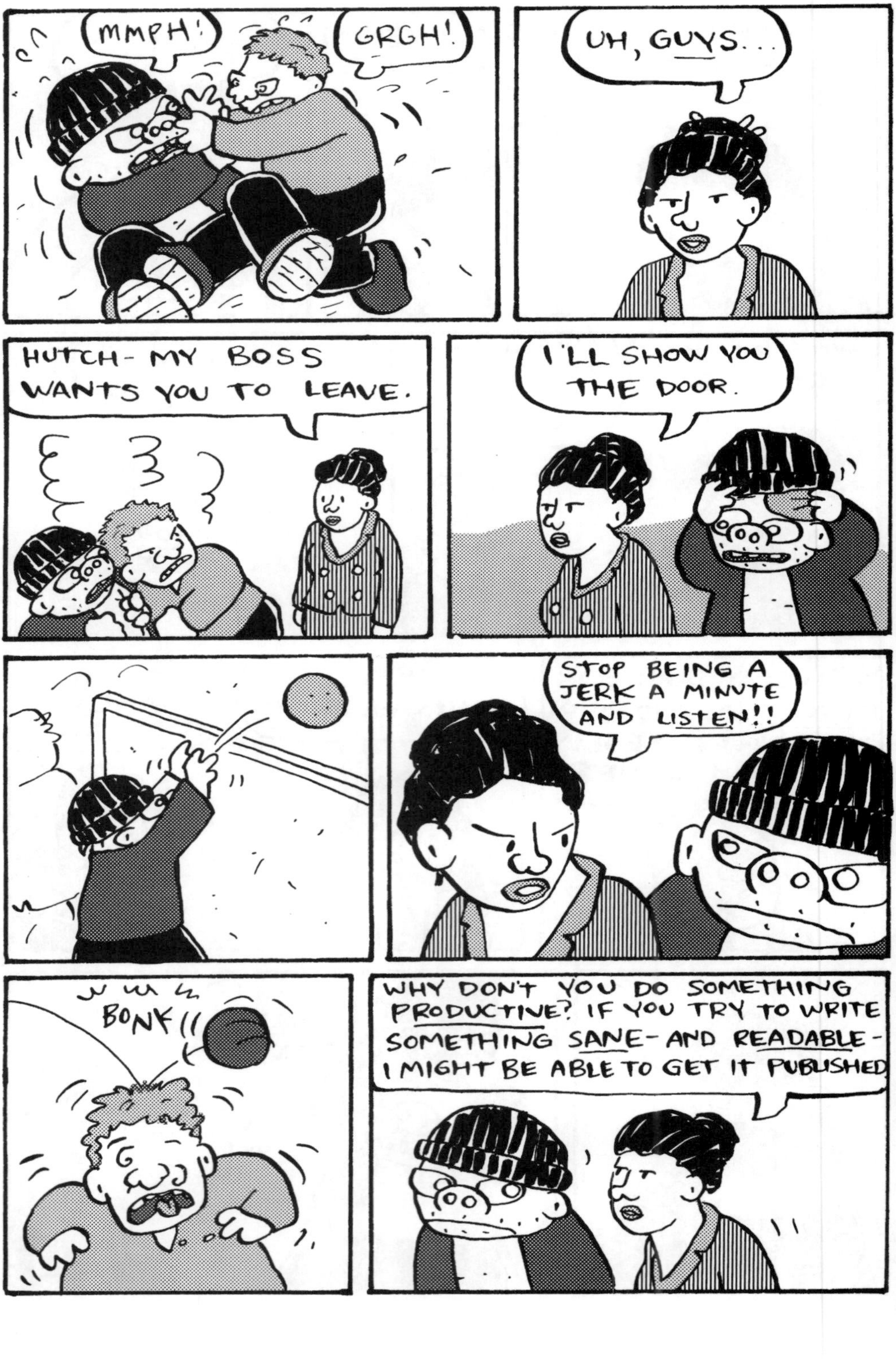
MMPH!
GRGH!
UH, GUYS...
HUTCH- MY BOSS WANTS YOU TO LEAVE.
I'LL SHOW YOU THE DOOR.
STOP BEING A JERK A MINUTE AND LISTEN!!
BONK
WHY DON'T YOU DO SOMETHING PRODUCTIVE? IF YOU TRY TO WRITE SOMETHING SANE- AND READABLE- I MIGHT BE ABLE TO GET IT PUBLISHED

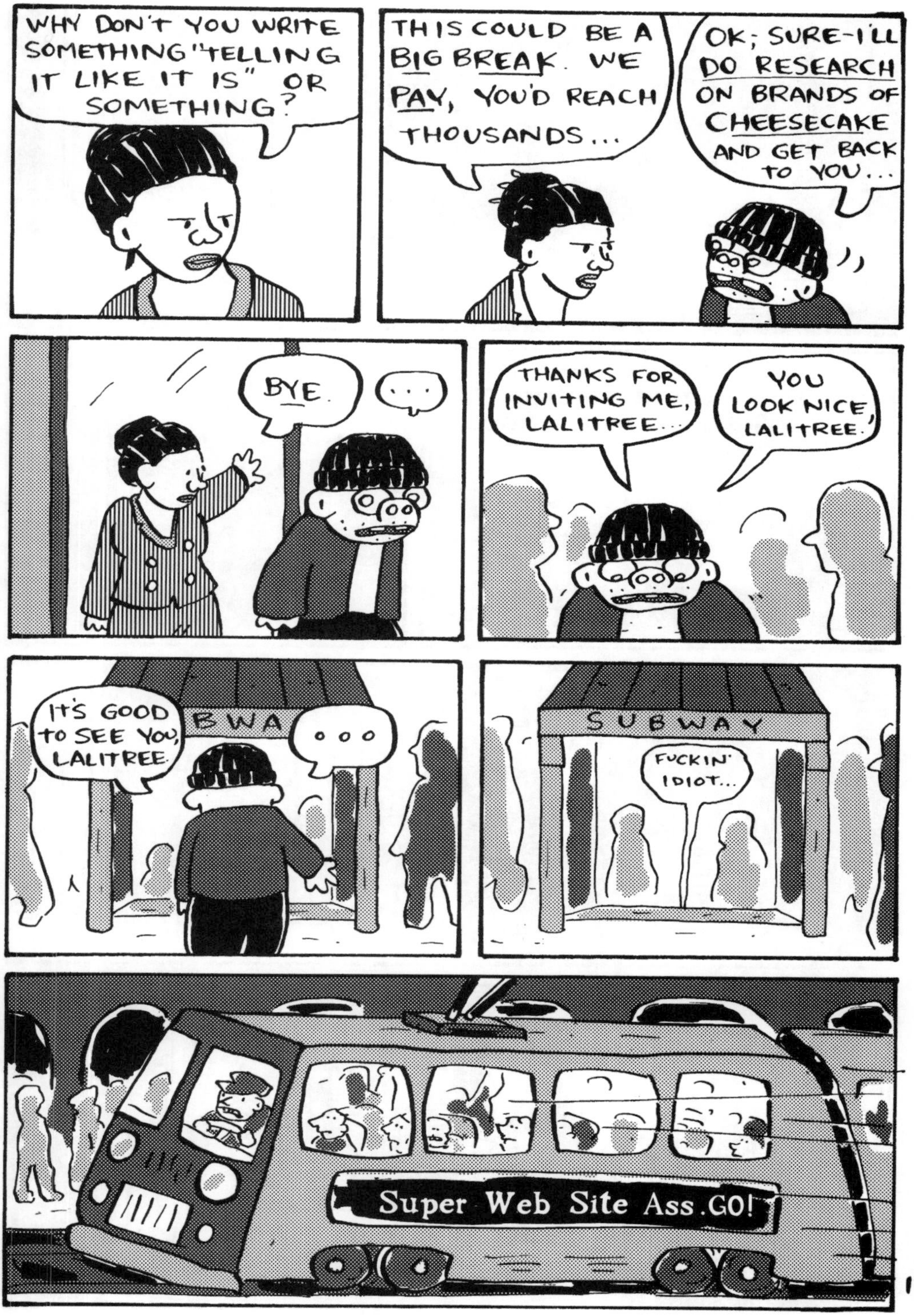
WHY DON'T YOU WRITE SOMETHING "TELLING IT LIKE IT IS" OR SOMETHING?
THIS COULD BE A BIG BREAK. WE PAY, YOU'D REACH THOUSANDS...
OK; SURE-I'LL DO RESEARCH ON BRANDS OF CHEESECAKE AND GET BACK TO YOU...
BYE.
...
THANKS FOR INVITING ME, LALITREE...
YOU LOOK NICE, LALITREE.
IT'S GOOD TO SEE YOU, LALITREE.
BWA
ooo
SUBWAY
FUCKIN' IDIOT...
Super Web Site Ass.GO!

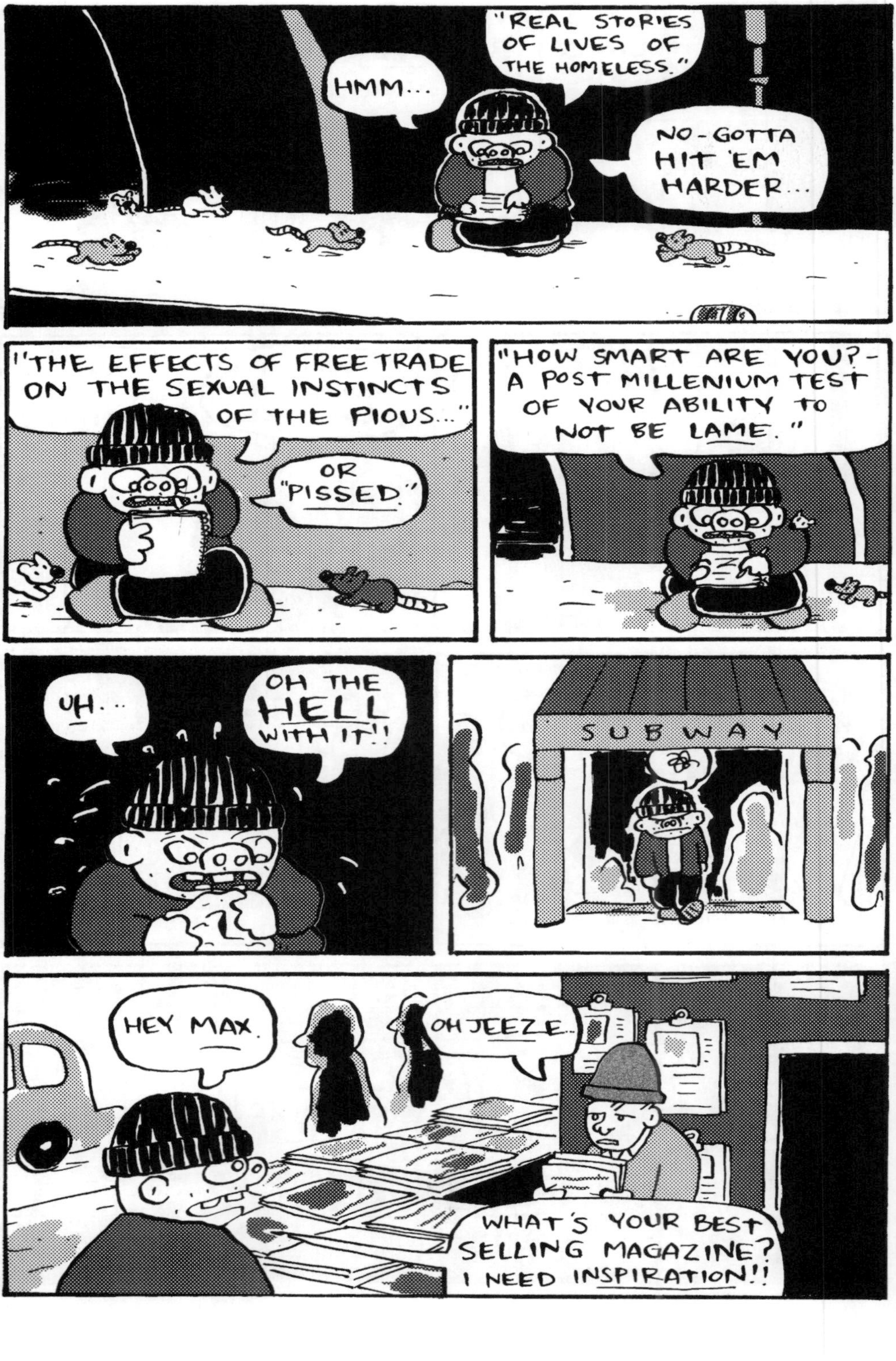
HMM...
"REAL STORIES OF LIVES OF THE HOMELESS."
NO-GOTTA HIT 'EM HARDER...
"THE EFFECTS OF FREE TRADE ON THE SEXUAL INSTINCTS OF THE PIOUS..."
OR "PISSED."
"HOW SMART ARE YOU? - A POST MILLENIUM TEST OF YOUR ABILITY TO NOT BE LAME."
UH...
OH THE HELL WITH IT!!
SUBWAY
HEY MAX.
OH JEEZE...
WHAT'S YOUR BEST SELLING MAGAZINE? I NEED INSPIRATION!!

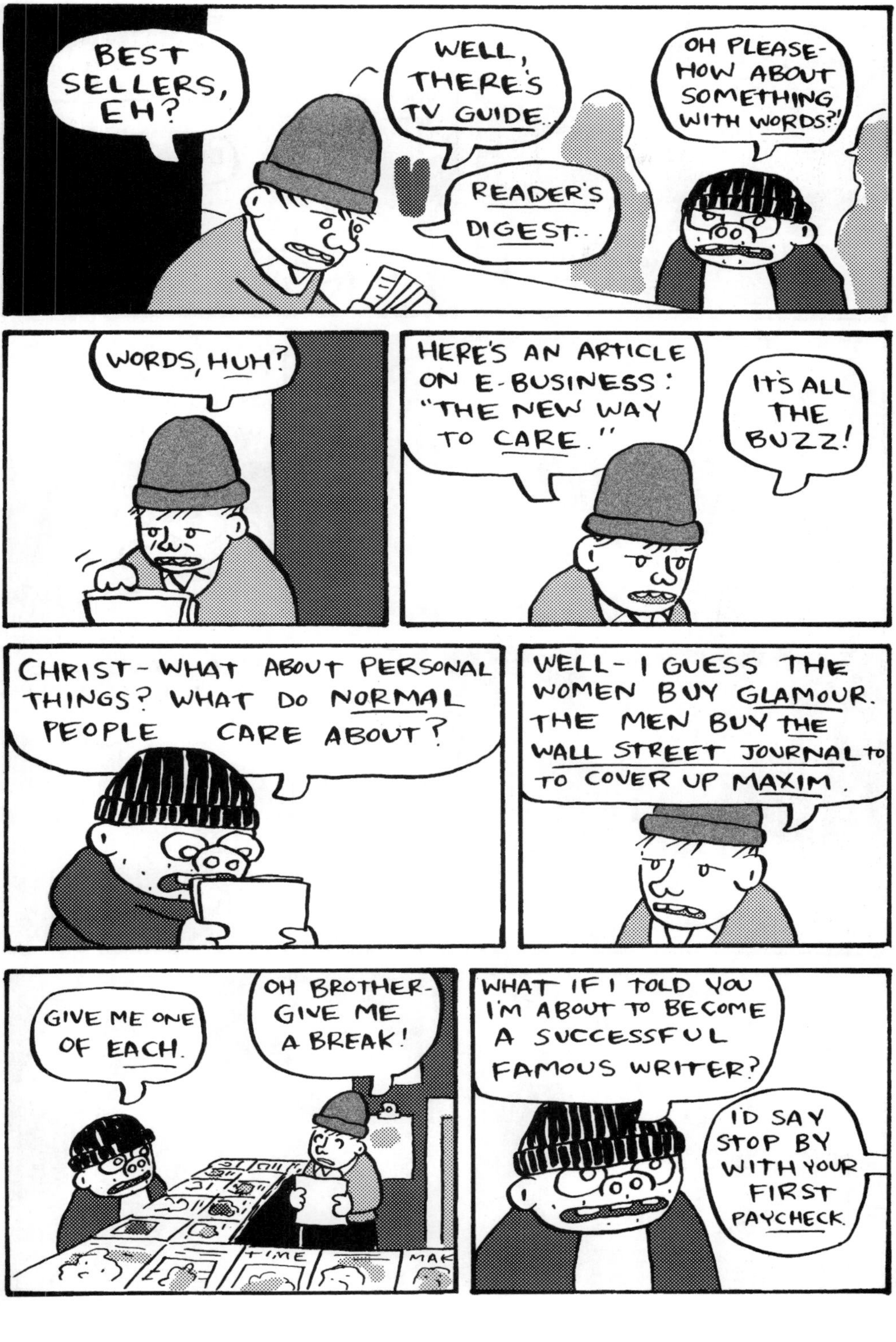
BEST SELLERS, EH?
WELL, THERE'S TV GUIDE...
READER'S DIGEST...
OH PLEASE- HOW ABOUT SOMETHING WITH WORDS?!
WORDS, HUH?
HERE'S AN ARTICLE ON E-BUSINESS: "THE NEW WAY TO CARE."
IT'S ALL THE BUZZ!
CHRIST- WHAT ABOUT PERSONAL THINGS? WHAT DO NORMAL PEOPLE CARE ABOUT?
WELL- I GUESS THE WOMEN BUY GLAMOUR. THE MEN BUY THE WALL STREET JOURNAL TO TO COVER UP MAXIM.
GIVE ME ONE OF EACH.
OH BROTHER- GIVE ME A BREAK!
TIME
WHAT IF I TOLD YOU I'M ABOUT TO BECOME A SUCCESSFUL FAMOUS WRITER?
I'D SAY STOP BY WITH YOUR FIRST PAYCHECK.

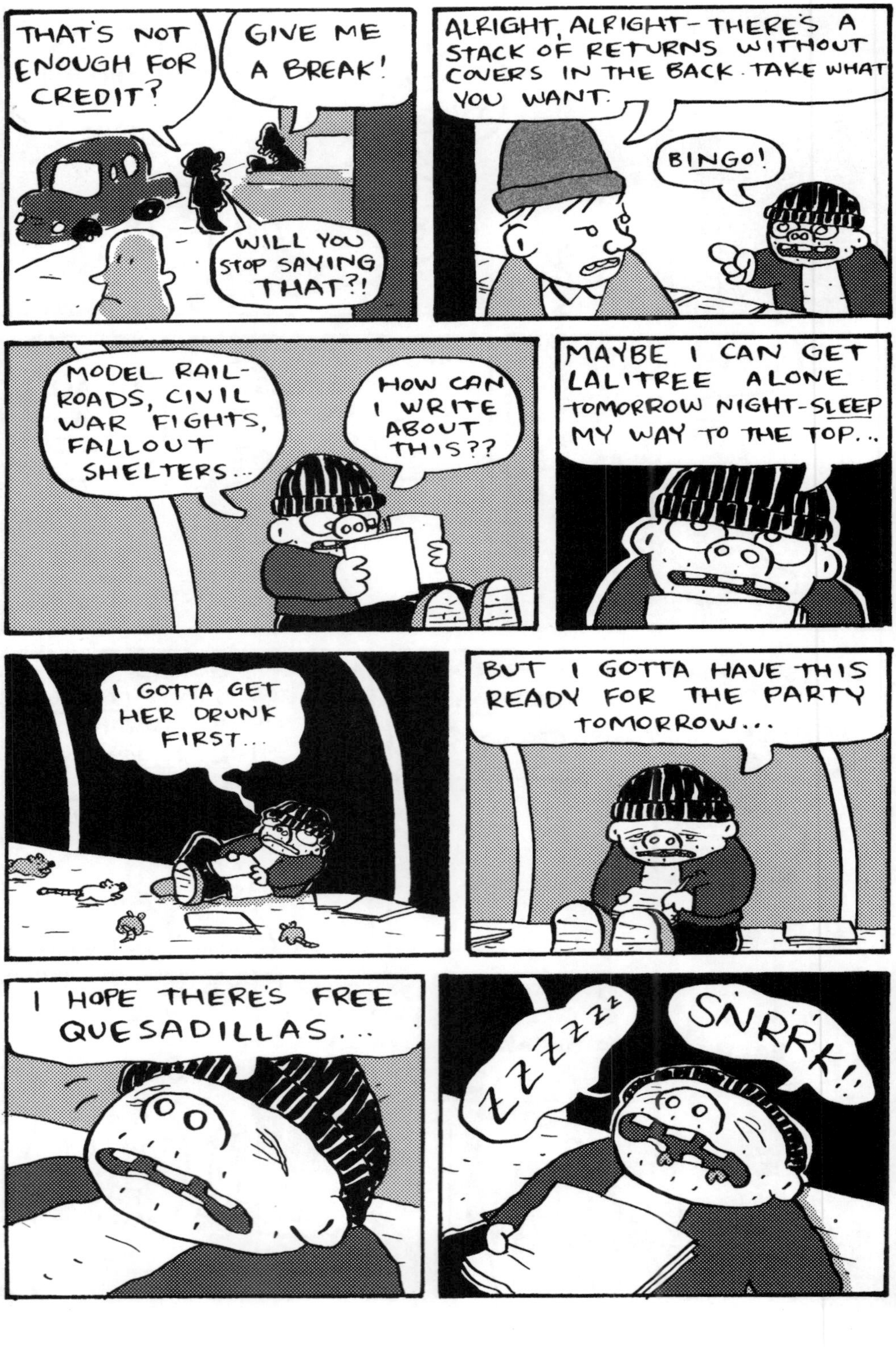
THAT'S NOT ENOUGH FOR CREDIT?
GIVE ME A BREAK!
WILL YOU STOP SAYING THAT?!
ALRIGHT, ALRIGHT- THERE'S A STACK OF RETURNS WITHOUT COVERS IN THE BACK. TAKE WHAT YOU WANT.
BINGO!
MODEL RAIL-ROADS, CIVIL WAR FIGHTS, FALLOUT SHELTERS...
HOW CAN I WRITE ABOUT THIS??
MAYBE I CAN GET LALITREE ALONE TOMORROW NIGHT-SLEEP MY WAY TO THE TOP...
I GOTTA GET HER DRUNK FIRST...
BUT I GOTTA HAVE THIS READY FOR THE PARTY TOMORROW...
I HOPE THERE'S FREE QUESADILLAS...
ZZZZZZZ
SNRRK!!

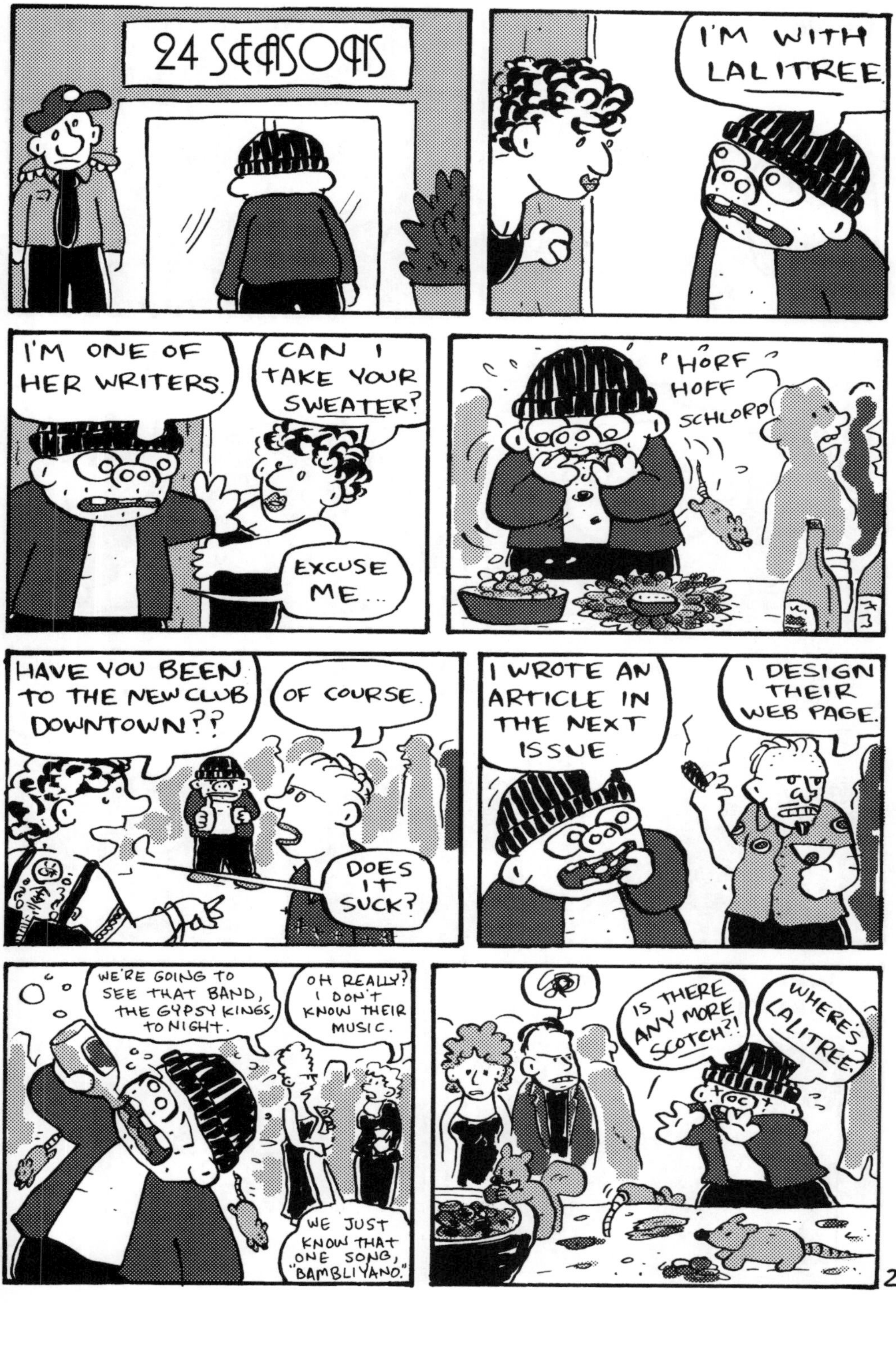
24 SEASONS
I'M WITH LALITREE.
I'M ONE OF HER WRITERS.
CAN I TAKE YOUR SWEATER?
EXCUSE ME...
HORF HOFF SCHLORP
HAVE YOU BEEN TO THE NEW CLUB DOWNTOWN??
OF COURSE.
DOES IT SUCK?
I WROTE AN ARTICLE IN THE NEXT ISSUE
I DESIGN THEIR WEB PAGE.
WE'RE GOING TO SEE THAT BAND, THE GYPSY KINGS, TONIGHT.
OH REALLY? I DON'T KNOW THEIR MUSIC.
WE JUST KNOW THAT ONE SONG, "BAMBLIYANO."
IS THERE ANY MORE SCOTCH?!
WHERE'S LALITREE?

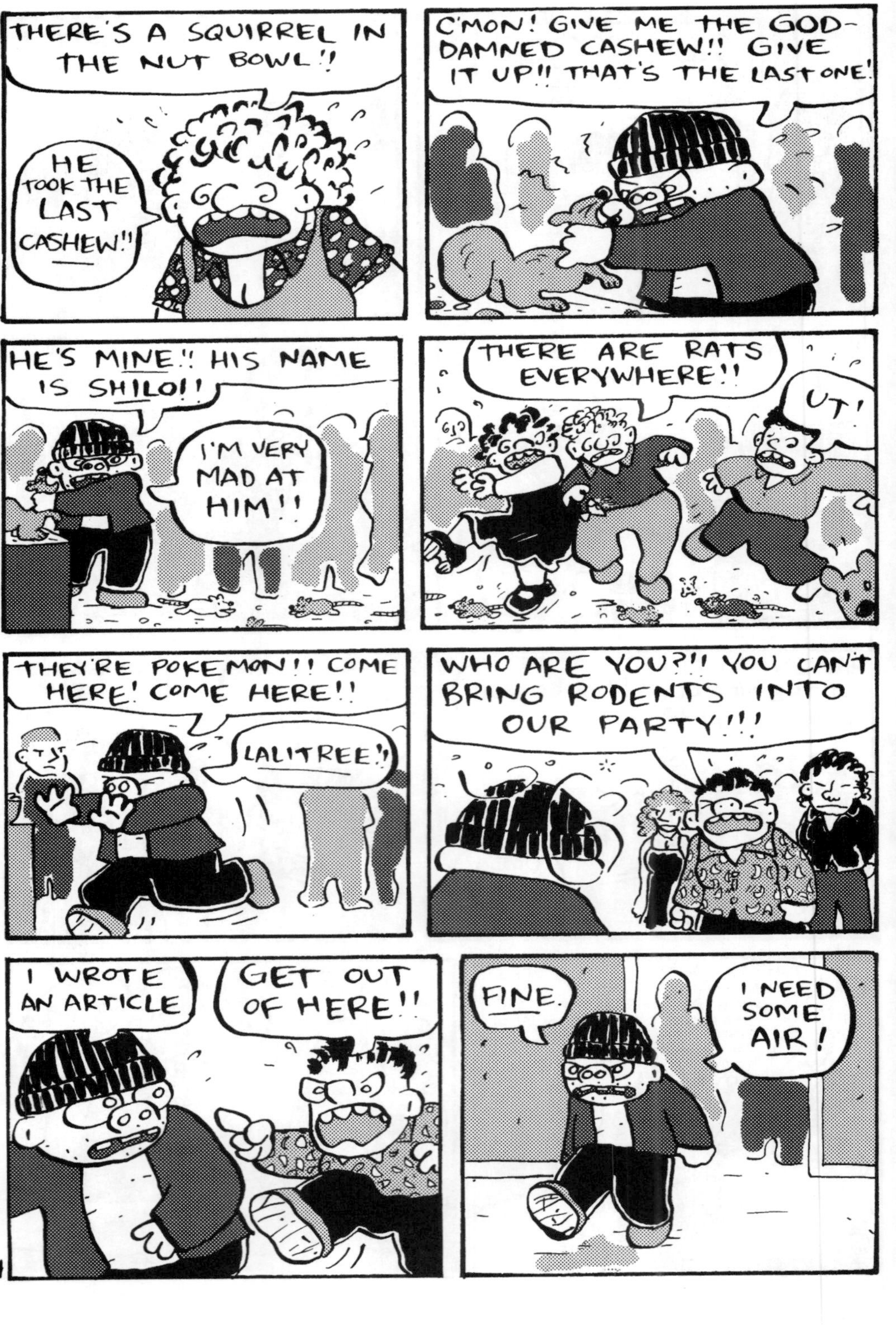
THERE'S A SQUIRREL IN THE NUT BOWL!!
HE TOOK THE LAST CASHEW!!
C'MON! GIVE ME THE GOD-DAMNED CASHEW!! GIVE IT UP!! THAT'S THE LAST ONE!
HE'S MINE!! HIS NAME IS SHILO!!
I'M VERY MAD AT HIM!!
THERE ARE RATS EVERYWHERE!!
UT!
THEY'RE POKEMON!! COME HERE! COME HERE!!
LALITREE!!
WHO ARE YOU?!! YOU CAN'T BRING RODENTS INTO OUR PARTY!!!
I WROTE AN ARTICLE
GET OUT OF HERE!!
FINE.
I NEED SOME AIR!

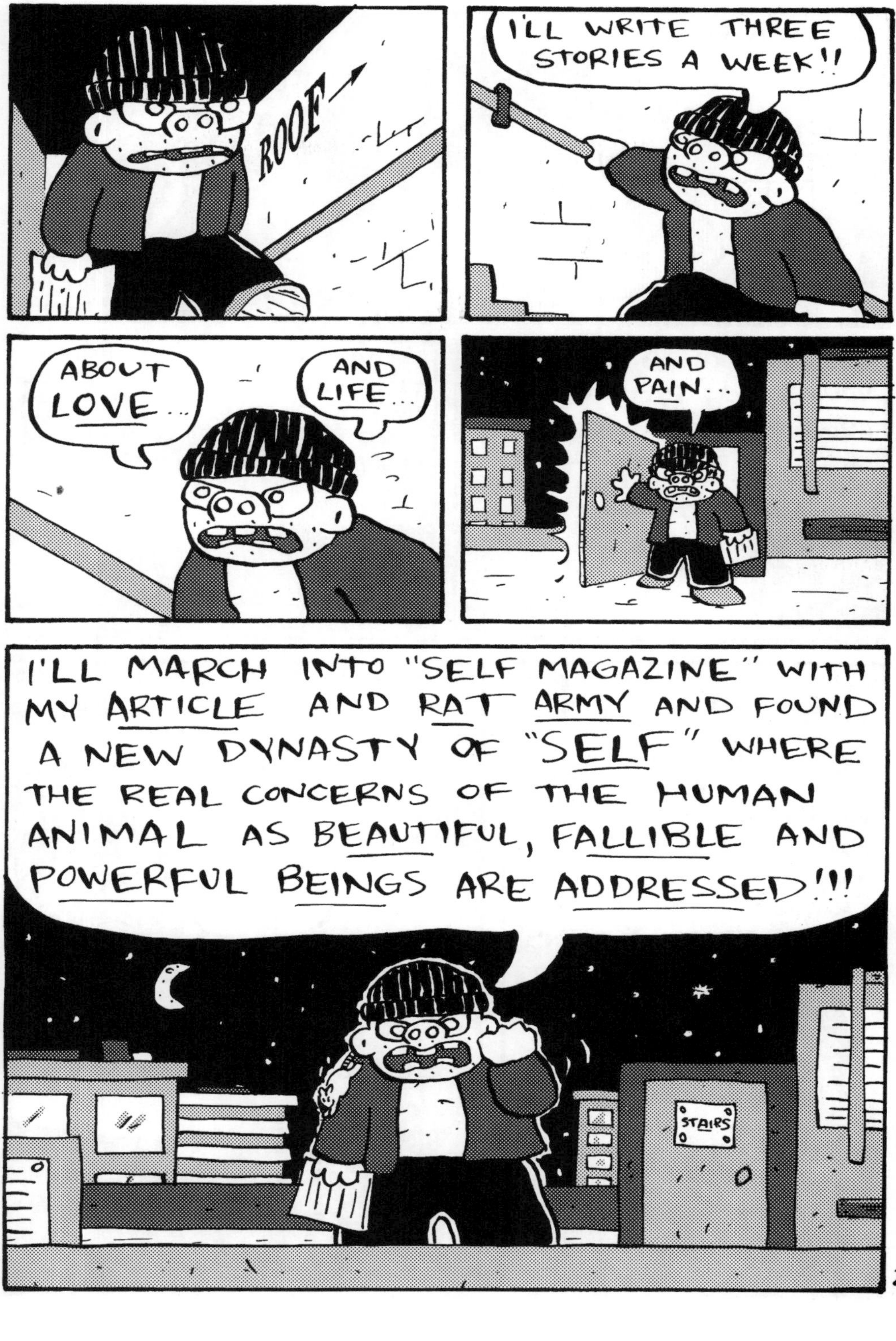
ROOF
I'LL WRITE THREE STORIES A WEEK!!
ABOUT LOVE...
AND LIFE...
AND PAIN...
I'LL MARCH INTO "SELF MAGAZINE" WITH MY ARTICLE AND RAT ARMY AND FOUND A NEW DYNASTY OF "SELF" WHERE THE REAL CONCERNS OF THE HUMAN ANIMAL AS BEAUTIFUL, FALLIBLE AND POWERFUL BEINGS ARE ADDRESSED!!!
STAIRS

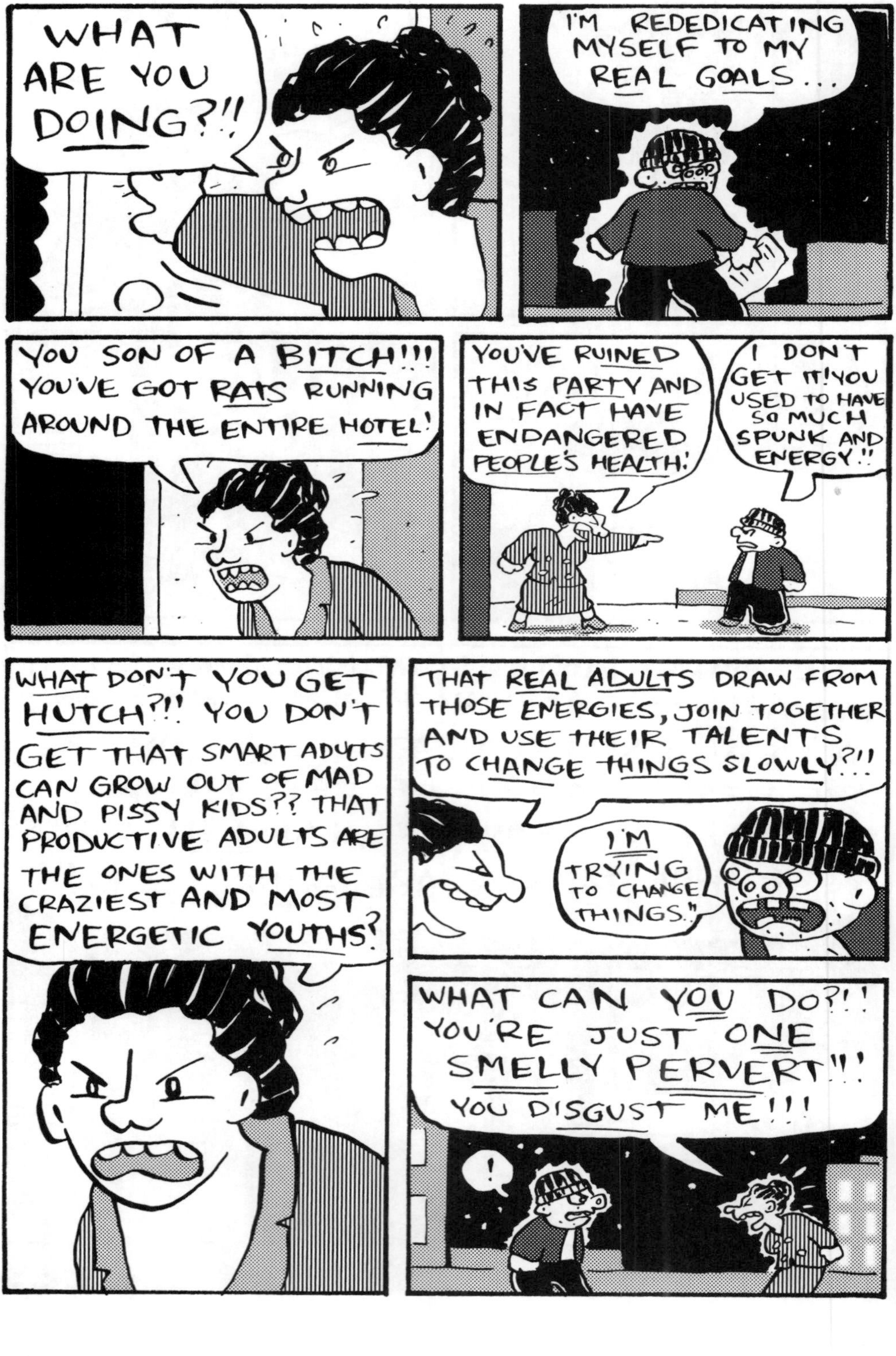
WHAT ARE YOU DOING?!!
I'M REDEDICATING MYSELF TO MY REAL GOALS...
YOU SON OF A BITCH!!! YOU'VE GOT RATS RUNNING AROUND THE ENTIRE HOTEL!
YOU'VE RUINED THIS PARTY AND IN FACT HAVE ENDANGERED PEOPLE'S HEALTH!
I DON'T GET IT! YOU USED TO HAVE SO MUCH SPUNK AND ENERGY!!
WHAT DON'T YOU GET HUTCH?!! YOU DON'T GET THAT SMART ADULTS CAN GROW OUT OF MAD AND PISSY KIDS?? THAT PRODUCTIVE ADULTS ARE THE ONES WITH THE CRAZIEST AND MOST ENERGETIC YOUTHS?
THAT REAL ADULTS DRAW FROM THOSE ENERGIES, JOIN TOGETHER AND USE THEIR TALENTS TO CHANGE THINGS SLOWLY?!!
I'M TRYING TO CHANGE THINGS.
WHAT CAN YOU DO?!! YOU'RE JUST ONE SMELLY PERVERT!!! YOU DISGUST ME!!!
!

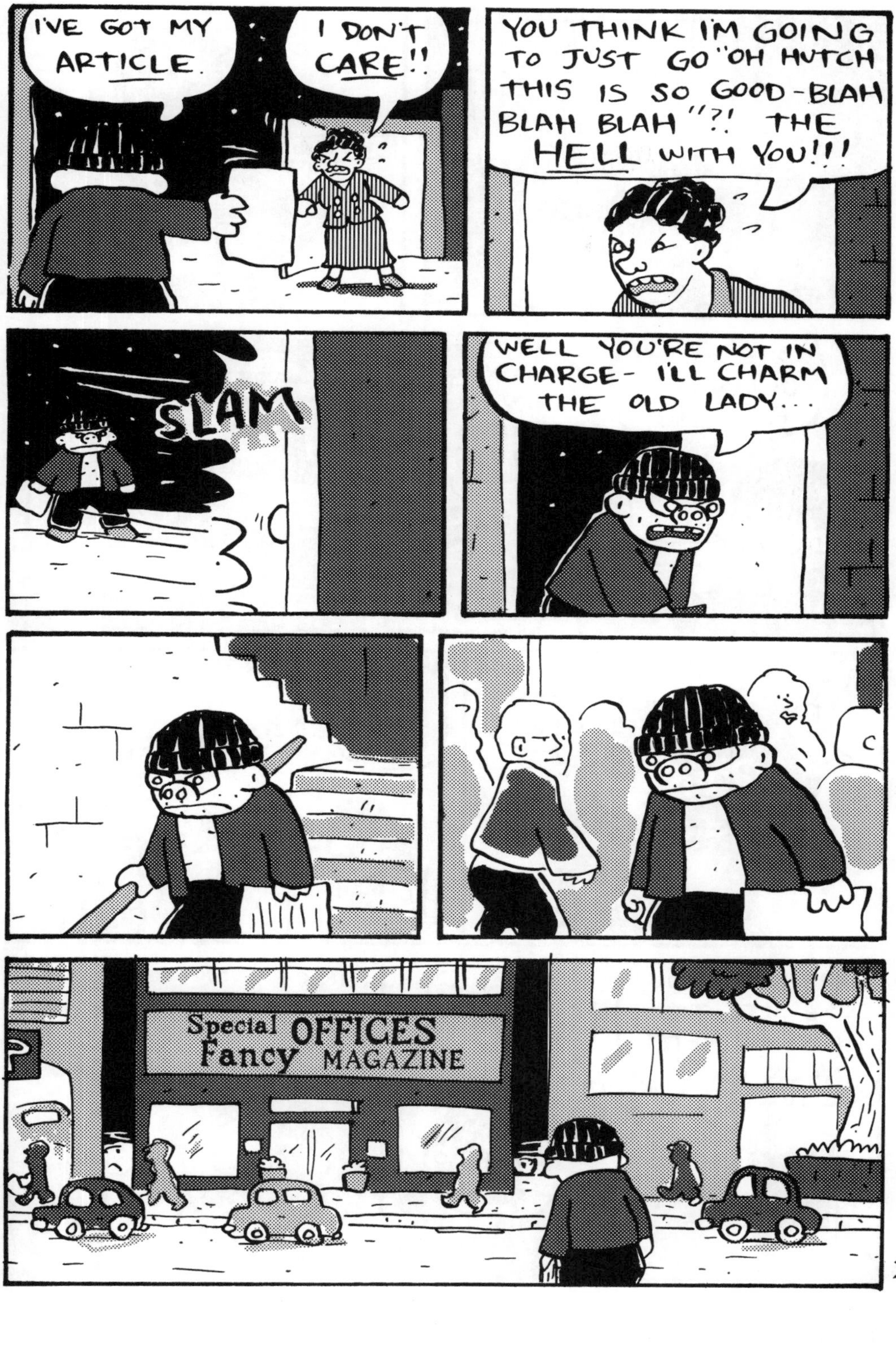

I'VE GOT MY ARTICLE.
I DON'T CARE!!
YOU THINK I'M GOING TO JUST GO "OH HUTCH THIS IS SO GOOD-BLAH BLAH BLAH"?! THE HELL WITH YOU!!!
SLAM
WELL YOU'RE NOT IN CHARGE- I'LL CHARM THE OLD LADY...
Special OFFICES Fancy MAGAZINE

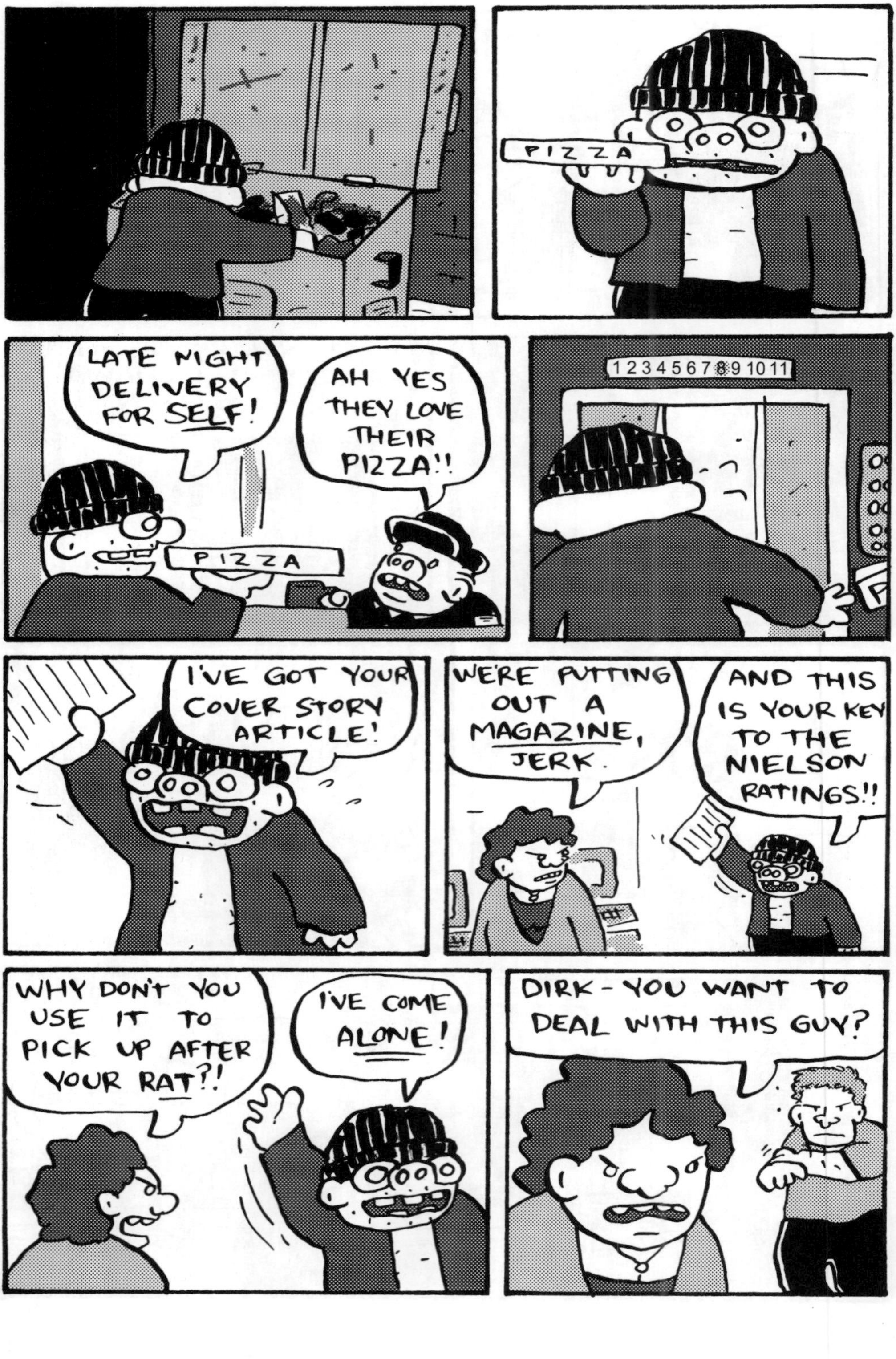
PIZZA
LATE NIGHT DELIVERY FOR SELF!
PIZZA
AH YES THEY LOVE THEIR PIZZA!!
1234567891011
I'VE GOT YOUR COVER STORY ARTICLE!
WE'RE PUTTING OUT A MAGAZINE, JERK.
AND THIS IS YOUR KEY TO THE NIELSON RATINGS!!
WHY DON'T YOU USE IT TO PICK UP AFTER YOUR RAT?!
I'VE COME ALONE!
DIRK - YOU WANT TO DEAL WITH THIS GUY?

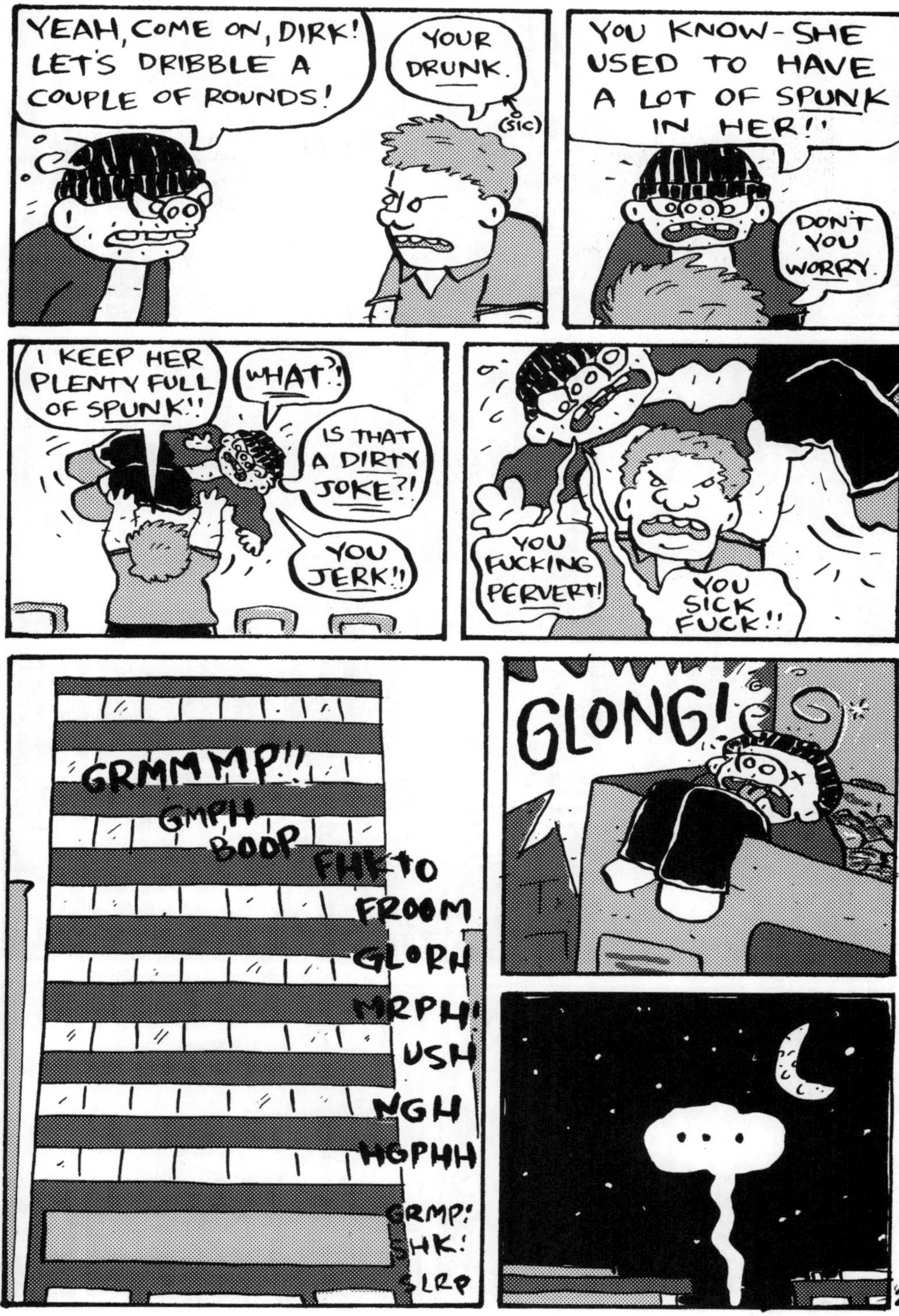
YEAH, COME ON, DIRK! LET'S DRIBBLE A COUPLE OF ROUNDS!
YOUR DRUNK.
(SIC)
YOU KNOW-SHE USED TO HAVE A LOT OF SPUNK IN HER!!
DON'T YOU WORRY.
I KEEP HER PLENTY FULL OF SPUNK!!
WHAT?!
IS THAT A DIRTY JOKE?!
YOU JERK!!
YOU FUCKING PERVERT!
YOU SICK FUCK!!
GRMMMP!!
GMPH
BOOP
FHKTO
FROOM
GLORH
MRPH
USH
NGH
HGPHH
GRMP!
SHK!
SLRP
GLONG!
...

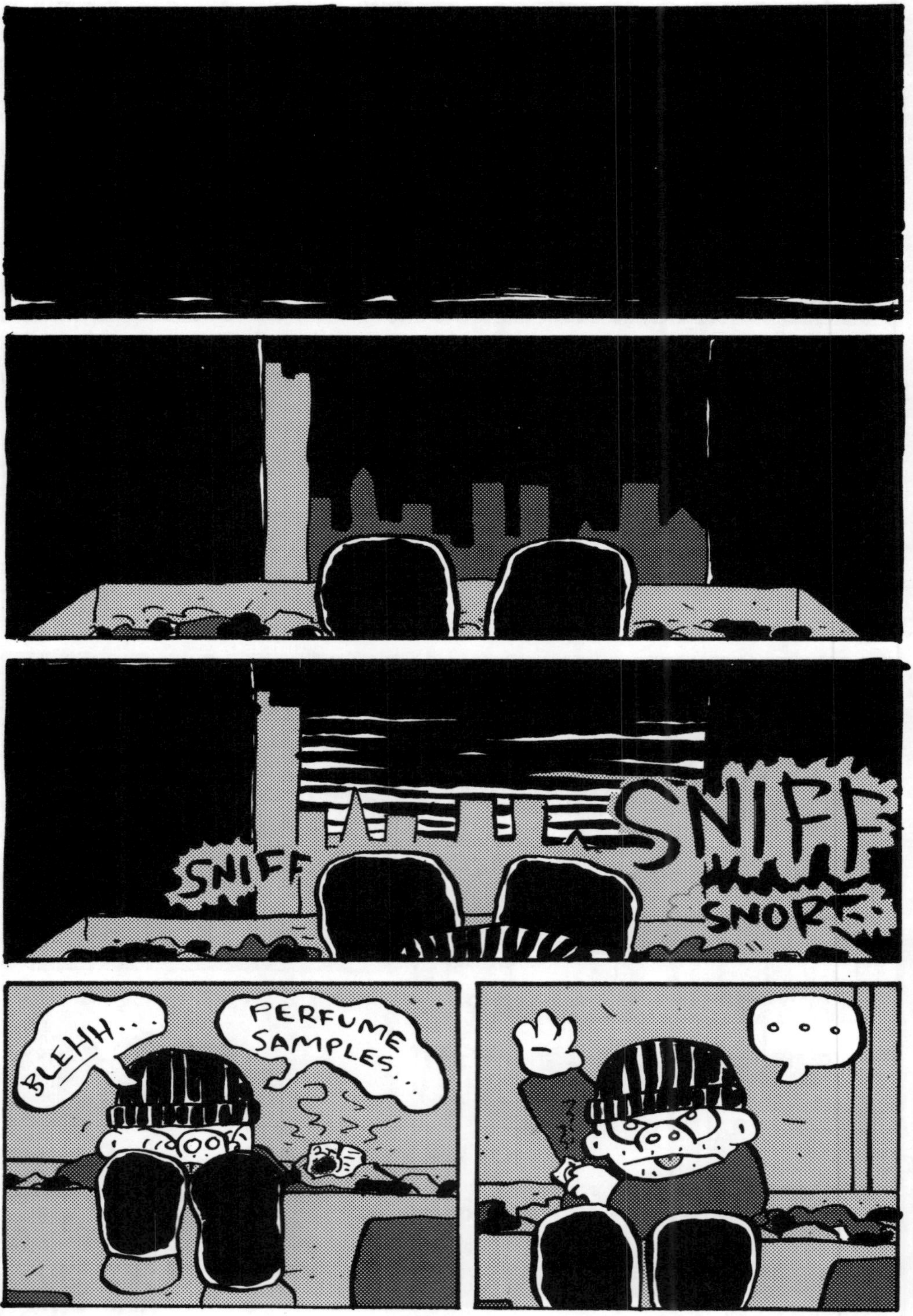
SNIFF
SNIFF
SNORE
BLEHH...
PERFUME SAMPLES...
...

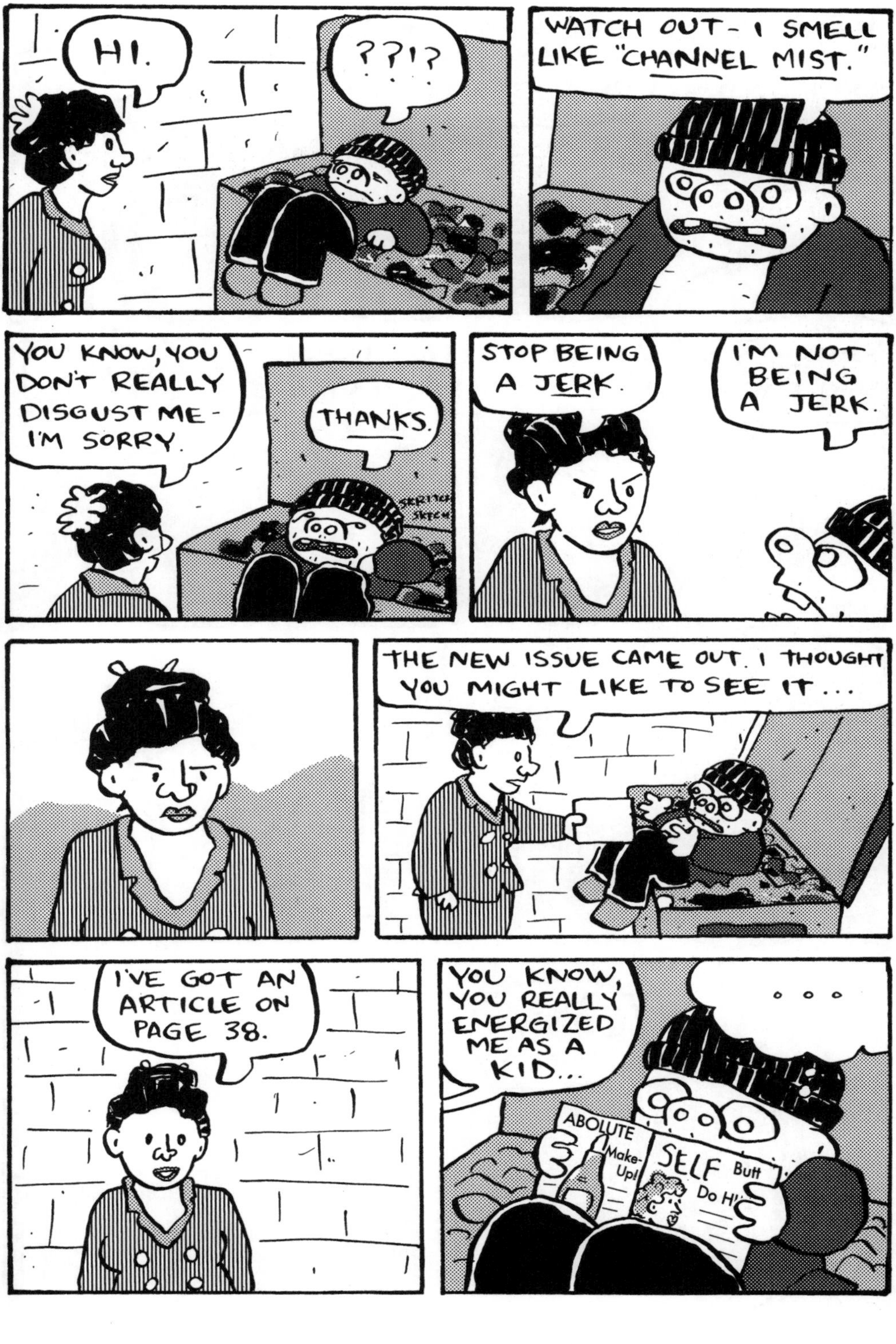
HI.
??!?
WATCH OUT - I SMELL LIKE "CHANNEL MIST."
YOU KNOW, YOU DON'T REALLY DISGUST ME - I'M SORRY.
THANKS.
SKRITCH SKRTCH
STOP BEING A JERK.
I'M NOT BEING A JERK.
THE NEW ISSUE CAME OUT. I THOUGHT YOU MIGHT LIKE TO SEE IT...
I'VE GOT AN ARTICLE ON PAGE 38.
YOU KNOW, YOU REALLY ENERGIZED ME AS A KID...
...
ABOLUTE
Make-Up!
SELF
Butt
Do H'

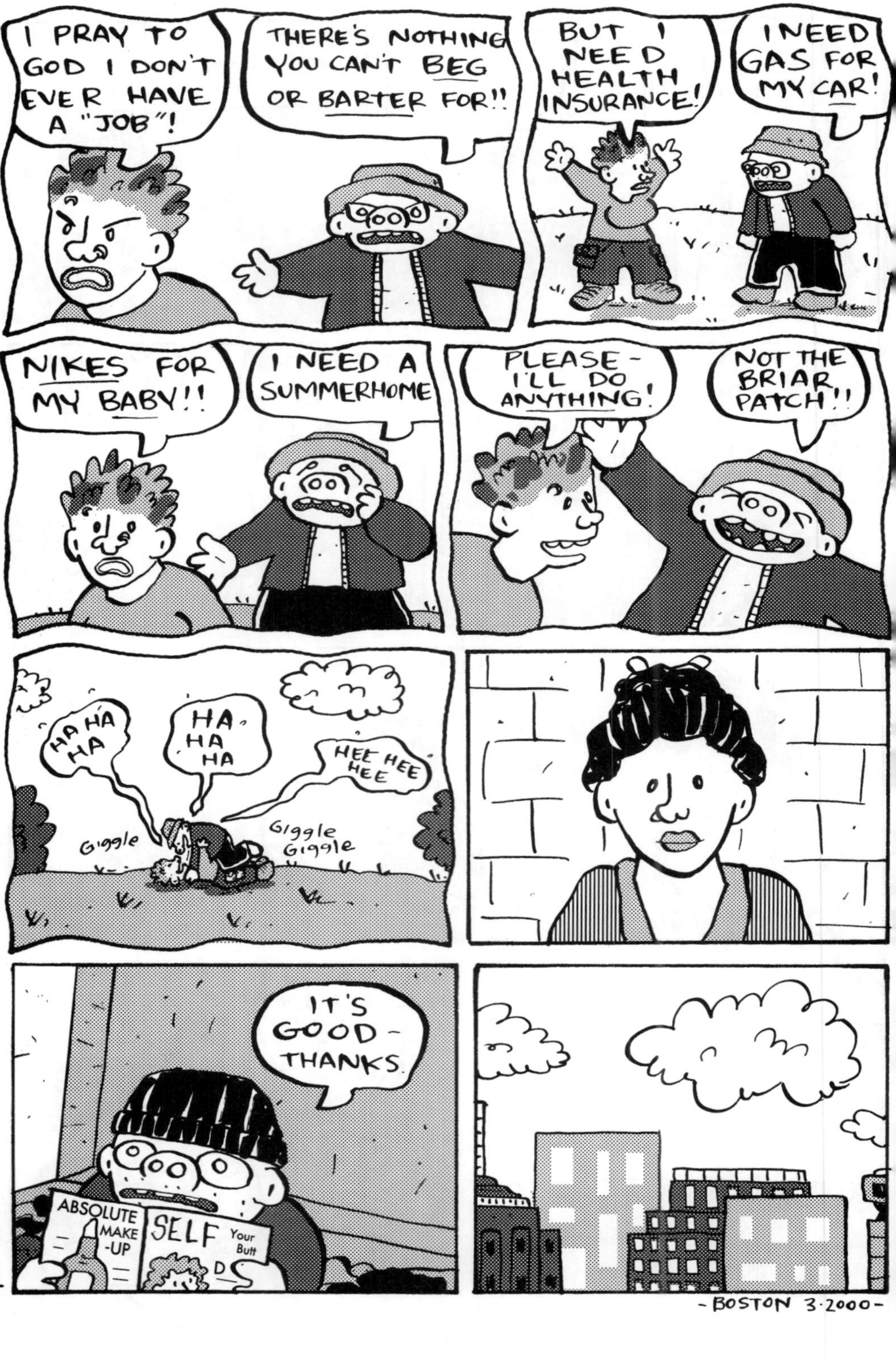
I PRAY TO GOD I DON'T EVER HAVE A "JOB"!
THERE'S NOTHING YOU CAN'T BEG OR BARTER FOR!!
BUT I NEED HEALTH INSURANCE!
I NEED GAS FOR MY CAR!
NIKES FOR MY BABY!!
I NEED A SUMMERHOME
PLEASE - I'LL DO ANYTHING!
NOT THE BRIAR PATCH!!
HA HA HA
HA HA HA
HEE HEE HEE
Giggle
Giggle Giggle
IT'S GOOD - THANKS.
ABSOLUTE MAKE-UP
SELF
Your Butt

-BOSTON 3·2000-

Tom Hart was born and
raised in Kingston, NY.